*The Politics
of an
Emerging
Profession*

THE POLITICS OF AN EMERGING PROFESSION

The American Library Association, 1876–1917

WAYNE A. WIEGAND

CONTRIBUTIONS IN LIBRARIANSHIP AND INFORMATION
SCIENCE, NUMBER 56

GREENWOOD PRESS

NEW YORK
WESTPORT, CONNECTICUT
LONDON

Library of Congress Cataloging in Publication Data

Wiegand, Wayne A., 1946–
  The politics of an emerging profession.

  (Contributions in librarianship and information
science, ISSN 0084–9243 ; no. 56)
  Bibliography: p.
  Includes index.
  1. American Library Association—History.   2. Library
science—United States—History.   3. Libraries—United
States—History.   4. Trade and professional associations
—United States—History.   I. Title.   II. Series.
Z673.A52W53   1986   020′.622′73   85–12679
ISBN 0–313–25022–7 (lib. bdg. : alk. paper)

Library of Congress Catalog Card Number: 85–12679
ISBN: 0–313–25022–7
ISSN: 0084–9243

First published in 1986

Greenwood Press, Inc.
88 Post Road West
Westport, Connecticut 06881

Printed in the United States of America

The paper used in the book complies with the
Permanent Paper Standard issued by the National
Information Standards Organization (Z39.48–1984).

10 9 8 7 6 5 4 3 2 1

Copyright Acknowledgments

The author and publishers gratefully acknowledge permission to use the following:
Some sections of chapter 2 are reprinted by permission of the American Library Association from
"The Wayward Bookman: The Decline, Fall and Historical Obliteration of an ALA President,
Part I" by Wayne A. Wiegand in *American Libraries*, March 1977, pp. 134–37; copyright
© 1977 by ALA.
Passages from Wayne A. Wiegand, "Melvil Dewey and the American Library Association,
1876–1907" are reprinted by permission of Forest Press. From *Melvil Dewey: The Man and the
Classification*, edited by Gordon Stevenson and Judith Kramer-Greene (Albany, NY: Forest
Press, 1983), pp. 101–128.
Quotations from the Richard Rodgers Bowker papers are reprinted by courtesy of the Rare Books
and Manuscripts Division, The New York Public Library, Astor, Lenox and Tilden Foundations.
Quotations from the Melvil Dewey Papers are reprinted by courtesy of the Melvil Dewey Papers,
Rare Book and Manuscript Library, Columbia University.
Appendix I and Appendix II are reprinted by permission of Munksgard International Booksellers
and Publishers, Ltd. From Wayne A. Wiegand, "American Library Association Executive Board
Members, 1876–1917: A Collective Profile," *Libri* 31 (August 1981), pp. 155, 156–159.

For
Shirl
a fellow traveler in life

Contents

Preface

"The best reading for the largest number at the least cost." When Melvil Dewey formulated this motto for the American Library Association (ALA) in 1879,[1] he unknowingly characterized the historical development of the association's first 41 years. Throughout this four-decade period, efforts to assist librarians in collecting "the best reading" represented the association's primary goal; these efforts also served as a necessary thread binding the association together during its tenuous, sometimes tempestuous embryonic years. ALA executive board members holding office between 1876 and 1917 were a highly homogeneous group whose social rank reflected the "character" of the dominant culture. As members of the "cultivated" classes, these library leaders intuitively "knew" what "the best reading" was. They regarded it as their professional goal to collect this literature and to make it available to a public which they confidently believed would eventually manifest the constructive social behavior, the zeal for material progress and the elevated cultural understanding which "naturally" followed exposure to good reading. The association's belief in this dictum remained unquestioned throughout the period under study.

For the first decade of its existence most ALA leaders thought the *esprit de corps*—that common spirit generated by annual ALA conferences which recited the social benefits of the goal and gave attendees an opportunity to fill up on library "religion"—was sufficient *raison d'être*. But Melvil Dewey disagreed, and as time passed he recruited a growing number of like-minded professionals (who eventually abandoned his leadership after the turn of the century) to dispute the means implicit in the last eight words of the motto. Just how should library collections best reach "the largest number at the least cost"? This study concentrates most of its attention on these disputes because it was the arguments over means which preoccupied ALA attention between 1876 and 1917. Agreement and continuity in the association were reflected in the unquestioned professional goal which had evolved from a set of enduring values held by a highly homogeneous group with a tradition of using libraries. Disagreement and de-

mands for change were almost always reflected in the varying methods that ALA
members advocated for achieving that goal. The profession's purpose has always
been comfortably and firmly housed in the goal. Most of its history, however,
is housed in the means, and because of this fact ALA's struggle to accommodate
shifting pressures and power groups within the world of librarianship naturally
emerges as the major theme of this book.

In subsequent pages the reader will note that the author has carefully avoided
the question "What constitutes a profession?" He does so deliberately. Since
1876 the library profession has unfairly compared itself to older, more established
professions like law and medicine, and come to questionable conclusions based
upon criteria historically established by other groups. Charles Rosenberg wisely
counsels a different approach:

Each profession constitutes a unique configuration of social and intellectual and institutional tools, evolved through a unique historical development . . . Each discipline presents
a different potential for social relevance—and thus a different order of sensitivity to social
pressure.[2]

Appendix I and II identify certain socioeconomic and professional characteristics of ALA executive board members over a 41-year period. The reader should
note that no detailed attempt is made to compare these leaders with the leaders
of other professions. If Rosenberg is right, that would not be the next step in
the process of building a historical foundation for understanding the direction
and activities of a profession during its formative years. Instead, the library
profession would be better served if the historian used the data as background
material for further analysis of the historical record available in the more traditional document formats—primary source materials available in archival dep-
ositories throughout the country. Tracing a profession's "unique configuration"
through "a unique historical development" in order to discover its "different
order of sensitivity to social pressure" might prove a better means to understanding the historical roots of the contemporary library profession in the United
States than contributing to the endless, largely fruitless debates over "What
constitutes a profession?"

The Politics of an Emerging Profession has two secondary purposes. First,
the author hopes his effort may stimulate a few more historians to explore the
field of library history, its institutions and professions. Library history represents
an area rich in research possibilities, especially for scholars exploring the new
fields of social and urban history, women's and family history, *histoire du livre*,
and for practitioners of newer research methodologies like oral history, psycho-
history, and quantitative history. Second, the author hopes to reiterate to the
library community the benefits of historical research into all relevant primary
source materials. Much of the detail, many of the patterns, and most of the
politics of the ALA's development discussed in subsequent pages represent new
information derived from analysis of primary source collections heretofore little

used in library history research. This experience will explain the author's decision to include an essay on primary source materials in the "Bibliography," and his decision to "load" the notes with citations mostly to primary sources.

In the research and writing of this book, the author incurred many debts. For financial assistance he owes thanks to the American Library Association for the 1975 Herbert Putnam Award, the University of Kentucky Research Foundation and the University of Kentucky Graduate School. Occasional released time from some teaching responsibilities between 1978 and 1983 was graciously granted by Dr. Timothy W. Sineath, Dean of the University's College of Library and Information Science; the College's secretarial staff has been exceptionally patient, understanding, and prompt with the manuscript's numerous drafts. Librarians and archivists at the many institutions holding the primary source materials listed in Part I of the "Bibliography" were very helpful, but a special word of thanks must go to the Interlibrary Loan librarians at the University of Kentucky's Margaret I. King Library. Six people read the entire manuscript: Gene Trani, whose counsel and advice as mentor have always been sound and much appreciated; Mike Harris, whose active mind constantly challenges scholarly convention; Mark Jones, whose friendship has sustained since graduate school in the early 1970s; Lee Cooper, whose red pencil and critical eye improved many of these pages; Ed Holley, whose busy schedule never prevents him from helping a young library historian; and Fran Miksa, whose careful, precise and rigorous critique consumed two weeks of his life. Errors of fact and interpretation, of course, belong to the author alone.

*The Politics
of an
Emerging
Profession*

1   An Auspicious Beginning: The Philadelphia Conference of 1876

In the fall of 1876 much of Philadelphia still sported the red, white and blue bunting which seemed to wrap the entire city when the nation's Centennial Exhibition had opened the previous May. The perpetual hum of exposition machinery, the bustle of the crowds, and the clatter of trains which ran from downtown Philadelphia to a depot just opposite the main gate marked a country on the move. Several blocks away from the fairgrounds a group of 103 people interested in libraries had assembled at the Historical Society of Pennsylvania in a room with a "cheerful garden vista" which was adorned by "solemn portraits and venerable books." The date was 6 October 1876. Those present voted a preamble to a still unwritten constitution. "For the purpose of promoting the library interests of the country, and of increasing reciprocity of intelligence and goodwill among librarians and all interested in library economy and bibliographic studies," the preamble stated, "the undersigned form themselves into a body to be known as the AMERICAN LIBRARY ASSOCIATION."[1] Shortly thereafter, the centennial "Conference of Librarians" adjourned.

The forces which brought these conference participants together in October 1876 were diverse, and the chronology of events leading to the conference not always clear. Twenty-three years earlier 53 people had met in New York for the first library conference on the North American continent. Conference participants discussed catalogs, indexes, government documents and popular libraries, and pledged themselves to meet again.[2] But the initial enthusiasm which sparked the conference soon dissipated, and within a year Congress passed the Kansas-Nebraska Act. It represented one more step toward a civil conflict which eventually tore the nation apart and preoccupied the attention of its citizens for an entire generation. Nonetheless, the conference of 1853 was not a total failure. Although it did not generate "the formation of a permanent Librarians' Association" that a conference resolution promised, its existence served as a precedent. Librarians had met once; they could meet again.

In 1867 Congress established the Department of Education. Two years later federal legislators demoted the department to a bureau, and transferred functional control to the Department of the Interior. Under John Eaton's direction, in 1872 the bureau agreed to develop a comprehensive list of libraries in the United States with 1,000 volumes or more. By April 1875, Eaton decided that the "Special Report on Public Libraries" on which the bureau had been working for the past three years ought to be published to coincide with the nation's centennial celebration.[3]

Commissioner Eaton was always eager to raise the bureau's visibility among constituents. As the deadline for gathering data for the report neared, he contemplated ways to advertise its publication. When Thomas Hale Williams, a librarian at the Minneapolis Athenaeum who had participated in the 1853 conference, recommended a centennial conference of librarians, Eaton saw a possibility. On 2 July 1875 the commissioner suggested to Justin Winsor, Superintendent of the Boston Public Library, that perhaps librarians ought to meet during the centennial, like other scientific, educational, and professional groups. Winsor himself had called for some "formally organized society of librarians" under the auspices of the American Social Science Association in his 1869 annual report, but in this case it appears he did not even respond to Eaton's 1875 letter.[4]

While Eaton had his own reasons for quietly recommending a meeting, he was not alone. Frederick W. Leypoldt, coeditor of *Publisher's Weekly* with Richard R. Bowker, demonstrated his continuing interest in libraries by reinstituting on 6 November 1875 a "Library and Bibliographical Notes" column he had dropped in January. Then, on 22 April 1876, he published a letter from a British correspondent which noted that "in these days of International Congresses, it is strange that no attempt should have been made to convene a Congress of Librarians."[5] Like Eaton, Leypoldt also saw an opportunity for personal and professional gain if only librarians could be convinced to meet during the celebration. But the opening of the centennial exhibition on 10 May passed without concrete action on a librarians' conference. Although two publishers and one well-placed government official wanted a meeting, no well-known, highly regarded librarian had as yet publicly stepped forward to make the same call.

Fortunately, the letter in *Publisher's Weekly* had not escaped the attention of the youthful, energetic, and ambitious Melvil Dewey, at one time assistant librarian at Amherst College, but in the spring of 1876, a self-employed entrepreneur attempting to establish a library supplies manufacturing company in Boston. On 17 May 1876 he ascended the stairs of the Porter Building at 37 Park Row in New York to discuss several matters with Leypoldt and Bowker in the editorial rooms of *Publisher's Weekly*.[6] He said he had been discussing the possibility of establishing a periodical devoted solely to library affairs with several Boston publishers and librarians; he also indicated his interest in producing standardized library equipment and materials in order to make library service more efficient. Leypoldt replied that he was not interested in the latter, but he did want to publish a general library periodical out of New York. He asked whether Dewey would be interested in becoming editor. Leypoldt offered him $500 a year, 20 percent of gross receipts, and advertising space at cost for his library supplies venture.[7] Leypoldt then recommended that the periodical be launched to coincide with a librarians' conference which could be scheduled later that year in Philadelphia.

Dewey would not commit himself to Leypoldt's offer until he talked to his Boston contacts, but he did enthusiastically second Leypoldt's suggestion for a library conference. All three men recognized that if they wanted to take advantage of the excitement generated by the centennial exhibition, they would have to issue the conference call in the next number of *Publisher's Weekly*, already at the printer. Bowker quickly prepared a preliminary announcement of a library conference to be held in August 1876, and Leypoldt and Dewey immediately cabled copies of the announcement to scores of librarians. They identified themselves as "connected with the library interests of this country," and after stating their belief "that efficiency and economy in the library would be promoted by a conference of librarians which should afford opportunity for mutual consultation and practical cooperation," they asked librarians to endorse the conference call.

Both Dewey and Leypoldt hoped the call would win endorsement from at least a few of the nation's leading librarians, but their efforts received a mixed response from two of the nation's most prominent library administrators. Winsor replied cautiously that although he could not make an August meeting, he was "willing to do anything helpful for the cause of public library interests." William F. Poole, director of the Chicago Public Library, was more circumspect. He wrote Winsor that "a party in New York whom I do not know" had asked support for a library conference, but he was inclined not to sign a circular until he knew more about it.[8] *Publisher's Weekly* went to press without the endorsement of any library leaders.

Dewey was not discouraged. On 19 May he met with Commissioner Eaton in Philadelphia. Since Eaton was already predisposed to encourage a conference, he readily agreed to help Dewey, Leypoldt and Bowker, and he also suggested that the official call for a conference go through bureau offices. With the commissioner firmly behind the project, Dewey returned to Boston. Next day Leypoldt announced the forthcoming library journal in a *Publisher's Weekly* editorial on "Library Cooperation." He also reported the preliminary call for a centennial congress of librarians at Philadelphia, which, he wrote, was "being signed by several gentlemen connected with the library interest." He did not elaborate. Although plans for a conference were now public, the library community was still suspicious and reluctant to endorse the idea. Not until 22 May, when Dewey returned to Boston, was he able to persuade influential Boston librarian Winsor, Boston Athenaeum Librarian Charles Ammi Cutter, and Harvard College Library Director John Langdon Sibley to join the call.

Poole proved more stubborn. He wondered if Winsor had "authorized" use of his name, and he worried "there were axes to be ground" by commercial publishers. He would not commit himself without Winsor. Dewey and Leypoldt recognized they had better defer to Poole if they ever hoped to solicit the Chicago librarian's endorsement. In a letter of 25 May Leypoldt apologized for sending a telegram "point blank at you," explaining that pressing publication deadlines had dictated his ill-advised and hasty course of action. Still Poole balked. He wrote Winsor on 31 May that Librarian of Congress Ainsworth Rand Spofford had "declined" to sign the call, and that unless Winsor attended the conference, "I shall follow his example." He also reported to Winsor a conversation Spofford had with Amherst Professor (later President) Julius H. Seelye, who said Dewey was "a tremendous talker, and a little of an old maid." Poole warned Winsor, "It won't pay for you and me to attend that barbecue." But Dewey persisted. He acknowledged Poole's importance when he wrote the Chicago librarian on 5 June: "Your name is always mentioned among the very first, and it would look all wrong not to see it in the list we now have." Cutter had already assured Poole on 2 June that Dewey was "no imposter, humbug, speculator, dead beat, or anything of the sort." This careful combination of prodding and praise finally worked. When the first printed call was issued on 9 June, Poole's name was included, although near the bottom of the list. Other signees included Winsor, Cutter, Sibley, Dewey, Eaton, Reuben A. Guild of the Brown University Library, Lloyd P. Smith of Philadelphia's Library Company, and Henry A. Homes of the New York State Library.

Noticeably absent from the list was Spofford's name. On 29 May he wrote Leypoldt that conventions were "mere wordy outlets for impracticables and pretenders." Nonetheless, he promised to "cooperate with any well-organized endeavor to aid the whole profession by solid publications . . . I may also find it possible to look in upon the Conference." Like Poole, Spofford later relented as planning for the conference gained momentum. He agreed to lend his name to a subsequent call. Others were less reluctant. Among those who answered the first printed call with words of praise and approval were Hannah P. James, librarian of the Newton (Massachusetts) Free Library, and Samuel Swett Green, librarian of the Free Public Library in Worcester.

Once an endorsed call had been issued, preparations for the conference accelerated. In July, Winsor, Poole and Smith formed a committee of arrangements. Smith suggested switching the dates for the conference to 4–6 October, in part because he could schedule rooms at the historical society at no charge to conference participants. Dewey took advantage of Eaton's offer to print and distribute the signed call from Bureau of Education offices. He also asked the commissioner to include a prospectus for the *American Library Journal* in the forthcoming *Special Report on Libraries*. Eaton consented, but only if his name was removed from Dewey's prospectus to avoid any appearance that he was using public office for private gain.[9]

On 28 July the bureau issued a second printed call specifying the conference dates as 4–6 October. Dewey used the verso to solicit papers. He tempted potential speakers by mentioning that Winsor, Poole, Cutter, Spofford and Smith were already on the program. Subsequently, he had the complete program printed for inclusion in the first issue of the *American Library Journal*, and by forwarding advance page proofs of the program to over 2,000 libraries during the last week in September, he took advantage of an opportunity to advertise both the advent of the *Journal* and conference. Dewey's energy kept conference planners from procrastinating, but when he pushed the arrangements committee to hire a stenographer for the conference, Poole objected. He wrote Winsor on 18 September, "Dewey needs looking after or he will pile up expenses. Please apply a breeching to [him] and hold him back."

Publisher's Weekly formally announced the program and the *Journal* in its 16 September issue, and Boston's *Daily Advertiser* told prospective conference attendees that the Library Company was "expected" to tender "an elegant entertainment."[10] At the end of the month the *American Library Journal*, which Dewey suggested was "meant to be eminently practical," issued its first number. Its pages announced the Philadelphia conference and suggested several positive outcomes, "not the least" of which "should be the proposed national organization."[11] In an article entitled "The Profession," Dewey equated the "high calling" of librarianship with the teaching profession, for "the largest influence over the people is the printed page," and a new breed of librarian who chose his collection wisely "may soon largely shape the reading, and through it the thought of his whole community."[12]

With the first issue of the *American Library Journal* on hand, several advance copies of the Bureau of Education's *Special Report* available for perusal, and all arrangements completed, the second library conference on the North American continent prepared to convene. The initiative for holding it had come not from the library community, but from the publishing and governmental sectors. Leypoldt, Eaton, and Dewey, who between them mailed more than 5,000 items advocating a conference, had much more to gain than camaraderie. Melvil Dewey, whose zeal and tenacity impressed everyone, served as the link among the three groups. He stood to gain the most professionally and financially as managing editor of a new library publication and as chief stockholder in a company which would specialize in marketing basic library supplies. Librarians had not even been involved in the initial conference planning stages, but once the idea took hold, they showed eager acceptance. When Dewey successfully enlisted Winsor's support, Poole followed and ultimately brought in others like Spofford with him.

Most conference participants registered at local hotels, but Lloyd Smith decided to host Dewey and the arrangements committee at his house in Philadelphia's Germantown section. Poole had been close friends with Smith for some time; both shared a conventional approach towards librarianship, and both were warm acquaintances of Winsor. Dewey was the newcomer. He later recalled that when he was being escorted into Smith's parlor after arriving late in the evening of 3 October, Poole rose from his chair, and as he extended his hand to Dewey, he remarked laughingly, "Well, Dewey, you are a better looking man than I thought you were. I had a clear picture in mind of you as about 70

years old, with white hair and glasses and round shoulders.'' Dewey remarked
he was also surprised. Poole was a generation younger than he "had been
prepared to meet.''[13] For the moment, the two men were friends. Together with
Winsor and Smith they sat down to discuss the conference which was about to
open the next day.

At 10:15 the next morning Justin Winsor called the meeting to order. He
seemed a natural choice to lead the conference. Poole had admonished Dewey
as early as 15 June, "Make Winsor the head and a mistake will not be likely
to occur.''[14] At 45 Winsor was commonly regarded as the nation's leading
librarian. A Harvard graduate who had already attained an enviable reputation
for his publications in American history, Winsor had presided over the nation's
foremost public library system in Boston since 1866. He was of average height,
but compactly built. His eyes, one of which required an eyeglass, suggested the
confidence of a proper Bostonian sure of his lot in life. His demeanor gave him
a commanding presence. He sported a well-trimmed beard and mustache under
a prominent nose. His low-pitched voice was not loud or especially distinctive,
but its resonance carried Winsor's message to the far corners of the conference
meeting room.[15] After appointing a committee on organization, Winsor introduced John William Wallace, president of the Pennsylvania Historical Society,
who welcomed conference participants to Philadelphia. Wallace called for a new
science—a bibliothecal science—and admonished those present to use the conference to establish an organization which could "promote" it. After the audience
awarded Wallace an enthusiastic response, Winsor invited the committee on
organization to nominate a slate of officers for the conference. The results were
not surprising: for president, Justin Winsor; for vice presidents, Poole, Smith,
Spofford and James Yates, public librarian from Leeds, England; for secretary,
Dewey, Guild, and Charles Evans, librarian at the Indianapolis Public Library
and one of Poole's protégés. After the conference approved the slate unanimously, Winsor took the chair, thanked conferees for their "compliment," and
deferred to Smith's motion for the appointment of three committees, one on
order of business, one on resolutions, and one on permanent organization. The
motion carried. After Dewey announced that a representative from the Bureau
of Education was en route from Washington with more copies of the *Special
Report on Libraries*, Smith moved that the conference recess until 3:00 P.M. It
had been a successful morning, and the conference seemed to run smoothly under
Winsor's steady hand, with able assistance from Poole, Smith and Dewey.

Winsor reconvened the conference at 3:20 and after Dewey read several letters
of regret from prominent individuals who could not attend, Winsor introduced
the scheduled section of the program which was devoted to formal papers. First
on the program was Poole, whom Winsor had called "the Nestor of our body
in experience." Next to Winsor, Poole was the most prominent librarian in the
United States. Born 55 years earlier in Salem, Massachusetts, he had graduated
from Yale in 1849. He had held the chief administrative post at the Boston
Athenaeum from 1856 to 1868, after which he left the East to organize the

Cincinnati Public Library. In 1874, he went to Chicago for a similar undertaking. Although a well-traveled librarian, he became best known for a periodical index he had completed while a student at Yale. The prospect of updating his index was sure to be raised at the conference.

For the moment, however, Poole had a captive audience for his talk on "Some Popular Objections to Public Libraries." Unlike Winsor, Poole's demeanor was "bluff, hearty, breezy," a manner more characteristic of a man of the West than of the East. Poole retained a mild aversion to eastern librarians for most of his life. He was six feet tall, loosely built, but with broad shoulders. Eyeglasses which covered his gleaming brown eyes sat upon a large nose, which stuck out from a face full of sandy-colored hair. Only the exaggerated length of his side-whiskers balanced the prominent nose. He tended to stutter when he became excited, and had a slight speech impediment. He also possessed a streak of vanity which occasionally translated into frequent, open, and vocal opposition to any innovation or movement in which he did not take a leading part. Bowker once referred to him as "our dear scoffer." Most contemporaries agreed he was a stronger bookman than administrator, but Poole never perceived this as a weakness. He thought it more important to foster "the spirit" of library work than to emphasize its mechanics and techniques. Poole also chewed tobacco, and on occasion smoked.[16]

Like Winsor, Poole was attracted to historical studies, but in the paper he delivered at Philadelphia he attributed a value to fiction in libraries which generated the "most earnest discussion" of the conference. Poole saw the issue as subordinate to another more important goal for public libraries: fostering the reading habit. If the acquisition and circulation of fiction of "marginal quality" was the only way to achieve that goal, Poole was willing to take the risks. Although he would not tolerate "immoral or vicious" books, he did not believe that patron consumption of fictitious works might lead to immorality, irresponsibility, or reckless living. Instead, Poole suggested, once these people formed a habit of reading they would more often than not seek to "elevate" their tastes and thus come under more direct guidance by the librarian.

When Poole concluded, Winsor opened the floor to discussion. The comments which followed demonstrated that librarians had been thinking about the fiction issue for some time; battle lines were quickly drawn. All present acknowledged that the printed word definitely had an impact on social behavior. Good literature led to good behavior; bad literature led to bad behavior. Few argued about what was good literature, but defining and identifying bad literature drew little agreement. Poole's most vociferous opponent was William Kite, librarian of the Friends' Free Library in Germantown, who argued that libraries need not stock novels at all. Most other conferees who spoke to the issue fell between Poole's and Kite's positions. James W. Ward of the Grosvenor Library in Buffalo, New York, seemed to express the vague sentiments of a majority. "If a novel is a good book, and accomplishes any good purposes, it is entitled to its place in a . . . public library. If in any sense it is a bad or even a useless book, it should be rejected." He did not specify criteria for determining the difference between the two. Others directed their comments to the need to "elevate" the reading tastes of the public.

Winsor joined Poole in his argument for placing novels in public libraries,[17] and both won support from Samuel S. Green, who reminded conferees that "popular libraries are not established merely for instruction. It is meant that they should give entertainment also. They are regarded as a means of keeping order in the community by giving people a harmless source of recreation." Green also complimented Winsor for compiling an annotated list of history and biography at the Boston Public Library which, Winsor had earlier reported, increased circulation in these two categories by 200 percent "without withdrawing fiction."

While conference attendees did not resolve the fiction question at Philadelphia, the positions they took reflected the thinking of leading professionals at the time. Most agreed that the mass reading public was generally incapable of choosing its own reading materials judiciously. Libraries should intervene for the benefit of society by acquiring and prescribing the best reading materials for the reading public's consumption. This approach represented a significant break with the past when the library's societal role was to acquire and preserve.[18] By adding a new dimension—advocating the efficient use of the collections under their care—librarians at the conference placed themselves in the vanguard of their profession. But the function of "prescribing" use, which was supported by principles of materials "selection," automatically placed these librarians in a socially patronizing position which was heavily influenced by their own social backgrounds and cultural value systems. Librarians charged with the responsibility for prescribing and selecting reading materials seldom questioned these values, for they instinctively assumed what was good for them as a group would be good for society in general, and would function as a passive control mechanism to maintain societal order.[19]

From the touchy fiction question, conference speakers then passed to more practical, less polemic issues.[20] Cutter's talk on "The Preservation of Pamphlets" led conferees to share so much practical information that the discussion had to be carried over to the evening session. Dewey, who had not even participated in the debate on fiction, championed the cause of small public libraries by reminding conferees that smaller institutions "cannot afford to treat the mass of pamphlets as books." Others contributed their views on book theft and mutilation, binding, government documents, duplicates, card catalogs, and finding lists. The discussion centering on cooperative indexing and especially Poole's *Index to Periodical Literature* led Dewey to move that the conference appoint a committee on cooperative indexing, and after that motion carried Dewey also moved that the newly formed committee report a plan for cooperative cataloging. Dewey impressed upon fellow conferees that progress in both areas would enhance general library efficiency. His motion passed unanimously.

Poole once again demonstrated his distrust of commercial publishers and booksellers by offering a resolution. He argued that an American Booksellers

Association (ABA) rule which forbade members from offering library discounts greater than 20 percent was discriminatory, "unjust and impolite, and is a rule which no librarian is bound to respect." Several conferees chafed under the harshness of the resolution's language. Other librarians pointed out that the ABA rule had not affected their discounts. Some booksellers present argued the resolution did not properly consider problems they had with publishers' prices. Despite objections, however, Poole's prestige and influence carried the motion, although not unanimously.

A committee on sizes of books issued a report to which Poole took exception. "I am not aware that we adopted all the points in the report which has just been read." Dewey quickly interjected that the missing points probably had been agreed to when Poole and Smith "felt constrained to retire—shall I say it?—to smoke." Smith then confessed he had given his proxy to Dewey when he left the room. The report was adopted, but Poole undoubtedly bristled at the way Dewey had handled the matter.

The committee on permanent organization reported a constitution for an American Library Association, but difficulties with identifying a consensus led Dewey to move that "we organize ourselves into the Association; elect a board of Officers, and entrust the preparation of the Constitution and By-laws to them, in order that there may be full opportunity for discussion and comparison of views." Dewey's motion carried just after another conferee moved that the secretary and treasurer's office be combined in the new organization. A nominating committee reported a list of officers including Winsor as president, Poole, Spofford and Homes as vice presidents, and Dewey as secretary and treasurer. Smith's motion to make the *American Library Journal* the official journal of the association was also adopted.

Most of the remainder of the conference focused on Dewey's new decimal classification scheme. Because "the prominent part which I have had in calling this Conference makes me unwilling to use any of its time for a matter in which I have so much personal interest," Dewey consented to talk about his scheme only after Smith prodded him. Following a brief discussion of the system, Dewey invited "those desiring to become members of the new library organization to sign the articles of association which were on the table." He signed first. Dewey also asked conferees to sign requests for copies of the *Special Report on Public Libraries* which had arrived on the morning of 5 October. He asked that librarians send him copies of library forms and applications so that all ALA members might benefit from the successful practical experiences of individual members. Winsor then indicated that conferees were free to tour neighboring libraries during the afternoon, but that they were invited back to the historical society that evening for a social occasion which would officially end the librarians' conference.

The 1876 conference set the tone and direction of the American Library Association for the next 15 years. The establishment of the association symbolized a break with an era when librarians were expected to acquire and preserve

socially beneficial and culturally substantive knowledge. The new breed of librarians, represented by such notables as Winsor and Poole, looked to create a
missionary spirit among fellow professionals that would encourage and facilitate
use of the sources of knowledge they acquired. These librarians believed that
public exposure to good literature would inevitably lead to a better informed,
more orderly society. While they marched forward with conviction, however,
these professionals failed to recognize they were also products, and in many
ways captives, of a socioeconomic and cultural value system in which they had
been raised and educated. This system automatically imposed parameters on the
types of library services they were willing to provide, and to a significant extent
dictated the activities and directions in which these librarians took their professional association.[21]

Evidence suggesting reasons for these limitations may be found in a collective
profile of ALA's first officers. All were white, Anglo-Saxon Protestant males
born in the Northeast, from families which had been living on the continent
three generations or more.[22] Most were educated in northeastern schools, and
most were chief administrators of large libraries. Public librarians predominated
among the ALA leadership, even though they comprised only 30 percent of the
103 conference attendees. Only Poole lived west of the Alleghenies; all lived
north of the Mason-Dixon line. Most were reared in middle- and upper-class
families where fathers were white-collar workers. Mean age of ALA officers in
1876 was 46.

Melvil Dewey was the baby of the group, and if significant differences are
evident among the ALA's early leaders, perhaps they can be found in Dewey's
complex character. While he shared his fellow ALA officers' belief in the power
of the printed word and the educational mission of the library, he was much
more interested in technical matters which would standardize internal procedures
and make library services more efficient. These interests closely coincided with
his activities as managing editor of the *American Library Journal* and his attempts
to launch a library supplies company. They may also explain Dewey's energetic
and enthusiastic efforts to get ALA organized. Throughout the conference Dewey
was the only prominent participant to focus upon the needs of small libraries,
which, he realized, stood to gain the most from standardization and systematization. And if the ALA Committee on Cooperative Indexing found the Dewey
Decimal Classification scheme a useful foundation for cooperative cataloging,
Dewey's fortunes would not be harmed.

For 15 years, however, Dewey would remain a maverick among ALA leaders.
He did not even look like the others. His six-foot frame was lithe and wiry and
he manifested a tendency to talk rapidly from his clean-shaven face. Although
he maintained a low profile during the first days of the conference, he could not
contain himself towards the end when questions concerning library efficiency
and standardization were on the floor. So confident had he become that he risked
alienating the influential Poole by patronizingly chiding him about his use of

tobacco. But Dewey was a minority in the leadership group. Winsor and Poole were more typical, more respected, more influential.

The conference itself reveals several characteristics about leading members of the library profession in 1876. Librarians were more concerned with practical and technical matters than with substantive philosophical questions. They believed that if the ''best reading'' collections they acquired were used by the general public, libraries would fulfill a valuable (though passive) societal role. But librarians could hardly be called reforming radicals. Although 13 women attended the 1876 conference, none ventured to speak except through male peers. Unlike the ALA, even the conservative, male-dominated Democratic and Republican parties ''allowed'' several women to openly voice opinions on political matters during their 1876 conventions. While the birth of the American Library Association in 1876 did not foretell a crusade to correct social inequities, it did provide an organization which would function as a locus for a professional *esprit de corps* and as a center for information exchange.

2   Rallying around "The Best Reading": The Formative Stages, 1876–1886

The American Library Association was almost a decade old when it met in Milwaukee, Wisconsin, from 7 to 10 July, 1886. Many members traveling from the East to Milwaukee gathered in Chicago on 6 July, where they were greeted by ALA President William F. Poole, still director of the Chicago Public Library, who had arranged a tour of Chicago's major sites. Shortly after lunch the traveling parties listened to a brief address by Chicago's Mayor Carter Henry Harrison, who prophesied to this audience that the Windy City would be "the Athens of America, rivalling even Athens of old." A reporter who witnessed the scene noted that Bostonians present looked "a little incredulous over the prophecy."[1]

Next day the party embarked on a leisurely three-hour train ride to Milwaukee, where they were greeted by Klas August Linderfelt, the hosting director of the Milwaukee Public Library, and William Plankinton, influential member of its board of trustees. It is probably not coincidental that most conferees checked into rooms at the Plankinton House, a short walk from the public library, at that time located inside the Germania Society's building.

The conference officially opened at 2:50 P.M. Both Emil Wallber, mayor of Milwaukee, and Harrison C. Hobart, president of the library's board of trustees, issued official welcomes. Poole genially replied that Milwaukee would not have to increase its police force during the conference; librarians were "peaceable and inoffensive folk. We are neither communists nor anarchists; although we are all knights of labor in the sense that we find it healthful to labor nights." Poole then delivered a presidential address in which he proudly noted that "no speculation or scandal has ever occurred in connection with the management of a public library. If every department in the corporation affairs in cities . . . were managed as well as their public libraries they would be model municipalities."[2]

Melvil Dewey, who in 1886 was library director at Columbia College in New York City, read the secretary's report. Although he delivered it in the same oral English used by everyone else at the conference, when the official proceedings were issued, the report was written in the simplified spelling style which Dewey had been advocating for ten years. Poole, Winsor, and Smith disliked it intensely; they successfully resisted Dewey's attempt to impose it on ALA, but they felt compelled to a compromise with Dewey that "neither side had any right to dictate how the other should spell."[3]

Dewey used his report to digress on several of his own schemes. He noted that the cooperation committee, consisting of Ellen M. Coe of the New York Free Circulating Library, C. Alex Nelson of the Astor Library, Walter S. Biscoe, Dewey's cataloger at Columbia, B. P. Mann of the U.S. Department of Agriculture, and chairman William I. Fletcher, director of the Amherst College Library, had met at Columbia a few weeks prior to the conference. The committee had solicited the opinions of over 20 New York librarians, and had developed a plan for cooperation which would require ALA to establish a new "Publishing Section." Dewey promised the plan would be discussed later in the conference.

He also announced publication of *Library Notes*, a new quarterly he was editing, to be issued by the Library Bureau, a library supplies company under his direction. He said *Notes* would be much cheaper than *Library Journal*, which at the time was subscribed to by less than 10 percent of American public libraries. As in 1876 Dewey continued to manifest a special interest in the cause of the small public library, noting that the subscription price of the *Journal* (which he no longer edited) was "prohibitive . . . to these little institutions that so much need its help." He wanted *Library Notes* to "build up" the proposed publishing section, to expedite publication of an ALA *Catalog* which would identify a core collection for all libraries, and to facilitate the dissemination of preprinted catalog cards to reduce duplicate cataloging of widely used titles. Dewey acknowledged the Library Bureau had a pecuniary interest in the latter.[4]

ALA Treasurer James L. Whitney, assistant librarian of the Boston Public Library, followed Dewey with a treasurer's report. Samuel Swett Green moved immediately that it be referred to the finance committee for auditing rather than to the executive committee, because members of the latter were "now more scattered than ever." But Green exaggerated. In 1886 the executive committee had one member—Poole—who lived west of Buffalo; the finance committee had none. When no one arose to contest Green's statement, his motion carried.[5]

At the Milwaukee conference no one openly argued the fiction question. Most discussion centered on practical library matters, and especially on classification and cataloging, which occasioned a lively debate. Dewey was especially prominent here, constantly stressing the value of simplicity and efficiency which was characteristic of his own decimal classification scheme. "The young librarian must choose whether he will adopt the time-saving labor methods, or stick to the time-honored ways in which our grandparents made their reputation."[6] Cutter reported that the "School of Library Economy" which Dewey organized at Columbia was almost ready to open. Dewey himself added: "We wish the ALA to feel that this school is its school." He then asked association members to report on the cooperation committee's recommendations that ALA establish a publishing section. Although Dewey had suggested the move, Poole did not name him to the committee. Instead, the ALA president selected Fletcher, Coe, Biscoe, William Coolidge Lane, who was assistant catalog librarian at Harvard, and Josephus N. Larned, director of the Young Men's Library in Buffalo.

The Milwaukee conference manifested one change not evident ten years earlier. Women were more visible. Ellen Coe challenged several opinions during one of the discussions on classification. Papers by Hannah P. James and Caroline M. Hewins, director of the Hartford (Connecticut) Public Library, were read in their absence. Increased participation by ALA women in conference proceedings may have been more noticeable in 1886, but it still was not proportionate to their numbers among conference attendees.

The day before the conference ended, the association voted to establish a publishing section "to secure the preparation and publication of such catalogs, indexes, and other bibliographical helps as may best be produced by cooperation." After passing a publishing section constitution, the next morning the association elected a slate of section officers which included Whitney as chairman, Lane as treasurer, and an executive committee consisting of Fletcher, Dewey, Bowker, Cutter, and Green. None lived more than a hundred miles from the Atlantic Ocean. The ALA executive committee reported its selections of association officers for the subsequent year, including Poole as president for a second year in a row, and vice presidents Spofford, Cutter, Providence (Rhode Island) Public Library Director William E. Foster and Mellon Chamberlain, who had succeeded Justin Winsor as superintendent of the Boston Public Library in 1877. Once again Dewey was named secretary, and Henry J. Carr, director of the Grand Rapids (Michigan) Public Library, was named treasurer.[7]

Although a close look at the association's leadership between 1882 and 1886 demonstrates little difference from the first group of executives elected at the Philadelphia conference in 1876 (see Appendix II), the statistical picture does not reflect struggles to alter the power alignments which were fought behind the scenes during ALA's first decade. For the most part the group in control was pleased with the structure, direction, and activities of the new library association. Melvil Dewey was not. During the last few minutes of the 1886 conference, for example, he moved two constitutional amendments which tested the strength of the control group: (1) "that no officer be reelected more than once"; (2) that "the A.L.A. shall annually elect, by written ballot, a President and an Executive Board, four members beside the President, who shall choose from the Association a Vice-President, a Secretary, a Treasurer, Finance and Cooperation Committee of three and any other needed officers or standing committees." In 1886 the energetic Dewey was not influential enough to get his motion passed.[8]

The day after the conference adjourned Horace Kephart, a Yale College Library assistant, wrote his longtime friend Henry L. Koopman of the Brown University Library that the meeting was "interesting." He reported that two people especially captured his attention. "My disrespect for Dewey has changed into a sort of wonder at his chic, gab and plausibility. He is really a remarkable human being," Kephart said. Then he continued:

Poole is splendid. We were old cronies in two minutes. Almost his first question (put with a searching look) was, "Are you one of those students of Dewey's?" When assured to the contrary he exclaimed, "Well, I'm glad to hear it." He asked me what I thought of Dewey, and I said, "He is a humbug." I think that Poole took a fancy to me at sight.[9]

Kephart's observations revealed more than he knew, and reflected a concealed history of infighting which had separated Dewey from the mainstream ALA leadership. The story behind these hidden struggles forms the foundation for a discussion in subsequent pages of the association's embryonic years.

Before conferees left the Philadelphia conference in October 1876, they had authorized their newly-elected officers to draw up a constitution and publish it in the *American Library Journal*. President Winsor, Vice Presidents Poole, Spofford and Homes, and Secretary Dewey submitted the ALA's proposed governing document to the membership on 31 March 1877. It was simple and straightforward. Article II stated the object of ALA "Shall be to promote the library interests of the country by exchanging views, researching conclusions, and inducing cooperation in all departments of bibliothecal science and economy; by disposing the public mind to the founding and improving of libraries; and by cultivating goodwill among its own members." ALA efforts would be directed toward improving practical, not theoretical, librarianship. The association would not attempt to foster the establishment of a body of theoretical knowledge upon which to found the library profession.[10] Rather, it would provide a forum in which technique would be fairly aired, and the constitution reinforced this mission in Article IV, Section 6, which determined that a "Co-operation Committee shall consider and report upon plans designed to secure uniformity and economize in methods of administration."

More important, however, was the controlling mechanism of the young association—the executive board. "The Association shall annually elect an Executive Board of five members, who shall have power to add to their own number, and from the board thus constituted they shall choose for the Association a President, Vice-President, a Secretary, a Treasurer, Finance and Co-operation Committees of three each, and any other needed officers or standing committees."[11] The power of the executive board was total. Because the president appointed a nominating committee at the beginning of each conference to identify a slate of executive board nominees by the end of that same conference, he effectively deprived the membership of any opportunity to contribute to the nomination process. And the nominating committee seldom presented more than five names for membership approval. As a result of this practice, the official leadership during ALA's early years became in large part a self-perpetuating body of men who were unusually homogeneous in socioeconomic and cultural backgrounds. They imposed their personal attitudes and values, as well as their professional goals and aspirations, upon ALA simply by virtue of the positions they occupied on the executive board.

Three names constantly surfaced among executive board officers throughout ALA's first decade: Winsor, Poole, and Dewey. Winsor and Poole were conservative by nature, serenely satisfied with the progress of the profession which had awarded them national reputations. While Poole retained his suspicions about the motivations of "Eastern librarians," he found it easy to work with Winsor since they both agreed that the association's mere existence was a major benefit to their profession's progress. Dewey, on the other hand, was the maverick of the group who seldom found allies among his fellow executive board members to push the association into new ventures. He wanted the association to participate actively in generating a variety of cooperative schemes to systematize and make more efficient practical routines in libraries across the country. He also demonstrated more concern for small libraries than Poole and Winsor. Although Dewey could not muster much support on the executive board, he used his position as managing editor of the *American Library Journal* to exert constant pressure upon the association to become more active. The *Journal* regularly carried editorials reciting the benefits of the cooperative, systematizing, and efficiency schemes which Dewey championed.

While these differences of opinion occasionally surfaced at conferences, most of the membership seemed blissfully unaware of—or, perhaps more accurately, indifferent to—opposing views. The membership undoubtedly recognized that the association needed Dewey's drive, energy, and free labor to survive an uncertain embryonic period characteristic of any professional association's growth. But ALA members also realized they needed the steady hand of leadership provided by individuals like Winsor and Poole who could command respect both inside and outside the profession.

Dewey's dual role as managing editor of the *American Library Journal* (ALJ) and secretary of the American Library Association is crucial to understanding ALA's early years. On the one hand, he had definite obligations to the *Journal*. His contract with Leypoldt specified an annual salary of $750 plus another $450 per year "for postage, stationery and incidentals, traveling, office, editorial and other expences incurred" for the *Journal*. For his part Dewey agreed to "assume the entire expenses" of his Boston office.[12] The ambiguity of these two contractual clauses would cause both men difficulty in the coming years. Richard R. Bowker had a much keener business mind than his publishing partner. Because Bowker was concerned that the *Journal* turn a profit as soon as possible, he frequently scolded Dewey for pushing measures that increased *Journal* production costs. After Leypoldt admonished Dewey on 20 October 1876 not to be afraid "that you may lose more or less by yielding in form to our sincere friend and well meaning counsellor,"[13] Dewey invited Bowker "to give me a blowing up for my weaknesses. I like it as I do a cold bath. It makes me shiver, but I know the final effect is good, and am grateful."[14]

Concurrent with his duties as ALJ managing editor, Dewey also exercised his influence as ALA secretary. For example, in the spring of 1877 he wrote John Shaw Billings, librarian of the National Medical Library, that the *Journal* needed more subscribers. "In this we think you will agree with us, that if it is impossible to continue the *Journal*, it will be more impossible to complete Poole's Index, prepare title slips for common use, or to do any of the cooperative work."[15] Similarly, in a circular sent to "Library Members of the Public" about the same time, Dewey encouraged his readers to join the professional organization whose object was to "make the libraries still more efficient, and at the same time to reduce their expenses largely." Several sentences later he stated that after "consulting my list," he found "your library has not yet subscribed" to the *Journal*, despite the fact that "it was chiefly for the smaller institutions that the *Journal* was undertaken."[16] To a keen businessman reading these letters, two questions would automatically surface: Who was paying for this correspondence? Who was Dewey representing—the *Journal*, ALA, or a minority within ALA—when he talked of efficiency, cooperation, and the interests of smaller libraries? In ALA's early years, when individuals were more concerned with fostering good relations among various organizational interests in librarianship than in defining territorial autonomy, this was not a problem. But Dewey's strong personality was always a force behind the winds of change.

The first annual meeting of the American Library Association was held in the lecture room of the New York Young Men's Christian Association on 4 and 5 September 1877. Only 66 people attended, little more than half the total in Philadelphia 11 months before. Although attendance was light, the conference was no less enthusiastic, for a number of conferees had planned to leave together from New York to attend a conference in London called by British librarians. Most anticipated the latter meeting would lead to the establishment of a British library association.

In New York President Winsor opened a conference which reflected ALA's overriding concern for practical matters. The fiction question was seldom raised, and whenever someone alluded to it, others did not comment sufficiently to generate extended discussion. Caroline Hewins of the Hartford (Connecticut) Public Library became the first woman to speak out at an ALA conference. She asked whether dog taxes were being used to support public libraries in states other than Massachusetts. Other topics aroused greater interest, and led conferees to establish committees to explore publishers' discounts to libraries, exchanging duplicate books between libraries, and distributing public documents issued by the federal government. Poole's paper on "Library Legislation" convinced the association to appoint a committee "to propose recommendations on legal provisions in regard to the establishment and management of public libraries." The move was sparked by Winsor's resignation as superintendent of the Boston Public Library the previous summer, when the Boston Common Council squabbled over the salary awarded the library director and the level of expertise needed to run the institution. Although Winsor was quickly appointed to direct the Harvard College Library, ALA members continued to exhibit a deep desire to depoliticize selection procedures in public library posts across the country.[17]

Poole delivered a progress report for the committee on the continuation of

Poole's Index, and Dewey enthusiastically read the cooperation committee's report on proposed rules for cooperative cataloging. Poole dissented. "I do not propose to be bound by anything that this Association may do in this matter. . . . I would rather the ALA should not commit itself to any particular style."[18] Despite Poole's opposition, however, other conferees saw enough merit in the proposed rules that Winsor appointed a special committee on uniform title entries. After Dewey cited the need for ALA to add to its membership roles, the conference adjourned.

In an editorial probably penned by Dewey, the *American Library Journal* summarized the conference as "no less successful" than its immediate predecessor. It gently reminded Poole, "the Martin Luther of the Conference," that an ALA-endorsed code of recommendations for uniform cataloging was not intended to be binding. "It is not expected that large existing libraries should revolutionize settled systems for the sake of ideal but inconvenient uniformity."[19] Dewey's concern for the small public library and his suspicions that administrators of large libraries generally lacked a wholistic perspective of the library world continued to surface in his editorials. But if the *Journal*'s columns reflected a refracted vision of the conference, the New York *World* was more perceptive, perhaps even sardonic:

As in all conventions, a slight division is apparent. The party of young librarians was eager for the adoption of Continental methods, for decapitalization in French style, and uniformity of labels, indexes and calendars, to which the conservative majority gave guarded encouragement. To hear the frank, mirthful Dewey . . . or the earnest, enthusiastic young Arthur W. Tyler [librarian at The Johns Hopkins University Library] enlarging on the advantages of omitting all capitals possible in a catalogue of books, one was fain to look upon it as a chief earthly interest, while the emphatic Spofford, who has charge of the Congressional Library, or the deprecatory Homes of Albany, and Poole of Chicago protest against any such neo-republicanism of letters and beheading of capitals.[20]

Shortly after the conclusion of the conference, members of the association sailed from New York to attend a meeting of British librarians in London. This session resulted in the establishment of the Library Association of the United Kingdom. En route Winsor took particular delight in observing that Dewey was "playing his first game of cards." Dewey had confided to Winsor that he had been "entrusted" to care for Wellesley College Librarian Annie Godfrey by her mother, but because he did not want others to know, Winsor observed in a letter to his wife, Dewey "pays little attention to her." Apparently Dewey could not contain himself for long: on the return trip Winsor noted that Godfrey "seems to be Dewey's particular."[21] Winsor himself was not above shipboard banter as he joined with Poole and Smith to "protect" a young Scottish woman named "Pussy," who was returning home from the United States. Each of the three conservative librarians took turns "promenading" the deck with the young lady "on his arm."[22]

The executive board elected at the New York conference held two meetings before returning to the United States. At the first, held on 13 September, the board reappointed the same officers who had served the preceding year with one exception; they added another vice presidential position and named John P. Dyer, librarian at the Mercantile Library of St. Louis, to fill it. At the second meeting, held on 29 October, board members decided to hold the association's next general meeting in Boston in June 1879, to allow time to arrange "an especially attractive and noteworthy convention." Everyone agreed upon the need to increase ALA membership.[23]

Shortly after returning from England Samuel Green wrote Winsor that he was pleased with the "added dignity" awarded American librarians because of the reception given them in England. He hoped this would induce more "thoroughly educated young men" to join the profession. He asked Winsor "why should there not be instruction given at Harvard in library work and library economy, and the best resources of the country be thus utilized to give the general culture and special training needed by librarians." It is not known whether Winsor answered.[24] In the meantime Dewey complained to Bowker about delays in obtaining proof copy of speeches delivered at the last ALA conference, whose proceedings were to be incorporated into future pages of the *Journal*. He was especially annoyed with "that old rat" Poole, who had "burned his copy as soon as he read it through!" He lamented, "I have to write to these fellows a second time generally."[25]

While Dewey struggled with his contributors, he also sought to renegotiate his contract with his publishers. The *American Library Journal*, which was renamed *Library Journal* (LJ) after the London conference, had lost over $1,100 its first year of operation. Because part of Dewey's income was tied to the periodical's gross receipts, he asked Leypoldt to renegotiate his contract. On 24 January 1878 Leypoldt reluctantly agreed to four new clauses. Almost immediately, however, the complexity of the contract spawned additional problems. Both Leypoldt and Bowker quickly grew to dislike "the clogging business complications" which Dewey "insisted upon."[26] The *Journal* continued to do badly. As managing editor, Dewey persistently emphasized "those topics which concern the librarian as an administrator rather than as a scholar," and he continued to court small libraries in an attempt to increase subscriptions. His efforts largely failed, and by late 1878 Bowker felt compelled to cut expenses by insisting that business management of the *Journal* be returned to New York.[27] Dewey reacted sharply. He wrote Bowker on 8 January 1879 that unless *Journal* publishers arranged a contract more favorable to him, he might start an "opposition journal" with the help of "the leading men" of ALA who had met in Boston that same day. He also implied that Bowker and Leypoldt were trying to ease him out of his position as managing editor.

Bowker was incensed. He reminded Dewey on 9 January that everyone "understood" from an editors' meeting the previous summer that the *Journal* "could not continue running into debt by covering the rent of the Boston office and services." He also argued against Dewey's implication that he was being ousted, and he promised Dewey if he continued these objectionable activities, Bowker would show Cutter and Winsor Dewey's letter of 8 January. Bowker recognized that Dewey was using his ties with ALA to pressure the *Journal* into a more favorable contract. He clearly resented Dewey's tactics and was willing, "if necessary," to call Dewey's bluff. On 13 January he wrote Cutter that Dewey could not possibly see "what a breach of faith is implied in this letter." He told Cutter that he wanted to keep this imbroglio within "the family," and because he did not want to write Winsor directly about the matter, he asked Cutter if Dewey's threat had "any foundation." Cutter reassured him about ALA's commitment to the *Journal*. Nonetheless, for some reason not evident in existing correspondence, the matter did go before the ALA executive board for advice "as to proper relations, pecuniary and otherwise" between the *Journal* and Dewey. To clarify the situation Bowker wrote Winsor on 15 January that "the difference with Dewey as we look at it, is simple, as to how much the *Journal* can afford to pay him." Unfortunately, available evidence does not reveal how the conflict was resolved, nor the final terms of that resolution.[28]

The incident does demonstrate a set of circumstances which would have a significant impact upon ALA for the next several years. Since October 1876, Dewey had served as the link between ALA and the *Journal*. On the one hand, he used *Journal* columns as a forum to keep his ideas of expanded library cooperation and efficiency before the eyes of the library public. On the other hand, Dewey used his ALA ties to evoke a better financial deal for himself with LJ. By mid-January 1879, as the rest of the executive board began to recognize this, Dewey's effectiveness with both groups steadily diminished. Increasingly, Bowker came to rely on Cutter to assume more editorial responsibilities for the *Journal*, and to serve as the unofficial link between ALA and LJ. The situation evolved naturally. Cutter's interests, ideas, and professional responsibilities occupied a more comfortable middle ground between Dewey and the ALA leadership. If Dewey recognized this changing situation, he did little to regain lost ground. In June 1879, as ALA officials prepared for the summer conference in Boston, Dewey worded an announcement for a conference reception at the home of Boston Public Library Trustee George B. Chase as if a conference arrangements committee had extended the invitation, and not Chase. When Chase protested, Dewey suggested that Bowker had neglected to catch this error before sending the preliminary program to the printer. Dewey did not mention that he had been responsible for proofreading the program. When Bowker learned of Dewey's implication, he immediately wrote to Winsor that he felt "righteously indignant . . . at being made a scapegoat."[29] The incident with Chase made Bowker even more cautious of the ALA secretary.

In the meantime, several association matters moved along more smoothly. The ALA's committee on title slips proposed a plan for issuing uniform title-entry slips which publishers could use in advertising their books and which libraries could use selectively as catalog cards. The scheme fit ALA's mission to educate the public to better reading. Members believed that if librarians highlighted the best books, the public would read them. The effort to update and expand *Poole's Index* also continued. At the 1877 London conference a group of English librarians had volunteered to index a series of British publications. LJ published a symposium on the forthcoming index in its June 1878 issue.[30] The ALA "Supply Department," which had grown out of cooperation committee activities and was largely housed in and run from Dewey's Boston office, also attempted to raise its profile.[31] Another activity which received attention—perhaps because Dewey pushed it so hard in ALA correspondence and LJ editorials—was work on the "A.L.A. Catalog."

In August 1877 Dewey suggested in a LJ article entitled "The Coming Catalogue" that librarians needed a cooperatively compiled catalog of 10,000 annotated books which could be used as a collection guide for any general library and as a reading guide for library patrons. He recommended that the work be undertaken by the association, and cited two precursors which had already benefited librarians—Winsor's annotated class list at the Boston Public Library and a pamphlet entitled *Best Reading* by Frederick Beecher Perkins. In response to Dewey's prodding, the ALA cooperation committee, whose members included Cutter, Frederick Jackson of the Newton Free Library, and Frederick Beecher Perkins of the Boston Public Library, decided to commence work on "a select catalogue, suitable to the purposes of the average library, including satisfactory annotations." The committee narrowed the scope of the catalog to 5,000 titles, decided to arrange entries in a subject classification, and asked for a guarantee against loss by soliciting advance subscriptions of $2.50. In summer 1879, the committee identified the catalog's three specific objectives: (1) to suggest the best books for a "proposed library"; (2) to eliminate the expense "of preparing a new separate catalog for each new library"; and (3) to guide readers to the best books on a given subject.[32] Committee members promised to report at a later date.

Reflecting the slow progress made by a few committees, the association itself did not grow as rapidly as Dewey had hoped. He kept pushing for ALA in LJ columns, and continually reminded readers of the potential of a strong association backed by funds generated from increased membership rolls. He constantly stressed that the public library had to assume responsibility for the general education of the masses after they left school, and he called for philanthropists to help the association in its work. To augment the association's image, he also devised an ALA motto while commuting by horse between his home in Newton and his office in Boston: "The best reading for the largest number at the least expense."[33] As the association prepared for its summer 1879 conference in Boston, however, Dewey forewarned Winsor that except for the cooperation committee, most others "are not doing anything." He suggested Winsor should not have high expectations.[34]

The American Library Association opened its second annual meeting on 30 June 1879. No one seemed to notice that Mary Abby Bean of the Brookline (Massachusetts) Public Library became the first woman listed on an ALA program. She spoke on "The Evil of Unlimited Freedom in the Use of Juvenile Fiction," a subject which received most of the press attention. Bean's talk was part of a symposium on fiction and children's reading that was debated by librarians like Foster and Green and nonlibrarians like Charles Frances Adams, Jr., trustee of the Quincy (Massachusetts) Public Library, and Robert C. Metcalf, headmaster of the Wells School in Boston. As in 1876, conferees could not agree on a consistent policy concerning fiction for public libraries. Cutter summed up the problem accurately in his report to the *Nation*. "There is, in fact, no single remedy."

As Dewey predicted, most committees reported little or no progress since the last conference. Nonetheless, he used his secretary's report to review general ALA progress, which in fact had been born exactly one thousand days before. "Our President shows his suspicion to the decimal character of my coincidence," Dewey joked with his audience, "but I plead innocence on any knowledge of the fact till last evening." Poole followed Dewey with a report on the progress of *Poole's Index*. He could not let an opportunity to tease Dewey escape. He gleefully noted the *Index* would cover "current periodicals down to January 1, 1880, an even decimal period, and stop there." Unfortunately, Dewey's reaction was not recorded.

Homes read a paper on "Legislation for Public Libraries," and followed it with a report from the committee on library legislation, which recommended that all state legislatures adopt laws to maintain public libraries. Conferees agreed. Cutter reported that the cooperation committee had decided to transfer the "stock and goodwill" of the ALA supply department to the newly formed Readers and Writers Economy Company, whose president and chief stockholder was none other than Dewey himself. The nominating committee reported Winsor, Poole, Whitney, Green and Dewey for selection to the executive board. All "were unanimously approved."[35]

When the conference adjourned at 10:00 P.M. on 2 July 1879, it was obvious that veteran librarians continued to restrain the direction in which Dewey wanted to take the association. Except for *Poole's Index*, under the direct guidance of its namesake, the remaining schemes which Dewey had been pushing were not much farther along in 1879 than they had been in 1877. And one scheme, a library supplies department, he had taken out of ALA entirely.

The association did not meet again until February 1881, but a series of events leading to that conference had a profound impact on ALA. The first few months following the Boston conference, however, showed the same mixed progress which had characterized the previous three years. On the one hand, three areas witnessed marked success. First, in fall 1879 Dewey recommended that the association consider incorporation. In a letter to Winsor, he cited four reasons to make the move. Incorporating, he said, would (1) give the association a "permanence and dignity not to be secured under our present organization"; (2) allow ALA to "hold property legally and without taxation . . . "; (3) permit ALA to become an individual under the laws, thereby eliminating the liability of members reluctant to undertake cooperative schemes like the ALA *Catalog* without legal protection; and (4) encourage contributions from "the wealthy quarter" of society. The executive board agreed with Dewey and approved the move without consulting the membership. On 10 December 1879 the American Library Association became incorporated under the laws of the State of Massachusetts.[36]

Second, in 1880 *Publisher's Weekly* adopted the ALA uniform title catalog code and honored an ALA request to include annotations with titles it listed. Third, work on *Poole's Index* moved along rapidly, although Poole became particularly piqued at Spofford, who procrastinated on the indexing responsibilities he had volunteered to contribute. Poole threatened to take over the assignment himself, or "what was most likely, omit it altogether, and make a full statement of the reason and the facts in my preface." Spofford fulfilled his obligation within two weeks. By November 1880, Poole told Dewey, the work of all volunteers had arrived and was now being arranged.[37]

In other areas, the association witnessed either limited or no success. Work on the ALA *Catalog* seemed to keep pace with *Poole's Index* for a while. On 15 October 1879, the ALA executive board proudly announced $1,207 had been pledged to develop the *Catalog*, thereby enabling ALA to retain complete control and simultaneously deprive profit-seeking publishers of any opportunity to "modify its character." The board appointed Frederick Perkins to "take direct editorial charge." By 24 January 1880, Perkins announced that a provisional list of 5,000 books would be subdivided by subject and soon sent "to the best authorities for revision and annotation." On 23 February he issued a circular inviting specialists to participate. That summer, however, after Perkins had accepted an offer to become director of the San Francisco Public Library, work on the *Catalog* ceased. Perkins complained he was geographically separated from the center of ALA activity, and he refused to do anything more until he was compensated for his efforts. On 9 November he wrote Dewey, "If I can draw pay I'll go on with the ALA Catalog with pleasure. You know I never agreed to do it without the cash."[38]

But Dewey was in no position either to help Perkins or to assume responsibility for the work himself. In December he became embroiled in yet another controversy, this time with the ALA executive board, concerning control of ALA books and funds. Throughout his life Dewey exhibited a careless attitude towards basic business practices; he was especially reckless and self-serving in keeping budget books and accounts. After Dewey was appointed temporary ALA treasurer to fill a vacancy in summer 1880, he began listing ALA and LJ funds in the same account books used to record the financial activity of his own Readers and Writers Economy Company. In December one of Dewey's partners in the company accused Dewey of dishonest business practices and threatened to take him to court. When Dewey hired a lawyer to represent him, he told Winsor about his practice of combining accounts in the same books. Winsor was appalled and felt he had to move quickly to make sure ALA funds, accounts, and books were divorced from any litigation involving the Readers and Writers Economy Company. He suggested Dewey tender his resignation as ALA treasurer at an executive board meeting to be held on 5 December 1880. When Dewey did not appear for the meeting, the board accepted a resignation he had never tendered, and empowered Samuel S. Green, chairman of the finance committee, to take control of ALA funds and books. On 11 December Winsor also ordered finance committee member James L. Whitney to retrieve all ALA supplies, books, and funds from Dewey's possession.

Dewey had been cornered, but on 13 December protested the executive board's action as an unfair "judgment against me" which was made without a foundation of facts concerning a matter "outside" the "province" of ALA. He demanded an apology. Winsor was not intimidated. "It is by no means an assumption by the board of your guilt which makes them take a position, quite as much for your interest as for theirs at the time when investigations in the Economy Company are pending and rumors are afloat to your discredit." Winsor argued that the board was justified "to take action looking to be disconnected with you officially in this interim of uncertainty," and that Dewey's troubles were not "outside its province. Consider! The ALA had a sum of money in its Treasurer's hands, it was originally on its books to his credit by his act. It no longer appears there as such but is in the books of the Economy Company as part of his individual credit. Is solicitude for the money 'outside our province'?" The ALA leadership had taken the proper course by asking Dewey to resign, Winsor argued, because wisdom "dictates for your own sake that you should have as little as possible connection with the ALA." Dewey continued to contend that he would return all ALA papers and funds on his own, but Winsor said the association could not take that chance. He wrote to postal authorities on 21 December that all correspondence to ALA or its secretary be delivered to Whitney instead. Again Dewey protested, but to no avail. "We argue to no purpose," Winsor wrote him on 23 December.

Before Whitney could act on Winsor's order, however, Dewey managed to separate ALA papers from the Economy Company's, thereby eliminating the possibility that the association would be drawn into a court battle and its funds needlessly tied up in litigation. Fortunately for Dewey, all of this happened before the Washington conference in February 1881. Winsor suggested that at the conference Dewey turn over all ALA funds and accounts to Green, who, in turn, would "simply report your resignation and handing over of accounts and cash, just as if there had been no delay of it." He also urged Dewey to make no public statements at Washington concerning the affair. "Let us assume there never has been any cause of inquiry, reasonable and unreasonable, and all will be alright. Do not let your convictions of your own ill treatment lead you to attempt an unwise procedure." He reminded Dewey he was still ALA secretary with the full authority inherent in that position. Green told Dewey he agreed with Winsor's advice.[39]

But as the Washington conference approached Dewey was losing ground on another front. In the November-December 1880 LJ issue, Leypoldt announced that Dewey "withdrew" from the *Journal* as of 1 January. Although he followed the announcement with praise for Dewey's contributions to the periodical, he could not disguise the fact that the move had not been voluntary. He identified no specific problems between the contending parties, nor did he acknowledge that Dewey's difficulties with the *Library Journal* had not diminished after the Boston conference of 1879. At the heart of the matter was Dewey's questionable bookkeeping and his complicated contracts, which he had consistently reinterpreted to his own advantage.

On 10 January 1880 Bowker had issued a circular forewarning LJ subscribers that "unless the increase of support this year fully covers the cost of publication, the enterprise will thereafter be suspended to await a more promising stage of library development." He reported that the *Library Journal* still had not showed any profit after four volumes. He also said he and Dewey would continue to edit LJ, but he announced that Cutter and Whitney would also be contributing special columns. Bowker simultaneously wrote a letter to ALA explaining the *Journal*'s dismal financial situation and, after reminding the association that LJ had supported it faithfully since 1876 and continued as the association's official organ, he asked ALA to contribute $200 towards the publication of the association's conference proceedings. ALA refused.[40]

In June, the *Journal* announced it was suspending publication and consolidating with *Publisher's Weekly*. Reactions from the library community were mixed. Some were angry that the *Journal* would break off publication in midyear. Others were sad that the profession would be losing an effective voice. Dewey reacted by suggesting four possible alternatives in a circular to prominent librarians: (1) assess ALA members $1 per year so the association could assume publication of the *Journal* on its own; (2) establish a sinking fund of $2,000 by asking ALA members to contribute $25 each; (3) reduce the price of the *Journal* by cutting printing and production costs; and (4) consolidate LJ with *Literary World* or *Publisher's Weekly* (PW). Responses revealed no consensus. William E. Foster and Jacob Schwartz of the New York City Apprentices' Library favored the first alternative; Homes and John Edmands of the Philadelphia Mercantile Library liked the second; William I. Fletcher preferred the third; and Lloyd Smith and Frederick M. Crunden, director of the St. Louis Public Library, advocated the fourth. Poole was generally surly about the entire situation. He complained of "an obscurity about the business management of the *Journal*," and the "disgrace" of ceasing publication in the middle of a volume. He claimed that the publishers owed subscribers the remaining issues of the current volume, after which another publisher could take the *Journal* and reduce the subscription fee. And he was adamantly opposed to providing direct financial assistance. "As a member of the American Library Association Executive Committee I can never consent to the Association being mixed up with the pecuniary affairs of the Journal." Poole also sent a letter to the Library Association in England openly criticizing *Journal* publishers for their action. His letter was read at an association

conference session just before Bowker, who had recently taken a full-time position in Great Britain, arrived to deliver an address. The ill-feeling which Poole's
move created permanently tarnished Bowker's attitude towards the Chicago
librarian.[41]

With Bowker out of the country, however, concerned librarians had a better
chance to work on Leypoldt, the weaker of the two PW editors. Dewey himself
recognized this; he had always attempted to renegotiate his contract with Leypoldt, not Bowker. Shortly after the June announcement, "discontented librarians" began protesting Leypoldt's decision. They repeatedly begged the aging
publisher to reconsider. The campaign apparently struck a responsive chord.
Leypoldt eventually relented and agreed to continue at least to the end of the
volume year, but at a reduced production cost. He would use smaller print and
shorten each issue to 16 pages. Although Leypoldt's move made librarians happy,
his business partner bristled. Leypoldt tried to minimize Bowker's anger by
writing a very defensive letter on 11 August to explain his decision. He especially
cited the added costs of consolidating *Journal* matter into *Publisher's Weekly*
columns. In the end, he concluded, continuing the *Journal* "will not cost me
much more money and trouble than the consolidation." He anticipated Bowker's
suspicion of Dewey, but informed his partner that Dewey "had no hand in this."
Leypoldt was now "consulting Mr. Cutter on the most important points." His
comment was telling; Dewey's influence on LJ was obviously diminishing.
Leypoldt's wife, who repeatedly told her husband that consolidation "won't cost
you a cent more," was less charitable. "I never believed in the *Library Journal*,
because I knew it would not pay and I thought Dewey about as miserable a
specimen of a gabbling idiot as I had ever beheld."[42]

Although Dewey made no apparent moves to press Leypoldt to continue the
Journal, his efforts to work a complex contract to his advantage and his propensity to mix LJ accounts with his other ventures continued to color their
relationship. By 4 October Leypoldt had had enough. "I am completely mystified
concerning your mode of doing business," he wrote, and he informed the Boston
entrepreneur that at the end of the current contract year "it would be better to
drop hereafter all business connections. . . . the fact is that your peculiar way of
doing business has cost this office more in time than all that you claim could
amount to." Simultaneously with this decision Leypoldt made two others. He
would continue the *Journal* for another year in the 16 page, small-print format.
He also asked Charles Ammi Cutter, who had been *de facto* LJ editor since
summer, 1880, to succeed Dewey. Cutter agreed to Leypoldt's offer on two
conditions: (1) the *Journal* could not use Cutter's name on the title page; and
(2) he would take the assignment only on a six-month trial basis. If pressed, his
obligations to the Boston Athenaeum had to take precedence over the *Journal*.
In December 1880 Leypoldt accepted Cutter's conditions.[43]

Leypoldt's action was just one more in a series of incidents that seriously
weakened Dewey's influence in ALA on the eve of the Baltimore/Washington
conference. He had lost a means of communication with the library community

that had lent credibility and prestige to his ideas for cooperation, standardization, and efficiency. But his troubles did not stop there. Within ALA, Dewey's sloppy accounting and questionable ethics had forced his resignation as treasurer and severely damaged his reputation within the association. ALA leaders became much more cautious and suspicious of his activities and motives. They were not about to give him the same freedom nor allow him to exercise the same power within ALA that he had enjoyed prior to the fall of 1880. He could still undertake the detailed clerical work of an ALA secretary from his Boston office, but Winsor, Poole, Cutter and other librarians of similar persuasion would set the tone and direction of the association as long as they held office. Without a political base, a supporting constituency, or an organ of communication, Dewey was powerless to do anything about it. He would have to suffer through the conference.

There were times when the ALA executive board doubted if the Washington conference would ever take place. For local arrangements they had to rely upon Spofford, who, when confronted with a choice between fulfilling his obligation to ALA and attending to the minute details that he was reluctant to delegate to subordinates, invariably chose the latter. On 15 January, just three weeks before the conference was scheduled to begin, Foster complained to Dewey, "If you could see the letters which both Mr. Winsor and myself [sic] have been sending Mr. Spofford for the last four weeks, many of them pathetic, and some quite the reverse, you would see why we can't 'make bricks without straw.' " After persistent prodding and much "drumming up,"[44] however, the fourth general meeting of the American Library Association came to order at 10:00 A.M. on 9 February 1881 in the library of the Army Medical Museum.

The conference was carefully programmed, and provided conferees little opportunity to celebrate advances within the library profession. Among its cooperative projects, *Poole's Index* was making satisfactory progress, but work on the ALA *Catalog* had ceased. Dewey remarked that the cooperation committee had not met since the Boston conference, and the committee on an index to subject headings had nothing to report. Conferees heard discussions on library architecture, the Library of Congress, and the different systems of shelf classification. Poole's comment on the latter demonstrated a strong opinion. He said he had failed to pay much attention to discussions of classification schemes because "I have not felt the need of more light on that subject." Rather, he said, "I find it more profitable to do other work, and follow other lines of investigation."

In other areas the conference enjoyed more success. By directing a public documents committee to petition Congress to improve public documents distribution, ALA demonstrated a desire to develop a more rational, informed electorate. Like other middle-class leaders of emerging professions, ALA members were suspicious of the political machines which were gaining strength in postbellum America. The membership also formally ratified the executive board's incorporation of ALA, and Dewey moved that ALA "establish . . . a library bureau as a center for library interests" to facilitate the collection and dissemination of products generated by ALA cooperative activities. After the finance committee issued a report which said nothing about Dewey's problems, Henry Homes moved to secure enough funds to hire an ALA secretary who would work full-time for "a sufficient endowment for the purpose of sustaining the agency." He met considerable opposition from Billings and Green, each of whom argued the association could not afford this proposed scheme at the expense of other ventures which promised more success. Homes allowed his motion to be tabled, but in the process predicted "the time would come when the Association would recognize the value and expediency of the measure." The conference adjourned on 11 February 1881, just 12 hours after a nominating committee named the usual slate of executive committee members: Winsor, Poole, Whitney, Green, and Dewey. All were unanimously elected.[45]

While conference participants judged their meeting a success, another less subjective observer gave it a mixed review. J. K. Hoyt wrote for the *Newark Daily Advertiser*:

I was really impressed with the gathering, but . . . there was from the beginning an overpowering sense of Cambridge, Harvard, and Boston—a feeling among the inferior planets that they were revolving around the Hub. There was too much attention paid to the great libraries and altogether too little to the lesser. There was much learned and elaborate advice given which will never be followed, and not much of the breath of life fell upon the seed scattered by the wayside. It was shown how large institutions should be arranged, managed, and housed, but not how books can be brought within reach of the toiling masses who need them the most; not a word for the embryonic library, not a word for the farmer's boys and girls who, lacking the advantages of the city, too often supply the place of solid reading with illustrated papers and stale novels. . . . Princeton and Yale can take care of themselves, and essays written for their benefit might as well be unwritten. What we need above all things is the multiplication of free libraries under intelligent direction, and their adaptation to the growing industries of the country, or to the expansion of the human mind where it is unreached by the strong current flowing through the concentrated centers of activity.

The *Library Journal* admitted Hoyt was "partly right," especially "that the smaller libraries did not get their due share of attention." But Cutter, who penned the editorial, confessed a dilemma. Several conference registrants represented smaller libraries, but did not speak up when given the opportunity.[46] Cutter offered no comment concerning the alleged influence of the "Hub."

The executive board met in Boston on 28 February and elected Justin Winsor as president; William Poole, Ainsworth Spofford, H. A. Homes, Lloyd P. Smith, J. L. Whitney, Frederick Beecher Perkins, and Daniel Coit Gilman (president of The Johns Hopkins University) as vice presidents; Melvil Dewey as secretary; and Frederick Jackson as treasurer. For some unexplained reason the board also named 17 additional individuals, including two women, as "Councillors." The position of councillor was not even mentioned in the constitution; members who occupied the post held no power and their exact responsibilities and obligations were never clarified. In subsequent years several ALA members would speculate that the board's purpose in naming councillors in 1881 was to involve more people in association matters. They recalled how several members had complained that the same individuals were elected to ALA offices year after year. In other action the executive board also authorized finance committee chairman Green to pay $200 for the outstanding expenses Perkins incurred on the ALA *Catalog*. The board also instructed Dewey to obtain ALA *Catalog* materials from Perkins and hold them until the board decided an appropriate course of action. And against Poole's objections the board then voted to pay the cost of typesetting conference proceedings in the *Library Journal*.

The board met again 10 November 1881 to appoint an arrangements committee for the forthcoming Cincinnati conference to be held in May 1882. It also referred the ALA *Catalog* problem to the cooperation committee for resolution. In the same LJ column which carried the summary of board activities, the editor also reported a new committee project designed to discover whether withdrawing from library shelves all books by authors whose works of fiction "are sometimes excluded from public libraries by reason of sensational or immoral qualities" had much effect on general circulation statistics. The committee promised a report in the future.[47]

Although ALA was preparing for its first conference west of the Alleghenies, librarians in the Midwest decided to strike out on their own. On 22 and 23 November 1881, a small number met in Springfield, Illinois. Dewey immediately questioned the advisability of forming a regional library association "lest the A.L.A. should consider it a rival," but midwestern librarians nonetheless decided to establish the Western Library Association and elected Poole as president. Perhaps they were partially motivated by the dominance of "Hub" librarians within ALA.[48]

The ALA executive board met again on 1 January 1882 to hear the cooperation committee's report on the ALA *Catalog*. As chairman, Cutter had contacted Perkins for information, and after discussing Perkins's written response the board decided to direct the committee "to select specialists to edit the A.L.A. Catalog in sections" and to place the activity under cooperation committee supervision. Several weeks later the committee reported that the results of its "questionable fiction" survey were inconclusive. Only 30 of the 70 libraries polled had responded, and, of the 30, 23 did not say whether restricting access to certain authors had affected total circulation figures.[49]

The ALA meeting in Cincinnati which convened on 24 May 1882 represented a sparsely attended "missionary" venture intended to alert the West to the library's social benefit. The most obvious absentee was Melvil Dewey. Only 47 people came, 12 of whom were women who chose to speak through Smith and Poole. The latter was especially active throughout the conference. He proudly informed conferees that the manuscript for *Poole's Index* was at the printer. "We, the editors, have done all that we promised to do, and even more." Cutter reported limited progress for the cooperation committee, and noted that activity on the ALA *Catalog* had stopped because not enough specialists had volunteered their expertise. The public documents committee indicated that congressional bills "embodying the wishes" of the association had been prepared to correct the inequitable and inefficient distribution of public documents. More general matters followed committee reports. Conferees identified several objections to the architectural drawings for the proposed new Library of Congress building; they also discussed classification, restricting the use of special materials (e.g., rare books), fiction, and the role of schools and libraries. Poole reminded Winsor of the birth of the Western Library Association, and the ALA president extended it "a hearty welcome."[50]

The conference ended on 27 May as quietly as it had begun three days earlier. Poole had been unusually active and positive throughout the proceedings. Three reasons may explain the prominent role he decided to assume: (1) his success with the *Index* placed him in the limelight; (2) as the West's leading librarian, he may have felt the need to project himself at the first ALA conference west of the Alleghenies; and (3) Dewey's absence created a vacuum he seemed eager to fill. Whatever his reasons, however, from this conference forward Poole began to contest Dewey more frequently, perhaps because of his own vanity, perhaps because of Dewey's abrasive ambitions, and perhaps because he and Dewey disagreed about the fundamental direction which ALA should take. It was obvious that Poole did not want ALA to champion most of the schemes Dewey advocated.

With Dewey maintaining a more restrained profile, ALA activity between conferences slowed. Executive board meetings occurred infrequently, usually only to elect officers or to fill committee assignments. In December 1882 the board asked the finance and cooperation committees and Dewey as ALA secretary to continue work on the ALA *Catalog* "without incurring any obligation on the Treasury."[51] The public documents committee continued to push Congress to reform methods for distributing public documents, but most interim activity was aimed at preparing for the ALA Buffalo conference in August 1883. Josephus N. Larned, librarian at the Buffalo Young Men's Library and chairman of the program committee, was especially concerned about securing a good attendance. He wanted to draw more western librarians than previous conferences located in the East, and to generate interest he sent out more than 200 program copies. Dewey was not satisfied that Larned had paid enough attention to the East. He repeatedly complained that Larned was ignoring the New York City area. Larned flared. "I have had plenty of fault finding and grumbling from you," he chastised Dewey. "Of needful information I have received little enough."[52]

ALA's sixth general meeting, which convened on 14 August 1883 in the Executive Committee Room of the Young Men's Library at Buffalo, had in-auspicious beginnings. Nonetheless, the 72 conferees did receive a generous dose of library "religion." The report of the public documents committee led the association to pass a resolution requesting that Congress investigate and develop an equitable method for distributing federal documents. Boston Public Library Director Mellon Chamberlain spoke about "Fiction in Public Libraries," but his presentation generated little discussion. Cutter admitted the cooperation committee had made no progress since the last conference, but he reported several cooperative endeavors not connected with ALA, including a newspaper obituary indexing project and cooperative library buying from foreign booksellers.

Dewey attempted to reassert himself at the conference, perhaps because he thought his new position as Columbia College's head librarian would give him more credibility within ALA and provide a better foundation to push his favorite schemes. In his secretary's report Dewey cheerfully noted how many libraries benefited from philanthropic attention over the past year. He also summarized progress on his independent activities, including the Library Bureau (organized in place of the Readers and Writers Economy Company), and a forthcoming *Library Manual*, which "will go to press, I hope, before our next meeting."

Poole continued to assert himself at ALA conferences. He argued for an index which would provide bibliographic access to the essays in many good anthologies currently in library collections. Several conferees disliked making research too easy for the library user, but Dewey strongly supported Poole's suggestion. "I am a champion of every labor-saving device, and have no sympathy with the theory that students are made superficial and weak by having aids." While the two men agreed on an index of essays, on almost every other issue they sparred openly. When Dewey reported that a lack of progress on the ALA *Catalog* had led the executive board to appoint a new committee in December 1883, Poole responded, "Committees are not worth a farthing to do such work." Poole wanted Dewey to take direct responsibility for the *Catalog*. "The problem which has vexed us for these many years will then have been solved." Dewey quickly reminded "our Nestor of librarians" that work on the ALA *Catalog* had a four-year history; *Poole's Index* took 30 years to complete. Conferees ultimately voted to ask the Bureau of Education for assistance in publishing the *Catalog*.

After reading a report on library architecture, John Edmands quoted several extracts from a letter Spofford had sent explaining the proposed new Library of Congress building. Spofford especially applauded the "grand central hall." Poole took issue immediately and vociferously criticized the congressional librarian's "great hall" concept as a waste of space characteristic of poor library architecture. Several conferees, including Green and Guild, defended Spofford in his absence. Winsor subsequently named a committee to consider resolutions on the LC building. Wisely, he appointed neither Poole nor Dewey to the committee.

A final issue over which Poole and Dewey sparred concerned the latter's report on a "School of Library Economy" which the Columbia College Board of Trustees had under consideration. Dewey wanted an ALA endorsement of the school, which would strengthen his case before Columbia's board. Poole opposed him. "There is no training-school for educating librarians like a well-managed library," Poole said, but he later added, "I do not wish to throw cold water upon the scheme." Guy A. Brown of the Nebraska State Library could not resist a rejoinder. "It seems to me that the gentleman has thrown a whole pool." Conferees laughed. Dewey said he welcomed the "cold water" as a "tonic," then immodestly and inaccurately reminded his audience that "when I proposed in 1876 to organize this Association, and to found the *Library Journal*, I was assured, by the same element that questions the school idea today, that there was no room for either." Dewey said that "element" later had to admit he was right, and Dewey predicted the "chief hydraulic factor in this discussion" would probably have to admit error again. Fortunately, no one challenged Dewey's questionable statements on the origins of ALA and LJ, but neither did the association endorse his school. However, with the exception of one dissenting vote (not identified in the proceedings) ALA did resolve to "express its gratification that the trustees of Columbia College are considering the propriety of giving instruction in library work, and hopes that the experiment may be tried."

The conference ended on 17 August as inauspiciously as it had begun. Cutter delivered a fascinating paper entitled "The Buffalo Library in 1983" at the last session, and several conferees called for more efforts to enlist state librarians into ALA ranks. Except for Poole, the nominating committee had reported the customary slate of executive board officers (Winsor, Dewey, Whitney, Green and Cutter), and although Green had suggested that "some western men be put on the committee," the slate was accepted without other additions, and the conference adjourned.[53]

As in previous years, association matters between conferences languished. The executive board did not meet until 21 December when it reelected Winsor ALA president. Spofford, Poole, Homes and Smith remained as vice presidents, Dewey as secretary and Whitney as treasurer. The board also voted to hold the 1884 conference in Toronto.

While the association seemed quiet on the surface, privately two of ALA's most prominent members decided to challenge Dewey for past transgressions. On 17 December 1883 Poole asked who was "the chief hydraulic factor" to which Dewey had referred at the Buffalo meeting. Dewey responded that he "was surprised that you should ask"; he thought it "perfectly clear" that it was Poole, but Dewey quickly added he "depended upon your taking it . . . in as good part as I always take the hits you enjoy giving me." Poole was not appeased. He disagreed with Dewey's recollection of the events leading to the 1876 conference, and in a lengthy letter written 28 December he recounted the chronology from his perspective. Dewey's charge that Poole said the profession had no room for ALA in the summer of 1876 he called "absurd and impossible." Poole then paraphrased much of the correspondence sent to and from his office in 1876. He told Dewey he had preserved it all, and he threatened to "give the public some extracts from these letters if it is necessary. . . . I won't be attacked by you in this way." He reminded Dewey that Leypoldt "comes in for a strong claim as the originator of the idea" of a national library conference, and he concluded menacingly, "Now my view of the case is that you have done me a great wrong, and owe me an apology, and a retraction in the *Library Journal*."

Dewey's response indicates why peers found it so difficult to work with him. First, he delayed answering Poole for nine weeks because "I have been simply driven to death with work and could not get at any personal matters." He told the Chicago librarian his "points" were "well-taken," but he was magnifying "the importance of a matter about which everyone else has long since forgotten." Dewey did not acknowledge that he had raised the issue in the first place. He indicated his desire to write with "utmost frankness," for he had no "time for circumlocution." He then proceeded to circumlocute freely in a lengthy letter. Dewey seemed incapable of admitting the possibility he might be incorrect, or that he might have distorted the truth. In fact, he skirted details on the series of events and resorted to generalities about the circumstances in which they took place. He promised not to repeat the incident again "in print or orally," and offered to disclaim "anything that reflects on your loyalty to the ALA" at the forthcoming Toronto conference. He then concluded, "I hope you will be able to send me word that you accept my friendly assurance and that the little hatchet you have whetted for my scalp is safely buried." Nowhere in the letter did he suggest that he had done Poole a "great wrong," nor did he feel the need to apologize or offer to retract anything in the *Library Journal*. Apparently Poole decided to let the matter pass. He responded to Dewey's "amiable letter" and its "pacific sentiments" by saying he had "no hard feelings" towards Dewey. "I will allude to the late unpleasantness only to say that you were mis-taken. . . . " Unwilling to budge on any point, even in private, Poole indicated he was "willing to let it go unsettled."[54]

Dewey had won an uneasy truce with Poole; he was not so fortunate with Bowker. Dewey always felt Bowker and Leypoldt had not fairly recompensed him according to the terms of his contract as LJ managing editor. In January 1885 he decided to press for "vindication." When Leypoldt died on 31 March 1884, Dewey had to negotiate with Bowker to win "restitution" from the Ley-poldt estate. But Bowker denounced Dewey's tactics. The LJ publisher castigated his former managing editor for writing "one of those letters which purports to be friendly and really is most unfriendly"; he added that any claim had to be made against the business since the estate was not solvent. Bowker urged Dewey to "put your claim in such simple written shape as to be evident to the ordinary businessman," and mail it to him. He did not want to see Dewey at LJ offices for fear of "reopening" a "painful" experience for Leypoldt's widow. He concluded, " . . . if you had really desired to be as friendly to him as you state, you would have been content with the lion's share of the early proceeds of the *Journal*, in connection with which as you know he lost so much money which went to you."

Dewey sent his claim, but Bowker judged it without merit. When Dewey continued to press, Bowker encouraged him to "bring suit as early as possible that the matter may be settled once and for all." Bowker said he would refuse to carry Library Bureau advertising in the *Journal* because Dewey's contractual requests represented "a complicated system"; he would have no more "double back action patent elliptical business complications of the old sort!" Dewey refused to bring suit. Instead he explained that he wished to settle his claim in face-to-face negotiations, or submit the entire disagreement to a neutral referee. If Bowker refused both courses of action, Dewey stated, "I am *forced* to believe you conscious of your unfairness and taking this course to avoid justice." Bowker gave no ground. "I cannot but distrust a 'friendship' which can descend to such abuse." He indicated he was glad Annie Dewey was "not cognizant of this attack upon me, for I regard her good opinion highly."

But Annie Dewey soon learned about the dispute. "I chanced to pick up your note . . . as his letters and papers have always been so free to me." She expressed sadness that the two friends fought so bitterly. "I am not blind to Mr. Dewey's faults," she admitted, but the situation "requires a little putting aside of pride" for both men. She urged Bowker to select a referee and said that her husband would not be aware of her letter to Bowker until the latter replied. Bowker must have agreed. Five days later, Dewey wrote Bowker that "I don't care a show what the decision is—it is only to get it and bury all memory of the thing forever." Bowker was probably unconvinced; if experience was any teacher, he had reason to be cautious. Dewey further promised "never to let a thing get so snarled again" and also pledged to "scrub away for LJ and put through a scheme for increasing its and the ALA list." He made no mention of *Library Notes*, still in the planning stages. For the moment neither man pressed his point, but the scars would remain. The ALA secretary was not wedded to the *Library Journal*; Bowker remained suspicious of Dewey's ambition and self-interest.[55]

While Dewey fought with Poole and Bowker, association matters proceeded at a snail's pace. For a short time it appeared the ALA *Catalog* might be published by the Bureau of Education, which had agreed to print the work from prepared copy and to distribute separately issued sections of the *Catalog* free of charge. ALA only had to organize the work, "secure the necessary cooperation," and oversee publication. Although Dewey had refused to edit the *Catalog* several years earlier, by the summer of 1884 he had several reasons to change his mind. First, more than three years now separated him from the unpleasant events of early 1881; Dewey once again showed a strong desire to move the association in directions he had defined as early as 1876. Second, as librarian of Columbia College he could tap a small army of volunteers on campus and within the New York City metropolitan area. He had no trouble convincing C. Alex Nelson, librarian at the Astor Library, to help because of "the *boom* and *position* in the library world" that "getting the ALA *Catalog* out" would give him. Third, Dewey wanted closer ties with the Bureau of Education. If cultivated properly, the relationship promised many advantages to the nation's libraries, ALA, and Dewey's own interests.[56] Fourth, annotated recommended book lists remained popular within the library community. Caroline Hewins's very successful *Books for the Young: A Guide for Parents and Children* (1882) and Frederick B. Perkins's *Best Reading* were still considered staple fare for building library collections. And finally, by organizing the entire *Catalog* in DDC, which at the time was being revised for publication in a second more comprehensive edition,

Dewey would expand the use of his own classification scheme.[57] Dewey decided to take on the assignment.

In the meantime, the association itself took a calculated risk. It cancelled the 1884 Toronto conference because of too many scheduling complications. On 20 October the board voted to meet at Harvard in June 1885 if a large delegation of librarians from Europe wished to attend, or at Lake George, New York, if they did not. Because the former situation did not materialize, board members eventually settled on the latter meeting place. In the process, they successfully resisted pressure from several western librarians, who wanted another conference on their side of the Alleghenies, and from Commissioner Eaton, who urged the association to meet in New Orleans in conjunction with an international exposition.[58]

By the time ALA met in Lake George in September 1885, it was nearly nine years old. The association had been led by the same people throughout that period, and its activities had been quite limited—in large part because the leadership of the organization wanted it that way. But some members thought it time for some changes. Frederick M. Crunden, director of the St. Louis Public Library, suggested that the ALA conference "divide into sections" to save time and offer "greater thoroughness and increased capacity for expression and absorption of various interests by the ALA." Justin Winsor suggested "the affairs of the Library Association might progress better if it has a president whose time was not heavily mortgaged to other engagements." The ALA's only president recognized the position he occupied, for when Dewey argued it was too close to the Lake George conference to honor Winsor's request, the Harvard librarian responded, "Very well—for the present. When we change, work should be made the condition of the position: no more figureheads."[59]

If arrangements for the Lake George conference did not go smoothly, it should have surprised no one; Dewey and Bowker had joint responsibilities for scheduling a program. Dewey wanted a series of 10 or 12 five-minute talks on predetermined subjects. Many potential speakers chaffed under such severe time restriction. A more serious problem arose when Dewey and Bowker realized that the ALA conference was scheduled for the same days the American Historical Association would be meeting in Saratoga, New York, and Winsor was committed to present a paper at the latter. Understandably irritated at the scheduling mix-up, Winsor suggested Dewey ask Spofford or Poole to preside at the ALA meeting until he could get there two days later. Bowker worried over the alternatives. He wrote Dewey that "I wish you could get Spofford as the acting vice-president, for Poole would be very likely to set everybody wrong instead of right for a send-off, and might then consider himself in line of succession for the presidency, which would be most unfortunate."[60] Memories of Poole's 1880 missive to the Library Association of the United Kingdom may have been running through Bowker's mind.

But Dewey had less confidence in Spofford than Poole. When the conference convened on 11 September 1885, Poole presided. As Bowker suspected, Poole's opening remarks were much more polemical than conferees were accustomed to hearing from Winsor. Poole made frequent reference to the differences between the East and West, especially in terms of the latter's support of public libraries. While he conceded that the New England states were leaders in public library support, he noted that New York, New Jersey and Pennsylvania had no statute enabling cities or towns to tax citizens to support libraries. "It is a phenomenon I am not able to explain."

Dewey followed Poole's opening comments with a secretary's report that was a rallying cry for increased association energy. He called for more activity in cooperative cataloging, a new set of officers each year, increased membership, a campaign to divorce all library appointments from the political spoils system, a permanent paid ALA officer (perhaps funded by the government in Washington), and more professional contributions to the *Library Journal*. Cutter next gave a cooperation committee report which covered two years of limited activity. He continued to boast *Poole's Index* as a major accomplishment, but also mentioned a newspaper obituary index and modifications in the ALA code on title entries as measured successes. His subsequent report for the transliteration committee sparked a sharp exchange which questioned the reason for ALA authority over such matters. When Cutter moved that the association endorse the committee's report, Poole responded, "We do too much voting. I have never asked the Association to endorse by vote any of my hobbies in methods of library work." Quickly, Dewey disagreed. He argued that ALA had to take official positions at its conferences because "there are hundreds of the smaller libraries who wait to learn the results of the meetings. . . . the old and experienced libraries are not the ones to whom these meetings are most useful." A more conciliatory Cutter may have perceived an emerging split. After he suggested, "I do not think that a definite vote at this time is desirable," the motion was withdrawn.

William Foster gave a brief report on Columbia's forthcoming School of Library Economy; his remarks evoked no open comment. Much of the remainder of the conference concentrated on topics Dewey had scheduled into the program. Conferees discussed such practical matters as book supports, book sizes, typewriters, handwriting, cataloging costs, small library buildings, galleries, stacks and shelves. In its report, the public documents committee demonstrated more aggressiveness than at previous conferences, and Dewey announced a cooperative agreement between ALA and the Bureau of Education to publish the ALA *Catalog*.

At the beginning of the conference, Poole had appointed a nominations committee consisting of two westerners, two easterners, and Larned of Buffalo as chairman. When the latter reported a slate of nominees for the executive board, he remarked: "We have concluded that it will be better to bring forward entirely new names, and that those names should be made representative of the different sections or different portions of the library interests of the country." The committee also recommended the reelection of the ALA secretary (Dewey) and treasurer (Whitney), and announced its nominations for executive board membership: Poole, Bowker, Foster, Fletcher, and B. P. Mann. After Bowker withdrew in favor of Dewey, the committee's "recommendations carried unanimously." Before the conference adjourned Dewey moved to commit the association to meet annually, and Linderfelt asked that the next conference be held in Milwaukee. Bowker agreed; " . . . for once we Easterners should put ourselves at inconvenience instead of asking our Western brothers to come here and meet us." The executive board then named ALA officers for 1885–1886: Poole as president; Spofford, Homes, Cutter and Foster as vice presidents; Dewey as secretary; and Whitney as treasurer.

E. C. Richardson, librarian at the Hartford Theological Seminary, then delivered the final conference paper which he titled "Bibliothecal Science and Economy—Article II of the A.L.A. Constitution." He openly asked the association to become "*the* authority in *all* matters relating to libraries," and suggested several specific questions ALA ought to address. He called for an "authoritative statement" from ALA leaders like Winsor, Poole, Cutter, Whitney and Dewey "as to what its field is, what has been done in it, what is to be done, and how?" Obviously Richardson wanted the association to evaluate itself, study its past, and set some realistic goals for its future. He also demonstrated a sense of frustration at defining the association's purpose in library affairs, and concluded "I think there are a great many in the same position." He asked for a report at the next conference so other ALA members would have a "clear idea" of the association's national role. No one moved Richardson's suggestion, and no discussion followed his presentation. The conference adjourned shortly thereafter.[61]

As the membership dispersed from Lake George, they left an association which obviously had not changed much in its nine-year existence. Winsor was no longer president, but Poole, who now stood at the helm, was just as properly placed and ready to advocate conventional librarianship. His greatest immediate goal as association president was to increase "western" participation within ALA. On 3 October 1885 he wrote Dewey, "We shall do our level best to give our Eastern friends something of Western hospitality next summer. . . . Our purpose is not only to show Milwaukee, but to give them some idea of the great Northwest—this 'Garden of the Lord, this paradise.' "[62] While Dewey was not at this time strongly opposed to Poole's goal for expanding geographic influences within the association, his hopes for ALA's future addressed broader professional issues—library efficiency, standardization and cooperation, and especially championing the interests of small public libraries which were springing up all over the country. In the fall of 1885, however, he still lacked a strong constituency from which to push his causes. He needed time to enlist the help of more people like Frederick M. Crunden and E. C. Richardson.

3   Pushing for "The Least Cost": Dewey's Resurgence, 1886–1893

Excitement hung in the air when ALA members gathered at the Chicago World's Fair in 1893. Not only could conferees share experiences with professional peers from all over the country, they could also peruse the highly touted Columbian Exposition. Chicago intended to use the fair to announce to the rest of the world that it had arrived as a cultural center. Led by a young, energetic group of businessmen and professionals who held prominent positions on the boards of the Chicago Symphony Orchestra, the Art Institute and the University of Chicago, the fair communicated youthful exuberance, a break with the past, and a look forward to an exciting future. Gathered around the Great Basin in Jackson Park on the shores of Lake Michigan were such impressive monuments as the Machinery Building, the Agricultural Building, the Electricity Building, the Manufacturers and Liberal Arts Building, and the Administration Building. On the east end of the Basin stood Columbia, presiding with arms stretched upward over her man-made architectural wonder. On the west side was the magnificent Columbia Fountain. Frederick Faxon, who was attending his first ALA meeting, later recalled:

The fascination and beauty of that exposition will always remain with me—the myriad of lights at night reflected on the lagoons, the bands playing, the gondolas silently gliding by—it made an impression that will never fade,—a vision of some foreign country set down in the center of the United States.[1]

The president of the American Library Association for the conference was Melvil Dewey, director of the New York State Library and Library School, and secretary of the Board of Regents of the University of the State of New York. In planning the conference Dewey had been assisted by a committee consisting of two women—chairman Mary S. Cutler, vice-director of the New York State Library School and library examiner for the University of the State of New York, and Hannah P. James, librarian of the Osterhout Free Library in Wilkes-Barre,

Pennsylvania—and five men—Frank P. Hill, librarian of the Newark (New Jersey) Free Public Library; Weston Flint, statistician at the U.S. Bureau of Education in Washington, D.C.; C. Alex Nelson, assistant librarian at Columbia College in New York; Charles A. Cutter, librarian of the Boston Athenaeum (until April 1893); and Frederick H. Hild, director of the Chicago Public Library. The name of William F. Poole, who had left the Chicago Public Library to organize the privately endowed Newberry Library in 1888 and in 1893 was busying himself with a variety of non–library-related exposition commitments, was conspicuously absent from the committee. Cutter represented the committee's sole link to the old guard. Except for Hild, who acted as liaison to the city in which ALA held its conference, the remaining members of the committee were close to Dewey. Poole called them the "Albany regency." ALA leadership had changed considerably since 1886.

Dewey opened the conference on 13 July in the Art Palace, but declined to give a formal address. Instead, he asked ALA Secretary Frank P. Hill to report on ALA's "Model Library," a 5,000-volume collection of the "best books" which the association recommended for every library. Hill noted that this long awaited collection "will probably interest more members than will any other exhibit at the fair." He complemented the exhibit committee for its work, and especially Cutler, who almost single-handedly had pushed a catalog of the collection through the Bureau of Education so that conferees would have copies before the conference concluded. The ALA *Catalog* had finally been published. During the previous ten days, Hill reported, Cutler had been reading proof of the *Catalog* at bureau offices with her assistant, W. S. Burns, a cataloger at the New York State Library.

The exhibit to which Hill referred was located northwest of the Government Building's rotunda in space assigned to the Bureau of Education. It consisted of four divisions: (1) an exhibition on the history and statistics of American libraries, which was prepared by the bureau; (2) exhibits presented by individual libraries; (3) a comparative exhibit of library models, blanks, forms and equipment which was prepared by Dewey's library school; and (4) the ALA model library, including a collection of the 5,000 new volumes listed in the ALA *Catalog*, which had been sponsored jointly by ALA and the Bureau of Education. One-half of the collection was classified by DDC, the other half by Cutter's Expansive Classification (EC). Separating these two rival schemes were the fiction and biography sections. A dictionary card catalog governed by rules adopted at earlier ALA conferences served to record titles in the collection. The 5,000 volumes were shelved in six separate types of bookstacks which were donated by library suppliers from around the country, including one set from the Library Bureau, which had recently opened an office in Chicago. Titles selected for the model library, which for the most part had been donated by publishers, were scheduled to go to the Bureau of Education in Washington for permanent display after the conclusion of the exposition.

After ALA Treasurer Henry J. Carr, still director of the Grand Rapids Public

Library, submitted his financial report, the conference settled down to a pattern of activity Dewey had deliberately programmed into the schedule. By assigning subjects to specific authors, he hoped that the published proceedings would ultimately serve as a "handbook of library economy," another goal towards which he had been working for over a decade. He had already arranged for the Bureau of Education to publish the handbook and distribute it free, along with the ALA *Catalog*, to requesting libraries and librarians. Because of this goal, the conference once again devoted most of its attention to practical matters such as shelves, fixtures, binding, furniture, accession policies and procedures, and librarians' salaries. Spirited discussions focused upon technique, not theory. An exception occurred when Samuel Swett Green recommended that libraries follow a consistent policy of weeding their collections. William F. Poole, who was not highly visible at the conference, responded, "I . . . wholly disagree. . . . If he should go through my private library I am sure he would weed out all the books which I most value; for I am not much interested in common books like those in the A.L.A. collection."

Peter Cowell, librarian of the Liverpool Free Library, prefaced his remarks on "Lectures, Museums and Art Galleries" by noting how many women now attended ALA meetings. "It is very evident that in this country ladies are a force, and in library work I believe a very strong force indeed." James G. Bain, Jr., director of the Toronto Public Library, noted that on the matter of open access to library shelves, "the question divides itself into large and small libraries." He surmised it would be easier for the latter to follow an open stacks policy. George Iles, an independently wealthy journalist from New York City with a strong interest in libraries, urged the wide dissemination of expertly composed annotations on newly issued books. He wondered if ALA might supervise a central bureau for annotation of books by university professors. Dewey responded immediately, "We want the United States government in Washington to cooperate." Iles suggested that if 500 libraries subscribed as little as $20 per year the scheme could be accomplished. When Tessa L. Kelso, director of the Los Angeles Public Library, moved that the association appoint a committee to explore this suggestion with the bureau, she was reminded that the new constitution, approved at the last conference, provided that "no important action of this kind can be taken by the association without action first by the Council."

The new constitution received some attention. Section 10 outlined the manner in which new officers were to be elected, but because it had not been fully settled at the 1892 conference, conferees still had to consider it at a special meeting of the 1893 conference. Green noted that the vote the previous year had been "very close," but he reminded association members that the old method of electing a five-member executive committee which chose all ALA officers had prevailed. E. C. Hovey, former trustee at the Brookline (Massachusetts) Public Library and treasurer of the recently established ALA endowment fund, objected vehemently. "I am distinctly in favor of this Association electing its officers by ballot. I am also distinctly in favor of having nominations for all the offices made openly." William Coolidge Lane, Cutter's successor at the Boston Athenaeum, disagreed. He worried that "if we are to ballot for the different officers it will take up a great deal of our time." Weston Flint noted that "I belong to a great many associations, and this is the only one that does not elect the officers by popular vote. I feel a good deal as Mr. Hovey does."

Dewey's position appeared opportunistic. He admitted that before 1892 he was "in favor of electing the president by general ballot and letting the other officers be elected by the executive committee," but after the 1892 conference (when, perhaps not coincidentally, he was elected ALA president), "I came back to the old view held from the beginning in 1876." Like Lane, Dewey worried about time. The constitution had already provided for the election by ballot of the five executive board members, four councillors and the trustees of the ALA endowment fund. "If you add a half dozen more we shall spoil a whole half day for this whole body on these wearisome and profitless elections." But Hovey was adamant. He moved substitutes for Sections 10 and 11 of the constitution, which provided that the officers of the association would consist of a president, three vice presidents, a secretary and a treasurer, each of whom would be elected by ballot at the annual meeting. The executive board would consist of these officers plus the immediate past-president, and would "have power to act for the Association in intervals between meetings on all matters on which they reach unanimous agreement." The executive board would also select the members of the finance and cooperation committees, and any other committees the board deemed necessary to conduct association business. When put to a vote, Hovey's motion carried.

The fiction question raised its hoary head again. Crunden suggested that ALA send out "a list of questionable novels for use of librarians." When Ellen M. Coe of the New York (City) Free Circulating Library reminded him that for any novel judged "questionable there is a certain class of our readers that is immediately anxious to get that novel," Crunden moved that the ALA publishing section "print a list for private circulation." His motion passed.

George Watson Cole, librarian of the Jersey City (New Jersey) Free Public Library, submitted a report for the library school committee. He pointed out that most of the New York State Library School's effort during the preceding year "has largely been given to the preparation and cataloging of its own exhibit and that of this Association." The success of the exhibits gave ample testimony to the quality of student work. Cole also noted that five other library schools had opened their doors in the last several years: the Pratt Institute Library School in Brooklyn, the Drexel Institute Library School in Philadelphia, the Armour Institute Department of Library Economy in Chicago, the Los Angeles Free Public Library Training School, and a summer school at Amherst College directed by William I. Fletcher.

Cutter reported for a "committee on the next meeting" that in keeping with "the unwritten law to meet alternately at cities and watering-places in the East

and West,'' the 1894 conference should be located in the East. The executive
board chose Asheville, North Carolina. Gardner M. Jones, librarian of the Salem
(Massachusetts) Public Library, reported progress by the committee on an index
to subject headings. He requested that the committee not be asked to compile a
list of subject headings. Rather, Jones explained, committee members should
spend their time ''upon matters about which there is some question, such as
synonymous headings, schemes for subjects which have sub-headings, etc.'' The
membership would not bend. It voted that the committee pass its list of subject
headings to the publishing section for printing and publication ''as soon as
practicable.''

Three sections within ALA which met coterminously with the parent organization experienced light attendance. The college library section elected G. W.
Harris of Cornell as chairman and Clement W. Andrews of M.I.T. as secretary.
The publishing section elected Dewey as president, Lane as secretary-treasurer,
and Fletcher, Bowker and Iles as the remaining members of the section's executive board. All were from the East. Finally, the Association of State Librarians, originally organized in 1889, met for the expressed purpose of disbanding
into two sections, a law library section and a state library section. The latter
elected Dewey its president.

Another group of librarians which met with ALA did not fare as successfully.
The World Congress of Librarians had been Poole's idea. He had hoped that
the Columbian Exposition would attract a score or more of important European
librarians. Cutter later reported in *The Nation* that ''the title World's Congress
was justified rather by the invitations which had been sent out than by the response
received, which consisted of 1 German, 1 Canadian, 2 Englishwomen, 2 Eng-
lishmen, and 200 Americans.'' To make matters worse, the few foreign librarians
who did present papers were seldom heard above ''the puffings, ringing, and
shrieks of a railroad which ran almost incessant trains directly under the win-
dows'' of the meeting room.

As always, conferees also enjoyed a social side. They could roam the exposition grounds, join a tour of the city, or attend Buffalo Bill's Wild West Show,
which the Chicago Library Club sponsored. Finally, the reception at the New
York State Building on the evening of 20 July included ''a little dance.'' Two
days later the conference adjourned.[2]

By any reasonable measure the Chicago conference was a smashing success.
The association could claim numerous victories, including the publication of the
ALA *Catalog* and the forthcoming ''Handbook of Library Economy,'' closer
ties between ALA and the Bureau of Education, and the successful exhibits.
The association also seemed to be closer to establishing a central source which
would aid librarians in selecting the best books for their libraries, perhaps even
privately circulating a list of ''questionable'' novels. By Dewey's design, practical matters dominated the program. The Chicago conference also represented
the first time ALA had operated under its new constitution, which was made
even more democratic through E. C. Hovey's efforts. For the most part, however,

the conference was Dewey's show. He had organized it; his people had carried out his dictates. Poole and his western associates were not highly visible at association meetings, a striking fact considering that the conference was held in their own backyard.

What had happened to ALA between the Milwaukee conference of 1886 and the Chicago meeting of 1893 to allow these changes to take place? Part of the answer to this question is reflected in a collective profile comparing ALA executive board members who held office between 1892 and 1896 with predecessors who occupied office between 1882 and 1886. Careful statistical analysis reveals both similarities and differences, the latter suggesting subtle but consequential shifts. For both five-year periods most ALA board members had been born into Protestant families who had emigrated from northwestern Europe four or more generations before. For the most part, they were still chief executives of large public libraries. In the latter half-decade, however, 25 percent were born outside the Northeast, 20 percent were women, and less than half came from families whose fathers were professional managers. Ten percent had graduated from Dewey's New York State Library School, and for 25 percent, the post they currently occupied represented their first professional position. Sixty percent were employed in public libraries, and 65 percent were located in the Northeast. Thirty percent had posts in the Midwest, up 13 percent from the previous half-decade.[3] The composition of the ALA executive board had changed in socio-economic and professional characteristics within a ten-year period. Recounting the manner in which Dewey capitalized on these changes and tracing the altered direction which ALA activities took between 1886 and 1893 presents a fascinating chapter in the association's history.

While ALA plodded along following the Milwaukee conference, Dewey did not. On 5 January 1887 he opened the first library school at Columbia College. "Its aim is entirely practical," he said, "to give the best obtainable advice with specific suggestions on each of the hundreds of questions that rise from the time a library is decided to be desirable, till it is in perfect working order, including the administration." Twenty students matriculated, including 17 women. Two months later Dewey was already cultivating potential employers so he could place his graduates in important library positions across the nation. Several "librarians of weight" considered the school "a foolish fad of his." Dewey was not bothered. He also asked the Commissioner of Education to provide his students with free copies of all bureau publications on libraries.[4] Melvil Dewey was never bashful.

While the fledgling library school struggled through its first years, Dewey also busied himself establishing a New York (City) Library Club, an organization which gave him yet another constituent base. The club met monthly; Dewey served as its president. In addition to these activities Dewey still retained his financial interest in the Library Bureau and continued to push acceptance of the DDC on a wider basis.[5] He also promoted his pet periodical, *Library Notes*, which automatically won him the umbrage of R. R. Bowker, who resented its "sudden appearance . . . in my absence." Bowker indicated that he could "not see why the *Library Journal* should not be adequate" for Dewey's needs.

Because Dewey's claims against the *Library Journal* still had not been settled to his satisfaction, he continued to press his case with Bowker. By the fall of 1886 the dispute had become general knowledge in ALA circles. Fletcher asked Bowker if "it has not got so that you and he cannot comfortably meet to work on this thing [the ALA publishing section] together with me." Bowker also learned from Henry R. Tedder, an English bookseller, that Dewey had encouraged the English *Library Chronicle* to duplicate for England what his own *Notes* was intended to do in the United States. If the *Chronicle* would "push the *Notes* a little on your side," Dewey wrote the editor, "we will do all in our power to extend your circulation here." While such activities hardly endeared Dewey to Bowker, both men finally agreed to submit their financial differences to referees for final, nonbinding resolution.[6]

Against this backdrop of Dewey's hyperactivity, ALA moved towards its forthcoming conference at Thousand Islands, New York. Between conferences ALA standing committees were not very productive, with one exception—the ALA publishing section. Even the ALA executive board, under Poole's direction, accomplished very little. The board met towards the end of 1886, appointed a program committee for the 1887 conference, and informally discussed how to streamline the conference while making it more coherent and substantive. Board members reached no agreement, however.

But the publishing section moved ahead. Under the direction of Chairman William I. Fletcher, in the fall of 1886 the section pledged to print catalog cards of leading new publications, to coordinate the work duplicated in libraries across the nation, and to publish an "Essay Index," an index to scientific serials, transactions and monographs, an index to bibliographical lists, and a pocket-sized handbook tentatively entitled "How to Use the Library." The publishing section's executive board selected Frederick J. Soldan, director of the Peoria (Illinois) Public Library, to write the latter, while William C. Lane of Harvard would compile the bibliographical lists. Interest in issuing the ALA *Catalog* in sections through the Bureau of Education continued, but ALA still had difficulty locating competent volunteers willing to select and annotate titles.[7]

On 30 August 1887, 186 people met at Round Island House at Thousand Islands, New York, for the eleventh ALA conference. For the first time in ALA history over half the conferees were women. Dewey proudly noted that "for the past three years the largest single delegation has come from Columbia College Library." Two-thirds of the conferees came from North Atlantic states. Poole, who had recently been appointed to organize the Newberry Library in Chicago, presided. In his presidential address he was much less polemical than he had been in 1886; he addressed the relationship between public libraries and public schools. Poole saw the former as a logical extension of the latter.

Dewey followed Poole with an abbreviated secretary's report. He indicated that conferees too shy to ask questions in open session could now write them down and deposit them anonymously in the ALA question box. He proudly digressed that his own library school at Columbia had "arranged and displayed" the ALA "Bibliothecal Museum" of library devices, catalogs, and blanks and he invited conferees to examine the display. Carr, who followed Dewey with a treasurer's report, complained that the association's contribution to the cost of publishing conference proceedings was steadily increasing because the total number of pages necessary to reprint the proceedings had increased by 125 percent since the Cincinnati conference. Cutter said the cooperation committee had "to confess that nothing has been done," but Green delivered a glowing report on Columbia's library school; it "fully justified the opinion of those persons who favored its establishment." Nonetheless, he warned against "certain dangers," namely provincialism and "the exaggeration of the importance of instrumentalities by its pupils." Green also reported that the public documents committee was still pushing Congress to pass a law instructing the public printer to place a bound copy of the *Congressional Record* in every government depository.

Conferees pledged the association to support civil service reform, and also endorsed a resolution inviting state librarians to form an Association of State and Law Libraries section within the ALA. The latter move may have been designed to keep more members of the library community under the ALA umbrella. Other splinter organizations had fizzled during the previous year. The Western Library Association had not met since Poole assumed the ALA presidency, and when it appeared the California state librarian might call a separate conference 'or far-western librarians, Cutter editorialized in LJ that "much more effective work can be done with and through the organized committees of the Association." Far-western librarians did not meet.

As in previous conferences, conferees devoted much attention to practical matters. They heard papers and participated in discussions on the effects of burning gas on leather, on lettering books, on notations for small libraries, on adjustable periodical cases, on duplicates and on library architecture. The ALA publishing section met on 2 September. Fletcher reported progress on all undertakings announced the previous fall, and indicated the Bureau of Education would issue the ALA *Catalog* in sections. Caroline Hewins's *Books for the Young* would be revised and issued as the first section, to be followed by "Travel" by Annie Dewey and "Political Science" by Bowker.

The ALA executive board decided to alter slightly the method for electing an ALA president. First, the current executive board voted that future boards should not nominate the same person two years in a row. Second, members directed that "an informal ballot be taken and put in the hands of the committee without announcement, as a guide to the preferences for president." Dewey was among the majority which openly supported both moves.

At an afternoon session on 2 September the executive board announced that Cutter had been elected president; Green, Chamberlain, Larned and Crunden vice presidents; Dewey secretary; and Carr treasurer. Winsor, Poole and Spofford were listed as councillors, an amorphous body still in search of function. The elections did not please everyone. Guild recognized that "old stagers" like Poole and himself were losing influence, but Guild was reconciled to it. He wrote Poole, "Let us enjoy each other's help and company while we can." Charles Evans, who had not attended an ALA conference since 1877, complained to Poole, "your successor should, naturally, have been Spofford, and not Cutter." He complained that "the manner in which the latter was put through seems to call for a reform in the manner of voting for officers."

But Evans was viewing events from a distance, probably receiving information from Poole, hardly a disinterested observer. He apparently did not realize that a minor reform in voting practices had already taken place when the executive board had decided upon an informal preliminary ballot to indicate the association's preference for president. Cutter had been a leading participant in association activities for over a decade and for the past six years was editor of the association's official organ of communication. Although Spofford directed one of the nation's largest libraries, he had never been a moving force within the association on the same level as Winsor, Poole, Cutter and Dewey. While Evans obviously had his own priority list for candidates, his criteria hardly matched those of active ALA members who recognized their interests would be better served with Cutter as ALA president.[8] The conference adjourned with plans to meet in St. Louis the following summer.

Once again ALA activities stagnated unexpectedly between conferences. Dewey created a minor controversy when he proposed that Green be switched with Crunden as first vice president. The ALA constitution did not rank vice presidents, but common practice dictated that the order in which the nominating committee reported vice presidents constituted an unofficial ranking. Dewey may have thought that by moving Crunden's name to first on the list of vice presidents, Crunden would stand a better chance of being elected ALA president at the St. Louis conference. The executive board voted four to one to defeat Dewey's motion.[9]

The turn of the year brought gloomy news for other ALA members. First, the publishing section abandoned its experiment with catalog cards because "the cards are not of sufficient practical use to librarians to make an adequate demand." Then a public dispute between Crunden and one of his subordinates at the St. Louis Public Library threatened to disrupt the summer conference. Dewey himself continued to squabble with several groups. The Columbia College Board of Trustees resisted his efforts to develop the library school, and although he continued to recruit students, some of his professional peers criticized Dewey's motives. Evans snidely referred to Columbia's library school students as "cheap help." In addition, Dewey still had not settled his dispute with Bowker.[10]

The *Library Journal* publisher continued to bristle over Dewey's many schemes. When Dewey suggested that LJ subscription fees be included in the cost of ALA membership, Bowker told him, "your plan would be ruinous to the *Journal*." Dewey had also tried to mollify Bowker by suggesting the Library Bureau and

Library Notes would greatly increase *Journal* subscriptions if the former acted as agents in the *Journal*'s behalf and received a commission for every new subscription. In December, however, Bowker complained that during the past year the bureau had acted as an agent for only nine subscriptions "old and new— which rather deranges your theory that *Library Notes* would help the LJ." Bowker later claimed that Dewey even convinced one regular *Journal* subscriber to go through bureau offices in the future rather than communicating directly with *Journal* editors. Then, in May 1888, the bureau suffered financial reverses which forced Dewey to reduce his majority stock and delay publication of *Library Notes*. That same month the ALA executive board announced the St. Louis Conference had been cancelled.[11]

Although the formal conference had to be cancelled, Cutter and the ALA executive board decided to call an informal meeting. Thirty-two people (18 of whom were women) showed up at Kaaterskill Falls, New York, when Cutter opened the substitute conference on 25 September. One conferee was from Louisiana, one from Colorado; the remainder came from the New England and Mid-Atlantic states. Cutter delivered an extemporaneous address, described the conference as "an informal, intermediate meeting" and promised the association would meet in St. Louis in the spring of 1889. After commenting on the increase of library philanthropy and the advance of civil service reform, he threw the conference open to informal discussion on subjects ranging from open shelves, cataloging, and providing answers for prize contests, to combining Cutter's numbers with DDC class numbers, proper title entries for female authors, and compiling an index to portraits. Fletcher reported that the publishing section was making slow progress on an *Index to General Literature*, and that the manuscript for Soldan's library manual had been destroyed by fire. He was unsure when it would be published, but Lane's index to bibliographies was completed and was scheduled to appear within the year. Fletcher also proudly announced that the section had drawn less than $100 from its treasury, while collecting $500. No other committees reported at the conference, and the association elected no new officers. The membership adjourned on 28 September.[12]

ALA leaders considered the Catskills conference disappointing and quickly began to plan for St. Louis to erase the bad feeling. Consistent with his behavior over the past two years, Dewey assumed the vanguard role. For a variety of reasons his position at Columbia became untenable, and he began to negotiate with New York State University Regent Whitelaw Reid for the position as secretary to the board and director of the state library. On 26 November 1888 he issued a circular marked "STRICTLY CONFIDENTIAL" to "a few men whose opinion I most value" to solicit their advice. He immodestly listed his accomplishments and indicated he was willing to make sacrifices by leaving New York City "for the work which promises still higher usefulness." He also said that unless replies to his circular were marked "private" he would show the regents the extent of his support, but he wished his own letter would be kept "strictly confidential" in case he chose not to accept the position if offered.

"The new state librarian would prefer not to know I had declined." Responses to Dewey's confidential circular came in from such library luminaries as Charles Cutter, S. S. Green, Mellon Chamberlain, J. N. Larned, Frederick M. Crunden, E. C. Richardson, Henry J. Carr, William E. Foster, C. C. Soule, H. M. Utley, Reuben Guild, W. I. Fletcher, and K. A. Linderfelt. Nonlibrarians who encouraged Dewey included Professor Herbert Baxter Adams of The Johns Hopkins University, President Francis A. Walker of the Massachusetts Institute of Technology, and Henry Barnard, the first U.S. Commissioner of Education. It appears Winsor and Bowker were not asked. Some chose not to respond at all. C. Alex Nelson, whom Dewey had earlier convinced to stay in New York to help on the ALA *Catalog*, wrote Bowker, "I have no confidence in his forwarding anyone's interests except his own—*entre nous*."

But Dewey's campaign ultimately proved successful. He accepted his new position on 12 December 1888. Several months later he convinced the state board of regents to transfer the Columbia library school to Albany. The Columbia Board of Trustees was not sorry to see the library school or its director leave New York City. Neither was Bowker. The referees considering the dispute between him and Dewey had just issued their recommendation, a mixed but complex decision which favored Bowker. Dewey accepted it and pledged his "word not to open the old matter in any way again."[13] As the St. Louis conference approached, Dewey was steadily gaining stature in the library community. His new position offered him an opportunity for more influence, and the number of graduates issuing from his library school promised to broaden his constituent base within ALA.

Crunden was worried about the St. Louis conference. He told Dewey that he had done "a good deal of 'blowing' about the intellectual and social culture of its [ALA] members and the men and women of distinction among them," and he admonished the New York state librarian to "induce our *best* men and women to come out." He was planning a "public meeting" where ALA luminaries would address an open St. Louis audience on the benefits of the public library for the community, and he needed to make a favorable impression. "It is quality, not quantity, I'm after."[14] Crunden's anxieties proved groundless. One hundred and six people registered for the conference, 49 of whom were women. Of the total, 39 came from the North Atlantic states, 57 from Great Lakes states. Massachusetts sent 19, New York 10, but Illinois sent 18, and Ohio and Missouri contributed 11 each. Spofford failed to attend, but "old stagers" like Winsor, Poole, Cutter, Green, Bowker, Foster, Fletcher, Linderfelt, and, of course, Dewey were conspicuously present. Cutter, who was actually serving a second term as ALA president by default because the 1888 informal conference did not elect new officers, opened the meeting at the Southern Hotel on 8 May with an address on "common sense." After Dewey offered an extemporaneous secretary's report, conferees settled back to hear and discuss a mixture of committee reports and papers. Green reported for the public documents committee that Congress had failed to pass a bill requiring the federal government to send a bound copy of the

Congressional Record to each depository library. The ad hoc committee on Dewey's library school gave good reviews. "The experiment is now an assured success," Green said. "The excellent assistants sent out prove that it has been of great advantage to have a course of technical education." He asked the executive board to establish a standing committee on the library school; his motion passed unanimously.

The cooperation committee reported it had considered many issues since the last conference, "but the pressure of regular library duties upon all the members has prevented much being done along those lines." The fiction question received little attention, but a lengthy discussion followed a paper on "Sunday Opening" by Mary Salome Cutler, instructor at the New York State Library School. Dewey supported her, but openly opposed any movement to demand extra pay for Sunday work. "Such a spirit has nothing in common with the modern library movement, which is nothing if not missionary in its character." He was glad ALA had been "singularly free from the stigma of being a trades union." Dewey's use of religious terminology and negative inference about unions was deliberately designed to put distance between librarians and members of other socioeconomic groups. Other conference papers followed on more practical problems like scrapbooks, charging systems, aids and guides for readers, and library architecture.

Conferees precipitated a minor argument when Arthur W. Tyler of the Quincy (Illinois) Public Library asked why the word "accepted" had been changed to "adopted" concerning the cooperation committee report. Fletcher stated forcefully that "if there is not value to the votes, there is not value to the ALA." An ALA endorsement had to carry power, he argued. Dewey agreed, and pressed conferees to adopt Fletcher's point of view as general policy. Although Winsor was quickly made chairman of a "Special Committee on Recommendations of Methods for the A.L.A. to Consider the Matter of ALA Endorsement," his committee subsequently refused to take action, reporting "the whole subject back to the Association for action in the future in a larger way." When ALA members adopted Winsor's report, Dewey pushed once more. "I move that a special committee of five be appointed by the chair to report at least three months before the next meeting a revised form of the constitution and by-laws covering all these points." Dewey's motion was approved and Cutter appointed Bowker, Dewey, Fletcher, Linderfelt and himself to the committee.

The issue of "ALA endorsement" was not the only point on which Dewey attempted to modify the ALA constitution. He also moved that the executive board be selected by a procedure using two ballots, the first informal, the second formal. At the beginning of the conference the membership would identify five people capable of exercising the "large powers" which the constitution invested in the executive board. A teller would compile a list of ten persons receiving the most votes and conferees would then elect five by formal ballot. "This system gives every member an equal chance to express his preference for the government of the A.L.A. for the next year, and is all there is left to us of democracy in an election." Dewey's motion passed, and shortly thereafter the informal ballot was taken. Among the top ten, four came from the Midwest. The formal vote which followed elected an executive board consisting of Poole, Cutter, Dewey, Fletcher and Crunden. The board later selected a slate of officers, including Crunden for president, Green, Chamberlain and Larned for vice presidents, Dewey for secretary, and Carr for treasurer.

At St. Louis the association added two new sections to its organizational structure. On 9 May ALA officially accepted the Association of State Librarians into the fold. Next day college librarians met to discuss the feasibility of organizing; they formally voted to assemble themselves into an ALA unit at the next conference. The increasingly diverse interests of librarianship and groups of members within ALA were beginning to change the association as it expanded its form to accommodate emerging specializations.

The publishing section met on 9 and 10 May to report its progress. While the experiment on printed cards had been scrapped, and Soldan had not yet started rewriting his "handbook for readers," three other projects were moving forward. John F. Sargent's *Reading for the Young*, an annotated booklist for young people, was ready for publication. A completed "bibliographic list" already prepared by James L. Whitney was being consolidated with another prepared by William F. Beer of Leadville, Colorado. Progress on an "Index to General Literature" languished because the publishing section needed more volunteers to index the 1,000 remaining titles. The section made no mention of the ALA *Catalog*.

Their work almost completed, conferees prepared to adjourn for another season. Custom dictated that their next meeting would be in the East and because it was a "college year" (as opposed to a "public library" year), the meeting would take place in late summer or early fall. Crunden had his "public meeting" on 7 May, and judged it a success. Dewey's presence was felt throughout the conference, and although the "old stagers" continued to monitor ALA through the executive board, their numbers and power was steadily waning with each conference.[15]

Between conferences ALA members struggled with a variety of problems. Although Dewey and Bowker had both agreed to a referees' decision to settle their private dispute, bad feelings lingered. Bowker complained that starting *Library Notes* constituted "objectionable treatment" and because the Library Bureau failed to render ALA's major organ of communication "adequate" support, he added, "I do not feel that you are fully and unreservedly the friend of the *Library Journal*." Dewey was still working on moving his library school from Columbia to Albany. Potential employers continued to contact him about graduates. Ever the opportunist, he also made several attempts to tap Andrew Carnegie's philanthropic inclinations, but Carnegie politely refused. "I have taken occasion to inquire of several parties about the supply of proper persons for libraries," he wrote Dewey," and find that there is no difficulty in getting persons naturally adapted for this work." Carnegie did not elaborate.[16]

ALA member Azariah S. Root, director of the Oberlin College Library, puzzled over the issue of association endorsement. He expressed interest in remarks made by Winsor and Poole at the St. Louis conference, but suggested that the two ALA veterans elaborate in LJ columns ''where we 'younguns' can have them to study.'' T. L. Cole, a lawbook seller from Washington, D.C., pressed Dewey to lead a movement within ALA to contest the dismissal of state librarians for political reasons. Paul Leicester Ford, co-managing editor with Cutter of the *Library Journal*, tried to solicit a series of articles on the subject ''librarianship as a profession'' which would address such questions as financial remuneration, health benefits, time demands, basic body of knowledge, and prospects for the future. He scrapped the plan when he failed to get enough authors to join a symposium.

Sectional attitudes began to surface more frequently. Foster admitted to Poole a ''certain tendency'' among easterners to look upon Chicago ''somewhat as you Chicago people 'look upon St. Joseph [Missouri],' '' but he speculated that ''this tendency is very plainly declining.'' Dewey wrote Cutter that an ALA circular authored by Crunden was ''a little western in its flavor, but I can stand it if you can.'' Other attitudes expressed in private were more familiar. Mary Bean, director of the Brookline (Massachusetts) Public Library who had apprenticed under Poole at the Boston Athenaeum, purposely asked Poole and Charles Evans for ''a dispassionate and just opinion'' of her professional efforts because they were not ''Dewey worshipers,'' but instead knew ''what library work is when they see it.''[17]

Although John Vance Cheney of the San Francisco Public Library was already pushing the association to meet on the West Coast in 1891, preparing for the 1890 conference seemed more important. ALA President Crunden was particularly careful about his appointments, making sure that scheduled speakers and program participants came from different geographical regions and especially requiring that ''new men should be put in the traces and not have all the work left to the old wheel horses—Cutter, Green, Foster, Larned, Fletcher, and one or two others.'' He said he preferred to save them ''for more original and important work,'' but he did not elaborate. Those Crunden did assign to speak on progress in various areas of library work at the next conference promptly began soliciting information from others.[18]

The summer of 1890 witnessed the beginning of a trend in the nation's library community which would have a subtle impact on the future of ALA—the establishment of state library associations. Again, Dewey was in the vanguard of this movement, helping to establish and then serving as first president of the New York Library Association in July. He privately assured Bowker that the state association would ''supplement and not share the work of the ALA,'' and that no one contemplated a state library association journal. Bowker probably remained skeptical. The New York Library Association quickly became a model for librarians from other states, including Iowa and New Jersey, both of which established associations within a year. William T. Harris, new Commissioner of Education, encouraged the trend, and also applauded efforts within ALA to form a trustees section. In other ALA matters, the publishing section issued its first publication, *Reading for the Young*, in September 1890. The *Library Journal* openly hoped that other such publications would soon follow. J. P. Dunn, director of the Indiana State Library, told Dewey that the association should push for reform of the publication and distribution of public documents, which he considered "of more importance than all the rest of the stuff the Association and the *Library Journal* devote their attention to."[19]

But the conference which met at the Fabyan House in New Hampshire on 9 September 1890 devoted its energies to more than public documents. One hundred fifteen of the 242 people who registered for the conference were women; 75 percent of the total came from North Atlantic states. In his presidential address Crunden happily noted the "inauguration of the movement to form" state library associations, which he judged could only benefit ALA in the long run. Dewey used his secretary's report to outline a specific plan of action for ALA. "Our iron is now hot. Let us strike hard." To move ALA's work forward, he called for the organization of more state library associations, more assistance from the national government (especially from the Bureau of Education), a doubling of ALA membership, and the creation of biennial national meetings. In off-years the association could divide into four or five sectional meetings. Although he did not openly address the issue, Dewey's recommendation reflected his fear of growing sectionalist feelings within ALA ranks. He hoped biennial meetings might provide a partial solution to a potentially destructive trend.

Walter S. Biscoe, Dewey's cataloger at the New York State Library, reported that the cooperation committee was confused about its true role within the association. On the one hand, the committee's traditional task of reporting on cooperative work had been transferred to an annual reporter appointed by the ALA president. On the other hand, the publishing section increasingly usurped the committee's bibliographical work. Biscoe asked association members for "brief statements of such work as they desire to have done by cooperation." E. C. Richardson and Caroline Hewins gave glowing reports on the library school, which by this time had taken up new quarters in the New York State Library and was again under Dewey's direction. Richardson did, however, suggest several areas for improvement. He called for more attention to library science, and less to library economy. He indicated that students operated under "dangerous high pressure," and that bibliography was "still disproportionately subordinate" to other more practical areas of curriculum.

Samuel S. Green reported for the committee on public documents that the move to systemize the distribution of public documents had again stagnated in a congressional committee. Green also asked the association's support for the bill to appoint an official indexer of public documents. While Dewey was not opposed to the ends desired by the committee, he did take issue with the means. "We may get together and pass resolutions, write them out, and send them to Congress," he said, "but it will do no good." Rather, he argued, "we should try to send the right men there; follow the matter up by individual effort till we get strong men to push it through." No one supported Dewey's suggestion.

On 10 September the association addressed several thornier issues. Green noted that ALA had appointed a constitutional revision committee at St. Louis to report a revised constitution three months before the Fabyan House conference. But because the committee had not issued a report, Green moved to replace it with a committee of five which would include Crunden and Dewey. After Green's motion passed, Dewey urged the association to elect its president, vice presidents "and perhaps one or two other officers, by a direct vote of all the members." Again, his recommendation to open the process of officer selection seemed to fall on deaf ears. Conferees took no action on Dewey's suggestion. They did, however, move to have all matters relating to bibliography referred to the publishing section, which they determined would consist of three people from the same section of the country. Consensus assumed the section would be more productive and effective if section members could meet more often. At the end of the conference Crunden appointed a publishing section executive board composed entirely of Massachusetts men—and Dewey.

The topic which won most conference attention, however, focused on the association's finances. After Treasurer Carr reported on ALA accounts, he suggested that the constitutional revision committee also consider methods to increase revenues and reduce expenditures. The finance committee expressed concern about ALA's future if it kept spending the subsequent year's revenue on the current year's bills. Carr urged "that some steps be taken to relieve us from the printing that absorbs our limited revenues," and Dewey suggested the association approach the Bureau of Education for financial support. Weston Flint volunteered to explore this possibility with bureau superiors.

E. C. Hovey, whose profile within the association increased with each conference, had another idea. He proposed the establishment of a permanent endowment fund, utilizing interest gained from its investment to add to ALA revenue or to defray existing expenses. "I move we raise this money before the first of January, and not be content with any sum less than $10,000." He resisted any motion to appoint a committee to study and report on the matter. "And when they do, I can hear even now the president say: 'The report has been received and will be placed on file.' " Like Dewey, Hovey wanted results. Conferees then adopted a series of resolutions which established a permanent endowment committee, and selected as members Hovey, Norman L. Williams, president of the trustees of the Crerar Library in Chicago, and Pliny T. Sexton, a regent of the State University of New York. Hovey immediately called for pledges, and before the conference passed to another subject, $5,000 had been committed, including a promise from Poole that "Chicago will give as much as Massachusetts." ALA's financial future suddenly looked brighter.

Conferees also heard a report from Frank Hill, director of the Newark (New Jersey) Free Public Library, on ALA's plans to participate in the Chicago World's

Fair in 1893. Rather than leaving exhibits to individual libraries, he urged ALA to coordinate a comparative but comprehensive general library exhibit which would contain a model library and samples of library plans, blanks, and methods. He also suggested that the association appoint two committees, one drawn from the general membership to supervise and prepare the exhibit, the other drawn from the Chicago library community to insure that ALA's best interests would be protected while preparing for the exposition. Association members approved a permanent committee of five, consisting of Mary S. Cutler, Florence E. Woodworth and Melvil Dewey of the New York State Library, Frederick Hild, director of the Chicago Public Library, and Hill. The permanent committee would be assisted by an advisory committee consisting of Poole, Flint, Coe, Brookline (Massachusetts) Public Library Trustee Charles C. Soule, and C. Alex Nelson, now of the Howard Memorial Library in New Orleans.

Members used the same method as the last conference for electing the executive board. Those selected included Crunden, Poole, Cutter, Dewey and Fletcher. Dewey tried to get the association to identify a consensus for president by authorizing an informal ballot to guide the executive board, but he failed. The executive board ultimately selected him as the next ALA president, Fletcher, Linderfelt, Soule, and W. T. Harris as vice presidents, and Carr as treasurer. For the first time in its history the association had a new secretary. W. E. Foster was selected to the office Dewey was forced to vacate for his new position. The remainder of the conference concentrated upon practical matters. Before adjourning, conferees selected San Francisco as the site for their next meeting.

The conference also clearly demonstrated continued growth of other professional library organizations, both inside and outside ALA. In addition to the meeting of the Association of State Librarians, the New York State Library Association held its first conference. The college library section formally established itself and library trustees, led by Hovey, Pliny Sexton, and J. M. Glenn, manager and treasurer of the New Mercantile Library in Baltimore, took the first steps towards organizing themselves into a third ALA section. The publishing section reported continued progress on an index to general literature (which the executive board renamed the "A.L.A. Index") and cheerfully announced *Reading for the Young* as its first publication.

Although the conference officially ended on 13 September, a post-conference excursion included a stop at Boston. There several ALA members were invited to address a publishers and booksellers dinner. Poole used the opportunity to criticize severely what he considered the mistakes and useless features in the architectural plans for the new Boston Public Library building which was nearing completion. His harsh remarks caused a furor in the local press, and especially irritated the library's board of trustees. Ill feelings between the Newberry Library Director and the Boston Public Library lasted for several years.[20] Some ALA members thought Poole had been needlessly offensive, and they wondered how much harm he had done the association.

With the unpleasant Boston dinner behind them, many ALA members approached the idea of a San Francisco conference with mixed feelings. While most recognized the need for "missionary work" on the West Coast, everyone acknowledged that the next conference would be sparsely attended. They did not anticipate much progress in sessions conducted so far from the center of library activity.

In the meantime, other work pushed forward. Members of the publishing section's executive board, all of whom resided in the Boston area, predicted that *Reading for the Young* would soon turn a profit for the association. They reminded interested librarians that by joining the section and subscribing $10 they could obtain all section publications at a 20 percent discount and also "share in the good work of cooperative bibliography"—a rather dubious benefit, but an excellent means to introduce a plea for more help on the "A.L.A. Index" which "is now well under way toward publication."[21]

The public documents committee continued its efforts to push a documents distribution bill through Congress, but enjoyed only limited success. George Chandler, first assistant secretary in the Department of Interior, asked Dewey if the library community really wanted *all* government documents included in a bill. He also wanted suggestions for classifying documents to maximize their utility. The committee responded with a special report to the ALA executive board just prior to the San Francisco conference.[22]

Planning for the San Francisco conference met several snags. On 31 October 1890 Arthur W. Tyler suggested that Dewey concentrate the program on subjects of interest to the West and "let the 1001 questions of interest to the smaller libraries of the East and the interior . . . go by." Dewey began to have second thoughts about taking ALA to California in 1891, but Soule reminded him that he had no choice. The previous conference had declared unanimously for California in 1891, and since ALA was pledged to Chicago in 1893, it was necessary to meet in the East in 1892. A generous turnout in 1892 would allow ALA to plan for and promote the forthcoming World's Fair conference. Still Dewey balked about the 1891 conference. Again Soule prodded. "If you do not soon act, I am afraid it will also injure your influence. This I should dislike to see, for I want your leadership clear and unquestioned for the World's Fair exhibits." Several days later Fletcher scolded Dewey for not acting. Finally Dewey committed himself to a fall, 1891, meeting in San Francisco, but he complained to Soule that a continued bout with hay fever might prevent him from attending the conference.

Then, on 11 July, he resigned the ALA presidency for "reasons of health," claiming his doctor forbade a cross country trip in October. The executive board met in Boston on 16 July, accepted Dewey's resignation and appointed Samuel S. Green as president and Frank P. Hill as secretary to replace Foster, who had also resigned his office. Green may have been deliberately picked to provide an incentive to the association's "old stagers" to make the trip to California. Hill wrote Dewey on 27 July that A. W. Whelpley, director of the Cincinnati Public Library, might be induced to go to San Francisco by "intimating" that "we

will try to elect him" to an office "just as Mr. Green was 'brought over.' "
Dewey wrote Whelpley two days later: "I have suggested to some of our prominent people that we should have a western man for president of the ALA next
year and that the place naturally went to you." In the meantime Green quickly
sent letters to Poole and Billings, encouraging both to attend; Hill contacted his
friends, and the *Library Journal* reminded readers how important it was to attend
ALA meetings.[23]

While the executive board struggled to finalize its list of officers and to obtain
promises to attend a West Coast conference, the newly named endowment committee was experiencing problems. The committee had carefully prepared a letter
introducing prospective donors to the purposes and benefits of subscribing to the
endowment fund, but money came in slowly. Although Massachusetts had given
$2,200 by the beginning of September 1891, the sum collected totaled just over
$3,000. John Glenn gently reminded Poole of his promise that "Chicago would
give as much as Massachusetts." Glenn noted that so far "nothing has come in
from the great Western metropolis." Hovey echoed Glenn's statements, and
forewarned Poole that he would identify Chicago's shortcomings in his report
on the endowment fund at the San Francisco conference.[24]

Planning for an ALA exhibit at the World's Columbian Exposition continued.
Commissioner Harris had informed Crunden on 3 March 1891 that final appropriations for the bureau's exhibit had not yet been determined. A month later
Harris appointed C. Wellman Parks of the Rensselaer Polytechnic Institute of
Troy, New York, as special agent to the Bureau of Education for work in the
exposition. He asked ALA to work through Parks. In the meantime the exposition
committee continued to solicit advice on classifying, arranging and collecting a
model library. While much of the preparation for the ALA exhibit occurred in
Albany, Poole chaired another Chicago-based group which posed potential conflicts because of overlapping responsibilities. Called the General Committee on
Literary Congresses of the World's Congress Auxiliary of the World's Columbian
Exposition, this group had responsibility for "arranging a series of international
conventions, or congresses" during the Chicago exposition. The committee
divided its attention into four areas of concentration—historical literature, philology, authors and imaginative literature, and libraries—and promised "to ask
the cooperation of, and to act largely through, the national and other societies
now existing for promoting these several objects." To the "Library Committee"
Poole appointed three Chicago residents: Frederick H. Hild, Daniel L. Shorey,
and Norman Williams. Hild was probably chosen to coordinate the activities
between Poole's and Cutler's committees.

On 16 August 1891 the ALA Columbian Exposition Committee issued a
preliminary report containing three parts—a plan, an estimate of costs and suggestions for raising money to cover costs. The committee wanted to invite all
libraries—domestic and foreign—to contribute to a general exhibit of library
architecture, appliances and fittings, bindings, and library history, and to set up
a model library of 3,000 to 5,000 volumes appropriate to the "general collection

of a small town library." The committee estimated the cost at $5,000 to $10,000, "probably the latter," and suggested five potential sources of revenue—state legislatures, the U.S. Congress, an ALA fund similar to its own endowment fund, individual libraries, and the Bureau of Education. Regarding the latter, ALA promised that in return for the bureau's help it "might leave the model library to the department." Harris was pleased with the preliminary report, and especially welcomed the suggestion that "each State lay aside a small portion of its appropriation for the purpose of aiding the library exhibit."[25]

While ALA planned for the future, other segments of the nation's library community were also active. Many states followed New York's lead and established their own state library associations. The Iowa and New Jersey Library Associations organized in the fall of 1890, the Connecticut Library Association held its first meeting in January 1891, and the Kansas Library Association first met nine months later. When H. M. Utley, Director of the Detroit Public Library, proposed a similar organization for Michigan to R. C. Davis of the University of Michigan Library, the latter responded "I am conscious that the National Association does not meet the wants of the newer and less experienced libraries. There is a disposition (and the thing seems inevitable) to discuss broad questions, and the meetings afford scant time for this, alone." He continued by hypothesizing that "it is possible that the information of state branches, where the details of library work can be discussed, is the remedy for the existing trouble." The Michigan Library Association was established on 1 September 1891.

In Massachusetts the approach was different. There the governor established a state library commission to coordinate and assist public library activity across the state. Soule complained to Dewey that because of State Librarian C. M. Tillinghast's influence "the ALA has been almost ignored (and apparently by intention) in this formation of the [commission] board." Soule wanted both Cutter and Green on the board, but only Green was appointed. Soule suggested, nonetheless, that Cutter "commend the commission as warmly as possible in the *Library Journal*. . . . If it lags or fails, it will be time to find fault next year." One reason for Tillinghast's position might be found in the establishment of the Massachusetts Library Club. Cutter wrote Dewey that Tillinghast did not want to admit public library trustees as members, but Cutter marshalled the club's executive board to issue a "vigorous protest." Cutter continued: "I find there is among smaller libraries a very strong dislike and distrust of the ALA. For that reason it is a pity that the executive board [of the Massachusetts Library Club] are all ALA men. We must live it down."[26]

Such private correspondence between association leaders demonstrates that strong anti-ALA feelings often helped to foster the organization of state library associations. Frequently these feelings were obscured behind arguments about the differing needs of small and large libraries. The former felt that ALA was run by directors of large libraries who primarily used ALA conferences as forums to address their own immediate problems. Dewey had perceived this early, and acted quickly to harness its potential in order to broaden his constituent base.

Small libraries wanted more systematization and uniformity, more guidance in the form of acquisition aids, and more advice on library routine. Ever since 1876 Dewey had urged ALA to focus on these matters, but for more than a decade his ideas found little support from an older, more experienced, and better known group of the nation's leading professionals who directed large libraries. Slowly the pendulum had swung to his point of view, and the weight of events increased its momentum.

Dewey was not among the 83 people who attended the ALA conference in San Francisco between 12 and 16 October 1891. Men outnumbered women among the registered conferees 44 to 36. North Central states sent 13 representatives, but sparse attendance seriously affected the entire conference. ALA President Green had to name substitute reporters for the ALA secretary, treasurer and finance committee. Fletcher introduced conferees to an ALA folder designed to advertise the association to potential members. Bowker read a majority report (Hovey, Green, Bowker and Flint) from the public documents committee which indicated Congress was no closer to a more equitable system for distributing government documents than the year before. The majority saw some hope, however, because House and Senate members had agreed to refer the question to a joint committee. J. P. Dunn, Indiana state librarian, said in a minority report that a joint committee should not be interpreted as progress. He thought the situation showed no improvement over past years.

Charles R. Dudley, librarian of the Mercantile Library in Denver, read a gloomy report from the endowment committee. "As a committee whose duties are to draw money out of other people's pockets, we regretfully admit that we do not appear to have been a signal success." He noted that ALA had received pledges of $7,665 at the last year's conference, but only $3,125 had been raised. A budget which accompanied Dudley's report revealed one notable success and two notable failures. Hovey had raised the $2,000 he had promised, but Poole had raised none of the $2,000 he had pledged and Dewey and Sexton submitted only $110 of the $2,000 they had pledged.

The report of the cooperative committee reflected its reduced role in association matters. Cutter said the committee had agreed to recommend a particular manufacturer's clips and binders for general library use, shields for movable electric lamps, and Cutter's own large initial colored labels for card catalog drawers. The Boston Athenaeum librarian also reported that the committee on revision of the constitution "had done nothing," after which Green appointed Soule, Winsor, Cutter, Crunden and Dewey to a committee to make suggestions for revising the constitution. Their deliberations would be considered at the next conference.

George E. Wire, superintendent of the medical department at the Newberry Library, read Frank Hill's report on Dewey's library school. Again the school received high marks. Hill wrote that the profession obviously needed the school; "of all the graduates who wanted library positions, only one failed." Dewey's students were increasingly populating the profession as the years passed. Green then called on Mary Wright Plummer to report on the recently established Pratt Institute Library School, and on William I. Fletcher to report on his Amherst College summer school course on library economy.

Soule indicated that the meeting of the trustees section would be postponed until the following year. President Green announced that E. C. Hovey, as member of the Massachusetts Commission on the Columbian Exhibition, had convinced the governor of Massachusetts to give ALA $1,000 of the $10,000 the Bay State awarded the commission. D. V. R. Johnston, reference librarian at the New York State Library at Albany, reported that the Bureau of Education had placed C. Wellman Parks in charge of the Columbian Exhibition's educational exhibit. Parks would be the association's contact with the bureau for obtaining exhibit space and for securing federal funds. Johnston remarked that Parks "is certainly a very competent man, or he would not be selected to take this . . . exhibit." Cutter noted the birth and growth of numerous state library associations, and encouraged the California librarians present to establish a similar group in their state. Perhaps the ALA leadership decided to bow to the inevitable; at least the formation of state library associations posed less threat to ALA than the formation of regional associations.

When Green introduced the subject of electing officers for the ensuing year, he commented that a revised constitution would probably provide for election by direct ballot in the near future, but since the old constitution was still in effect he called for the election of an executive board of five members. Conferees informally suggested 16 names. From that list they cast formal ballots and elected Hill, Cutter, Linderfelt, Dudley, and Fletcher as executive board members. Dudley wondered whether tradition dictated that the president be elected from the ranks of the executive board. Green replied "it has been commonly so"; Cutter indicated "it has been an unbroken custom"; Fletcher noted the one instance when conferees cast an informal ballot for president "merely for the guidance of the Executive Committee." The board then elected Linderfelt ALA president, thereby confirming Dewey's earlier prediction to Whelpley that the office would go to a "western man." Dewey had merely guessed the wrong man. Appointments as vice presidents included Fletcher, Soule (who later resigned and was replaced by Utley), Caroline M. Hewins (the first time a woman had been named as an ALA vice president), Lewis H. Steiner, director of the Enoch Pratt Free Library in Baltimore, and Joseph C. Rowell, librarian at the State University of California at Berkeley. Frederick Hild was added as a sixth vice president later on. Hill was reelected as secretary and Carr as treasurer. Dewey's name did not appear among the officers except as a councillor, a position he automatically merited as an ALA ex-president.

The publishing section met briefly on 15 October. President Fletcher proudly announced the *ALA Index* was in press. The Association of State Librarians chose not to meet, but it did submit a report to ALA on its activities. As chairman of the subcommittee on libraries for Poole's Chicago-based committee on literary congresses, Frederick H. Hild asked if ALA had officially declared its 1893 conference for Chicago. He indicated that the general committee intended to organize an international congress of librarians "on the largest scale possible" and that his subcommittee had already selected an advisory council of 150 librarians "in all parts of the world" to help. ALA later officially declared Chicago its 1893 conference site.

John Vance Cheney caused a mild stir when he announced that A. J. Rudolph, his first assistant at the San Francisco Public Library, was almost ready to introduce a new method of cataloging "which bids fair to amount to something like a revolution." Cheney indicated Rudolph's innovation would eliminate the card catalog and make cataloging a book a one-day process in which one assistant could do the work of five laboring under the old system.

Although the association's last session in San Francisco took place on 16 October, the conference did not adjourn for several weeks. Conferees reconvened in Santa Barbara on 21 October, on the train returning east on 30 October, and finally in Chicago at the Newberry Library on 2 November, where Green thanked Chicagoans for inviting ALA to their city in 1893. Green then declared the conference adjourned.[27]

The *Library Journal* judged the San Francisco conference a qualified success. Because Pacific Coast librarians were "a very wide-awake set of people," a LJ editorial declared, it was a "gratifying surprise . . . to find out how little, after all, [ALA] missionary efforts were needed." *The Nation* was even less excited. An editorial (probably penned by Cutter) noted that the San Francisco conference was "much quieter" than its predecessor and carried "less of the enthusiasm of the crowd." Many old subjects were rehashed; little new information offered. The editorial especially complained about the conferees' repeated tardiness— "the defect of the whole convention"—and concluded that "sight-seeing proved too strong for business." The San Francisco conference accomplished little beyond fostering the organization of the Southern California Library Club on 9 November 1891.[28] Dewey had been conspicuously absent, attendance was sparse, and an air of obligation to visit the West Coast hung over the assembly like a wet blanket. Their obligation fulfilled, ALA members now turned their attention to preparing for the 1892 conference in the East, and, more important, the 1893 Chicago World's Fair.

In subsequent months momentum for establishing state and local library associations continued. The Indiana State Library Association was formed in December 1891, one month after the Massachusetts Library Association had been organized. Eighteen Chicago librarians met at the Newberry Library on 17 December 1891 to organize the Chicago Library Club. Those present elected Poole president, Hild first vice president. Edith E. Clarke, Poole's head cataloger at the Newberry and a former Dewey student, complained to George Watson Cole that unlike the New York Library Club, the Chicago group "lack[ed] enthusiasm and outspokenness at our meetings." Poole tended to dominate.[29]

Elsewhere, in January 1892 the public documents bill finally cleared the congressional joint committee. The *Journal* urged all librarians to write their representatives to support the bill. Superintendent of Documents John G. Ames also canvassed ALA members for their support, but J. P. Dunn thought any official response from the ALA executive board "a trifle cheeky" since the public documents committee had done the work. Nonetheless, Fletcher said he would "boost" the bill. He also announced in LJ columns that the *ALA Index* was due "the middle of this year," and he especially encouraged libraries "which have so few sets of periodicals as not to require Poole's Index" to subscribe early. He promised that "nothing could do more to enable a librarian to 'make the most of a small library.' "[30]

Progress in preparing for the World's Fair stuttered as it ran into several difficulties. In January 1892 Hild asked Frank Hill to come to Chicago to discuss the exhibit before the next ALA conference, which was scheduled for Lakewood, New Jersey, in May. Why Hild did not first ask Cutler, on whose committee Hill was serving, would only become evident later. Hannah James, also on Cutler's committee, complained to Dewey about being "lonesome. I have not heard a word about the WF [World's Fair] in a long time." She suggested that it would be a "good idea for our committee—*your* I mean—to confer" with Poole's Chicago committee so the two bodies would not duplicate efforts. In February Commissioner Harris forewarned Dewey that the rules of the federal government's supervisory World's Fair Committee had created so much "red tape" for the bureau it would be "unwise" for ALA "to depend upon" it for financial assistance. Harris did say, however, that if ALA relinquished ownership of its exhibit to the bureau after the exposition closed he would give as much financial assistance as possible. In a circular dated 1 April 1892 the ALA executive board announced that the only thing necessary to conclude plans for a successful exhibit "is agreement among members of the ALA as to details." Harris suggested to Dewey on 5 May that ALA should make its participation in the Chicago World's Fair a subject of major discussion at its forthcoming conference in order to erase any points of disagreement between librarians with conflicting obligations to the exposition. Hill strongly advised Dewey that "we do not want it to appear that [Cutler's] committee has *decided anything*." Harris's and Hill's comments tacitly acknowledged a growing split between the Poole and Cutler committees. The split was exacerbated at a meeting of the Chicago Library Club on 6 May.

Club President William F. Poole indicated that although Windy City librarians were "very much in favor" of an ALA exhibit, he thought the "generous response" from foreign librarians to his own committee's invitation for an international conference suggested that ALA would not have sufficient room to display examples of library architecture, appliances, blanks and bindings, and especially a model library. Besides, he digressed, "I object to its being given that name by the A.L.A. I do not think the A.L.A. should be burdened with the expense of buying, arranging, and cataloguing such a library." He also did not think the collection should be called a model library since it "seems intended to be simply a small circulating library for the country town. Let it be known by that name." Hild publicly calculated the square footage the model library would consume, and then deferred to S. H. Peabody, chief of the Division of Liberal Arts for the exposition, who reminded club members that "space is going to be very limited." Because the first priority was "a complete exhibit of all library appliances," Peabody suggested book lists rather than books. Only Newberry Assistant Librarian C. Alex Nelson protested, arguing the exhibit ought to include the actual volumes.[31]

An open conflict over the ALA's Columbian Exhibit seemed imminent for the association's forthcoming Lakewood conference, but an unexpected incident occurred in late April which radically changed the situation and profoundly affected the American Library Association. In effect, it subtly tipped the delicate balance of power away from the old guard and towards Dewey and other librarians of similar persuasion. On 28 April 1892, ALA President Klas August Linderfelt was arrested for embezzling funds from the Milwaukee Public Library over a seven-year period. On 29 April ALA Secretary Hill asked Dewey if an executive board meeting should be called. Hill thought H. M. Utley should preside at the forthcoming conference, "as he is a western man, and we want Fletcher for next year." On 30 April Hill informed George Watson Cole that the ALA executive board would meet informally and unofficially at his house on 2 May to discuss the ramifications of "Mr. Linderfelt's troubles" on the forthcoming conference, scheduled later in the month. Poole took a more personal interest in Linderfelt's plight. He had watched Linderfelt's rise in the profession since 1881, and had encouraged him to participate in ALA in part to counter the power of eastern librarians, and especially Dewey. Poole scanned the Milwaukee papers for news of Linderfelt's difficulties, clipping articles freely and sending them to notable librarians across the country. Samuel S. Green thanked Poole for a clipping and noted, "I should have as soon suspected myself as Linderfelt." Larned, who also received a Poole clipping, stated, "The Linderfelt affair is dreadful beyond words. . . . It does not seem possible that so cleanly seeming a man has always had a twist of dishonesty in him."

Winsor worried about ALA's national profile. "It would be a pity to have notices respecting the coming conference go out with his name attached," he wrote Poole. Like Winsor, Dewey worried about ALA's public image. He suggested that Linderfelt resign as ALA president so the association could elect First Vice President Fletcher at the first meeting of the conference. Cutter concurred. "Fletcher was my preference for ALA president next year," he wrote Dewey, but he worried that "as it is a western year, would it be better for Utley to preside at some of the sessions? The westerners won't like it if we have three eastern presidents in succession." On 6 May Hill wrote Dewey that Fletcher ought to be elected at the executive board meeting rather than during the full session in order to attract less publicity. On 10 May Hill informed Bowker that Linderfelt had resigned as ALA president and that "naturally the position falls to the first vice-president, Fletcher."[32]

President Fletcher called the ALA conference to order at the Laurel House in

Lakewood, New Jersey, on 16 May. Although association members smoothed over the Linderfelt affair quickly and quietly, and Fletcher's only reference to it in his presidential address was "the peculiar circumstances under which I assumed this office," the incident hung over the entire conference like a dark cloud. Nonetheless, conferees pressed on. In his secretary's report Hill cited the need for extended discussion of the ALA Chicago exhibit. "If we go into this affair at all it must be with the united determination to make it a pronounced success," he said, but he did not specifically mention Poole's committee. Carr followed with his treasurer's report, which was passed on to the finance committee for examination. John Glenn of the finance committee informed conferees that ALA was incurring its usual annual deficit, drawing from money generated for the subsequent year's expenditures to pay off the current year's bills. He pointed out that ALA needed $800 for annual expenses but could count on only $625 of annual income. The ominous financial condition of the association led Green to ask the finance committee to propose solutions.

The committee gave its answer the next day. Increase annual dues from $2 to $3. Members noted that printing the conference proceedings consumed nearly three-fourths of all ALA expenditures. By previous agreement with the *Library Journal* the association turned over enough copies of the proceedings to the editor to supply each LJ subscriber with one copy, which in turn served as a monthly issue of the *Journal*. LJ would reimburse ALA only for the cost of paper. Since the committee did not see any fair way of reducing these costs, a dues increase was the next logical solution. Dewey argued vociferously against the move, speculating that ALA would lose members. But he offered no alternatives. Once again the problem went back to a special committee, which later presented a compromise. In lieu of a dues increase, the committee proposed to raise the annual dues for institutions to $5, to establish a list of life members for a flat fee of $100, and to create a new class of members called "Fellows," whose annual dues would be $5. Dewey raised no objection, and the report was adopted.

The New York State Library School once again received a glowing report, this time submitted in three parts by three different people; Mary Wright Plummer of Brooklyn's Pratt Institute, Willis K. Stetson of the New Haven (Connecticut) Free Public Library, and George E. Wire, superintendent of the medical department at the Newberry Library. J. P. Dunn reported for the public documents committee that the documents bill had finally passed the Senate and was currently being considered in the House. Conferees adopted his motion requiring ALA to petition Congress to pass the Senate bill. The endowment committee reported total subscriptions paid at $3,560.50, far below the $10,000 goal set at the 1890 conference.

Two issues which merited most attention at the conference were preparations for the ALA Chicago exhibit and revision of the ALA constitution. Cutler introduced the former when she read her committee report to the conferees on 17 May. She suggested that the ALA exhibit be made part of the Bureau of Education exhibit since the latter had offered both space and money. All other suggestions for raising money were "impracticable." The committee also recommended that the exhibit be divided into four parts: (1) exhibits by individual libraries; (2) a comparative exhibit which would include demonstrations of library architecture, appliances, fittings, and bindings; (3) historical and descriptive material on American libraries; and (4) a model ALA library set up in working order. The committee further suggested that the exhibit be placed under a permanent exposition committee with power to appoint "necessary superintendents and assistants," subcommittees on selection and collection of books, architecture and library statistics, and to "carry out such plans as will in their judgment best promote library interests and insure the success of the exhibit." Finally, Cutler recommended that the permanent committee report its progress monthly in LJ columns.

Green suggested that the association take up the committee report section by section. When conferees addressed the first section, C. Wellman Parks forewarned the association that both space and money would be limited. The bureau was assigned only 4,000 square feet, half of which would go to ALA. D. V. R. Johnston replied for Cutler's committee that the space "is fully ample for any reasonable exhibit," and that $5,000 would be "sufficient to make a satisfactory exhibit." Hill asked if New York could be counted on for $1,000 from money allocated by the state legislature, but Dewey could not promise. Green said ALA should depend only upon the $5,000 promised by the bureau. Poole objected. "This proposition to turn the matter over to the Bureau of Education is a new one; at least it is new to me." Hill quickly clarified that "the superintendence of the whole affair is to be in the hands of the committee appointed by the American Library Association. The bills go through the Bureau of Education but the management is in our hands practically. . . ." The published proceedings do not indicate that Poole responded. The association adopted the first section unanimously.

When conferees began discussing the second section, Green reconsidered the procedure which he had recommended. He surmised a section by section approval would bind a permanent committee to a specific course of action and greatly limit its freedom to react to unforeseen circumstances. Hovey and Fletcher agreed. Fletcher further suggested that the permanent committee "should include the committee that has already done the work on it." Since the ALA president would appoint the committee, Fletcher's suggestion was significant. Hill then reminded conferees that the committee "doing this work does not wish it to be understood that they consider themselves a permanent committee. The whole matter is now in the hands of the Association to make such decision as it may seem fit." Dewey, who had remained unusually quiet throughout the discussion, cited minutes from the previous conference, which demonstrated Cutler's committee already was "permanent." Utley moved that Cutler's committee be continued, and Dewey amended the motion to refer the whole issue "to a committee of five to be appointed by the Executive Board, with full power to carry out all the arrangements of this exhibit." The amended motion passed. It meant the members of the new executive board would determine the composition of the ALA World's Fair Committee. Poole moved that the ALA invite foreign library associations to attend the fair, and after his motion passed he described the efforts his committee on literary congresses had taken to schedule an international conference of librarians, many of whom had already been sent invitations. Hild advocated that Poole's committee work out a coordinated schedule of meetings with the ALA executive board. For reasons unmentioned which would only become apparent later, he did not suggest conferring with Cutler's exposition committee.

The second issue which commanded much conference attention was the report of the constitutional revision committee, whose members included Winsor, Cutter, Crunden, Dewey, and Soule as chairman. While several articles involving word changes met little or no comment, the committee's recommendations for electing officers and an executive board generated a spirited discussion. A committee majority had suggested electing by ballot an executive board of five which would transact association business and elect its officers. Soule substituted a motion to elect a president, three vice presidents, a secretary, and treasurer by direct ballot, and that these officers, together with the ALA president for the previous year, constitute an executive board. Hovey approved Soule's position and added that the Australian ballot system ought to be superimposed on the direct election of officers.

When the floor opened to discussion, Larned said he liked the majority report, but he worried that ALA's image would suffer from "an ambitious contest for the presidency." Lane, Crunden, and Dewey agreed. Dewey's response represented a reversal of positions he had assumed at previous conferences. "While I declared at Fabyan's for the direct election, I now incline to the old system." He gave three reasons for changing his mind: (1) the association was too evenly divided on the question; (2) anyone absent from the annual meeting would probably not be elected—even though "he is perhaps the best man for the place"; and (3) by direct vote the association might elect a president who "would not work in harmony" with the executive board and other officers. Soule dismissed Dewey's logic. "The direct election of the President specially prevents the accusation that the Association is being run by a clique." Hill said that some conferees opposed Soule's recommendation because they feared "one or two prominent members could get up here and sway the crowd and make it go whichever way they desired." His implication was harsh. It indicated that a number of ALA leaders had little confidence the membership was capable of choosing its own officials wisely. But Soule, Hovey, and Hill eventually lost the argument 19 to 18. Majority recommendations carried 17 to 11.

Sections mandating an annual conference and preventing an ALA president from succeeding himself were approved with little comment. Section 17 determined that the council was "to serve as an advisory board. No recommendation in relation to library administration shall be promulgated by the association, and no section shall be established under its name, until approved by two-thirds vote of the council.'' The section attempted to make the council a viable body with a specific organizational purpose. Previously it was considered "honorary," but Dewey looked upon the new council as "a kind of senate. It resembles the French Academy, and should be an honor to which the young librarian would look forward as the highest distinction." Conferees passed other minor revisions and then approved the new constitution for final action at the next meeting.

Several other familiar issues surfaced during the conference. George Iles repeated his call for a central bureau with a permanent staff to issue lists of annotated books which librarians and consumers could use for guidance. Fletcher said that "between the Publishing Section and the Library Bureau we have the beginning of the organization that is necessary." Dewey then pushed for the ALA *Catalog*, which he saw as a logical extension of Iles's ideas. Poole resisted. "That is not our purpose," he said. Poole thought indexing more suitable to association goals. Conferees ultimately appointed a committee "to see if the plan presented by Mr. Iles or some other is practicable." Dewey followed by urging the Bureau of Education to appoint "at least one officer . . . who shall devote his whole time to the general interest of American libraries." Although he kept his motive secret, Dewey wanted this individual to double as a permanent ALA secretary.

On 19 May the committee on nominations reported the results of its informal ballot for the ALA executive board; Dewey (105), Crunden (96), Hill (92), Soule (89), Cutter (86), Poole (17), Fletcher (17), Hild (12), Larned (11), and Hannah P. James (6). After Soule withdrew his name, Carr suggested "it is very desirable that a woman should serve" on the executive board. A formal ballot followed, and the final results showed Dewey, Crunden, Cutter, Hill, and James as members of the new board. The only "old stager" was Cutter; the others were philosophically aligned with Dewey. Few were surprised when the executive board subsequently appointed a Columbian Exposition Committee consisting of chairman Mary S. Cutler and members Hill, C. A. Nelson, Weston Flint, Hild and James. Crunden then listed the executive board's selections for ALA officers for the next year. He pointed out that the board had to overcome Dewey's "obstinacy and persuasive powers" to make him president, but Hill suggested the composition of the board and its desire to make the strongest possible showing at the conference the following year made the choice almost inevitable. As one condition for accepting, Dewey insisted that all ALA ex-presidents—Winsor, Poole, Cutter, Crunden, Green and Fletcher—be selected vice presidents. Hill was chosen secretary, and Carr treasurer. An informal ballot for council members showed the top ten as Poole, Dewey, Winsor, Cutter, James, Fletcher, Crunden, Lane, Green and Ellen M. Coe, all of whom were then elected.

Other smaller groups also met at the ALA Lakewood conference. President Dewey called the New York Library Association to order on 17 May. Chairman Fletcher directed the attention of the college library section to papers on "A Skeleton of Library Science" and "Teaching Bibliography to College

Students." As treasurer of the publishing section, William C. Lane cheerfully reported that the Omaha Public Library had ordered 500 copies of *Reading for the Young*, and section president Fletcher then noted that *ALA Index* was still not finished. New section officers for the coming year, all of whom came from the East (Fletcher, Lane, Dewey, Cutter and Soule), requested that ALA direct the committee considering Iles's plan for annotations to report to the publishing section.

For the first time in association history, ALA women organized a fourth group at a separate meeting to focus attention on women in the library profession. In her paper on "What a Woman Librarian Earns" Mary Cutler pointed out that "woman's fitness for library work is proved. She has already a recognized place in the profession. She has contributed somewhat to the literature of the subject and holds offices of honor in the American Library Association. This is due largely to the liberal spirit of the teachers in the library movement of the last twenty years." Conference proceedings do not indicate any objection to Cutler's gratefulness for the "liberal spirit" of her male professional predecessors. Chairman Coe appointed Hannah James, Annie Dewey and Harriet E. Greene, an instructor at the New York State Library School, as a committee to organize an ALA women's section.

When the new executive board met in Washington, D.C., on 21 May, the Linderfelt affair was the first order of business. Board members handled the matter so expeditiously that it was obvious they had predetermined a course of action. Secretary Hill reported he had received Linderfelt's resignation, and the board decided that, barring objection, Fletcher would assume the duties of president. Hill then moved that Linderfelt's resignation "take effect from the time of election." The motion quickly passed and "the Secretary was directed to record W. I. Fletcher as President for the entire term," thereby erasing Linderfelt's name from the official roster of ALA presidents. The *Library Journal* cooperated by making no mention of Linderfelt in its report of the conference. Thus, the American Library Association successfully erased the memory of a disgraced leader.[33]

Although most of the conferees left Lakewood after the association's work concluded on 19 May, the conference itself did not officially adjourn until 31 May, when a train departing from Jersey City carried the midwestern and western librarians home. Two hundred sixty people had registered for the conference; 150 were women. A geographical analysis of conferees shows 200 from North Atlantic states, only 29 from Great Lakes states. Fifty-eight attended from the New York State Library School, including administrators, faculty members and students. Little wonder that control of ALA was passing to Melvil Dewey as the association prepared for the Chicago conference of 1893. He dominated the executive board and commanded the exposition committee through its chairman, Mary S. Cutler, a subordinate at the New York State Library whom he often called "one of his special lieutenants." He also held an influential position on the executive board of the ALA publishing section. The Linderfelt affair had clearly hurt the western librarians, who had no one of Poole's former stature within ALA to counter the momentum the energetic Dewey was creating. The only official link between Poole's Chicago-based committee and Cutler's Albany-based committee was Frederick H. Hild. The conference had not reduced the potential for conflict between the two groups, but it did effect significant changes in the balance of power among competing interests.

Less than two weeks after the Lakewood conference Dewey's hegemony received its first test. Acting on behalf of Poole's committee, Hild formally requested C. Wellman Parks to ask Cutler to step down as chairman of the ALA Exposition Committee because as a woman she would not be as effective as a man. Hild suggested Cutter as a good substitute. When Parks communicated Hild's request to the ALA committee, Cutler agreed to the change, provided the rest of the committee consented. Weston Flint quickly concurred, and on 13 June Cutler offered to resign. Dewey saw through Hild's move and acted to counter it. He immediately issued a circular soliciting executive board sentiment. Hannah P. James objected, "I deny the right or justice of the demand made upon our committee to change the chairman." Hill was less kind. "This is nothing but a Chicago growl and should not be listened to," he said. If Cutler resigned, he would also. Crunden echoed Hill's sentiments. "When the cheeky Chicagoans present a formal request (practically a demand) it raises my combativeness." Crunden thought Hild "absurd . . . to object to work under a person so much his superior in intellect, character, and professional attainments." Cutler should not resign. He added parenthetically, "Glad Poole isn't President, or Hild, or Winsor, or anybody else especially."

Cutter told Dewey he would not vote "because it would be inconsistent with my promise to Mr. Parks. However, it makes no difference, there is little doubt how the other three will vote." Cutter also wrote C. Alex Nelson, another member of the committee, that Cutler saw Hild's move as "a slur upon her sex, which she naturally resented." On 22 June Dewey issued a circular to the ALA World's Fair Exposition Committee outlining the decision of the ALA executive board regarding Hild's formal request to replace Cutler as chairman. "We find ourselves unable with proper regard to the interest of the ALA to consent to the proposed change. This decision is clear, strong and unanimous." Dewey had won. Control of the committee would remain in Albany.[34]

Although the issue had been settled in Cutler's favor, she wasted no time repairing bridges to the Chicago group. On 8 July she asked Chicago Library Club Secretary G. E. Wire if the club would serve as a local committee for the exhibit. "Dr. Poole as President of the Club would naturally represent the Club and in that capacity become a member of the advisory board." Wire accepted on behalf of the club four days later. That same month the committee issued its first progress report in the *Library Journal*. A checklist of 5,000 volumes "common to a few public libraries" would soon be sent out in sections to 40 or 50 librarians for approval, additions, or deletions. Louisa S. Cutler, former librarian of the Aguilar Library in New York City and Mary Cutler's cousin, would ''take charge of the work.''[35]

A second test of Dewey's control came several months later. When he found out Hild and Poole wanted to schedule the international congress of librarians in advance of the ALA meeting, he immediately dispatched a circular to the association's executive board that the Chicago committee was attempting ''to get up a rival meeting the week before ALA and thus take the wind out of our sails.'' Dewey wanted a combined conference. He wrote Hild that two separate meetings would be counterproductive; both could not be successful. Instead, Dewey suggested holding them simultaneously, allowing ALA to meet in the morning and the international congress in the afternoon or evening. He also reminded Hild of an analogous situation involving the National Education Association (NEA). When a Chicago-based committee attempted a similar move against the NEA, the leadership decided the association would not recognize the committee, and would warn foreign educators against separate meetings if the Chicago committee continued its activities. Dewey said that although he ''did not approve that action . . . and I should oppose it even more strongly among the librarians,'' he was ''sure that we can agree on some satisfactory plan before any final circulars are sent out so that there shall be no appearance of any friction.'' Hill, Crunden and James wholly supported Dewey. ''I am for harmony—provided we don't have to do all the harmonizing,'' Hill said. ''That correspondence makes me sick—disgusted,'' Crunden replied. ''I can't help thinking that if Poole or Hild had been elected president there would have been no plan of this kind proposed.'' James was equally contemptuous. ''I am thankful you are at the helm, with a crew that will follow you in the straight path and will not be turned aside by false lights, or treacherous signals. All the storms we have will be of Poole's own raising—he'll soon find they will not wreck us!''[36]

Dewey called a meeting of the ALA executive board in Boston for 28 September. All agreed there should not be two separate conferences. He then reported the agreement to the Chicago committee, and followed that action with a personal visit in mid-October. By the time he left, the Chicago committee had agreed to schedule ALA meetings simultaneously with the international congress. The former would meet six to nine days in single sessions each morning; the latter would meet in the afternoon. Dewey had won another battle. In announcing the agreement on the joint conference, Dewey also said that because the program he planned for the forthcoming Chicago conference would be directed towards practical matters in librarianship, he had ''assumed to speak for the ALA'' by approaching Commissioner Harris. He asked the commissioner if the bureau would print the proceedings as a handbook of library economy and mail it free to requesting libraries. Harris agreed, and the ALA executive board subsequently officially endorsed Dewey's action.[37]

For a short time preparation for the conference went smoothly. At a meeting the last week in October Parks said the $5,000 allocated to the ALA exhibit seemed firm. The World's Fair Committee continued to issue rosy progress reports, and on 21 February, Dewey announced the tentative Chicago program, noting that because printed proceedings would comprise a handbook of library economy, contributing authors should provide a "judicial digest" of existing literature on the subject.[38]

That same day, however, Mary S. Cutler and several other committee members met with Commissioner Harris to complain that C. Wellman Parks was "incapable of dealing with reasonable people in a way that they can endure." Cutler was especially concerned with Parks's threats to modify the agreement struck between the bureau and ALA at Lakewood in May 1892, and with his treatment of the women who were preparing for the exhibit. "We must insist that hereafter the correspondence be carried on between yourself and the chairman of the exposition committee," she said. "We cannot consent that [the exhibit] be under the supervision of Mr. Parks; we would rather make no exhibit at all." Dewey echoed these strong words, although he claimed a role of peacemaker between Parks and "the ladies." Parks would not be allowed "to tamper with the exhibit at his own sweet will." Harris agreed that all correspondence between the bureau and the exposition committee should now go through him instead of Parks.[39]

Throughout the spring Dewey maintained pressure to publicize the conference. On 20 May he encouraged all ALA members to solicit new members and attend the conference; he also included copies of the new "ALA Yearbook" for 1893. On 1 June he asked major American newspapers for a favorable editorial on the conference by 10 June. After visiting Chicago the beginning of June, he reported to the executive board that Poole and Hild seemed "happy" and "cordial. If there are any clouds I have failed to find them in my weeks at Chicago." Crunden replied he was glad the ALA executive board insisted on Dewey as president at Lakewood. "I consistently return thanks that in deciding the question principle triumphed over policy and that the coming meeting is in the right hands." James was so pleased with Hild's reversal that she even suggested him as ALA's next president. On 29 June Dewey forwarded a copy of the ALA program to Harris with a request that he duplicate it and send it out, at bureau expense, to all libraries on the bureau's mailing list. On 11 July Harris forwarded a copy of the ALA *Catalog* to the Secretary of the Interior.[40]

Although wrestling with Poole, Hild, and Parks demanded most of Dewey's ALA time, other issues were not being ignored. The public documents committee continued to press Congress for a documents bill. Because Dewey considered meetings of the Association of State Librarians (ASL) as "a fizzle in the past," he encouraged ASL President J. P. Dunn to push for "our first full and successful meeting" in Chicago. In February 1893 Houghton-Mifflin published the *ALA Index* for the ALA publishing section. Dewey's suggestion that ALA arrange two special meetings in Chicago—one for library trustees only, the other for librarians only—in order to discuss relations with trustees received a mixed reaction. On the one hand, Bowker thought more would be gained by interaction than "segregation." On the other, James thought Dewey's idea "excellent," while Winsor admitted "I am not now enough in the swim of such things to have very definite ideas of what is best." Dewey decided to proceed and pressed E. C. Hovey to make sure enough trustees attended to make the separate meeting successful. Prospects for establishing a permanent ALA women's section were considerably dimmed when Los Angeles Public Library Director Tessa Kelso wrote an open letter to the *Library Journal* as "a protest against such a plan." She argued that "sex should have no weight where ability is equal" and that separation from the body of librarians which consisted of both sexes "is a serious mistake." Hannah James wrote Dewey that "personally I do not favor an organization, but only a little gathering to discuss informally any topics that would be interesting to women alone, such as health, hours of work, women's wages, etc." Although she did not explain how the first two categories were exclusive to women, she did say Coe and Annie Dewey agreed with her to drop efforts to establish the section. Only Cutler protested.[41]

As Dewey led the ALA into the Chicago conference, both the association and the profession had obviously changed. The organizational composition of the American library community had altered significantly over the last several years. For example, Illinois librarians were discussing the possibility of organizing a state association, the Colorado Library Association held its first meeting on 29 December 1892, the Minnesota Library Association met for the second time on 29 December 1892, and the Drexel Institute of Philadelphia announced it was opening a new library school. And in January 1893, the state of Connecticut passed a bill establishing the Connecticut Library Commission. The profession's leadership was also changing. By his own admission, Winsor spent most of his time on historical scholarship, very little on librarianship, and was "not now enough in the swim of such things" to make a difference in ALA. Cutter had resigned his post at the Boston Athenaeum in April 1893 as a result of a disagreement with Athenaeum trustees. In the Midwest, Poole was being openly criticized by his own board of trustees for spending too much time on materials acquisition and not enough on efficient library administration. His subordinates often complained he gave them no direction, and did not properly coordinate routine library work.[42] With Linderfelt gone, Hild humbled by his two recent defeats, the only other western librarian with enough stature to contest Dewey's growing influence was Frederick M. Crunden. But Crunden was a staunch Dewey ally who regularly agreed with the direction Dewey wanted the association to take.

As the Chicago conference opened it was obvious that ALA leadership had undergone significant change since 1876. The old guard no longer controlled; it had been replaced by a new breed of librarians, championed by Melvil Dewey, which was anxious to increase the efficiency (" . . . at the least cost") of librarians through their professional association. The ALA *Catalog* and the forthcoming handbook of library economy also reflected changes in ALA direction. More would be forthcoming in the future. Dewey's position was secured by a group of allies on the ALA executive board, by a loyal group of influential and hard-working subordinates at the New York State Library and the New York State Library School, and by the ever-increasing number of Dewey library school graduates who assumed positions in libraries across the country. He rode the crest into Chicago.

A Struggle to Identify "The Largest Number": The Pressures of Growing Factionalism, 1893–1901

The 100-degree heat was almost unbearable. Certainly it was unusual for Waukesha, Wisconsin, where 460 people attended the 23rd ALA conference at the Fountain Spring Hotel on 4 July 1901. Three hundred and twenty-four conferees came from the Midwest. By 1901 ALA boasted a total membership of 874, and at Waukesha the women in attendance outnumbered men two to one. Not only had the association itself grown, its meetings had changed in many ways since 1893. Conferees now sported badges; the 1901 conference badge was suspended by a red ribbon extending from a clasp shaped like a badger. In addition, the conference calendar had become so crowded that members of differing ALA groups and affiliates were forced to make adjustments. Several special committees and the ALA council met the morning of 4 July. The Wisconsin Library Association, the Illinois Library Association, and the recently organized Bibliographic Society of Chicago met that afternoon.

President Henry J. Carr, director of the Scranton (Pennsylvania) Public Library, finally called the first general session to order at 8:15 P.M. in Waukesha's Methodist Church. Carr had been a loyal member of the association, and since 1879 had attended every conference. For nearly 20 years he had served faithfully as either treasurer or secretary. The presidency had been his reward. "I'm glad you found out what a good fellow Carr is," Frank Hill wrote Springfield (Massachusetts) Public Library Director John Cotton Dana, just prior to the opening of the conference.[1] Carr entitled his presidential address "Being a Librarian," and emphasized to his audience they were members of a profession of professions because they were custodians of literature for all professions. Thomas L. Montgomery, director of the Wagner Free Institute Library in Philadelphia, next spoke on "What May Be Done for Libraries." He emphasized that the public library should remain an educational institution and not pander to the demand for light fiction. Herbert Putnam, in his second year as Librarian of Congress, announced that his institution would try to lend more books in the future.

At the association's first business session the following morning ALA Secretary Frederick W. Faxon, manager of the library department of the Boston Book Company, reported that during the past year the association had enjoyed the largest annual growth—225 members—in its history. He also announced that the new *ALA Handbook* was already two months old. Gardner M. Jones, director of the Salem (Massachusetts) Public Library, presented a treasurer's report showing a balance of $1,176.28. C. C. Soule, president of the Boston Book Company, read the report for the trustees of the endowment fund. He complained that the permanent fund "is not as large as it ought to be," and suggested "if any of you should be asked where an amount of say $100,000 could be placed with advantage to the general library cause, I hope you will bear in mind the inadequate funds of the Association." The allusion to Carnegie's library philanthropy was unmistakable. The cooperation committee issued an abbreviated statement because its report the previous year on cooperative cataloging had been "exhaustive." Routine reports from the committee on foreign documents, the committee on title pages and indexes of periodical volumes, and the committee on international cataloging of scientific literature were followed by a memorial to historian John Fiske, who had died just before the conference convened.

The third session was equally colorless. After Indiana State Librarian W. E. Henry reported for the committee on public documents, John Cotton Dana gave a report for the committee on cooperation with the National Education Association. "Libraries and librarians are as yet held in small esteem by the educational people of this country." He applauded the efforts of fellow committee member Mary Ahern, editor of a six-year-old periodical entitled *Public Libraries* that was published out of the Library Bureau's Chicago branch. Dana noted that Ahern had attempted to alert NEA members to the committee's program by sending announcements to 32 education journals. Only two had bothered to print the announcement. Dana then suggested that one method of penetrating the educational community would be to incorporate library-related courses into the nation's normal school curricula. He especially complimented the Wisconsin library community for its effort in that direction. But Dewey defended the educators. "The public teachers and the other teachers of this country are a badly over-worked class," he said. His remarks were followed by a report on uniform standards of book statistics from the committee on international cooperation, and an unusually quick statement from the committee on library training.

Papers dominated the fourth session, but the fifth session, held the morning of 9 July, proved much livelier. George Watson Cole's report on "Gifts and Bequests to American Libraries, 1900–1901" recorded Andrew Carnegie's generosity. Of $16,000,000 donated to libraries in the previous year, Carnegie accounted for more than $11,000,000. Cole also lamented that the ALA publication fund had no new money. "The Publishing Board is much hampered by lack of funds from carrying on its important work," he said. "If some philanthropically inclined person would present a fund, say $100,000, upon condition that all publications issued from its income should bear the name of the fund, it would not only be of inestimable benefit to the cause of libraries, but would also be a most enduring monument to its donor." This marked the second time conferees had heard an appeal for a $100,000 donation, although this one came from a second source and for a different purpose.

W. I. Fletcher followed Cole with a report from the publishing board. He briefly outlined an agreement with the Library of Congress to issue printed catalog cards for general library use. Conferees were excited at the prospect and Dewey was especially complimentary. Putnam privately described him as being "in rapture." Fletcher also identified several other board projects. He announced George Iles's $10,000 donation for J. N. Larned's annotated *Literature of American History*, scheduled for publication in the fall. He also cited a forthcoming second edition of the *ALA Index*, a supplement to the ALA *Catalog* edited by Mary S. Cutler Fairchild (she had married E.M. Fairchild in 1897), and an *ALA Portrait Index* by William Coolidge Lane and Nina E. Browne of the publishing board. The report ended by echoing Lane's previous pleas for salaried officers to meet the needs of the library community.[2]

Frederick J. Teggart indicated progress in his report for the committee on a handbook of American libraries, but he also said that the committee had not yet determined whether the publishing board or the Bureau of Education would actually publish the handbook. After conferees directed a committee of the children's librarians' section to prepare a "cooperative list of children's books," Putnam elaborated on the Library of Congress's decision to issue printed catalog cards along with the publishing board. He identified three reasons the library could undertake the task. First, the publishing board promised to act as a liaison between the library and ALA; second, *Publisher's Weekly* pledged to alert the library to recent publications; third, R. R. Bowker had pledged $1,000 to cover any potential deficit the first year of operation.

George Iles then delivered a paper on the "Trusteeship of Literature." He still wanted to establish a central bureau with a permanent salaried staff whose primary task was to appraise literature, but he said staff members could disseminate legislative information, assist in cooperative cataloging, and perhaps even prepare elementary guides called "library tracts." Iles hoped some benefactor would support his plan. Richard T. Ely, director of the School of Economics at the University of Wisconsin, took issue with Iles. "Have we a judicial body of men who could render these estimates?" he asked. Ely did not think so. He distrusted any organization which potentially threatened freedom of thought, learning, and science. He suggested that Iles's proposal might lead to an *index librorum prohibitorum* and an *index expurgatorius*. Putnam interjected that the selector decides "what represents this doctrine best—not whether the doctrine is right or wrong." He argued that this was one of the profession's least understood functions, although he did not elaborate on what criteria librarians used to determine "best." Putnam's words did not placate Ely. He still opposed any appraisals on catalog cards which might consolidate public opinion "along one line." The conference then passed to a discussion of the relationship between publishers, booksellers, and librarians. Bowker argued vociferously for maintaining a link between the library and book communities.

That afternoon Dewey chaired an informal meeting of the "State Library Commissions and Travelling Libraries Roundtable." The movement to establish state library commissions had gained momentum since 1893. Several midwestern commissions had been especially successful in establishing traveling libraries to service rural populations. In fact, the Wisconsin Library Commission often boasted about its employees' "personal contact" with people in "neglected communities," and to prove its claim, had one of its "travelling libraries" on display in the conference exhibit area. Later that afternoon the catalog section met. After Anderson H. Hopkins of the John Crerar Library identified the section's activities, participants argued over the format and issuance of Library of Congress printed catalog cards.[3]

Next morning tellers reported the election of officers. To the surprise of very few, New York Public Library Director John Shaw Billings was chosen president. Several people had wanted to nominate Putnam in order to enhance the possibility that the cooperative scheme on printed catalog cards would succeed, but Putnam had plans to tour Europe for three months. Billings, who was not present at the meeting, was the clear alternative because of his close ties to Carnegie. He directed a library system to which Carnegie had recently pledged $1,000,000 for the construction of 65 branch libraries. Billings was also a founding member of the Carnegie Institute scheduled to open in Washington, D.C., the next year. By placing a man Carnegie knew and respected in the president's chair, ALA leaders hoped to increase their chances for the $100,000 donation they had been hinting at throughout the conference. Unlike Carr, whose loyalty to the association won him a turn as president, Billings had been neither an active nor a very attentive ALA member. In fact, he disagreed with those ALA members who wished to harness the public library to the popular education movement, and he had argued that a library ought to be a reference institution for scholarly use. After Secretary Faxon telegraphed news of the election to him, Billings felt compelled to request an outline of his duties.

Other officers chosen included First Vice President James K. Hosmer, director of the Minneapolis Public Library (whose election suggested he would be Billings's successor), Second Vice President Electra C. Doren of the Dayton (Ohio) Public Library (who occupied the position among the officers which by this time was traditionally reserved for a woman), Secretary Frederick W. Faxon, Treasurer Gardner M. Jones and Recorder Helen E. Haines, assistant editor of the *Library Journal*. Council members elected included Henry M. Utley, Mary E. Ahern, Pittsburgh Public Library Director E. H. Anderson, Iowa State Librarian Johnson Brigham, and Philadelphia Public Library Director John Thomson. After thanking Wisconsin and its library community for courtesies and hospitality, ALA conferees adjourned, some to travel to an NEA meeting in Detroit, some to return home, and some to join a postconference boat trip through the Great Lakes.

The conference was also marked by meetings of numerous special interest sections. Besides those already mentioned, other groups which gathered at Waukesha included the National Association of State Librarians (NASL), the college and reference section, the children's librarians section, the trustees section, and roundtable meetings on "Instruction in Bibliography" (coordinated by Crerar Library cataloger Aksel G. S. Josephson) and "Work of State Library Associations and Women's Clubs on Advancing Library Interests." At the latter Ahern argued ALA "should take care of the technical side" while "smaller questions . . . should be taken up by the state associations."

The ALA council was particularly active. After recommending that the next ALA meeting should be held at a New England resort, the council voted that ALA ex-presidents constitute a nominating committee, that interest from the endowment fund be used for publishing board projects, and that ALA establish two new committees—a committee on relations with a book trade and a committee on express and postal rates. The council also directed the committee on cataloging rules for printed cards to work with the ALA publishing board and the Library of Congress to formulate consistent rules satisfactory to all parties.[4]

That the Waukesha conference did not openly manifest the political struggles evident in preparations for the 1893 Chicago conference should not suggest the association enjoyed a quiet life at the turn of the century. ALA changes since the 1893 conference had been just as painfully wrought as those during the half-decade preceding it. In fact, subsurface shifting of allegiances and interests pointed toward a future which promised even more significant changes. A few specific trends were already evident. ALA's organizational structure was more complex. New association sections reflecting specialized interests at the Waukesha conference suggested an emerging bureaucracy within the library profession. Other special groups had discussed organization at informal roundtable meetings. State library commission employees, whose strength had steadily grown in the Midwest, generated much energy and discussion. They agreed with Dewey that the public library must standardize and make its services more efficient, but they did not necessarily follow Dewey's leadership. Too many things had happened since Chicago which led them to question Dewey's sincerity.

The profession also sported a new periodical, *Public Libraries* (PL), published from the Library Bureau's Chicago office. PL and state library commissions primarily reflected the concerns of their rural western constituents by addressing the practical problems of library service to rural populations. Neither was much interested in large urban or research libraries. In contrast, the ALA publishing board continued to address the needs of large libraries, especially those located in the East. While library commissions aimed their efforts at whole groups, the publishing board continued to issue aids to satisfy the perceived information needs of individuals. Seeds of a potential dispute were evident. On the surface, however, the mood was universally optimistic. Membership was up, and the benefactions of Andrew Carnegie promised a rosy future for new members of the profession, perhaps even a sufficient endowment to fund the permanent ALA headquarters and staff which Henry Homes had first called for in 1881. And with Billings as ALA president, the prospects for obtaining a donation seemed even better.

The record of how the association adjusted to the pressures of a growing bureaucratic environment characterized by factionalism, sectionalism and special interests between 1893 and 1901 forms yet another chapter in ALA's early history.

Progress within ALA slowed in the wake of the highly successful 1893 conference. Outgoing Treasurer Carr was still angry at ALA's irresponsible practice of paying the current year's bills with dues supposed to cover the subsequent year's expenses. He complained to his successor, George Watson Cole, that the Chicago conference put ALA "as much in the hole" as the previous conference. He recommended as "a leverage to use in collecting the dues" that Cole not supply delinquent members with printed conference proceedings.[5]

Grumbling about the unsuccessful portions of the Chicago conference continued. Dewey complained to J. Y. W. Macalister of London that he "was ashamed the way things were botched" for foreign librarians. He blamed Poole and his Chicago associates, who were "the most touchy people we have." In addition, C. Wellman Parks continued to plague the ALA exposition committee. By prior agreement ALA had promised to send the model library to the Bureau of Education immediately after the exposition closed. But Parks objected. He wanted to exhibit it in New York City for a while, and had already contacted several book publishers to assist him. Members of the exposition committee were incensed. They were especially sensitive to any possibility that the very industry from which they purchased the tools of their trade might capitalize on ALA efforts. Since the association had not authorized Parks to use its name in the proposed venture, committee members complained to Harris. The commissioner acquiesced. When the ALA executive board met on 10 November 1893, members unanimously ratified the committee's action and authorized it to inform the publishing industry that the association would have "no further relations" with Parks.[6]

The board also appointed Larned and Hill to a program committee to eliminate duplication of presentation topics at the subsequent conference. The board also authorized the publishing board to keep the *ALA Handbook* up-to-date. Several months later the Bureau of Education finally published the ALA *Catalog*, Pratt Institute issued Mary Wright Plummer's 56-page pamphlet entitled *Hints to Small Libraries* (designed as a substitute for "the long desired A.L.A. manual"), and Roberts Brothers of Boston published William I. Fletcher's *Public Libraries in America*, a general survey of library conditions in the United States. The ALA publishing section had no direct responsibility for any of these three additions to the growing body of practical library literature. Nonetheless, the section continued to solicit money to expand its publishing activities.[7]

President Larned opened the 1894 ALA conference on 17 September at the

Grand View Hotel in Lake Placid, a resort village in the Adirondacks. Two hundred five people registered; 164 came from North Atlantic states, only 30 from the Great Lakes states; 120 were women. In his presidential address Larned argued that the public library must provide a check against dangerous political doctrines by collecting the best thought of the past and present. Higher education could not accomplish this task because too few citizens attended college, he said, and the press was too willing to play for sensational headlines to be trusted to exercise a beneficial social impact. Conferees were so impressed with Larned's remarks that they later decided to have the address separately printed for wider dissemination.

During the next five days the conference hosted ten sessions, plus two separate section meetings—the college library section and the publishing section. Participants in the former spent much of their time planning future activities. Participants in the latter enjoyed a more productive meeting. Section President Dewey reported no progress on the *ALA Manual*, to be published by the Bureau of Education, but the *ALA Index* was beginning to show a profit, and sales of *Reading for the Young* had almost matched publication expenses. A *List of Subject Headings for a Dictionary Catalog* was nearly ready for the printer, and Ellen Coe had almost completed an annotated list of books for girls' and women's clubs, which the section planned to publish. Fletcher then asked section members to identify directions for future publishing activities. Privately, he lamented to Dewey that the section was not receiving more money from the endowment fund.[8] Before adjourning, the section directed its executive board to "prepare for private circulation an annotated list of undesirable fiction."

The conference itself went smoothly. Secretary Hill reported that the Chicago conference had been a success, although the *ALA Manual* was still at the Bureau of Education awaiting an open spot on the printer's schedule. Hill also reported that William Frederick Poole had died on 1 March. Conferees later devoted their tenth session to eulogizing Poole. Treasurer Cole reported a membership count of 470, and the finance committee confirmed an ALA treasury balance of approximately $300. The cooperation committee called for consistency in generating library statistics, while the committee on library school and training classes rendered another glowing report on the New York State Library School. Committee member G. T. Little, director of the Bowdoin College Library, also described library schools at the Pratt, Drexel, and Armour institutes, the Los Angeles and Denver public libraries, and the Amherst College summer program. Little concluded by citing a survey of 100 libraries in which 77 reported that they preferred to train their own employees rather than hire apprentice librarians. The profession at large still believed the skills necessary to practice librarianship could be learned on the job. Veteran librarians did not see the need for formal library school education.

A committee on foreign documents discussed problems concerning document exchange agreements with foreign countries, and the committee on public documents argued that a public documents bill before a joint congressional committee encouraged political patronage. Eight speakers discussed the "selection of books." St. Louis Public Library Trustee James K. Hosmer suggested Iles's plan for a central bureau was unnecessary; reviewers were generally reliable. Others argued that Iles's plan would minimize the need to read reviews. Five speakers also addressed "Common Novels in Public Libraries," but the topic generated less discussion than its predecessor. A symposium on "Supplying Current Daily Newspapers in Free Library Reading Rooms" met a different reaction, however. Frederick M. Crunden remarked "so far as I have observed, the people who come to the newspaper reading room only are the people who really do not count for much anyway. They are the driftwood of society that has little influence one way or another." The elitism in his remarks went unanswered. At the same session the committee on an index to subject headings reported its work was almost complete. After conferees heard a short description of contemporary library architecture, they joined in a lengthy discussion on the topic of flooring materials for library buildings.

On 19 September, ALA opened its sixth session with a symposium on periodical library bulletins. Denver Public Librarian John Cotton Dana called for the publication of "library tracts" which librarians in remote areas of the United States could use to "arouse library interest." He complained that "the *Library Journal* is expensive, and cannot expect a wide circulation" and that "it is doubtful if the American Library Association itself uses sufficient printer's ink." Later Dana argued that the publishing section should press commercial publishers to print library editions of popular books which could withstand heavy use, and he called upon the section to compile "a dictionary of library economy" which in a concise manner would give "direction in regard to the minor details as well as the more important subjects in library work."

After Dana took his seat, ALA members elected their officers, for the first time in their history using the Australian ballot to choose among a slate of nominees which included Milwaukee Public Librarian Theresa West, the first woman ever nominated for the ALA presidency. Tellers reported the results of the voting three sessions later. For president, Detroit Public Librarian Henry M. Utley received 64 votes, Cleveland Public Librarian William Howard Brett 43, West 20, and Caroline M. Hewins two write-in votes. West withdrew and on the second ballot Utley won a majority. Dana, Mary S. Cutler and Ellen Coe were elected vice presidents, Hill repeated as secretary, and Cole as treasurer. West, Hewins, William Coolidge Lane and Caroline Garland of the Dover (New Hampshire) Public Library were added to the council.

Several ALA members were dissatisfied with the Australian ballot. Crunden believed the substance gained from an ALA conference too valuable to sacrifice to a time-consuming electoral process. Dewey suggested the association give the ballot a three-year trial period. Crunden remained adamant. He moved that the next ALA conference consider a constitutional amendment which would reinstitute the old method of electing officers. His motion passed. Other issues which generated conference discussion included reports on public access to library shelves, public libraries and university extension, and the functions of a university library. Just before adjourning, conferees voted to meet in Denver in 1895. On 27 September, the executive board appointed Mary Cutler to chair a committee on a supplement to the ALA *Catalog*.[9]

Perhaps it was inevitable that the conference following Chicago would be less than spectacular and concentrate on more routine matters. The disputes which had characterized ALA matters during the previous three years had subsided, and the association had become more introspective. While Poole was no longer alive to exert leadership for western librarians, others had emerged to fill the vacuum. John Cotton Dana, a New Englander transplanted to Colorado, was perhaps the most vocal, and ALA was scheduled to meet in his state in August 1895. Preparation for the Denver conference was casual; the association continued to suffer some lethargy in the wake of the Chicago conference. Consensus regarded the trip to Denver as another missionary venture west of the Mississippi River. But Dewey continued to work behind the scenes to push ALA for more progress. On 21 January 1895 he precipitously scolded Harris for taking too much time with the *ALA Manual*, which consisted of papers presented at the Chicago conference. Harris responded sharply that many considered "the printing of this document a liability" and some congressmen had openly wondered why the Commissioner of Education's annual report "should give so much space to the details on management of libraries." Dewey quickly retreated, saying he understood Harris's problem.[10]

Undaunted, Dewey pushed ahead on other fronts. He convinced William Coolidge Lane, who had recently become director of the Boston Athenaeum, to remain as publishing section secretary-treasurer. Any "plan to turn over the publishing of the proceedings to our section," Dewey suggested, makes it "doubly important to have our most careful strong men in the Publishing Section." On 9 April he suggested that the section expand its scope of activities to include: (1) the completion of Soldan's handbook on library use; (2) the printing of catalog cards; (3) the publication of an index to scientific serials, transactions and monographs; (4) the completion of an index to bibliographical lists; (5) the coordination of bibliographical work between libraries to minimize duplication; (6) additional annotations for the ALA *Catalog* supplement; (7) support for Iles's plan for evaluating books; (8) the preparation of a supplement to *Reading for the Young*, with an index to leading children's periodicals; (9) the establishment of a gifts exchange and distribution agency; and (10) the preparation of a list of inexpensive children's books.[11] The years had not tempered Dewey's ambitions for ALA.

A month later the Massachusetts Library Club formally announced that it would publish a "monthly list of selected fiction." The number of library selection tools and aids was growing, and although ALA lagged behind, plans were afoot for more. During the summer of 1895 the publishing section issued a *List of Books for Girls and Women and Their Clubs*, edited by Augusta Leypoldt and George Iles (and funded by the latter), but distributed through the Library

Bureau in Boston. By this time Wisconsin and Vermont had also established
state library commissions, and Ohio and Vermont had founded state library
associations. The number of library organizations continued to grow at a greater
rate than the publication of library selection tools necessary to fill their needs.
Other ALA committees were less active than the publishing section. The public
documents committee lobbied for John G. Ames as superintendent of documents,
but the appointment eventually went to F. A. Crandall. The committee on foreign
documents experienced difficulty just gathering information.[12]

ALA President Henry Utley's prognosis that "the east will be sparsely represented" at the Denver conference proved to be accurate. When he called the
conference to order on 13 August he and Dana were the only executive board
members present. Not even Dewey attended. One hundred forty-seven people
attended, 35 from North Atlantic states, 39 from Great Lakes states, and 67
from Mountain states; 87 registrants were women. Utley told the gathering that
"the function of the public library is purely and wholly educational," that there
was "no limit to the concern of the free state in the education of its citizens,"
and that public libraries deserved state support in their efforts to educate the
masses and "to guide [them] in the path of highest progress." From that lofty
but seldom discussed philosophical position conferees again turned their attention
to more practical matters.

C. Alex Nelson, deputy librarian at Columbia College, gave an abbreviated
oral report for the absent Secretary Hill and Treasurer Cole. The finance committee reported a balance of $1,108.85— "the best financial showing ever made
by the Association." The executive board acknowledged a constitutional amendment making the ALA recorder an executive board member. Bowker reported
for the committee on public documents that the bill signed into law on 12 January
1895 "is, on the whole, probably as satisfactory a first step, or rather stride, as
can be expected in a measure so entangled with many complexities and per-
plexities, bibliographical as well as political."

The next four sessions covered routine committee reports and formal presentations on practical library problems, but at the sixth general session ALA
members gathered to elect officers. To save time and to avoid the necessity for
a second ballot, Utley announced that candidates receiving a plurality would be
elected. While votes were collected and tallied, conferees chose Cleveland for
their 1896 conference site. Tellers then reported the results of the election: John
Cotton Dana as president, Henry Carr, Theresa West and Denver City Librarian
C. R. Dudley as vice presidents, St. Joseph (Missouri) Public Librarian H. L.
Elmendorf as secretary, and George Watson Cole as treasurer. New council
members included Utley, Katharine Sharp of Chicago's Armour Institute, Minneapolis Public Librarian Herbert Putnam, and Pittsburgh Public Librarian E.
H. Anderson. None of the new officers were from northeastern libraries.

Perhaps because the number of new faces among ALA officers reflected such
a decidedly western bent, the discussion of the constitutional amendment on
electing officers which followed generated lively debate and occupied the greater

part of two sessions. The amendment which Crunden had pushed at Lake Placid provided that the association "elect by ballot a president and an executive board of five" which would in turn select the remaining ALA officers—in short, a return to the method practiced before 1893. Crunden said that the new balloting method took too much time and relied upon a "popular assembly" which was often largely ignorant of nominees' abilities. He worried about the roles that emotions and politics would play in future elections. "There are no cliques in this Association, but there are minor sentiments; that we all know," he said. "It is perfectly natural that the librarians in the West should act together since they know each other better than they know the librarians in the East. The same is true in the East." Utley countered that the association ought to have a democratically elected government. Although C. Alex Nelson attempted a compromise by suggesting that members of each of five sections of the country elect one person to represent them on the executive board, his comments fell on deaf ears. Utley closed discussion, and after declaring "the membership itself, and not a clique or junta, ought to control the Association," forced a vote. Thirty favored the amendment, 26 were opposed. Crunden was far short of the two-thirds majority necessary to carry. The problems of balancing obviously growing sectionalist sentiments against the reality imposed by the democratic election of association officers at conferences held across the country continued to divide and perplex ALA leaders.

At the final session on 21 August, Utley read Dewey's report for the cooperation committee. Dewey suggested seven topics (some of which had been discussed many times over the years) for future consideration: (1) the organization and coordination of state and local library associations; (2) the compilation of "a list of 500 books for the use of small libraries, many of which are simply dazed and confused by the wealth of the A.L.A. library"; (3) interchangeable membership among library associations; (4) promotion of the publishing section's new subject heading list; (5) the possibility of relinquishing the editing, printing and publication of the conference proceedings to the publishing section; (6) cooperative selection and annotation of books based upon a model provided by the Massachusetts Library Club fiction list; (7) promotion of a plan for printing catalog cards to be distributed by the Library Bureau; and (8) exploring and evaluating the potential of various library appliances. After reading Dewey's report Utley entertained a series of reports and resolutions and adjourned the meeting.[13]

The election of officers and subsequent dispute on the constitutional amendment caused some consternation among the membership. Incoming Secretary H. L. Elmendorf wrote Dewey that he feared "it was a mistake to make the new organization so decidedly western. There is, if I'm not mistaken, a reaction after Chicago and Lake Placid." Dana also wrote Dewey apologetically that he only accepted the ALA presidency because Brett "preferred having the meeting next year in Cleveland to being elected President this year." To both men Dewey replied, "I believe it well to have tried a decidedly western organization. We want to make the ALA national and not let the idea get abroad that it is a New England affair.''[14] Despite Dewey's reassurances, however, sectional dissension continued to surface as ALA significantly expanded its membership beyond the North Atlantic states.

Expansion of library interests was evident in other organizations. By the end of the year library associations had been established in Vermont, Ohio, Indiana, Nebraska, and Central California; Vermont and Wisconsin had also organized state library commissions. Within a few months the *Library Journal* noted that Chairman Frank Hutchins and Secretary Lutie Stearns had turned the Wisconsin Free Library Commission into one of ''the most effective educational agencies in the state.'' Other associations were not idle. In March 1896 the New Jersey Library Association, the Connecticut Library Association, and the New York Library Club petitioned Congress to reprint the *ALA Catalog*.[15]

Undoubtedly ALA President Dana wanted to make a point when he called the executive board together 1,300 miles east of his Denver home at the Cleveland Public Library on 10 October. Besides himself, other board members present included Utley, Carr, West and Elmendorf, and observers Brett and George B. Meleney of the Library Bureau's Chicago office. The board filled the remaining positions on the ALA's many committees, set the dates for the 1896 conference at Cleveland, replaced the ill ALA Treasurer Cole with E. H. Anderson of Pittsburgh, and directed Dewey to pull the *ALA Manual* out of the Bureau of Education unless the latter could publish it promptly. While the actions of the board were not controversial, the fact that members met in Cleveland, and that subsequently Dana, West and Elmendorf traveled east on a ''general visit'' to libraries, did not go unnoticed.[16] Westerners were obviously trying to ease some of the tension created by the recent Denver elections.

Dana also had a second purpose in mind. When he and West visited Bowker in New York, he identified ''our desire for some means of communication with the smaller libraries''; he asked Bowker ''if it could not be reached by a supplement of the Journal or something of that kind.'' Specifically, Dana wanted ''a circular of information on the starting of libraries in small towns.'' But Bowker manifested no interest in this project. Perhaps he remembered how Dana had openly complained at the Lake Placid conference that the *Library Journal* was too expensive for the smaller libraries growing up all over the trans-Allegheny frontier, and that LJ generally ignored their unique problems.

It was no coincidence that Meleney attended the 10 October ALA executive board meeting. If Bowker was not interested in satisfying the needs of smaller libraries, Dana wondered if the Library Bureau would help. Meleney expressed interest, but said he would have to check with the bureau's president and chief stockholder, Melvil Dewey. In 1895 Dewey and Bowker still feuded over their interpretations of the origins of ALA and LJ. Each would open old wounds rather than concede a point, but each kept the argument out of the *Library Journal*. Bowker still bristled over the duplicitous manner in which Dewey had introduced *Library Notes*, an inexpensive periodical Dewey hoped would serve the needs of the smaller libraries. *Notes* had never been successful and in 1895 was issued infrequently. Dana's suggestion to Meleney reopened publication possibilities for Dewey.

By Christmas, 1895, Dewey and Meleney had decided to issue a new periodical entitled *Public Libraries* from the bureau's Chicago offices. It would be cheaper than *Library Journal* and would address the needs of the smaller public libraries of the Midwest which were beginning to proliferate. Dewey admonished Meleney to assemble a board of editors of "ten or a dozen of your best people," and suggested Crunden, Utley, Dana, Brett, Whelpley, Elmendorf, West, Sharp, and Stearns—all westerners. He thought Lutie Stearns ought to be managing editor, although he complained that writing out her first name in full would reflect on her poorly—just as "if Mr. Dana printed on his letterhead 'Tootsie C. Dana.' " He also suggested that the first number of *Public Libraries* carry Dana's recently completed *Library Primer*, a tract which the ALA publishing section for some reason seemed reluctant to publish when Dana had initially offered it the previous summer. Meleney agreed with all Dewey's recommendations, but when he attempted to negotiate a salary with Stearns, she demanded twice as much as he was willing to pay. Mary Ahern got the job instead.[17]

By February 1896 rumors of the new periodical began to reach Bowker's office. He wrote Dewey on 7 March that a new periodical "limits the field of the Journal seriously and prevents the development it should have in importance, extent and circulation." Dewey responded that the "new western monthly" should not be regarded as a "rival" to LJ, but a complementary publication. Bowker strongly disagreed, and complained not only to Dewey, but also to Elmendorf, Cutter, Fletcher, Dana, Secretary of the Wisconsin State Historical Society Reuben G. Thwaites, and Library Bureau Manager H. E. Davidson that the bureau had treated the *Journal* discourteously because it had not identified "the desire of western librarians for a separate periodical."[18]

In mid-March Meleney asked Cutter and Fletcher to join the *Public Libraries* board of editors; both men declined the invitation. Dewey later scolded Meleney for his mistake, reminding him that both Cutter and Fletcher had business connections with Bowker through the *Library Journal*. He warned Meleney that "we must move carefully so as to avoid an L.J. party and a P.L. party. We want everybody heartily for the P.L." He then wrote Ahern: "Bowker is on the warpath and will criticize every page you print in these early numbers. You must be doubly careful." To Theresa West he wrote that "Bowker need not trouble you a particle. He will influence a few of the ALA people to his point of view at the beginning, but simply be sweet and serene and take hold and make the success of Public Libraries possible." The *Library Journal* dispassionately announced *Public Libraries* in a May 1896 editorial, and suggested that "whether the American library field is large enough to support three library periodicals remains to be seen." The first issue of *Public Libraries* appeared in May and carried Dana's "Library Primer." Its subscription price was $1 per year, $4 less than LJ. An introductory note said the periodical would fill "the need for a publication which shall give special attention to the more common details and trials of the small and new public libraries.'' Dana was excited about the first issue. *"Public Libraries* . . . will do, I firmly believe, the things we expected it would,—arouse interest in the library business among small librarians [sic] in the middle west.''[19] The manner in which western librarians, Dewey and the Library Bureau began *Public Libraries* had created ill feelings between East and West. The mere existence of *Public Libraries* showed that the Midwest/ rural library advocates were dissatisfied with *Library Journal*, which they claimed always catered to Northeast/urban library advocates. Cracks in the national library community were widening.

Dana made one move which received universal approval, however, when he established a formal link between ALA and the National Education Association (NEA). He had initiated the move by writing a letter to NEA's board of directors and convincing the ALA executive board to endorse it. On 7 July NEA directors unanimously voted to establish a ''library department.'' Two days later a group which met to organize the department elected Melvil Dewey as president, Denver Public School Superintendent J. H. Van Sickle as vice president, and Ahern as secretary. Dana was pleased. He wrote Dewey on 20 July, ''We are the people! All the news from Buffalo [where NEA met] is that the Library Department went through with a hooray, and that we made a ten strike in calling the matter up.'' Further ALA action awaited the forthcoming ALA conference.[20]

The ALA publishing section pushed forward with its activities. On 12 December 1895 the executive board voted to prepare a supplement to the ALA *Index*, to thank Iles for funding the *List of Books for Girls and Women*, and to accept his offer to fund two more selective bibliographies, one on music and one on fine arts. In spring, 1896, the Bureau of Education finally issued the ALA manual, which was formally entitled ''Papers Prepared for the World's Library Congress'' and published as part of its annual report for 1892–1893. Board members examined a copy when they met again on 10 June 1896. Dewey, Fletcher, Bowker and Lane attended what proved to be a testy session. Most discussion surrounded Lane's suggestion that the section be discontinued so ALA could constitutionally identify a publishing arm and define its duties. Board members finally agreed to present an amendment at the Cleveland conference. They also agreed to publish the monthly fiction lists of the Massachusetts Library Club as long as the club continued to prepare them, and they authorized Lane to hire a part-time bookkeeper at no more than $50 per year to account for publishing section activities.[21]

Dana took preparation for the Cleveland conference seriously. He had deliberately scheduled the October 1895 executive board meeting in Cleveland, and shortly after the new year, began pushing for active, interesting sessions and section meetings. Dana especially wanted Iles on the program. ''Would he not make a stirring appeal to librarians to come down out of their catalogs and off their shelves, and get at the people of this world?'' he wrote Dewey. Carr forewarned Brett that New England librarians seemed ''indifferent'' to Cleveland. He traced the reason to the planning of a trip to the international conference of librarians in England in 1897 which was "being engineered chiefly from the Mississippi Valley, instead of the seaboard as should have been done." Brett's fears were relieved when he learned that the recently appointed and highly respected Boston Public Library (BPL) Director, Herbert Putnam, planned to attend. No one from BPL had attended an ALA conference in the previous five years. To stir support among southern librarians Bowker offered to cover travel expense for Anne Wallace of the Atlanta YMCA Library. Theresa West predicted that because of the treasury balance "there will be a concerted action for a paid official for the ALA" at the forthcoming conference. She told Dewey that Anderson and Elmendorf would push for it. Finally, Mary Ahern reminded her PL readers that the conference was "in the neighborhood of so many of the new libraries in the middlewest." Because of the scheduled session "specially devoted to beginners," she expected the Midwest "should be fully represented."[22]

By the time ALA members gathered for an informal social meeting at Cleveland's Hollenden Hotel on 1 September 1896, specialized interest among association members were beginning to cluster around clearly identifiable groups. Midwestern librarians were primarily concerned with small and rural public libraries; they were especially attracted to ideas Dewey had espoused for years. Northeastern librarians were primarily concerned with large urban public libraries, but were convinced that addressing their needs would also benefit smaller libraries. These two groups competed for control of the association for the next 15 years. Since ALA's future would be determined by its officers, and since the officers were now elected by a plurality at annual conferences, attendance became vitally important—especially to midwesterners who needed ALA support and publications to maintain the momentum of their public library movement. Three hundred sixty-three people attended the Cleveland conference, 140 from North Atlantic states, 194 from Great Lakes states; 217 were women.

Dana officially opened the conference on the morning of 2 September. After dispensing with initial niceties towards his hosts, he startled his audience with a presidential address entitled "Hear the Other Side." "A free public library may be other than a helpful thing," he told conferees. It might provide shelter to indolents and tasteless fiction to the idle. It might also create an indifference among parents who neglected their children's reading. Dana identified only one way to attack these problems. "A library is good only as the librarian makes it so." He placed the burden for correction on his fellow professionals, admonished them to grow personally, to participate in community affairs, to convince others of the benefits of the library profession, and to participate in important associations like ALA and the library department of NEA. Librarians, he argued, controlled their own professional destiny. Dana's words irritated many listeners who looked to a presidential address for professional self-justification. Dana was not the type to heed traditional expectations. The speech immediately won him a reputation as a "maverick" in the library profession. Frederick Faxon later called him the "Bernard Shaw of librarianship."

Fortunately, the next speaker was less polemic. Josephus Nelson Larned delivered a paper in which he castigated the evil influence of the American newspaper on a vulnerable public opinion and forecast a dire future if this force remained unchecked. One agency, however, stood out as a force for good. "I rest my faith in a future of finer culture for mankind upon the energy of free public libraries in distributing good books, far more than upon any other agency that is working in the world." It was the kind of address conferees wanted. The *Library Journal* called it "beyond question, the event of the Conference." When conferees recessed for five minutes, Larned received most of the congratulatory and adulatory attention.

After the recess, the program became more routine. Superintendent of Documents Crandall explained the ramifications of the proposed new documents bill. Iles delivered a paper on the "Appraisal of Literature," after which Elmendorf announced an executive board decision to reissue Dana's "Library Primer" as a publishing section document. Acting Treasurer Anderson reported that ALA had 512 members and a treasury balance of $1,558.14. Caroline Hewins read a paper on "Gifts and Bequests," and Elmendorf reported on curricula for the committee on library schools and classes.

Lane then read a report for the publishing section. He summarized its publications, indicated (but did not explain why) the section had decided not to compile a list of undesirable fiction, and identified other works in press or in progress. Other activities which the section would consider at the conference included issuing manuals on cataloging, government documents and reference books, reissuing the "Library Primer," taking over printed catalog card distribution from the Library Bureau, and reorganizing itself. Lane then asked the membership to consider a change which would allow the section to use the interest earned from the endowment fund for publishing activities. He also proposed a constitutional amendment creating a publishing board of five members to be appointed by the ALA executive board for three-year terms. The "object" of the new board "shall be to secure the preparation and publication of such catalogs, indexes, and other bibliographic and library aids as it may approve." The publishing board would appoint its own chairman, secretary, and treasurer, and its treasury would be independent of the ALA treasury. Lane's comments generated little discussion. A constitutional amendment recognizing the ALA publishing board passed at the next session.

At the fifth session Ahern read an invitation to ALA from the executive board of NEA's library department "to cooperate in the work of the Department." The membership voted to accept the invitation and directed the executive board to appoint a cooperating committee of five. Lutie Stearns read a paper on "Advertising a Library" (LJ called it "one of the most notable papers of the Conference"), and C. R. Dudley followed with a paper on "Library Editions of Popular Fiction." In the discussion which followed, Frank Hutchins, secretary of the Wisconsin Free Library Commission, spoke emphatically to the needs "of the small libraries . . . in isolated hamlets."

That evening conferees engaged in the "most novel incident" of the confer-ence. Cutler had divided ALA members into groups to review bibliographic lists recommended for the ALA *Catalog* supplement. Lists were subdivided by subject areas such as sociology, science, useful arts, history, children's books and fiction. The last occasioned the most spirited discussion and demonstrated the profes-sion's persistent inability to decide what was "quality" literature. Two books especially aroused consternation—Stephen Crane's *Red Badge of Courage* and Harold Frederic's *The Damnation of Theron Ware*. The majority agreed the two books were well-written, but because neither was true to fact most participants thought both should be removed from the list. Hannah P. James later wrote Brett that the session was "invaluable" because of "the tremendous weight of the influence of the Association in favor of purity in fiction. . . . I doubt not many 'feeble knees' were strengthened and many backbones stiffened by the vote taken that evening." Before the session ended participants rejected one-third of the fiction titles.

The Illinois, Indiana, Michigan, Ohio and Wisconsin Library Associations also held meetings during the Cleveland conference. Before adjourning, ALA members cast their ballots for ALA officers for the ensuing year. Later that evening tellers announced that Brett would serve as president, Elmendorf, James and Hosmer as vice-presidents, Ohio State Library Commissioner Rutherford P. Hayes as secretary, and Cole as treasurer. New council members included Dana, Dewey, Carr and Mary W. Plummer. The executive board had retained its western majority.[23]

The animosity which had surfaced before the conference was not evident during the proceedings. Since a majority of registrants came from the Great Lakes states, since librarians from trans-Allegheny America retained control of the ALA leadership structure for the second successive year, and since addressing the practical needs of small, rural public libraries was becoming a recurrent theme with each conference, midwestern librarians had little reason to complain. The association was gradually adjusting to their presence.

Just prior to the removal of the Library of Congress (LC) into new quarters, Congress charged the Joint Committee on the Library to investigate LC conditions and make "such recommendations as may be deemed desirable." Among the prominent librarians called to testify were Brett, Hayes, Dewey, Spofford and Putnam.[24] During the course of the hearings Pennsylvania Congressman Lemuel Ely Quigg suggested to Putnam that the American Library Association might benefit by reincorporating as a national body under U.S. laws. This would permit the association to offer valuable advice to the Library, perhaps through a formal ALA board of visitors. Quigg offered to introduce a bill of incorporation at ALA's request. Putnam favored the suggestion, and together with Fletcher, Dewey and Columbia College Librarian George H. Baker, he petitioned the ALA executive board on 2 December to consider Quigg's offer. The board met the following day and appointed a committee of three (Putnam, chair, Dewey and Bowker) to study the matter. But Hayes quickly introduced a resolution which stated that reincorporation under U.S. laws "with headquarters in Washington" was "desirable." The resolution passed unanimously. In other action the board voted to hold the 1897 conference in Philadelphia in June, and to appropriate $200 for the expenses of the publishing section (plus $50 for the treasurer).[25]

Reincorporating the association as a national body posed several advantages. First, the federal government would be more inclined to provide funds for a permanent headquarters. Second, any allocated funds would likely include a salary for a staff member. ALA members hoped this person could coordinate ALA activities to increase membership and relieve some of the pressure on volunteer help. Third, the Government Printing Office could publish ALA manuscripts. This would save the association thousands of dollars, yet permit the expansion of the association's publishing program. Fourth, locating ALA headquarters in Washington would enhance cooperation with the Library of Congress to develop the kinds of joint ventures that the association had been talking about for two decades.

Putnam told Bowker on 29 December that he thought a decision to reincorporate had to be made by the membership, not the executive board. Bowker concurred, but counseled patience. "I do not believe that anything will be gained by rushing this thing through." Dewey disagreed. A bill should be pushed through, he argued, before the current session ended in March. Putnam supported Dewey's position, and immediately asked Brett to call a special ALA meeting. The ALA president set it up for 6 February at Columbia University in New York.[26]

Although Bowker initially thought a motion to reincorporate "would be ratified almost unanimously," a formidable opposition quickly emerged. Winsor warned Dewey on 28 January that Billings "and others are going to antagonize the scheme." Winsor himself disapproved any official connection between ALA and LC. Almost simultaneously another seemingly unrelated problem arose which unexpectedly complicated the situation even further. In January, John Cotton Dana circulated a note to ALA members which recommended that the association secure more members by allocating $500 to Secretary Hayes for "such propaganda work for the Association as to him and the president [Brett] deem advisable." *Public Libraries* endorsed his recommendation in an editorial. Because Dana asked that the issue be placed on the agenda for the special meeting in February, Bowker, Dewey, and Putnam may have suspected ulterior motives that could be traced to subsurface sectionalist feelings which had been evident in association activities over the past several years.

As the special meeting neared, they plotted strategy. Bowker suggested that the committee write a bill of incorporation similar to that of the American Historical Association which would allow ALA to report either through the Smithsonian Institution or the Bureau of Education. Bowker was adamant that the bill empower ALA to visit the LC only "*on request.*" He worried a "mandatory provision" would turn Winsor against reincorporation. He also expressed "doubts" to Dewey about Dana's request. Several days earlier Bowker had met with Putnam, Soule, and W. R. Eastman of the New York State Library. All agreed that the request needed "some specific statement of how the money should be used" before the executive board approved it. They also worried that if the recruitment money Dana had recommended was used to increase membership primarily in the West, "the ALA would presently take shape more as a federation of state and local organizations than as a body of enormous membership." Dewey disliked blind appropriations, but was nonetheless inclined to support Dana's request. "It would be a great misfortune . . . to give our western friends the idea that we wish to muddle them in their work," he wrote Bowker. "Some have suggested that this was a device for rolling up a western membership so large as practically to exclude the easterners who organized and carried on the ALA so many years." Dewey suggested that the incorporation bill authorize LC to employ a full-time salaried officer who would serve as ALA secretary. He did not share Bowker's fear of Winsor's opposition. ALA "should never do our fullest work till we are attached to Washington interests," he wrote Putnam.[27]

Forty-nine people attended the special session at Columbia on 6 February; 44 came from the North Atlantic states. Putnam's report on reincorporation, which included a draft bill, "was accepted." After a brief discussion, Carr offered a substitute motion which authorized the executive board to "take under consideration the matter of procuring reincorporation" and report at the next annual conference. The motion carried unanimously and the meeting adjourned one-half hour after it started. Since reincorporation constituted the only "official business," the association did not consider Dana's request. The *Library Journal* suggested that the membership deferred action on reincorporation because "the present time and circumstances did not seem auspicious for such reorganization, and the American Library Association could certainly not afford to put itself in the position of seeking aggrandizement for itself by a crusade in its own behalf. The special meeting was unanimous in this judgment."[28] More likely, the specter of division in the ranks, which included opposition from Billings and Winsor, did not promise enough support to push the bill through Congress.

Sectionalism began to surface in other areas as well. On 5 December 1896 "A Member of the A.L.A." scolded the *Library Journal* for stating in its November issue that "the feeling of the West against the East, so rampant before election day, is directly contrary to the national spirit." The letter-writer said she deplored a national spirit "that does not include a recognition of the right of the producing classes to at least enough of the products of toil to support life." She complained that the national spirit was not "restricted geographically to the East." On 19 February 1897 E. P. Salender of Beloit, Wisconsin, wrote Frank Hutchins that the Wisconsin Free Library Commission had to do more with traveling libraries. "The neglected backwoods family life calls for as much careful study as the slums of our large cities," he said, and argued that the library profession should devote equal attention to "rural homes."[29]

The following month Charles Soule responded to the *Public Libraries* endorsement of Dana's recommendation. "Are you quite sure we want to recruit the A.L.A. up to big numbers?'' he asked the editor. The periodical calmly rejected his argument in an editorial and invited other interested parties to debate the question in its columns. Dana was angry. He wrote Brett privately on 26 April that Soule's implication ''is one that might much better never have been made. There is sufficient tendency already on the part of our colleagues to indulge in a little sectional feeling.'' He reported that several people had already advocated ''a western or a central library association'' to counter the ''criticisms of myself and my particular friends from the good people from the other side of the Alleghenies.'' Later he told Brett that Soule's suggestion threatened efforts to make ALA ''popular'' and ''to draw into its ranks the librarian of the small library.''

In April *Public Libraries* began publishing responses to Soule's letter. Dana argued that ALA would be more powerful with a larger membership. Thomas L. Montgomery agreed, but both met opposition from F. M. Crunden and George Iles. It soon became obvious that the profession would not be able to resolve the question through the columns of *Public Libraries*. The debate awaited discussion at the forthcoming conference. In the meantime, Evanston (Illinois) Public Library Director George E. Wire wrote ALA President Brett that ''for the last three conferences the Chicago party has brought the president with it; I want to keep up the record.''[30]

In the midst of these public and private disputes the association moved forward in several other areas. On 2 March 1897 ALA formally protested a tariff bill which removed books imported for libraries from the free list. A month later Brett circulated a copy of an amendment to the bill approved by the executive board which restored such books to the free list. In the fall of 1896 the publishing section agreed to prepare printed catalog cards for the Library Bureau if the bureau would market and distribute them. Lane would supervise the preparation from a room which the Boston Athenaeum provided ALA free of charge. The section hired Nina Browne, formerly of the Library Bureau, to do the cataloging. The *Library Journal* asked all libraries, ''large and small, to support the enterprise.'' The section also issued supplements to *Reading for the Young* and Caroline Hewins's *Books for Boys and Girls: A Selected List*. Work continued on the ''Index to Portraits.''

Not everyone was happy with publishing section progress, however. In April 1897 Mary Ahern asked Brett ''what has become of the ALA primer?'' Brett asked Elmendorf, who responded that he and Dana were both piqued that the publishing section had taken no action on the matter. Elmendorf promised to investigate further. On 29 April Dana wrote Brett that ''I would prefer that the ALA should not do anything more about the primer.'' He was negotiating with the Library Bureau to print it in a separate number of *Public Libraries*. If negotiations fell through, he indicated that he would publish the work himself. Next day Elmendorf reported to Brett that because ''the Association seems never to have decided to publish'' the primer, the publishing section had refused to act. The section's inaction on Dana's small book gradually became a festering source of bad feeling among champions of small rural public library interests.[31] They perceived the section's passive attitude as just another indication of eastern control of ALA.

William Howard Brett opened the 1897 ALA conference at an informal gathering at the Pennsylvania Historical Society in Philadelphia on 21 June. Three hundred fifteen people registered, 229 from North Atlantic states, 53 from Great Lakes states, 24 from South Atlantic states; 194 were women. Not since 1894 had the eastern contingent been so large at an ALA conference.

Working sessions began the next morning. In his presidential address Brett took a retrospective look at the association which had first met in Philadelphia just over 20 years before. Hayes followed Brett's address with a secretary's report, and Fletcher read Lane's report for the publishing section. Lane called the printed catalog card project the section's "most considerable undertaking of the year." He also indicated that a committee appointed to consider publishing the "Library Primer" still had not communicated with the section, but he did not elaborate. Fletcher announced that the Carnegie Free Public Library of Pittsburgh had donated $100 to the section, and George Iles had agreed to contribute $1,000 to publish a historical bibliography. Conferees voted to thank Iles for his generosity.

Tillinghast reported for the cooperation committee that continuation of the Massachusetts Library Club fiction list was doubtful. Production costs had already exceeded income projections. Hayes read majority and minority reports of the committee on an American libraries clearinghouse, a central agency ALA hoped would gather and disseminate information about libraries. In the majority report Reuben G. Thwaites and J. F. Langton of the St. Louis Public Library argued that a clearinghouse was necessary, but since the Superintendent of Documents and the Bureau of Education refused to assume the task, the only alternative seemed to be the Library of Congress. The implicit connection with the reincorporation scheme was obvious. Adelaide Hasse submitted a minority report which argued that no government agency should become an information clearinghouse for libraries.

At the next session Mary Cutler argued in her report for the committee on a supplement to the ALA *Catalog* that the criteria for selection had to be "carefully stated" in order to insure the supplement's success and general utility. She once again divided conferees into groups to repeat the experience of the Cleveland conference, but generated less interaction. Even the fiction question aroused little debate. During the evening session Melvil Dewey offered his own interpretation of the association's 21-year history. Between 1876 and 1886 ALA had fostered the development of library methods to augment the impact of libraries at minimal cost, he said. Between 1886 and 1896 ALA had raised the profile of the public library as an essential part of the nation's educational system. In 1896, ALA was entering a "filtration period" which promised to filter bad literature and expose the public only to the good. His implied reference to selection aids which were published, in press, and contemplated by the publishing section was evident.

But his unwillingness to specify criteria for identifying bad literature merited no audience comment.

Next morning some conferees attended meetings of the college section. Others joined an experimental open discussion on various subjects such as classification and cataloging, charging systems, book pockets and book marks, and standard reference works. Brett had deliberately scheduled the session to counter complaints from directors of smaller libraries about the limited utility of ALA conferences.

Assistant Treasurer Nina Browne reported a treasury balance of $1,102.20, and total membership of 434. Billings reported progress on the "Proposed Building for the New York Public Library," but when Brett introduced the reincorporation question, discussion subsided. Dewey suggested that the executive board be authorized to reincorporate "when they deem it expedient." Larned objected. " . . . it seems to me it is an inopportune time for discussing it." Approval of Larned's motion to postpone discussion constituted the last action ALA took on the issue. The movement to reincorporate had died as quickly as it had been raised six months earlier.

Next afternoon Foster announced that the council had agreed to apply interest from the endowment fund towards publishing section expenses. Conferees voted to recommend an immediate transfer of $500. Ahern reported "progress" for the committee on cooperation with the library department of NEA. Larned announced that the Bureau of Education would probably be unable to publish the ALA *Catalog* supplement; his motion that the publishing section assume the responsibility carried. Before the session ended tellers announced the election of new officers: for president, Justin Winsor; for vice presidents, Hayes, James and Crunden; for secretary, Dewey; for treasurer, Jones; and for recorder, Helen Haines. New ALA council members included Fletcher, Foster, Bowker and Cutter. Once again the ALA hierarchy had a decidedly eastern profile.

While the college section met separately the following morning, other conferees enjoyed a session on "elementary library work," more evidence of Brett's desire to appeal to the interests of the small public librarian. In the afternoon conferees accepted Atlanta's invitation to host an ALA conference, though not until 1899. ALA would go to Chautauqua in 1898. Dewey then introduced a constitutional amendment. He wanted to increase the number of elected council members by 25 percent. In addition, each state or local library association would be entitled to "one councillor of its own selection, and to one additional for each full 100 members."

Dewey's motive for the amendment was not immediately apparent. By expanding council membership, it is likely he hoped to minimize the possibility of splinter groups forming separate rival library associations. The amendment would provide a constitutionally sanctioned superstructure under which specific and specialized library interests could find common ground. It also allowed for differences in geography as well as types or sizes of libraries. At this time he was not concerned with defining the council's function or role within ALA. He was more concerned with preserving the unity of the association itelf. Dewey asked for a vote approving the amendment so that the association could discuss it at the Chautauqua conference. Conferees agreed.

That the Philadelphia conference stressed the theme of perspective was not surprising; it was the first time ALA had met in the City of Brotherly Love since the association's birth just over two decades before. With model consistency members elected Winsor and several other "old stagers" to lead a delegation of American librarians to the international conference of librarians in London shortly after the Philadelphia meeting adjourned. At a meeting in Oxford, England, on 24 July, the executive board formally approved Dewey's suggestion to concentrate the Chautauqua program on two major topics—"the training of librarians and assistants" and "libraries as allied agencies for popular education." Dewey wanted to make sure conferees would not concentrate on issues which tended to divide them.[32]

In October 1897 *Public Libraries* suggested that ALA had been developing a distinctive "fraternal spirit among its members, a loyalty to and friendship for each other." The compromising spirit which the periodical alleged was short-lived, however. On 22 October 1897 Winsor died, and the ALA presidency fell vacant. Wire wrote Dewey four days later, "Now is the time to put in Mr. Carr. He has served long and well and deserves the presidency." He added, "I hope this *place* idea of president will be broken up for good and all."

Precedent suggested the vacancy should go to the vice president who had received the most votes in the previous election, Rutherford P. Hayes. When Linderfelt resigned in May 1892, Vice President Fletcher had succeeded him by executive board consensus. Dewey wholeheartedly supported that move, but in this case the ALA secretary chose a different approach. On 12 November he wrote other ALA executive board members that "after careful study [of the ALA constitution] and consultation with some of those most familiar with it, my first impression is confirmed that it is the duty of the executive board to elect a president for the balance of this year"; until that election, he continued, the ALA secretary would be in charge of the association. He suggested that Herbert Putnam would be Winsor's "natural successor in the presidency which had gone to Boston for the year." He also mentioned Billings, director of the New York Public Library, as a possibility, but because Billings was busy with New York Public Library building plans, "his term as president will soon come." Dewey obviously wanted to keep the ALA presidency in the east.

ALA Recorder Helen Haines, now associate editor of the *Library Journal*, balked at Dewey's suggestion. Haines normally asked Bowker's advice on all ALA matters, and Bowker may have cautioned her against trusting Dewey. She ultimately decided to request every board member's interpretation of the ALA constitution "before giving a final vote on the subject." Hannah James was equivocal, but not so suspicious. Although she thought the first vice president "had to be considered," she acknowledged "I'm pretty pleased at the idea of Putnam." But she had other motives also. "I was going to use the occasion to point a moral as to putting in women as VPs. I don't approve of it and never have." Hayes did not equivocate; he challenged Dewey directly. While he did not dispute the ultimate need to elect a new president, he was firmly committed to running the association himself during the interim. "My understanding of the constitution of the ALA is that from the time of the death of Dr. Winsor until the election of a president, I am the chief executive of the Association and that official notices of all kinds should be sent out by my direction."[33]

Dewey responded quickly, haughtily, decisively. "You are partly right and partly wrong in your interpretation of the A.L.A. Constitution. I can easily understand how one who has only recently been active in the association might get a wrong impression, and so give you the points with some detail." Citing his extensive experience in ALA matters, and his participation in the writing of the ALA constitution, he indicated that the ALA presidency was mostly ceremonial, and that the real center of association activity was the secretary's office, from which "all needed notices are sent out." He told Hayes that he had consulted an experienced lawyer who confirmed his interpretation that until the executive board voted for a new president, the ALA secretary should assume the president's duties. Dewey indicated that the executive board could elect a new president by mail if the vote was unanimous, and he asked Hayes to send a nomination. Dewey also circulated a copy of his letter to Hayes to other board members. Hayes wrote Brett on 20 November that he resented Dewey's haughty manner and patronizing tone.

Dewey continued to press for Putnam's election. On 23 November he reported to the board that four votes had been cast for the Boston Public Librarian, "three have not yet voted, and no other nomination has been made." He indicated indifference about who should fill the office, but argued against leaving it vacant, and against holding a special meeting. "Shall we make the vote unanimous electing Putnam, or nominate someone else, or leave the place open till later?" Brett shared Hayes's anger over Dewey's imperious move. He told Dewey on 26 November that Hayes did not want "to succeed to the presidency, but merely to act as president until a president is elected presumably by the executive board." Dewey's interpretation that the secretary was the "real executive head of the Association, and the secretary's office its headquarters, while the president is merely an honorary figurehead, seems to me absurd. . . . it certainly does not describe the condition of the last two years." He agreed the board had to elect a new president, but he objected to Dewey's campaign for Putnam. "What I do insist on is that the board shall decide this for itself." James repeated her vote for Putnam, but misinterpreted Hayes's position. "I am surprised at his lack of good taste and self-respect in demanding the place." Haines cast her vote for Putnam on 27 November.[34]

Hayes persisted. On 2 December he asked members of the ALA executive board to identify the ALA president for the balance of Winsor's term, and to determine whether the president or the secretary was the chief executive officer. Crunden answered the next day. "I had assumed that the first vice-president succeeded to the position of president on the death of the latter." Further, he thought that the ALA president was the association's only chief executive officer. James echoed Dewey's position on 4 December. In a marginal note on a copy she sent to Dewey, she wrote "What a goose the man is to want the place without having earned it." Dewey responded on 8 December, indicating that the association had no president at the moment, and that "the secretary is the working officer who executes the directions of the Association." He predicted that the association would soon change the wording of its constitution to avoid similar problems in the future. He concluded to Hayes, "I am sorry that you have thought it wise to stir up so much discussion." On the same day Hayes wrote "you may cast my vote for Mr. Herbert Putnam as president of the American Library Association." He did not address the question of who was the ALA's chief executive officer until the vote was official, however.[35]

But the issue would not die. Brett wrote Hayes on the tenth that "the vice-president first named" should assume the presidency until the board filled the vacancy, and he believed that Dewey had interpreted the executive powers of his own office too broadly. To Dewey Brett wrote that he would vote for a new ALA president only "when the question is properly presented." Brett's resentment of Dewey's high-handed treatment of the issue was evident throughout his letter. Hayes was also insulted at Dewey's accusation that he had unjustifiably caused internal dissension. He told Dewey that he regularly received telegrams and letters urging him as "chief executive officer" of the association to protest a movement to remove the Superintendent of Documents. Upon the advice of four "prominent" association members (whom he did not name) he felt he had to act for ALA. "To sum up the situation from my standpoint," he concluded, "from the death of Mr. Winsor until the election of his successor I am president and chief executive officer of the Association. On the announcement by you of an election by the executive board my term as president will end."[36]

Dewey's response was nasty. "Of course, you are totally wrong in the last sentence of your letter, but if it amuses you it does not hurt anyone else," he wrote on 14 December. "No one could question your signing as acting president, but you would only make yourself ridiculous by the statement or signature as president. . . . Your self-appointment as 'chief executive officer' is purely a figment of your imagination." In a postscript he added, "Merry Christmas." When Dewey sent copies of his letter to other ALA board members Haines showed it to Bowker, who called Dewey's comments "doubly unnecessary," and wrote in an LJ editorial that "Mr. Hayes, as the present first vice-president, has very properly assumed the duties of the presidency pending a settlement of the question." Bowker indicated that the executive board favored Putnam as president "should it be decided that the office was vacant," but the latter question had to be settled first.

Dewey then attempted to use the editorial to his own advantage. He wrote another circular to the board, claimed LJ had endorsed Putnam, and called for a unanimous vote to elect him. Haines responded immediately that the *Journal*

had in fact endorsed no one, and that she would refuse to vote until the vacancy
question was settled. Her letter placed Dewey on the defensive. He first wrote
Bowker, "I am awfully sorry about the LJ episode, but you evidently do not
quite understand my attitude." He explained that the suggestion of Putnam's
name was intended to be private "and certainly very humiliating to Hayes who
has made a great goose of himself on the whole matter." Dewey said he at one
time thought so much of Hayes he recommended the Ohioan to President McKinley
as a high-ranking assistant in the Library of Congress "in the belief he was the
best man we had found for permanent secretary without which the ALA will
never do its work properly." But, Dewey said, other ALA members (whose
names he did not mention) had changed his mind. He then complimented Bowker
on employing "an exceedingly clever woman" as his associate editor. With
Haines he was more aggressive. "Mr. Hayes and the others have sent in their
votes for Mr. Putnam, but I cannot announce it till you definitely give your vote
again." Still Haines was suspicious. "I should greatly regret to have my vote
counted as a telling one," she wrote Dewey "and thus influencing perhaps
someone who would not wish to vote against what was understood to be a
majority."[37]

Shortly thereafter Hayes informed Bowker he would vote for Putnam. When
Bowker showed Hayes's letter to Haines, she sent Dewey her vote for Putnam,
all the while assuming hers was the final vote which would make the election
unanimous. Bowker then asked Dewey for official notification of the unanimous
election, but when Dewey replied that Brett still had not voted, Haines was
certain that she had been tricked. "You stated that my vote was the *only* one
not received on the presidential question!" Dewey's sheepish response was
unsatisfactory. "You were right," he admitted, but Brett "had written three
letters, all of them very strongly supporting Mr. Putnam as his first choice . . .
and while he had voted three times I did not have the official vote which of
course he had a right to change at the last minute. Both statements, you see,
were correct." To Brett he was demanding. "Everything is blockaded because
you do not vote . . . at least be courteous enough to tell us." Brett was equally
incensed, calling Dewey's communication "entirely out of place." Nonetheless,
he acquiesced and made Putnam's election unanimous. The association would
not have to call a special meeting to elect a president. On 18 January Dewey
implored Putnam to accept the appointment, but Putnam balked. He was suspicious of all the political machinations implied in a letter Hayes published in
LJ which gave his side of the story. Dewey wrote Putnam a second letter which
stated "there is a screw loose in Hayes' makeup," but even his offer to forward
all correspondence on the fiasco did not curb Putnam's suspicions. Only a friendly
letter from Hayes offering "an expression of his personal desire that I should
accept the presidency" changed Putnam's mind.[38]

The incident was over, the matter settled, and the *Library Journal* applauded
Putnam's election to the ALA presidency in its February issue. But a residue of
bitter feelings remained, most directed at Dewey. The suspicions he had raised

in pushing Putnam's election did not quickly dissipate. From that time on Dewey's direct influence on ALA affairs began to diminish. *Public Libraries*, which had been one of Dewey's staunchest western supporters because of parallel philosophies of library service, openly declared, ''We think a mistake has been made'' in the way Putnam was elected. Frederick Crunden, a westerner who had backed Dewey on numerous occasions, wrote Carr: ''I think all the members of the ALA are pretty well agreed that we must, as far as possible, eliminate politics from the Association.''[39] As in 1880, Dewey had overstepped his bounds. His ends may have been worthwhile, but his means alienated many close friends, several of whom lived west of the Alleghenies.

Other events would further test the fabric of the association before the Chautauqua conference convened in October 1898. Bernard Steiner, director of the Enoch Pratt Free Library in Baltimore, suggested to Dewey that the association should establish a section ''for the large city libraries which have branches.'' In January, *Library Notes* died quietly and temporarily passed into the pages of *Public Libraries* as a column entitled ''Library Notes by Melvil Dewey.'' In February librarians from Michigan, Ohio, Indiana, Illinois, Iowa, Wisconsin and Minnesota held an ''Interstate Library Meeting'' at Evanston, Illinois, hosted by the Chicago Library Club. Lutie Stearns delivered a keynote address on ''How to Organize a Public Library in a Small Town.'' Illinois Library Association President J. W. Thompson said that the aims of the conference were ''to cultivate wide acquaintance among librarians, to strengthen interest in state organizations, and to bring about closer relations between the colleges and public libraries.'' And while *Public Libraries* lamented Dana's move to the Springfield (Massachusetts) Public Library, Stearns wrote him privately, ''I believe I've never congratulated you upon your eastern migration, and I don't believe I ever shall; for I think we westerners that love the west feel pretty selfish about any such transmigration.'' Similarly, Ahern implored him: ''Do not become part of the effete East whatever you do.''[40]

Between conferences ALA also tested its lobbying strength in the arena of national politics. A situation which had induced Hayes to commit on the ALA presidency early was the attempted removal of F. A. Crandall, superintendent of public documents. ALA had tried to mobilize the national library community against the move. Billings wrote President William McKinley in Crandall's behalf and Bowker wrote Assistant Secretary of the Navy Theodore Roosevelt and Librarian of Congress John Russell Young. Roosevelt and Young promised to work for Crandall; McKinley did not answer Billings's letter. ALA also attempted to press the Senate to pass Bill 2842, which provided that the office of superintendent of documents and the cataloging of documents be placed in charge of the Library of Congress. Neither effort succeeded.[41]

Although ALA could boast no successes on a national scale, the publishing section was quick to identify some of its own accomplishments. In November 1897 Lane announced that with the cooperation and support of Harvard, Columbia, the John Crerar Library and the Boston and New York Public libraries, the section would begin issuing printed cards "for articles contained in certain current society publications and other scientific, archeological, historic and economic serials, both in English and in foreign languages." On 19 April 1898 Iles announced that he would fund an American history bibliography which Larned would compile for the publishing section. Beer's bibliography on French fiction and the *List of Subject Headings* were published that summer, about the same time a commercial press issued a second printing of Plummer's *Hints to Small Libraries*. Lane reported that plenty of copies of *Books for Boys and Girls* remained in print, and also indicated that the *ALA Portrait Index* would be delayed. Cutler, who had married and taken her husband's name of Fairchild over the winter, called for more cooperation on the supplement to the ALA *Catalog*.[42]

As ALA secretary, Dewey carefully prepared the Chautauqua program. He consented to let large libraries meet in a separate section; he also asked the board to endorse an invitation to the new Librarian of Congress, John Russell Young, to address the conference. Hayes vetoed the recommendation. Dewey invited Young anyway, but the librarian declined. When Koopman suggested a topic outside the two themes Dewey had set the year before, Dewey refused. To Mary E. Hazeltine, director of the James Prendergast Library in Jamestown, New York, and chairman of the local arrangements committee, Dewey wrote, "You are doing splendidly and I am proud of you as one of my girls. Don't forget that we count on you as one of the family." Putnam scolded Dewey for inserting the phrase "the conference should be a time of rest as well as of business and pleasure" in preliminary program announcements. The Boston Public Library director said he had just convinced his board of trustees to grant employees leaves of absence with pay to attend. On 15 June Dewey informed conference speakers they were restricted to five minutes each. Bowker complained that 200 scheduled presentations were too many. Dewey's response was hardly diplomatic. "Neither you nor Miss Haines can seem to get it in your head that the names of the program do *not* represent papers." Bowker was not intimidated. "When you tell a man to describe 'all his tour around the world' in three minutes, you throw a lurid light on his whole business of crowding the conference program."[43]

But Dewey held the power; Bowker could only complain. The program was set when President Putnam called the Chautauqua meeting to order on 5 July 1898. Four hundred ninety-four people registered, 305 from North Atlantic states, 142 from Great Lakes states, and 30 from South Atlantic states; 320 were women. Like its predecessor, the Chautauqua conference was dominated by eastern librarians. The executive board had met the previous day. Putnam, Dewey, Jones, Crunden, James and Haines were present; Brett and Hayes were not. The board voted to hold the conference proceedings to 200 pages or less, to turn over the remaining stock of old proceedings to the publishing section, and to assign to the constitutional revision committee the tasks of "defining the duties of president and secretary" and of "specifying procedure in case of vacancy in the presidency."

Putnam's presidential address carefully avoided the controversies which had arisen since the last conference. He did make a special plea, however, that the Library of Congress assume a leading role in the national library community. "How gladly would we accept, if the National Library will assume this leadership!" Dewey used his secretary's report to caution all speakers not to exceed their five-minute allocations. Gardner Jones read the treasurer's report, identified a treasury balance of $776.16, a membership of 527, and a list of ALA publications for sale, including 990 copies of Larned's 1894 presidential address. Lane reported for the publishing section that W. Dawson Johnston was preparing printed catalog cards for new books on English history. Andrews concentrated his cooperation committee report on the international library conference of the past year. He also warmly noted the interstate library meeting in Evanston in February, and the efforts to generate a summary report on state library association activities. In a progress report for the committee on a supplement to the ALA *Catalog*, Mary S. Cutler Fairchild reported that in May 1898 the publishing section had accepted an offer from the New York State Library to print the supplement as a bulletin, which would be issued in the fall. Dewey had obviously tired of education bureau delays; he would publish the supplement himself. Following Fairchild's report Dewey had seven speakers scheduled in rapid succession to close out the session.

The afternoon session concentrated on the influence of library schools on the profession. Edith Clarke, cataloger at the public documents office, argued that the library professional had three qualifications: (1) executive ability; (2) technical knowledge; and (3) culture. Since the first could not be taught, and the third encompassed "that inward spiritual activity, with its characteristics of right feeling, of intelligence, of sympathy," library schools had to direct their attention to developing the second. At the third session Dewey convinced conferees to ask the executive board "to formulate a plan looking to a system of library examinations and credentials." The session ended with more discussion on library instruction. At the sixth session Utley and Larned agreed that the profession was responsible for "warning the public against untrustworthy books." The best way to exercise that responsibility, they suggested, was not to buy those types of books in the first place.

That afternoon Putnam invited discussion on the constitutional amendment which Dewey had quickly pushed through at the Philadelphia conference. Elmendorf agreed that the council had been "largely an ornamental body," but unless the amendment defined its duties more precisely, "it seems unnecessary to increase its size." Dewey answered that the proposed amendment was a response to "some of the older members of the Association" who had suggested membership ought to be restricted. Enlarging the council would enable ALA to recognize a group for "conspicuous public services. Beyond that, the query of how much the council shall do is still an open one." Hill objected. The amendment would permit local library associations to elect non-ALA members to ALA council. Crunden said he first thought the amendment had merit. "The method it suggested of enlarging the council and intrusting the business affairs of the association to that council offered the solution of our difficulties.'' But Dewey's explanation discouraged him, for the new council would have no ''particular reason for being.'' He moved that the proposed amendment be referred to a constitutional revision committee. When John Thomson moved the appointment of that committee, both Dewey and Crunden withdrew their motions and Thomson's motion carried. Putnam quickly appointed Crunden, Brett, Plummer and Register of Copyrights Thorvald Solberg to the constitutional revision committee. Although conferees could justifiably say they had addressed Dewey's proposal, the motions effectively stifled debate on a threateningly fractious issue, and postponed discussion to a more opportune time. Dana wrote Putnam shortly after the conference ended: ''You had your hands more than full, and there were . . . beneath the surface a few things ready to crop up and be disagreeable if the opportunity offered, and you were very far from permitting the opportunity.''

That evening the membership elected new officers for the forthcoming year: for president, William Coolidge Lane, who had replaced Winsor at Harvard; for vice presidents, Andrews, Sharp and Thomson; for secretary, Carr; for treasurer, Jones; and for recorder, Haines. New council members included Larned, Jones, Brett and Crunden. The conference adjourned to meet the following spring in Atlanta.

As in previous years the conference also scheduled time for section meetings, but the Chautauqua conference was unusual because it offered more meetings which were more active. Dewey's program planning had deliberately encouraged them. He had often argued that ALA should stretch its organization to cover specialized interests materializing within the profession. To ignore them would lead to numerous smaller professional associations outside ALA control, thereby muting the association's claim as the national voice for library interests. The Chautauqua conference hosted meetings of the large library section, the college and reference library section, the trustees section, the state library section, and the elementary section, which devoted its attention primarily to the problems of smaller libraries. The conference itself showed Dewey's hand throughout—tight schedule, short papers focusing on practical library problems, participation by as many members as possible, and restricted forums. Carr later complained that this focus was too restrictive.[44] But Dewey likely had another motive. Subsurface movements, cloakroom comments and subtle complaints had emerged too frequently over the last several years and threatened to shred the ALA fabric. By keeping the conference moving, by allowing minimal time for debate, and by providing separate forums for growing special interest groups, Dewey had effectively split dissident forces and deprived them of opportunities to join forces against the parent organization. Dewey acted to preserve the unified ALA momentum he had helped to build over the past decade. It remained the national voice for library interests.

When the ALA executive board met in Cambridge, Massachusetts, on 25 November, members decided that the Atlanta conference would have the same number of section meetings as Chautauqua. The board also read a letter from Fairchild suggesting that ALA publish a series of library tracts and recommending that the board commission two papers for the Atlanta conference which would provide "practical information regarding the scope and organization of the public library and of the college library." These papers could then be printed in leaflet form and distributed. President Lane appointed Soule, Plummer and Haines— all from the East, and none of whom represented small libraries—as a committee to consider the request. Lane also appointed Brett, Putnam and Hill to a committee to consider formulating a system of library examinations. He asked Brett to solicit information from library school directors around the country.[45]

Between conferences individual committees attempted to make progress. Dana tried to generate more interest for the NEA Library Department by suggesting to an NEA journal editor that he invite teachers to criticize librarians openly. The publishing section issued a revised edition of the ALA *Handbook*, and announced that subscriptions were being taken for Johnston's printed cards for new English history books. On 10 January 1899 Lane wrote a lengthy letter to trustees of the ALA endowment fund which detailed limitations under which the section labored due to lack of funds. "New work continually develops before us, but the gratuitous aid of librarians already overworked cannot always be given. The work of the Section needs to be reorganized on a basis of employing more paid service." Lane lamented that money generated by the ALA and the endowment fund was not sufficient to meet the need. Of course the trustees already knew this, but Soule hoped that the letter, if shown to the right people, might influence a few wealthy philanthropists in search of a good cause to endow.[46]

The publishing section could not issue everything it wanted, but its publications did demonstrate priorities. Not everyone was satisfied; some agencies began their own publishing programs to answer their own needs. In September 1898 the Wisconsin Free Library Commission issued a revised edition of its "Suggestive List of Books for a Small Library," and the following March the Library Bureau announced it would issue Dana's "Library Primer." Other challenges to ALA dominance over the national library community also emerged. In November 1898 state librarians met in Washington to organize the National Association of State Librarians which was, organizers said, "in no way opposed to the A.L.A. or any other organization of librarians; on the contrary, many members were very strong in their support of the State Library Section of the A.L.A." In February, Indiana started a state library commission, and on 19 April 1899 Lutie Stearns told a meeting of the Fox River Valley (Wisconsin) Library Association that librarians should make the library "the center of happiness in the community. It should be bright, clean and attractive. *Recreation* as well as *education* should be its aim." Within a few years the Stevens Point Public Library "exercised its social service instinct by supplying a recreation room for men and boys equipped with a billiard table." Librarians in the East seldom assigned "recreational" activities such a lofty place among public library service priorities.[47]

The committee to review the constitution was very active between conferences. In September Chairman Crunden solicited suggestions from committee members. Thwaites said he preferred a council of 50 to transact the business of the association. This would "simplify and dignify matters, . . . take them out of the hands of a town meeting such as our conventions have grown to be, and . . . make a seat in the Council worth having." Hill disagreed. He preferred that the executive board retain its power. Carr equivocated. He avoided the council question altogether and advised only that the duties of the president and secretary be more clearly defined, and a successor to the presidency in case of a vacancy be specifically identified. Crunden argued that the constitution should allow ALA to "grow indefinitely," but its business should "be transacted by a comparatively small number who know what they are about." If the association's business could not be conducted by a small body, Crunden favored extending members suffrage only after they had attended their second conference.

In January 1899, however, Crunden fell seriously ill and the committee chairmanship passed to Dana, who had replaced Brett on the committee the previous September. In February Dana summarized the sentiments of a "few" committee members in *Public Libraries*:

Make the council in part a representative body by sending delegates from state and city library associations.

Give more independence to the several sections, making of them in effect departments, with department officers, each section looking after its own program, and, in the main, all its own affairs.

Let the associations represented in the council contribute to the A.L.A.'s treasury.

Give the council power to establish departments, determine the place of and time of meeting; direct in some slight degree the work of the sections; fill all vacancies in office occurring between the annual meetings; determine the duties of officers when necessary; act as advisory board for the Association; hold meetings, not only at the time of the meeting of the A.L.A., but also on other occasions during the year if it seems advisable. This council should have from 50 to 75 members.

Public Libraries immediately applauded any move to give the council more power, and approved efforts to solicit money from other library associations.

On 3 March Dana outlined for committee members a report he intended to give at the Atlanta conference. Although its contents closely paralleled his summary note in *Public Libraries*, on one item he was much more specific. "Arrange to make the Association or some part of it a body representative of other and lesser library organizations: partly to strengthen the ALA; partly to assure the general unity of the library movement in this country." Bowker responded two days later in a lengthy memorandum that the association had to retain the "general meeting" concept to preserve "enthusiasm and inspiration." He said the most significant improvement program committees could make would be to cut down on the number of papers presented.[48]

Would Bowker consider assigning a "percentage of total conference time that shall be taken up by the general meeting?" Dana asked. That was not the point, Bowker replied. Rather, it was a question of "whether the whole body should be the Association or whether some representative organization should be practically the ALA with the other members tagging on behind." He distrusted a council with too much power, and preferred that the executive board "should have power between sessions." Dana agreed with Bowker's desire to preserve "the sensation of 'belonging' to the general body." A revised constitution ought to foster that feeling. He emphasized, however, that the committee had to move quickly. Nine days later he complained to Carr that his committee had not reached consensus. "If they do not before long, I shall be inclined to either print something myself, or make them stop me," he wrote Carr, "for I feel that it is very desirable that some move be made at Atlanta looking toward a consolidation of library interests East and West. We shall have a split if we are not careful."[49]

Under Dana's constant pressure the committee decided to issue a draft (largely written by Bowker) which the *Library Journal* ran in its April issue. The committee itself had not agreed to it, but hoped it would serve as a foundation for discussion at the conference. Bowker wrote Solberg on 12 April that "the whole scheme, as Dana, Miss Plummer and I have talked it out, is to maintain the general character of the Association while restricting any haphazard conference attendance from passing votes or making decisions of importance." He especially noted that the committee wanted to divide the council into two parts: "active" councillors, consisting of the executive board members plus 18 others elected by the association at staggered three-year terms, and "representative" councillors, consisting of "designated representatives of sections and affiliated organizations." It "may not be desirable to support that at Atlanta," Bowker informed Solberg, "but only to present it for discussion."

Utley complained to Carr that conferees would not have sufficient time before the conference to consider a document so important to ALA's future. He also predicted that a small attendance at the Atlanta meeting would automatically limit meaningful debate. "That is one of the reasons I opposed constitutional changes at Denver, and I observe that the amendments here proposed have not been revised even by this committee, dominated as it is by Dewey." Although Utley was wrong about Dewey's ability to dominate, Dana did express misgivings about "making two classes in the council." He doubted the necessity for creating a division "as a guard against hasty legislation." He told Bowker he could not attend the Atlanta conference, and gave the publisher his proxy to retain the division only if a majority approved; "otherwise, I should say no to it."[50] The committee's report promised to generate a lively discussion at the conference.

While Dana, Plummer, Solberg and Bowker struggled with the sticky problem of revising the ALA constitution, several others worked ALA's first significant accomplishment of national importance—the selection of Herbert Putnam as Librarian of Congress. When diplomat John R. Young had been nominated as Librarian of Congress by President William McKinley on 30 June 1897, members of the national library community were not pleased. They wanted a seasoned librarian to replace the aging Spofford when the library moved into its new quarters. Young subsequently surprised them with energetic leadership and judicious appointments to important subordinate positions, e.g., Spofford as chief assistant, David Hutcheson as Superintendent of the Reading Room, Solberg as Register of Copyrights, and J.C.M. Hanson as Superintendent of the Catalogue Department. When Young died unexpectedly on 17 January 1899, McKinley was forced to look for a successor.

Several politicians applied, but from the start Massachusetts lame duck Congressman Samuel June Barrows was the frontrunner. Lane, Bowker, Hutcheson and Solberg, however, wanted a librarian for the post. They agreed that the two most likely candidates were Dewey and Putnam, but neither wanted the post, and both had turned back inquiries from the administration when McKinley had decided to replace Spofford two years earlier. ALA leaders agreed that LC needed a librarian, but they were hard pressed to identify a qualified candidate among their ranks who would be willing to take the post. Through Massachusetts Senator Henry Cabot Lodge, Lane arranged an interview with the president for 4 February 1899, and invited Bowker to accompany him. Bowker arrived in Washington first, and while waiting in an anteroom at the White House, he encountered Barrows. He approached the retiring congressman to say that ALA really preferred a trained librarian for the post, but if no one should be found, Barrows's candidacy "seemed preferable" to others. "Mr. Barrows replied as frankly that if such a librarian were in the running he would not himself be a candidate." But Barrows had already committed himself, and had enlisted the support of political friends and allies in his quest for the post. Lane arrived a short time later, and together the two were ushered into the Oval Office. McKinley wasted little time. He said he wanted to nominate either Putnam or Dewey to the position, but since neither wanted it, he felt inclined to nominate Barrows. Nonetheless, Putnam was his first choice. Bowker quickly saw an opening and immediately pressed it. He told McKinley that "such word from the President of the United States was a command and it remained for us only to see that Herbert Putnam was prepared to accept the position." Lane echoed Bowker's sentiments, and after the two left, Lane returned to Boston to convince Putnam to accept the president's offer. On 6 February the Boston Public Librarian cabled McKinley that "I am prepared to place myself at your disposal." But one-half hour later Putnam withdrew his name because Barrows had not volunteered to withdraw. The congressman was openly asking why Putnam "was changing his mind," why he was "now entering the field," and why he was about "to seek the support of the ALA." Putnam would not engage in political infighting.

Although Lane and Bowker had wrongly assumed Barrows would quit his candidacy if ALA found a librarian, McKinley had not. He urged Putnam to reconsider, or he would have to nominate Barrows. Putnam respectfully refused, and on 15 February McKinley sent Barrows's name to the Senate for confirmation. But Lane would not give up. He worked closely with Lodge and senior Massachusetts Senator George F. Hoar to identify what he considered Barrows's "discreditable" behavior, and won their support to block Barrows's nomination. Congress adjourned on 3 March without acting on it. Although McKinley offered Barrows a recess appointment, the latter refused, recognizing that the confirmation process might be messy and not at all certain. McKinley then offered Putnam a recess appointment. Once comfortably assured that political maneuvering for the LC post had ceased, Putnam accepted.[51]

The episode is a curious one in American library history, for Putnam's initial refusal had given evidence of librarians' distaste for "politics." This revulsion carried over into ALA activities as association leaders worked hard to counter any impression that "politics" were an operational factor in organizational business. It demonstrated a myopia and misconception which continued to plague ALA, and in this case, almost cost the profession a large share in the future of the nation's foremost library, an institution begging for a sense of professional direction and a steady hand of leadership.

The Atlanta conference represented ALA's first venture into the Deep South. It was designed as a missionary effort to stir interest for establishing more southern public libraries. Anne Wallace, the director of the Atlanta YMCA Library, was responsible for local arrangements. Planning went smoothly until the middle of March when someone asked if a session on the library's role in the education of blacks would be appropriate for the conference. Lane grew cautious. "I am somewhat afraid to tackle [it] & sh'd not want to say anything about it at present." If the association decided to hold the session, however, Lane suggested W. E. B. DuBois, a Harvard graduate and Atlanta professor, as speaker. Carr was even more cautious, "unless it be a very broad minded paper." Wallace responded on 1 April. "To bring it in its crude shape before the national association, where partisans could make political capital out of it," she said, "would prove inimical to both white and negro [sic] interests." She might even lose the momentum she had generated to get Atlanta its own public library. Carr said he and Lane recognized "the need of being very careful and conservative on the negro [sic] question at this time and in the peculiar situation that the movement at Atlanta has brought about." On 15 April Lane wrote Carr that "the question of Negro Education, or the Negro in Relation to Libraries, we will leave untouched altogether."[52]

When Lane opened the Atlanta conference on 9 May, he looked over an audience of 215 registered white guests, 100 from North Atlantic states, 55 from Great Lakes states, only 53 from native South Atlantic and Gulf states; 116 registrants were women. New Englander Putnam was not impressed with his temporary surroundings—a "mongrel city," he told his wife, "a northern manufacturing town and a southern aristocratic town; a town that has boomed and a town decaying." He complained two days later that the hotel was "intensely uncomfortable to the purpose," and the business of the conference was "noisy, dirty, confused and tiresome" because the hotel was located next to railroad tracks. Ahern complained of the "dusty little closet over the streetcar racket which was dignified by the title of my room."[53]

In such an environment Lane delivered his presidential address—"graceful, sympathetic, and directly inspiring," LJ called it, a recounting of the events of the past year and a look towards the future. Lane noted the birth of several additional library associations, societies and clubs, especially the Medical Library Association and the National Association of State Librarians. "Such development seems to me wise if only the number of meetings to be attended is not too greatly multiplied . . . we hope that they will always also meet in conjunction with us." After conferees thanked Lane for his effort to make Putnam Librarian of Congress, Carr issued a gloomy secretary's report which cited financial difficulties. He admonished the association to exercise more fiscal restraint. Jones read the treasurer's report, identified a balance of $436.43, and cited a membership of 501.

Lane's report for the publishing section gave a summary of section publications, explained that work on the supplement to the ALA *Catalog* was again delayed, and indicated that Fletcher had almost completed another edition of the *ALA Index*. Lane urged the association to establish a guaranteed fund of $1,500 "to make good any possible deficit" so that the work the section had planned "could be pushed on vigorously and efficiently during the coming year." Soule read a report for the "committee on library tracts," which recommended a series of publications "intended not for experienced librarians but for communities where library interest is to be developed." The committee recommended that the publishing section consider seven possible tract subjects in priority order: (1) "why should we have a public library?"; (2) "how to start a public library"; (3) traveling libraries; (4) "suggestions for governing boards of libraries"; (5) library rooms and buildings; (6) book selection and purchase; and (7) "scope and management of college libraries." Conferees voted to continue the committee and made Andrew Carnegie an honorary ALA member before adjourning the session. Next morning Stearns described "how to organize state library commissions and make state aid effective." She argued that "conditions which obtain in the West are but little understood in the eastern part of the country." She also cited the need for more western and southern state library commissions because those states were not yet ready "to establish libraries through compulsory legislation."

The following morning members of the committee on constitutional revision entertained suggestions and criticism of their draft. The session occasioned so much response that Lane had to cut discussion short in order to return to the scheduled program. Montgomery then read the report of the cooperation committee which especially noted "cooperative measures" undertaken in the western and central states. After several papers were delivered, Crunden returned to the podium for a show of hands on crucial questions before his committee. He wanted membership guidance before preparing a final draft for association consideration, and he decided that a majority would rule in each case.

Shall the constitution recognize affiliated organizations?
No.

Shall the constitution alter the status of sections?
No.
Shall sections be specifically represented in the council?
No.
Shall the name of the Publishing Section be altered to Publishing Board?
Yes.
Shall the council include all ex-presidents of the association, *ex-officio*?
No.
Shall the council have the general management of the business affairs of the Association?
Yes.
Shall the council designate place of meeting?
Yes.
Shall the council elect the officers of the association?
No.
Shall they nominate officers, leaving any member with the right to make any nomination desired?
Yes.
Shall the constitution be changed, making the president eligible for re-election?
No.
Shall the ranking vice-president succeed the president in case of vacancy?
Yes.
Will the association decide to adopt the substance of the constitution at this meeting, the draft to be sent in print to each member by next October and finally adopted at the next meeting?
Yes.

As Crunden summarized his interpretation of membership response, his committee would have to revise the constitution to give more power to council but not to affiliated organizations, to decrease the powers of the executive board, and to assign more independence to the publishing section.

At the next session tellers announced election results: Thwaites for president; Anderson, Plummer, and Richardson for vice presidents; Carr for secretary; Haines for recorder; Jones for treasurer; and new council members including Billings, Lane, Andrews and Electra C. Doren. Later, conferees selected Montreal as the site for the next ALA meeting.

At the seventh session Crunden sought approval of his committee's revised draft of the constitution. After voting Dewey's motion to permit the committee to make minor stylistic and word changes, the membership considered the draft section by section. It ''was subjected to a cross-fire of amendments, counter-amendments and substitutes, from which it finally emerged, condensed and modified, but with less radical alterations than might have been expected.'' The compromise document created a new council consisting of 32 members (including the executive board) who would administer the association. The new constitution made no mention of affiliated organizations, but did provide that the ranking vice president should succeed to the presidency in case of vacancy. It also created a publishing board with a separate treasury, and, if funds were available, provided for the selection of a salaried secretary to serve as executive officer of the association for a three-year term. Conferees directed the committee to prepare a final draft of the amendments for the executive board, and adjourned.[54]

Public Libraries later called the compromise "as near the expression of a majority of the members as it would be possible to obtain." In essence it merged Bowker's "general meeting" concept and Dewey's desire to involve as many people and library organizations in ALA government as possible. The council, which would hold more power under the new constitution, still had vaguely defined duties, but its expanded membership allowed more representation from all regions of the country and helped to check the growing sectionalism within the association. By failing to provide a constitutionally sanctioned forum for other library associations, however, the compromise revision greatly limited avenues of communication from interests representing small libraries. Librarians from the Midwest seemed willing to give the new document a fair trial, even though it did not meet their most pressing needs. As a missionary effort to the South, the Atlanta conference enjoyed moderate success. As an effort to eliminate sectional division within the association, it only delayed the larger struggle to a later day.

Fortunately, the months preceding the Montreal conference were not as strained as the previous year. Henry Utley expressed surprise at Thwaites's election ("he is not a librarian and there are plenty of deserving people in actual library work who have been passed over too long") but *Public Libraries* thought "in view of the Montreal meeting, his selection at this time is peculiarly timely." Dana complained to Theresa West Elmendorf (who had married H. L. Elmendorf in 1896) that "it was a terrible mistake wrangling over the constitution" at Atlanta. He expressed particular surprise that the idea "of associating all library associations in the country with the ALA was turned down. I am firmly convinced that it will be a great mistake if this motion is not carried through." His fear of growing fractionalization among library interests was evident. In December Thwaites won a place for librarians on the list of professions recognized and counted by the Bureau of the Census, and in February 1900 Secretary Carr responded to an inquiry from the Baltimore Badge and Novelty Company. "The majority of [ALA] members would rather be found dead than wearing the usual convention badges," he wrote.[55]

In the fall of 1899 the association experienced a humorous episode involving George F. Nason of Franklin, Kentucky, who was marketing a small traveling subscription library under the name of "The American Library Association." On 10 October Carr asked Nason about the company he headed, and told him the name "American Library Association" had been incorporated under the laws of Massachusetts in 1879. Nason responded that he was not aware of the "other ALA," and that Carr's letter was his first indication a rival existed. He asked Carr to explain how use of the name "works an injustice to you," and promised to change his company's name to "National Library Association" if Carr's response was satisfactory. Carr replied several weeks later that it was "difficult to understand" Nason's ignorance, "considering the long-established and public work that has been carried on by the A.L.A." He also pointed out to Nason that his venture was not an association, but a company. Three days later Nason objected to the "high and mighty style" of Carr's letter, and informed the ALA secretary that he would change the name of his business enterprise to "American Library Company." He concluded "Should you for any reason wish to continue this correspondence, in which we have no further interest, kindly enclose stamp for reply." The stationery on which the letter was written had "Association" crossed out and "Company" stamped above it. Carr later thanked Nason for his response, but did not enclose a stamp.[56]

ALA committee work continued during the conference interim. While Bowker and his public documents committee pushed the Senate Committee on Printing to amend the public documents bill to improve their distribution, Thwaites convinced Dana to chair the committee on library schools because past committee reports were "rather perfunctory, being more synopses of the official reports of the schools themselves. Let us have a different sort, this year." Almost immediately the committee encountered difficulties. Fellow committee member Adelaide Hasse, documents librarian at the New York Public Library, was troubled over Thwaites's charge. "It is a delicate business," she wrote Dana. Alice Kroeger, director of the Drexel Institute Library School, did not see "much need of a library school committee of the ALA." In May Aksel Josephson, cataloger at the John Crerar Library, suggested that the committee investigate instruction in librarianship and bibliography, and visit all library schools annually at ALA expense. Dana politely responded that the association could not afford it, but Josephson argued that a large endowment would surely come if the profession upgraded its image by working towards higher salaries, shorter hours, scholarships, and inducing "more *first class men* to take up library work."[57]

On 6 December 1899 Lane wrote Putnam that he and E.C. Richardson of the Princeton University Library were meeting in Boston to discuss cataloging cooperation. "I wish you could make it convenient to be here at the same time so that we might look at the subject from the possible point of view of the Congressional library as well." Whether Putnam made that meeting or not is unknown, but on 8 March 1900, Columbia University hosted an ALA cooperation committee meeting "to consider printed catalog cards and cooperation." ALA members present included Putnam, Harris of Cornell, Richardson of Princeton, James H. Canfield of Columbia, Addison Van Name of Yale, Lane of Harvard, Andrews of the Crerar, Solberg of the Copyright Office, and Thwaites and Carr in their capacities as ALA president and secretary. Several days later Lane wrote Iles that the discussions "may lead to a much more extensive cooperative cataloging scheme on the part of the publishing section than anything we have yet undertaken." He did not elaborate.[58]

Another issue continued to fester. Shortly after the Chautauqua conference, Ahern asked Dana why he had not forwarded his "Primer" to ALA. "I can't exactly tell you why," Dana responded. "I think probably it's westernism—but

I don't quite want to ask the Publishing Section to print anything for me.'' In September, the Library Bureau published it. Three months later the Wisconsin Free Library Commission issued a supplement to the *Suggested List of Popular Books for Small Libraries*, and, in the meantime, *Public Libraries* urged ALA to issue a "Handbook of American Libraries." But the publishing section had other priorities. Because the section was told it would not be permitted to occupy space free of charge at the Boston Athenaeum for much longer, Lane and Soule recommended that someone in the association approach Carnegie for a contribution. Although Commissioner Harris advised the section to "make no bones of applying to him direct," Lane ultimately decided to work through Bowker. On 2 March 1900 Bowker wrote Carnegie that should the philanthropist "ever care to do anything further for libraries, . . . you might care to look into the work" of the publishing section. Carr wondered if Soule should also approach Carnegie to reinforce the section's needs. Soule suggested that no one else should interfere because Bowker was still seeking an interview with Carnegie.[59]

The committee on library tracts also experienced problems. As chairman of the publishing section Lane had refused to issue George Wire's *How to Start a Library*, which Lane considered "unworthy of publication in the form in which it was presented." In April Wisconsin Free Library Commission Secretary Hutchins complained to ALA President Thwaites that Lane had asked him to finish a tract on traveling libraries in a "feverish rush," but Hutchins had heard nothing since submitting the manuscript. Thwaites wrote Carr, "What is the status, *entre nous*?" Carr responded that the "hitch" was Lane. Manuscripts submitted were "not quite up to the *Harvard Standard*," and Lane had a "disposition to disregard and belittle anything done by and emanating from women." Helen Haines, who was "entirely discouraged in the matter," told Carr that she would recommend that the committee be disbanded at the Montreal meeting and the task of issuing tracts be reassigned to the publishing section. Thwaites became angry. "Our obstructionist friend [Lane] . . . neither knows nor cares anything of what those sturdy folk are doing who carry the gospel of good books into the city slums, the small villages, and the isolated farmsteads." He told Carr he would resist the committee's dissolution at Montreal.[60]

Irritations also surfaced elsewhere. Dana agreed with Josephson that ALA needed to publish its own organ. Dewey and Ahern feuded over a lack of communication between *Public Libraries* and the Albany Library School faculty and staff. "I find it requires more pride than I care to give to make them prepare material for you," Dewey wrote Ahern contemptuously. The fiery editor wrote to Dana on 19 February that "Albany is simply unbearable, with one or two exceptions, from top to bottom." Dana agreed. "The Albany world is a little bit removed from the rest of us, maybe exclusive?" Dewey's credibility with his western friends was gradually eroding. Alienating the editor of the western library community's chief communications organ did not help. On other matters, Dana's suggestion that the profession develop special library services for business earned a cold reception from Carr. "Undesirable and unadvisable," he said. Librarians should concentrate on improving existing services.[61]

Mixed emotions, mixed motives, and mixed allegiances brought 452 people to the ALA conference in Montreal on 7 June 1900. Two hundred eighty-seven came from North Atlantic states, 100 from Great Lakes states, 41 from Canada and England; 309 registrants were women. President Thwaites introduced the routine business almost immediately. Carr delivered his secretary's report, indicated the revised ALA *Handbook* had been issued, and noted that although the association was on a firmer financial foundation than previous years, it still could not afford a permanent paid secretary. Treasurer Jones reported a balance of $54.75 and a membership of 664, 61 greater than the previous year. Lane presented the publishing section report by noting that sales were down. Although printed catalog cards showed a profit, publishing section books continued to record losses. Soule indicated that the trustees of the endowment fund had obtained no additional money.

Dana presented a report for the committee on library schools which was critical of library education. "Too much attention, relatively, is given to the subjects of cataloging and classification," he stated. "How cruelly just!" murmured one unidentified member of the audience, probably echoing Dana's indictment of curricular emphases in Dewey's school and its clones. Dana concluded his report by reiterating the suggestions Josephson had made a month earlier. Conferees voted to send the recommendations to council for consideration. Hill reported for the committee on library tracts that three numbers of the series had been published, but he recommended that henceforth responsibility for publication ought to be passed to the publishing section and the committee disbanded. The recommendation was referred to council for action. In his report on gifts and bequests, George Stockwell of the Westfield (Massachusetts) Athenaeum noted that during the past two years Andrew Carnegie had donated $4,560,450 to library construction and development. In other matters, the revised ALA constitution passed its second reading. Members quickly voted that the new constitution should take effect immediately.

The next four sessions concentrated on customary committee reports and presentations dealing with practical librarianship. At the sixth session E. C. Richardson of Princeton reported for the cooperation committee. He recited progress on several projects, but focused attention on a two-point plan developed at the 9 March meeting at Columbia University. The scheme required that: (1) ALA should appoint a committee on cataloging rules; and (2) the publishing section should establish a bureau under its supervision to coordinate the necessary work. The membership apparently favored the plan immediately; the discussion which followed Richardson's report reflected nearly unanimous support for the venture. Dewey's motion that the executive board take action on the recommendations was voted. Lane later wrote Putnam, "Cooperative cataloguing on printed cards was given a boom and seems to be really on its legs and about to go if we can get the way plain before it."

Thwaites called the last session of the conference to order the following morning. First order of business was an amendment to the new constitution which attempted to clarify council duties. Under the proposed amendment council would be empowered to adopt all bylaws; establish new sections; "promulgate recommendations relating to library matters"; and nominate officers by a two-thirds majority. Concerning the last point, council also had to place all other names nominated by any five members 24 hours before the election on a printed ballot. The amendment was voted, but still required approval at the subsequent ALA conference to take effect. Tellers then reported the results of the election: Carr as president; Richardson and Fairchild as first and second vice presidents (the new constitution made this distinction); Faxon as secretary; Haines as recorder; Jones as treasurer. New members of the council included Soule, Gould, Hosmer, Putnam, Hewins, Sharp, Whitney, Hill and Iles. Once again, the officers of the association reflected an eastern majority.

With each successive conference the growing specialization within the profession became more apparent through the organization of new sections. Although the trustees section continued to languish, the college and reference section and the large library section enjoyed reasonable success, good attendance and varied programs. Competition with the National Association of State Librarians was evident in light attendance at the state and law library sections, but the newly formed cataloging roundtable drew 125 people who quickly agreed to petition council for a cataloging section. Two other groups met in "roundtable" meetings: officers of state library associations and officers of state library commissions. Several participants criticized program planners for scheduling their meetings simultaneously. The Montreal conference also provided the impetus and occasion for organizing the Canadian Library Association.

Because the new constitution gave the ALA council more power, council sessions attracted more attention than previous conferences. In accordance with the specific duties assigned them, council members voted to hold the next ALA meeting "in a summer resort in the middle west," to authorize the establishment of a catalog section, to recommend that the executive board appoint a liaison between ALA and individual state library associations, and to adopt a bylaw creating a committee of five which would visit and report on library schools and make recommendations for improvement. The executive board later appointed Dana, Crunden, Doren, Hill and Indianapolis Public Library Director Eliza G. Browning as members of that committee. The executive board was less active than previous conferences when it held more constitutional power. It made appointments and reappointments, transferred control of the library tracts series to the publishing board, and authorized the publishing board to create new committees to meet requirements of the cooperation committee's recommendations on cooperative cataloging.[62]

The Montreal conference was a comfortable success. The fears generated by sectionalist feelings, by disagreements between representatives of small and large library interests, by special interests not concerned with the "general meeting" concept—all subsided temporarily in order to observe the impact of the revised constitution. The publishing section, whose name was changed to publishing board, became more autonomous, but control of its products remained in the hands of New England librarians who directed large libraries. Thwaites's reaction to Lane's lack of progress on the library tracts series signaled future troubles for ALA. Progress in cooperative cataloging was easily the conference's most visible success.

Committee work continued between conferences. Andrews negotiated with Commissioner Harris to publish a *Handbook of American Libraries*. By October Putnam had decided to commit the Library of Congress to the cooperative cataloging scheme which the ALA publishing board had under consideration. Details were worked out over the winter, but when only 58 libraries had subscribed to the new service by spring, Bowker became skeptical about its future. While the publishing board struggled over the future of the cooperative cataloging scheme, the Minnesota Library Commission voted to join with state library commissions from Iowa and Wisconsin to publish "a suggested list of books for small libraries and handbook of library method and such other cooperative work as can be done more advantageously and cheaply together." And in the NEA library department Dana was becoming discouraged over lack of cooperation from NEA officers and members.[63]

More irritating to Dana, however, were difficulties experienced by his committee on library schools. He had accepted the chairmanship "because I did not like to decline to do any reasonable thing for ALA," but he protested to Carr that committee members should not be expected to visit library schools at their own expense. Then Hill asked to be removed from the committee in October because of an unexplained spat with Dewey. Crunden also resigned. Dana wondered why the committee "seems to be a hot buck which my compeers wish to drop." Carr wrote Dana on 7 November that Foster and Brett would replace Crunden and Hill. "Geographical distribution . . . is thus maintained and also a fair contiguity of location as among the East and West." Two weeks later Foster told Dana he could not serve. "Trouble, trouble, boil and bubble," Dana told Carr. The ALA president was also frustrated. Perhaps the committee should "go into the shade for a season," he said, despite the dictates of the new bylaw. Dana suspected that the critical report he had given at the previous conference might explain a reluctance to serve on his committee. In addition, Foster and Hill had both specifically cited their desire not to clash with Dewey, the New York State Library School Director. Still, Carr urged Dana to push ahead.

On 28 November another committee member complained to Carr. Because "there are too many Westerners on that committee for it to do effective work," Eliza Browning explained, and because "there should be at least two graduates of library schools in order to get a fair all-around view of the question," she wished to resign. "I am aware of the fact that there are a great many members of the ALA who are positive that there is a geographical limitation to the culture in the ALA," she added, "but this is not time to do missionary work with them to teach them better.'' Carr disagreed with her logic, but accepted her resignation. After an effort to induce J. L. Harrison, director of the Providence (Rhode Island) Athenaeum, to join the committee failed, Carr suggested to Haines that she ought to run an ad in LJ saying ''Wanted: Someone to serve on the Committee on Library Training. No reasonable offer refused!''

After Christmas, however, Browning relented and decided to return to the committee. Carr wrote Dana on 27 December that Harrison was unable to accept because he was already on a committee started by the library schools themselves ''for the purpose . . . of meeting and conferring with your committee.'' He knew nothing about this committee, but both men sensed Dewey's shadow lurking in the background. Finally, he told Dana that Faxon had asked the outspoken Assistant Los Angeles Public Librarian Mary L. Jones to join the committee. ''She is far enough away just now not to be dangerous,'' he noted. After Jones accepted on 19 January 1901, Dana circulated letters to library schools that the Montreal committee report had been interpreted as ''more critical of the schools than it really was,'' and he encouraged directors to cooperate for the sake of progress and improvement. He especially wanted to remove a consensus among library school graduates that they were superior to librarians who had received only apprentice training.

By spring Dana was wearing down. He had received so much criticism for his previous conference report, he wrote Fairchild sarcastically that ''perhaps the committee can this year make a compilation of reports from the different schools, which will be entirely satisfactory to all of them.'' To E. H. Anderson he complained that fellow committee members spend most ''good gray matter in telling me that they did not have any ideas . . . I get so confounded tired of the everlasting refrain 'Consider, old cow, consider.' '' He promised a report, but predicted his mood would not change before the Waukesha conference in July.[64] Dana's positive attitude towards ALA was obviously eroding. He saw the membership and leadership more interested in self-congratulation. They interpreted internal criticism as unnecessary and perhaps even harmful. And their attitude towards improving the status of librarianship by establishing standards for quality professional education obviously fell far short of a firm commitment.

In November 1900 Carr appointed ALA representatives to local library associations. *Public Libraries* welcomed the move, and admonished the newly appointed representatives to foster closer ties between state associations and ALA in hopes that a closer union would increase ALA coffers and enable the association to hire a full-time salaried secretary. PL also complimented NASL on its decision to meet coterminously with ALA in Waukesha in July. But while one faction seemingly returned to the fold, another was gestating outside it. Aksel Josephson, who was interested in starting a bibliographical society and publishing a bibliographical yearbook, made several inquiries to test interest. He wrote W. Dawson Johnston, who in turn asked George Parker Winship about Josephson's character. ''Josephson is a hustler,'' Winship responded, ''with national peculiarities which would unfit him for leadership. But he would do most of the work on anything he went into, and do it well."

In January, Ahern complained to Dana that Massachusetts subscriptions to *Public Libraries* were abysmally low. Was it "because the magazine was started in Chicago whereas Massachusetts librarians are in the east?" she queried sarcastically. On 17 May, Library Bureau Manager H. E. Davidson wrote Bowker that he was about to reorganize the bureau. It seemed "the only means of arriving at a satisfactory settlement with Mr. Dewey and eliminating him from the management pertaining to the Library Bureau."[65] Melvil Dewey had lost another foothold in the national library community.

Preparations for the Waukesha Conference began almost immediately after the ALA executive board met on 2 November 1900. The program committee decided to schedule time for the same sections and roundtables which had met at Montreal, with two additions—a section for library work with children, and a section for the discussion of cataloging and classification. Ahern suggested that Carr appoint an introduction committee to seek out "the small fry" and make them feel welcome at ALA's open sessions. In the past, she pointed out, introduction committee members "stood around and visited with each other" rather than welcoming directors of smaller libraries. On 19 February 1901 Thwaites suggested to Carr that the association "give more attention to the literary side of the program than it had heretofore." Faxon objected. Because the conference would be in the West, "something elementary was needed," he argued. Thwaites recoiled at Faxon's patronization. "We are all of us opposed to this thought. Local flavor appeared to us as essential when we went to Atlanta and Montreal, but Wisconsin and the West are not provincial!"

The month before the conference another controversy festered below the surface. In its June issue *Public Libraries* suggested that Putnam would make a good ALA president for the forthcoming year. Because the editorial represented the first time anyone had openly endorsed a candidate before a conference met, it set off a flurry of correspondence. Putnam responded quickly (but privately) that he did not wish to become a candidate. He thought "Billings should be the next President," although he had heard that Thwaites was pushing Hosmer's name. When Dana scolded Ahern for her open endorsement she responded that Hosmer was "in no sense a presiding officer." His occupancy of the chair at a Minnesota library meeting several years earlier was "most inefficient and ludicrous." Dana agreed with Ahern's assessment of the Minneapolis librarian, "but the custom has been to pass the presidency round in a complimentary sort of way, and on that basis it is very properly Hosmer's game." He warned Ahern not to interfere, and speculated that if the membership had to choose between Hosmer or Putnam at a conference held in Wisconsin, "Hosmer will win. You might conduct yourself accordingly." Ahern retreated.

On 13 June 1901 ALA charter member Samuel S. Green informed Dana he would not be attending the ALA conference. "I do not feel it to be a duty to go, for while I meet a few old friends whom I like much to see and who enjoy exchanging ideas with me, the great bulk of the members of the Association do not care anything about me.'' Green's comment was an open recognition that his generation of ALA leaders had passed. Dana argued that many more people were glad to see him each year than his letter implied, but he did not attempt to persuade Green to go to Waukesha. Carr hoped to have better success with Richardson, who had informed Faxon on 20 June he would not be attending the Waukesha meeting. Carr told the Princeton librarian the eastern contingent needed a strong showing, and reminded him that he was ''in line for the presidency of the ALA and should have it in 1903.''[66]

On the eve of the 1901 conference the American Library Association looked substantially different from eight years earlier. ALA manifested numerous growing pains. More sections, emerging roundtables, and special interest and type of library groups jockeyed for a place within the organizational structure to legitimate their existence. Differences in affiliations—geographic, type and size of library—all surfaced periodically to threaten ALA's image as a unified national voice for library progress. Pressures from outside the organization also increased. On 1 July 1901 ALA leaders looked over their shoulders at three special library associations with national constituencies, 18 independent state library commissions, 25 state library associations, and 12 local library clubs. All had specific needs; all sought to address constituencies which they thought ALA had not previously included in ''the largest number'' the association claimed it served. Sometimes their needs paralleled the direction the ALA leadership was taking the association; other times they ran counter to it. ALA struggled mightily to accommodate these complex pressures.

5   Forging a Professional Identity: Adjustment and Accommodation, 1901–1909

Six hundred twenty people registered for the ALA conference at Bretton Woods, New Hampshire, on 26 June 1909; 432 came from North Atlantic states, 117 from North Central states; 413 were women. But this attendance distribution did not reflect the membership at large. Members from North Atlantic states now comprised 45 percent of total ALA membership, North Central 22 percent. The East no longer held a majority.

Not only had the geographic profile of ALA membership changed, so had the national library horizon. At Bretton Woods the American Library Institute (ALI) met coterminously with ALA. ALI represented a self-elected national library elite who deliberated on library matters of national significance. Thirty-three states had their own library commissions by 1909. Many spoke to the profession through a League of Library Commissions, which, like the National Association of State Libraries and the American Association of Law Librarians, had affiliated with ALA. Thirty-eight states also had their own state library associations. Twenty-five intrastate regional and local library clubs complemented them, and on 8 June, librarians from several far western states banded together to organize the Pacific Northwest Library Association. Two more periodicals had made their appearance—the *A.L.A. Booklist*, issued by the ALA publishing board and advertised as "an annotated buying list of current books suitable for small and larger public libraries," and the *Bulletin of the American Library Association*, the ALA's new official organ. LJ and PL continued to publish monthly issues.[1] Seven more library schools had opened to enroll aspiring professionals.

On 26 June the ALA council had met to discuss routine matters. Included among its more important actions was a vote to establish a section on "Professional Training for Librarianship." The executive board met two days later to consider an offer from the Chicago Public Library Board of Trustees for free space in the library if ALA would relocate its headquarters there. Members present included the ALA's first Canadian president, C. H. Gould, McGill University librarian; N.D.C. Hodges, Cincinnati public librarian; Arthur E. Bostwick, director of the St. Louis Public Library; Purd Wright, director of the St. Joseph (Missouri) Public Library; Alice B. Kroeger, director of the Drexel Institute Library School; and James I. Wyer, New York State librarian. The executive board also invited members of the ALA publishing board to the meeting. Those present included Chairman Henry E. Legler, secretary of the Wisconsin Free Library Commission; Clement W. Andrews, director of Chicago's John Crerar Library, and Hiller C. Wellman of the Springfield (Massachusetts) Public Library.

Gould was especially careful to have ALA Secretary Wyer read verbatim the correspondence he had received from Harry G. Wilson, secretary of the Chicago Public Library Board of Trustees. After insisting that the letters be reprinted in the minutes, Gould turned to Carl B. Roden, acting Chicago public librarian. Roden read a letter from Chicago Library Club President Carrie L. Elliott, who offered on behalf of the club to furnish and refit the new quarters, and make all other necessary arrangements to move the executive offices from Boston to Chicago. Gould asked ALA Treasurer Wright for an estimate of normal ALA revenue, excluding income from the publishing board. "$5,500," Wright responded. How much would a permanent secretary and headquarters cost the association annually? he inquired. "$7,000" the executive board thought, figuring combined secretary and clerical salaries at $3,500, a contingency fund at $1,000, and allocations for the ALA *Bulletin*, conferences, and committee expenses at $2,500. Several board members felt sure that $500 in expenses could be pared on the *Bulletin* alone[2], but Legler had another idea. The publishing board wanted the executive offices in Chicago to assume four duties specific to board functions: (1) provide secretarial services for the publishing board; (2) conduct all correspondence beyond editorial responsibilities; (3) maintain business relations and arrangements between the board and outside sales agents; and (4) maintain a subscription list for *Booklist*. If the new executive offices agreed to assume these responsibilities, the publishing board would contribute $1,500 annually to maintain Chicago headquarters, with a promise of more if warranted. The ALA executive board then moved quickly. By accepting offers from the publishing board, the Chicago Public Library, and the Chicago Library Club, it committed the association to establishing a new headquarters at Chicago, where it has remained ever since.

Outsiders thought the meeting ran smoothly; insiders recognized that the steps and action had been carefully choreographed and rehearsed to hide the level of friction which had preoccupied ALA during the past six years. Like other events, the move signaled changes for ALA, and these changes characterized the Bretton Woods conference when President Gould gaveled the association to order for its first general session at 8:30 P.M.

After initial ceremonial greetings from local dignitaries, and a conciliatory presidential address on "Co-ordination, a Method in Co-operation," Secretary Wyer reported without explanation that Mary Ahern had resigned as recorder in September 1908, and had been replaced by Alice Kroeger. He also noted that

ALA had over 2,000 members, and that three committees now controlled ALA finances. Trustees of the endowment fund managed the $100,000 Andrew Carnegie had donated, plus $5,000 of general endowment monies. Income from the Carnegie fund yielded $5,000 per year, and was given to the publishing board, which used this money plus $8,000 from sales to fund its publishing activities. Finally, the executive board collected $4,700 per year for annual association memberships which it used to cover publication of the ALA *Bulletin*, conference proceedings, the ALA *Handbook*, and maintenance of the ALA executive offices. But Wyer forewarned: ''The removal of the Executive offices to Chicago and their organization upon somewhat broader lines will severely tax the present resources of the Association.'' He concluded by complimenting three executive board members who had represented ALA at seven state library association meetings during the past year. ''They have undoubtedly done much to promote professional intimacy and solidarity, and to make the Association better known and to bring to hundreds of remote library workers the sense that each of them has a part in its purposes and in its work.''

After Wright reported a balance of $5,070.90 in the ALA treasury, publishing board chairman Legler detailed the benefits of relocating headquarters to Chicago and passing the proposed new constitution. The publishing board, he said, had two tasks: to conduct the business of a publishing concern and to solicit and prepare publishable material. Both would be aided substantially by the establishment of an adequate headquarters located near a large public library. And the new constitution sanctioned a paid full-time executive officer who would serve as secretary of the association and the publishing board. The arrangement would ''render more compact and serviceable the entire business organization of the Association.'' The Secretary of the Wisconsin Free Library Commission was obviously much more optimistic about this turn of events than the New York State librarian. Legler also recited the advantages to the *Booklist*, which could guide the acquisitions of ''thousands of small public libraries whose book committees and librarians have not opportunity for personal examination of the product of the book press.'' Legler wanted to make *Booklist*

the nucleus for the editorial service which is now being given in the preparation of tools for the library world. This is especially advisable, in view of the fact that the active work of the Board prior to the establishment of the *Booklist* led to the publication of such valuable bibliographical tools, serviceable more particularly to the larger libraries, that the needs in this particular field are no longer insistent.

Legler's statement signaled a clear departure for the publishing board and hinted at subsurface friction. He noted that 80 percent of *Booklist* issues were distributed to libraries free of charge through library commissions. It was no coincidence that the secretary of the Wisconsin Free Library Commission served as chairman of the ALA publishing board.

Legler also reported that Elva Bascom of Madison, Wisconsin, who presently served as *Booklist* editor, would work on a second supplement to the ALA *Catalog*. Since neither the Bureau of Education, which had published the original ALA *Catalog* in 1893, nor the Library of Congress, which had published the first supplement in 1904, could contribute, the publishing board would have to assume the entire financial burden. Other activities which Legler mentioned included publication of the ALA catalog rules, guidelines to reference books, and continued progress on a list of subject headings and a manual of library economy. Treasurer Jones concluded the publishing board report with a detailed financial statement, and after the membership accepted the reports of the council and executive board, Gould closed the first general session.

At the second session animated discussion centered around the revised constitution, which was being presented for its second reading. The proposed constitution differed from its predecessor in three important ways: (1) salaried executive officers would no longer be elected, but appointed by a board of directors who would hold them accountable; (2) the executive board would assume more power and become a "true board of directors"; and (3) the council would be relieved of its business functions and made into a deliberative body. Librarian of Congress Herbert Putnam, who chaired the constitutional revision committee, asked conferees either to accept or reject the proposal, but not to tamper with it. The effect of his all-or-nothing recommendation was to force full approval. Purd Wright supported Putnam's strategy. Removal of headquarters to Chicago would be difficult enough, he said. Delaying approval of the revised constitution would unnecessarily complicate matters.

But William F. Yust, director of the Louisville Free Public Library, disagreed. He found certain portions of the proposed constitution objectionable, particularly Sections 15 and 16, where it was stated that council would consist of the executive board, 25 members elected by the association, 25 additional members elected by the council itself, and all ALA ex-presidents plus the presidents of affiliated associations. "A self-perpetuating body with power to control the policy of the Association," Yust charged, is "a fundamental defect." Scrap the whole council idea, suggested Cornell University reference librarian Willard Austen. New Bedford (Massachusetts) Public Librarian George Tripp was less charitable. "Sections 15 and 16 make this the most autocratic constitution I have ever heard of outside of Russia." Putnam bristled, "The injunction upon our Committee was in particular to center the control of your affairs in an Executive Board, a body selected by you annually, determined by you annually, acting, therefore, under constant monition, if you choose." The committee purposely designed a council which had almost no legislative powers, only advisory, deliberative powers, Putnam noted. Director of Baltimore's Enoch Pratt Free Library Bernard C. Steiner asked everyone's patience. Give the executive board the powers it will need to carry out the headquarters scheme successfully, he argued.

Legler was so anxious to get unanimity on the constitution in order to save the headquarters scheme that he moved approval without Sections 15 and 16. After Gould reluctantly agreed with Legler's move—both men had participated in the painful behind-the-scenes battle to move ALA headquarters to Chicago, and neither wished to let this opportunity slip away—Gardner Jones pointed out how intricately those sections were bound within the rest of the document. "It would be very undesirable to adopt a new constitution and still carry the old provisions about the function of the Council, with the friction between the Executive Board and Council which has existed in the past, and which is removed by the new constitution." Think of the positive features, Jones admonished conferees. The executive board would run the business of the association and appoint a secretary and treasurer "fitted to do the work in connection with the new headquarters." One member of the finance committee had to be an executive board member, thereby ensuring control over the association's financial affairs. Similarly, the new ALA secretary and treasurer would serve in the same capacity on the publishing board, thereby establishing a link between the two that had heretofore been lacking. Finally, correspondence votes between meetings no longer required perfect unanimity, but only a majority, provided no member objected to the correspondence vote itself. Next to these major benefits the council issue paled. Vote now, Jones said; the council matter "we can consider later." Jones must have been convincing. Legler withdrew his motion and then called for the question. The revised amendment passed "by a nearly unanimous vote." The second session adjourned.

The conference included three more general sessions, all of them less anxious than the second. Several people gave papers on education and the library, and a variety of reports came from such committees as international relations, cooperation with the National Education Association, library administration, library architecture, library work with the blind, bookbinding, bookbuying, catalog rules, library training, and public documents. At the final session tellers announced results of the election: N.D.C. Hodges as president; Wyer as first vice president; and secretary of the Iowa Library Commission Alice S. Tyler as second vice president. Other executive board members included C. W. Andrews, Theresa West Elmendorf, Lane, Legler, Putnam and Wright. This list duplicated exactly the slate of officers presented by the nomination committee. Because of the scheduled headquarters move and the new constitution, the secretary and treasurer would be appointed by the executive board after the conference.

Other sections and affiliated associations met between general sessions. The college and reference section, the catalog section, and the children's librarians section all had fruitful meetings. The section for the professional training of librarians held its first meeting after receiving council approval, but the trustees section continued to suffer light attendance and little action. The National Association of State Libraries met for the twelfth consecutive year, sharing one session with the American Association of Law Librarians, meeting for a fourth consecutive year. On 2 July John Cotton Dana, now director of the Newark (New Jersey) Free Public Library, organized a Special Libraries Association to help coordinate efforts among municipal, legislative, reference, commercial, technical and public welfare libraries. For the moment, Dana chose not to affiliate with ALA. That same day the League of Library Commissions held its sixth annual meeting. Chalmers Hadley, secretary of the Indiana Public Library Commission, read a report from the league's publications committee which had been prepared by Mary E. Hazeltine of the Wisconsin Library School at Madison. The paper identified progress on such publications as "Mending and Repair of Books," "Why Do We Need a Public Library?," "Children's Suggestive [sic] List," "Magazines for the Small Library," and "Graded List of Books and Reference Books for Schools." At the end of its second session the league appointed a new publications committee consisting of Clara F. Baldwin, secretary of the Minnesota Public Library Commission, Charlotte Templeton, secretary of the Nebraska Public Library Commission, and Hadley. The Midwest controlled the committee.[3]

Before officially adjourning the conference, the executive board selected its first full-time, salaried executive officer. This individual would be responsible for supervising the relocation of national ALA headquarters to Chicago. The appointment had been carefully considered, and although several persons had sought the position, the board ultimately settled upon Chalmers Hadley, graduate of Earlham (Indiana) College and the New York State Library School, and a former president of the League of Library Commissions (1907–1908). His credentials were largely midwestern.

Hadley did not have long to settle into his new position. ALA closed its old headquarters at 34 Newbury Street in Boston on 31 August and accepted the resignation of publishing board secretary Nina Browne. Next day it officially opened its new headquarters on the fifth floor of the Chicago Public Library building. On 2 September, the executive and publishing boards had their first official meetings in the new quarters, a room 50 by 60 feet in size, paneled in English oak, and adorned by nine chandeliers containing six lights each. The *Bulletin* cheerfully described the meeting, but quickly added:

The removal of the executive offices from Boston to Chicago will not mean the lessening in any way [of] those close connections which have always existed between headquarters and the library activities in New England and the East. It promises to mean in addition to these connections closer relations between the Association and increasing activities in the West and South.

The overriding concern with sectionalist feelings was transparent. Nearly a half-century later Louis Bailey remembered his friend Chalmers Hadley: "I saw him a number of times when he came to Chicago to open the A.L.A. office and know he had difficulty trying to keep harmony between East and West in those early days." On 4 September Clara Baldwin wrote Legler she liked "very much" Legler's suggestion "that the sale of [League] publications be transferred to ALA headquarters." And Bowker astutely noted "the way things are going as the star of empire takes its way westward." Fletcher later complained about "Legler and other westerners now in control of ALA matters."[4] The association had entered a new era and transferred leadership to a new group.

Painful Adjustment: 1901–1905

The story of the struggle preceding the Boston-to-Chicago transfer has its beginnings in the last half-decade of the nineteenth century, but momentum to establish a permanent ALA headquarters began to accelerate significantly after the 1901 Waukesha conference. Members frequently dubbed the activities "ALA politics" and referred to them often in their correspondence. Many began to worry about the proliferation of roundtables and sections, and a few retained suspicions of Dewey's power, though it was obviously diminishing, and his influence on the ALA's direction.[5]

On 30 September 1901, the ALA executive board met for a routine session. Board members had decided to hold the next conference at a "seaboard resort near Boston." They also filled vacancies on existing standing committees. Dewey received a three-year appointment to the publishing board, and C. C. Soule accepted an appointment to fill the vacancy left by Iles's resignation. The appointments followed a publishing board meeting at Lake Placid on 27 and 28 September, at which board members thanked Putnam for authorizing the Library of Congress to take over the cooperative cataloging scheme. Dana privately chuckled at the eastern establishment—"the grand phalanx of the ALA," he called it. He wrote Ahern on 17 October, "I should think Meleney would like to frame the list of the ALA Executive Committee which appears on the corner of the stationery and keep it ever before him."[6]

Undercurrents of dissatisfaction at ALA's direction continued to surface in the Midwest. Aksel G. S. Josephson argued that the ALA should concentrate more attention on bibliography. Josephson had been active in organizing the Bibliographical Society of Chicago, and proposed that the federal government fund a bibliographical society. Dewey disagreed; he considered it "simply breaking into the distinct field of the ALA and its Publishing Board." On 28 February William Stetson Merrill of the Newberry Library, who served as chairman of a Bibliographical Society of Chicago committee appointed to consider a national organization, circulated a memo which asked interested parties to respond to two proposals: "1st, that a national society should be formed at once, independently of the Chicago Society; and 2nd, that the present Society develop into national sections."

When ALA President Billings received a copy of the proposals, he responded quickly and decisively. "I believe in strengthening existing institutions and avoiding the creating of new ones whenever possible." He assured Merrill that if significant interest in bibliographical work existed, ALA officers would gladly consider commencing a bibliography section within ALA. Several days later ALA Secretary Faxon wrote Josephson that the ALA program committee wanted the bibliographical society "to take charge of a part" of the fourth general session of the forthcoming conference "for a report on and discussion of the question of a bibliographical institute." Several members of the Chicago bibliographical society remained unimpressed. Oberlin College Librarian Azariah

S. Root wrote Josephson on 13 March, "I do not believe there should be anything more than a cooperative connection between [the bibliographical society] and the ALA. I am not very greatly enamored of the ALA and think it is largely run by a certain set for the promotion of mutual interests."

Billings pressed on, however. He urged Josephson to try running a national organization as an ALA section. He also said the ALA executive board had appointed a committee to consider the matter, and incidentally mentioned that Librarian of Congress Herbert Putnam was a member. Three months later Putnam received an internal LC report entitled "Report on Bibliographical Work in the U.S., & Especially in the Library of Congress," prepared by W. Dawson Johnston of LC's Division of Bibliography. Putnam told Johnston to revise the paper in order to highlight two specific areas. First, as bibliographical work within LC evolved, "most of the things that Josephson proposes for his Institute of Bibliography" would "come to pass." Second,

Josephson has put on paper various projects that independently undertaken would involve an elaborate organization. They are most of them to be undertaken in ordinary course by the L. of C. I should like this to appear from your paper. You need not argue it out, but at least suggest it. Do not mention Josephson, as I cannot accept him nor be associated with his projects as his projects.[7]

Josephson was challenging the two most important institutions in the national library community—the American Library Association and the Library of Congress. Neither wanted to relinquish control over any part of the library community's professional activities.

Shortly after the Waukesha conference the secretaries of state library commissions from Minnesota, Wisconsin and Iowa agreed to issue a bimonthly list of books recommended for small libraries. Wisconsin would compile it, Iowa would print it, while Minnesota would edit a handbook of practical library work. The three commissions published the handbook in April 1902. In the meantime, the Wisconsin Free Library Commission issued pamphlets entitled "Fifty Books for a Child's Library" and "How May the Federation and the Commission Cooperate to Aid Our Library Interests."[8]

While midwestern library commissions published practical information for small libraries, the ALA publishing board focused its efforts in other directions. The board continued to work with the Library of Congress on the catalog card scheme, and in the fall of 1901 brought out the second edition of the *ALA Index*. The following spring the board published a fourth library tract, "Library Rooms and Buildings" by Charles C. Soule. Bureau of Education Commissioner William T. Harris sent a clear message to Dewey that although he shared Dewey's desire for a new edition of the ALA *Catalog*, the bureau would not be able to publish it. Dewey suggested to Putnam that the Library of Congress undertake the project.[9]

Billings's activities between conferences quickly showed why he had been elected ALA president. On 22 November 1901 he wrote Bowker that "the thing I wish immediately to talk to Mr. Carnegie about is the publication fund." He did not think it advisable to press for an endowment to establish a permanent ALA headquarters, but he did want a "concise statement" outlining the publishing board's plans for the future. Bowker responded quickly, then sent a "confidential" circular to members of the publishing board informing them of Billings's intentions. Since Carnegie often made his gifts in United States Steel bonds which yielded 5 percent, he said, "a gift of 100,000 dollars would thus give 5,000 dollars annually to the Board."

Lane was excited, but worried that all ALA members might not agree with the directions the Carnegie grant would permit the board to take its publishing program. By March, several months after Billings's initial visit, Carnegie had tentatively agreed to the ALA president's request, but he asked Billings to send him a letter outlining the specific purpose for which the donated funds were intended. Since Carnegie had just incorporated the Carnegie Institution in Washington, D.C., on 4 January, "to conduct, endow, and assist investigation in any department of science, literature, or art," he did not want to commit funds to two organizations competing to provide the same service. On 14 March Billings, who also served as trustee for the Carnegie Institution and who anticipated the scholarly, research-oriented goals the institution eventually would take, wrote the philanthropist that the interest for the special fund would "be applied to the preparation and publication of such reading lists, indexes and other bibliographical and library aids, which will be especially useful in the circulating libraries of this country." He added that "the results will be of great value in promoting the circulation of the best books among the people by the instruction which can thus be given continuously." Although Carnegie agreed in early May, Billings decided to keep news of the grant "strictly confidential" until the summer ALA conference.[10]

The 1902 ALA conference formally opened on 17 June in Magnolia, Massachusetts. One thousand eighteen people registered, more than double the attendance of any previous ALA conference. Charles Ammi Cutter explained the large turnout in a *Nation* column. "The reason is plain. They met in Massachusetts, where every town but two has a library and some have several. The rest of New England is almost as bibliothecal, and New York is catching up." Four of five in attendance came from North Atlantic states; three-fourths of total registrants were women.

The association spread its activities over seven general sessions, four section meetings, two roundtable meetings, four council meetings, and two executive board meetings. In addition, the Bibliographical Society of Chicago met separately. ALA Secretary Frederick W. Faxon reported the association now boasted 1,265 members, Treasurer Jones noted a treasury balance of $363.01, and Endowment Fund Trustee Soule announced a fund principal of $6,498.66. Routine committee reports followed.

At the beginning of the third general season Billings delivered his presidential address. He emphasized the educational role which the public library played in the lives of citizens, and especially children. He suggested that the profession should devote more time to working with school libraries and existing children's collections within libraries than to establishing "home libraries," small collections of books circulated to specified neighborhood homes. The latter, he thought, could more appropriately be handled by charitable organizations. What had the public library accomplished over the last quarter century? "It does seem [it] has lessened the power of the demagogue and unscrupulous politician to control votes, and that in public life the steadily increasing influence of educated men is, in part, due to the reading facilities which the people most enjoy." He offered no evidence to validate his speculation. Towards the end of his speech Billings announced to a surprised but pleased crowd that Carnegie had agreed to donate a $100,000 endowment fund to ALA for use by the publishing board, subject to the restrictions outlined in Billings's letter of 14 March. "It is a unique gift from a unique man, who deserves our best thanks," Billings stated. The audience applauded.

The fourth general session opened the following morning. George Watson Cole reported on gifts to American libraries during the past year and noted that of the $9,300,000 dollars donated for library buildings, Carnegie had contributed $7,600,000. Bostwick reported that the committee on library training still lacked direction and purpose, and requested that the membership provide the committee with more guidance in the future. Dewey announced that the Library of Congress had agreed to publish a new edition of the ALA *Catalog*. Fletcher gave a lengthy report of publishing board activities, and invited "special attention" to the board's decision to "issue cards prepared by the Bibliographical Society of Chicago indexing the contents of the leading bibliographical publications." That evening the Bibliographical Society of Chicago met. Among papers presented, Aksel Josephson read his "Plan for the Organization of an Institute for Bibliographical Research." The institute would systematically issue bibliographies "according to a preconceived plan," and would be funded by a large endowment. It was obvious Josephson silently hoped the proposed institute would somehow come under the sponsorship of the newly formed Carnegie Institution. Putnam then read W. Dawson Johnston's "The Work of the Division of Bibliography of the Library of Congress," which explained the division's many functions, while Fletcher elaborated on the bibliographical work and plans of the publishing board which the Carnegie grant would provide. The juxtaposition of these papers was probably not coincidental.

At the seventh session the secretary announced the election of new officers: James K. Hosmer as president; Columbia University Librarian James H. Canfield as first vice president; and Anne Wallace as second vice president. Frederick Faxon, Gardner Jones, and Helen Haines retained their seats as secretary, treasurer, and recorder. New council members included Melvil Dewey, E. C. Richardson, N. D. C. Hodges, Lutie Stearns, and William T. Peoples, director of the Mercantile Library of New York City.

Program planners also provided additional time for section meetings. Root presided over the college and reference section, while J.C.M. Hanson of the LC's cataloging department chaired the catalog section session. The trustees section and the children's librarians section both had fruitful meetings, but the state library roundtable considered disbanding to foster closer ties between ALA and the National Association of State Librarians. The state library commission roundtable, on the other hand, won council approval to become a new section. The executive board reappointed Fletcher as chairman of the publishing board. When it also appointed Hiller C. Wellman to succeed Bowker, who had resigned, the publishing board ended up with four members from Massachusetts (Fletcher, Lane, Soule, Wellman) and one from New York (Dewey). Control of publishing board activities would remain in the East.

The Bibliographical Society of Chicago met independently on 18 June. Josephson presided and introduced two papers: "The Scope of an American Bibliographical Society" by A. S. Root, and "A Plan for an American Bibliographical Society" by John Thomson. Josephson subsequently opened the meeting to general discussion. Marvin Busbee, Dartmouth College librarian, argued that the newly established Carnegie Institute in Washington, D.C., should support a national bibliographical society. Columbia Reference Librarian C. A. Nelson suggested the society should be affiliated with ALA, but should not be a section within the association. Billings argued that as a trustee of the Carnegie Institution he did not believe a bibliographical society would receive support from that quarter. Josephson reported results of a survey Merrill had taken in February. Of the 87 people contacted, 80 wanted a national bibliographical society and 67 of those wished this organization to evolve naturally from the Bibliographical Society of Chicago.

Society members then appointed a committee to draft rules and regulations governing a national bibliographical society. Although they carefully pointed out that "all steps taken during the current year shall be tentative only," and that the committee would "confer with the proper authorities of the American Library Association and the Bibliographical Society of Chicago to bring about the accomplishment of this project," the outcome was already predetermined.[11] The movement toward a national bibliographical society had acquired enough momentum to overcome resistance from ALA and the Library of Congress. At a meeting of the Bibliographical Society of Chicago on 29 January 1903, the executive board appointed William C. Lane as chairman of a committee to organize an "American Bibliographical Society." Josephson had won, although Billings successfully continued to resist his efforts to seek Carnegie funds for a bibliographical institute.

Just two months after the close of the Magnolia conference several prominent midwestern librarians, including Alice Tyler, Gratia Countryman and F. A. Hutchins, called a meeting of "librarians, trustees and all others of the West and Middle West interested in library work" for 28–30 August 1902 at the State Historical Society building in Madison, Wisconsin. One hundred fifty-four people attended, two-thirds of whom came from Wisconsin. The program provided much practical library information for attendees, but on 30 August representatives of the Illinois Library Association and the library commissions of Nebraska, Minnesota, Iowa, Indiana and Wisconsin discussed mutual problems and outlined proposed cooperative efforts for the coming year. Several months later the Wisconsin Free Library Commission published a *Buying List of Recent Books Recommended by the Library Commissions of Iowa, Minnesota, Wisconsin, Idaho, Nebraska and Delaware*. Simultaneously the Nebraska Free Library Commission issued a 16-page *List of Public Documents for Small Libraries*. Midwest librarians also watched progress on the new edition of the ALA *Catalog*. "The great aim should be simplification in the interest of small libraries and books," R. G. Thwaites reminded ALA *Catalog* Associate Editor May Seymour.[12]

After the Magnolia conference the publishing board began to determine how to spend interest from Carnegie's $100,000 gift. Dewey characteristically was quick to suggest that "a part of Mr. Carnegie's gift should be used to help on the ALA Catalog." Since the Library of Congress had already agreed to publish it, he recommended the publishing board allocate $100 per month to employ a full-time assistant. The publishing board approved his request. On 15 November 1902 he issued a circular outlining the general plan for a catalog listing 8,000 volumes which would be particularly adapted to "very small libraries" because citations would be ranked by order of importance. He pressed the publishing board to adopt the Decimal Classification (DC) scheme as the *Catalog*'s standard arrangement. Others continued to press for "appraisal" or "evaluation" annotations within the *Catalog*. On 1 December the publishing board moved its office to 10½ Beacon Street, a room on the first floor of the Boston Athenaeum which had formerly been occupied by the American Academy of Arts and Sciences. Nina Browne remained in charge. The larger quarters permitted her to handle all publishing board publications, which previously had gone through the Library Bureau.[13]

On 15 December 1902 W. Dawson Johnston suggested that the publishing board consider a "bibliographical periodical" entitled "Book Notes" which "shall be devoted primarily to a description of the most popular and useful books, and only secondarily to a description of scientific books of value chiefly to the specialists, and of rare books, of interest mainly to the collector." Lane said he and two other publishing board members "were a good deal impressed by the possible value of such a publication," but the board could not afford it since "our income for the present year [is] largely devoted to . . . a new edition of the American Library Association Catalog." But Putnam urged Johnston on. He discussed Johnston's scheme with Lane and Fletcher in April; several weeks later George Iles inquired about "the project Book Notes." Although he was "delighted" at the prospect, Iles told Johnston, "the main difficulty is financial. When we have threshed out the whole question of what a headquarters should be and do, we may be able to draw up a plan so clear and reasonable that it may obtain for us the endowment needed."[14]

Dewey misinterpreted Putnam's efforts for "Book Notes." He had suggested to Putnam in February that the Library of Congress issue a quarterly supplement to keep the forthcoming ALA *Catalog* current. Putnam replied that "the time is not ripe . . . to consider that thing." He may have been hoping "Book Notes" would win an independent endowment from someone like Iles. Dewey was anxious. Within a short time, he began telling people it was his "understanding" that a year after issuing the ALA *Catalog* LC would begin publishing quarterly supplements. Putnam became indignant, and scolded the New York State librarian soundly. "We have undertaken to publish the ALA Revised Catalogue. We have not yet undertaken to do more, . . . and I do not like to have it committed in fact by assumptions or 'understandings.' "

Dewey's response was characteristic: affected anguish at unjustifiably being thought dishonest or disloyal, then taking the offensive on unrelated issues. "When I got yours, I felt more tact than you," he said. "I have been so absolutely loyal to your work and you personally, and to the theory that you were to do your way in your own time that I felt deeply hurt at any suggestion like your implication of edging." He then admitted "pure carelessness" in using the word "understanding," but that was as much of an apology as Dewey could muster. Thereafter he took the offensive. Putnam should make LC the leader for *all* American libraries, not just of research libraries. Several years before, the congressional librarian had promised to include Dewey numbers on the printed catalog cards LC was selling, but Putnam still had not fulfilled his promise. Although Dewey ended on an aggressive note, he never again pushed Putnam on quarterly supplements to the ALA *Catalog*. "Book Notes," or a periodical of similar ilk, would not come from LC.

If Dewey could not move Putnam, neither could Johnston move the ALA publishing board. Chairman Fletcher wrote that the board was "very hospitable to the 'Book Notes' scheme," but Lane "is the one man in the boat who backs water somewhat earnestly." Fletcher promised to cite the need for a bibliographical periodical in his annual report to ALA at the forthcoming conference. Iles promised continued verbal support.[15]

Other association members also met obstacles between conferences. James Kendall Hosmer was not a dynamic ALA president. Although he lacked contact with Carnegie money, ALA leaders hoped somehow he would be able to locate enough to endow a permanent ALA headquarters. On 9 September 1902 he admitted his shortcomings to Herbert Putnam. "It is quite awkward to be so far away as I am from the center." More perplexing at the moment, however, was the position of ALA secretary. Faxon insisted on resigning, and to replace him Hosmer suggested Walter L. Brown, H. L. Elmendorf's assistant at the Buffalo Public Library. Putnam had another idea. He wanted to appoint C. H. Hastings of the LC catalog department as ALA secretary, and LC would underwrite part of his salary and give him released time to carry out his secretarial duties. Putnam felt he could justify this expenditure because Hastings was directly involved with the distribution of LC printed catalog cards for the ALA publishing board.

Hosmer took Putnam's suggestion to Lake Placid where ten members of the council met informally the end of September. Dewey told Putnam that the group agreed Hastings "was not adapted" to become ALA secretary. Instead, they suggested Putnam hire William F. Yust to a position on the LC staff for $1,200. "He would accept and as A.L.A. Secretary do a fine work." Hill echoed Dewey's suggestion two weeks later. On 22 October Putnam wrote Dewey that "I can now see my way clear to employ Mr. Yust in this Library." On 25 October Dewey attempted to clarify what he thought was Putnam's offer. "Is it clearly understood that if you appoint Yust or any other good man in the Catalog Department, that he is to have all the time he needs for A.L.A. work and to do that work on official time?" Would Putnam also allow Yust enough time off and sufficient travel expense to attend various state library meetings? Putnam responded that he could not possibly justify paying a full-time ALA secretary with government funds. Yust would have to render some service within the library, and the association would have to fund all clerical work. Unless the association was willing to accept this, Putnam could not hire Yust. But ALA could not afford even minor contributions toward maintaining a permanent staff member, so the matter dropped. Dewey still held out hope for Washington, however. "We want to concentrate this work on the spot and the essential thing is to have the man and the work there." When the ALA executive board met on 9 December it appointed University of Nebraska Librarian James I. Wyer to succeed Faxon.[16] Thus the ALA lost another opportunity to establish a permanent headquarters and paid staff because it could not cover even a portion of the necessary costs. Noticeably, ALA president Hosmer had been largely absent from all negotiations.

Hosmer failed on yet another matter. The association still hoped Andrew Carnegie would endow a permanent headquarters and paid staff position. Hosmer knew this, so he visited Carnegie in New York shortly after the new year. After being conducted into Carnegie's library, the ALA president presented him with a copy of Larned's *Literature of American History*. "Mr. Carnegie received it graciously, and talked freely about his interest in libraries and his gifts." Hosmer thought he saw an opening and suggested that another library cause beckoned "a liberal giver." Carnegie balked, "grew canny and wary, ran over rapidly the sums he had given to this, that and the other institution in America and Great Britain, making it very clear that he had often been begged, and that it embarrassed him." Hosmer wisely retreated, spent the remainder of the interview discussing mutually agreeable topics, and left Carnegie's mansion empty-handed.[17] The ALA would have to search for funds elsewhere.

Plans for the Niagara conference continued. Hosmer especially wanted Putnam to attend because ALA luminaries like Lane, Fletcher, and Andrews could not. When Wellman received a preliminary program, he noticed it was accompanied by a card advertising steel library stockroom equipment. "This is about the limit," he wrote Boston Athenaeum Director Charles Bolton. "Isn't it about time that we do something?" he told Putnam, Thomson, and Pennsylvania State

Librarian T. L. Montgomery. Together they petitioned the ALA executive board "that no form of commercial advertising be countenanced officially by the ALA, either through circulars sent out by its officers, or by permitting exhibits at headquarters during meetings of the Association." Hosmer decided to postpone a decision on the issue until the Niagara conference. The *Library Journal* admonished the association that advertising should be "carefully considered and regulated according to some definite principle."[18]

Six hundred eighty-four people attended the Niagara conference which Hosmer convened on 23 June 1903; 419 came from North Atlantic states, 162 arrived from Great Lakes states; 447 of the conferees were women. After official greetings from local dignitaries, Wyer noted in his secretary's report that ALA now boasted 1,350 members, but that the association needed still more members to augment its national impact. Treasurer Jones reported a treasury balance of $12.38. Wyer read Soule's endowment fund trustees report, which showed a balance of $103,876.01.

Wellman read Fletcher's report for the ALA publishing board. Fletcher acknowledged Carnegie's gift, but called for an even larger endowment to fund a permanent staff and headquarters. He thanked Dewey and the New York State Library staff for assistance on the new edition of the ALA *Catalog*, but reported slow sales of the ALA *Index, Literature in American History*, and the library tracts series, and cards indexing bibliographical serials. More successful were Alice Kroeger's *Guide to the Study and Use of Reference Books* and the ALA *List of Subject Headings for a Dictionary Catalog*. Fletcher concluded by announcing a plan for "the publication of a periodical devoted to notes upon current literature, so written, classified, and indexed as to assist the librarian in the labor of choosing books for purchase, of assigning subject entries in cataloging, of classification, and of reference work." He did not elaborate. A report on gifts and bequests, which showed Carnegie had donated $6,679,000 to libraries in the last year alone, ended the session.

The conference witnessed six more general sessions, most of which were noncontroversial. Hosmer delivered an uninspiring presidential address at the second general session, while most of the fourth session concentrated on library training. Mary Plummer read a report which related the results of a survey covering library school faculty entrance requirements, curriculum, tuition, practice, credentials, electives, graduate associations, summer schools, apprentice classes, college courses in bibliography, state normal school courses in library economy and correspondence courses. Conferees were so impressed with Plummer's work they followed her recommendation to establish a standing committee on library training. The eight-member committee would be carefully structured to represent the various library constituencies most directly affected by library training. Plummer also called for a tract on "Training for Librarianship." Lutie Stearns then argued for more summer schools, especially in the Midwest. "Library conditions in the west are not easily understood here in the east," she emphasized.

At the sixth session George Iles discussed "A Headquarters for Our Association." ALA needed one to collect library architectural plans; to aid library administration by keeping an accurate record of existing state library laws, bibliographic lists, etc.; to become a center for the "appraisement" of literature; and to serve as a catalyst for cooperation between public schools and public libraries. Iles argued that this new headquarters should be near a "great library," and might sponsor a library school.

A million dollars would provide a suitable site, building and equipment, and would leave for endowment a sum which would greatly lift the efficiency of our libraries as a whole, and add incalculably to the good that the printed word would do in America and the world. The man or men to give this large gift would undoubtedly assure its success by adopting a constitution so wise, and by appointing trustees of such ability and character, as to shed new lustre on the work and aims of us all.

The appeal to Carnegie, although not overt, was unmistakable. Subsequent discussion of Iles's paper demonstrated general agreement. E. C. Richardson suggested that as a temporary solution ALA should hire a permanent secretary to work with the publishing board out of the board's Boston offices. Just as soon as possible, however, headquarters should be moved to a "practical central point," preferably either New York or Washington. Putnam said that although he wanted LC to extend services, locating ALA headquarters within LC walls would overextend them.

Fletcher finished the session with a brief outline of publishing board plans. The board intended to concentrate on annotated bibliographies, perhaps "through the issue of a serial publication." The board also wished to publish the recommended list of children's books being prepared by the children's librarians section, and to consider extending "appraisal" work and enlarging the *ALA Index*. At a subsequent session the ALA secretary announced results of the election: for president, Herbert Putnam; first vice president, E. C. Richardson; second vice president, Mary W. Plummer; secretary, J. I. Wyer; treasurer, Gardner M. Jones; and recorder, Helen Haines. New ALA council members included Thwaites, Canfield, Countryman, Dudley and Little. Program planners had also provided time for meetings of the college and reference, the catalog, trustees, and children's librarians sections. In its first meeting ever the state library commission section focused upon the traveling or "home" libraries whose value Billings had questioned at the previous conference.

The executive board met twice during the conference, but accomplished little more than completing committee appointments. For the first time, board members felt the impact of a new constitution which assigned them less responsibility than the previous document. The council, on the other hand, was much busier. During five meetings council members addressed a variety of important issues. The first involved a decision on a bylaw outlining methods of nominating its own members.

The executive officers of the Association, i.e., the president, secretary, treasurer and recorder, shall be chosen solely with reference to their ability and willingness to serve the Association, without regard to residence or previous service, except as hereinafter provided. The vice-presidents, one at least of whom shall be a woman, shall be selected from ex-members of the Council. In general, nominations to the Council shall be made with a view of having it representative of all sections of the country and of the principal classes of the libraries included in the Association.

The bylaw openly reflected the association's desire to provide all factions within ALA with a means to participate in association decisions. The motive was more subtle—to minimize the possibility that any faction would break away from the parent organization.

The council also addressed the need for a permanent headquarters, and adopted an ineffectual resolution suggesting it was "highly desirable that steps be taken to secure a national headquarters for the Association." Members then asked the executive board to appoint a committee of five "to formulate a plan for permanent headquarters . . . to estimate necessary expense, to consider means by which this expense may be met, and to report on the whole matter as soon as possible to the Council." In other action council voted that all printed matter coming from local conference planning committees be approved by the executive board, and that a committee of three be appointed to "draft a bylaw or bylaws covering the whole question of the relations of the Association to advertisers and advertising." Wellman had won his point. Council delayed action on the recommendations from Mary Plummer's committee on library training, but instructed the library administration committee to develop a system of statistics gathering which librarians could use in compiling annual reports.

Two other associations met during the conference. The National Association of State Librarians (NASL) held its sixth annual meeting on 24 and 25 June. After New Hampshire State Librarian Arthur Chase convened the meeting by lamenting "the seeming indifference of some of the southern and western librarians toward the Association," N. C. Buchanan, New Jersey State librarian, introduced a "perennially interesting subject"—the possibility of "merger of the N.A.S.L. into the A.L.A." After recounting NASL history, he reported a three-member committee's unanimous opinion that it should remain separate. Most NASL members were already ALA members, Buchanan noted, and since NASL always met during ALA conferences, the groups could actually be no closer. Merger would not necessarily benefit ALA; and it would definitely hurt the state librarians.

The Bibliographical Society of Chicago met on 22 June to consider organizing an American bibliographical society. In his presidential address, Aksel Josephson again called for an endowed institute for bibliographical research. Wilberforce Eames of New York City's Lenox Library (now a part of the New York Public Library) read the report of a committee appointed at the previous conference to draft rules and regulations for a national bibliographical society. The report carried no surprises. It called for an "American Bibliographical Association" whose organization would "be left in the hands of the Bibliographical Society of Chicago."[19] Josephson had won, despite the efforts of Billings, who had championed ALA, and Putnam, who led LC. The Niagara conference ended with another group of special interest librarians organizing outside ALA.

As the association prepared for its next conference, which was to be held in St. Louis during the Louisiana Purchase Exposition of 1904, it was led by a president with a national reputation. As chief executive of the Library of Congress, Herbert Putnam stood at the center of action, able to exert influence over ALA's cooperative activities (printed catalog cards), its publishing efforts (the ALA *Catalog*), and its quest for a permanent headquarters and a paid secretary. While Putnam had a favorable attitude towards all these efforts, he was constrained by priorities imposed upon him by Congress. Not many ALA members understood this. ALA had made definite progress on cooperation and publishing, but a permanent headquarters and paid secretary continued to elude the association. Washington certainly seemed a logical choice for both; perhaps Putnam could succeed where Hosmer had failed and convince Carnegie of the importance of ALA's needs. As a member of the Carnegie Institution board, he appeared to stand a much better chance than his predecessor.

However, certain library groups continued a variety of activities which generated a momentum all their own. In the summer of 1903 the Wisconsin Free Library Commission issued its *Supplement to the Suggestive List of Books for a Public Library*, which concentrated on physics and economics. University of Wisconsin Physics Professor C. W. Mendenhall and Economics Professor T. S. Adams had selected and annotated all the citations. A month later the Iowa Library Commission issued Anne Carroll Moore's 22-page pamphlet entitled *A List of Books Recommended for a Children's Library*. At the same time the ALA publishing board announced continued progress on the *ALA Portrait Index*, scheduled for publication in the spring of 1904 in two volumes selling for about $10. In spring, 1904, Henry E. Legler succeeded the ailing F. A. Hutchins as secretary of the Wisconsin Free Library Commission.

As the year progressed several midwestern state library commissions began steps to force more attention on their unique professional needs. On 22 August 1904 they met in Chicago "to consider the desirability of forming a national organization," and resolved to organize it at the forthcoming St. Louis ALA conference. They thought a unified organization could accomplish five things: (1) press publishers to supply more durable binding on popular books; (2) commence lists of recommended books "which can be relied upon by the small libraries that are without bibliographies or other equipment for careful book selection"; (3) print suggestions on how to organize and run small libraries; (4) provide advice and counsel on library architecture; and (5) schedule a regular forum so libraries could devote more time to small library problems than "it is possible to give under the hurried conditions of a section meeting of the A.L.A." Three days after the meeting, the Wisconsin Free Library Commission announced it had reached an agreement with the H. W. Wilson Company of Minneapolis to publish buying lists compiled by the commission. Public libraries in Wisconsin, Minnesota, and Iowa would receive free copies, but other commissions would have to purchase these lists from Wilson. In the fall Alice Tyler asked all library commissions to respond to the five points identified at the Chicago meeting, and to comment on the advisability of forming a national organization. Fourteen replied. All approved cooperation, but several were "doubtful" about the viability of "a separate organization aside from the A.L.A. Commission Section." Tyler promised to take the responses to the St. Louis conference.[20]

The Bibliographical Society of Chicago continued to move towards a national organization. In January 1904 it issued a circular and draft constitution for an American Bibliographical Society. The circular promised a rosy future. "The possibility of an international bibliographical congress at St. Louis in connection with the World's Fair makes the present time especially propitious for the formation of a society representative of American bibliography." The society did not mention cooperation with ALA. When Josephson sent a copy to Bowker, he also asked for a *Journal* subscription list to maximize circulation of the announcement. Bowker refused, saying that as "a general rule" periodicals did not give out subscription lists. The Bibliographical Society of Chicago met once more on 23 April and resolved to "wind up its affairs . . . and to terminate its existence" once the organization of a national society was completed.[21]

As Putnam prepared the association for the St. Louis conference, he experienced routine difficulties with several committees. James H. Canfield, who had succeeded Dana as chairman of the committee of cooperation with the NEA library department after the 1902 ALA conference, resigned his position in July 1903. When Putnam polled the executive board for a successor, all agreed on Dana. Dana accepted Putnam's invitation to succeed Canfield, but also remarked, "I have long thought that the ALA needed to put more money and thought than they ever have into two things—the increase of its membership and the bringing of the units of that membership together by more cooperative work."[22]

A second group which caused Putnam problems was the committee on relations of libraries to the book trade. Wellman refused to serve on the committee because he thought ALA ought to refuse membership to anyone interested in purely commercial ventures. His attitude may have been fairly representative because Putnam had great difficulty filling committee slots. Wright refused because he was too distant, but he did recommend either Hill, Steiner, or Dana instead, even though the latter "has made some enemies by his outspoken position." Gardner Jones agreed, but Helen Haines thought Dana should definitely be on the committee because it "would please the more radical people." Putnam finally settled on Steiner and Dana, with Bostwick as chairman.

To assist the committee in fulfilling its duties, Bostwick subsequently requested a copy of LJ's subscription list from Bowker. He also asked if LJ would print committee reports critical of *Publisher's Weekly*, LJ's sister publication. Bowker reassured Bostwick that LJ "represents the library interests only." The periodical agreed to print Bostwick's reports verbatim. Nonetheless, Bowker would not give the committee a copy of LJ's subscription list. When Bostwick argued that Bowker's stance "was practically a refusal to allow the American Library Association access to the records of its own official organ," the publisher responded tartly that "the Journal is not subsidized by the Association, and does service rather than receive support." Only after continued pressure did Bowker agree to address and mail committee reports direct from LJ offices. But he continued to refuse any requests for an LJ subscription list.[23] Bowker apparently wanted it both ways; while he wished the *Journal* to benefit from association with ALA and status as official ALA organ, he also wanted the periodical to maintain some distance for the sake of objectivity. Several members began to feel the distance more than the association.

A third group which met mixed success was the ALA permanent headquarters committee. It was probably no coincidence that Putnam asked John Shaw Billings to serve as chairman, since Billings's ties to Carnegie money were so direct. On July 1 Billings outlined five questions the committee needed to address: determine (1) what a new headquarters should provide; (2) where it should be located; (3) how much it would cost to construct and equip; (4) what the annual cost of maintenance would be; and (5) by which means these costs should be met. He then gave his own answers. Headquarters should provide office space for the ALA secretary and the publishing board, and a room for architectural plans and illustrations of library buildings. He did not think headquarters should include a room for the collection of bibliographical aids, however. The association first had to decide if it wanted to maintain a model library. Billings insisted that headquarters be located in either Washington or New York. He favored the latter, but advised against housing it in a large library. He also estimated the cost of construction and equipment somewhere between $120,000 and $300,000, and the annual maintenance cost at $25,000. A $1,000,000 donation would provide and equip the building, and leave enough money in a permanent fund to yield sufficient interest to maintain and staff it. "How to get the means?—Ask for them," he concluded.

Putnam had also asked Anderson, Andrews and Bowker to serve on the headquarters committee. Since Andrews was the only member located west of the Appalachians, chances for discussion of locating headquarters anywhere outside the East were effectively minimized. Bowker quickly agreed to join the committee, but indicated he would "be rather a conservative" and suggested Dewey as a proper balance. Bowker agreed with most of Billings's suggestions, but elaborated on funding. "There seems to be only two ways: Private endowment in whole or in part; Congressional appropriation in part." Putnam responded that several people were adamant that Dewey should not serve on the committee. Nonetheless, he said, "I wish to make sure that this is on record that [Dewey] has been fully consulted." Bowker agreed, and proposed an ingenious method for making Dewey's ideas public. He offered ten pages of LJ's November issue for a symposium on "A National Headquarters for the Library Association:

Some Suggestions and Opinions,'' and invited seven people to contribute. Naturally, Dewey led the response symposium. He recited the benefits of locating ALA headquarters in New York, between the national library in Washington, and the Library Bureau headquarters in Boston. Iles, Bostwick, Thomson, Plummer, Wellman, and A. H. Hopkins also contributed, and all agreed that New York would be the best location. No symposium contributor came from a library west of Pittsburgh.[24]

The permanent headquarters committee met in New York on 25 November. Only Anderson was absent. Bowker argued that the permanent headquarters site should never become a permanent conference site. His colleagues agreed unanimously. They also agreed on the advantages of a central organization, but cautioned that ''an injudicious choice of a permanent secretary might injure the Association.'' Committee members compromised on other issues, however. A permanent ALA headquarters should provide eight services: (1) concentrate all ALA administrative work; (2) collect library plans and architectural drawings; (3) maintain a professional library collection; (4) extend publishing board work to prepare more ''library aids''; (5) furnish expert advice on library matters; (6) provide a placement service for librarians; (7) serve as a duplicate exchange clearinghouse (lists only); and (8) facilitate interlibrary loan through clerical assistance. Permanent headquarters should be located in New York, or in Washington ''if the Association is to be dependent upon governmental aid.'' It should not sponsor an ALA library school, certify or examine candidates for library positions, or provide meeting facilities for local library associations. Annual cost would be $50,000, while a suitable building and site was estimated at $250,000. A ''comparatively permanent secretary'' would have chief administrative control; an assistant secretary would perform routine clerical work.

After finishing its work the committee decided that minutes of the meeting should not be released in order to augment its chances of winning funds for ALA headquarters. Committee members then asked Putnam to take a copy of their confidential recommendations directly to Carnegie. Putnam reluctantly agreed. Unfortunately, he was no more successful than Hosmer. Although Carnegie expressed interest in the scheme, and admitted its benefits to the national library community, he did not invite Putnam to make a formal request for funds. Rejected, Putnam asked that the interview, like the recommendations he had carried to Carnegie, be kept ''confidential.'' The committee honored his request. When Billings later reported to council, he said that the headquarters committee had not yet considered ''how to raise the necessary funds to carry out the general scheme.''[25] Except for a set of plans, then, ALA was no closer to establishing a permanent headquarters and funding a paid executive than it had been in 1881, when Henry Homes first suggested it.

Dewey was noticeably absent from efforts to secure a permanent headquarters, perhaps because he was deeply involved in getting the new edition of the ALA *Catalog* published before the St. Louis conference in October 1904. Because the Library of Congress would publish it for ALA, Putnam also became involved.

On l0 July 1903, he ordered W. Dawson Johnston to represent LC "in aid of the general editorship of the publication." Knowing how Dewey often misinterpreted orders to his own advantage, Putnam was very precise with Johnston. Avoid using "a standard, test, or method so highly scientific as to overlook the function of the List as a list for small libraries," he told his subordinate, and reject "questions of prerogative which may delay or complicate the work." The final source of authority, Putnam argued, should be the ALA publishing board.

Johnston contacted Dewey four days later, indicated that Putnam wanted all material ready for press by 1 November, and asked Dewey to assemble a corps of experts who would select and describe the titles included. On 16 July C. H. Hastings told Johnston that *Catalog* entries ought to be alphabetized by main entry and then numbered consecutively. This would facilitate the library's obligation to provide printed catalog cards for each entry. Next day Lane told Johnston he feared a "weakness" in the scheme lay in "not having anyone in its own (Publishing Board) employ who could act as a general editor." This forced the board to rely on Dewey to do most of the work at Albany. On 17 July Dewey welcomed Johnston to the project and offered to add his name on the ALA *Catalog* title page as associate editor.[26] It appeared the project was off to a harmonious start. Not for long, however.

On 17 August, May Seymour, Dewey's assistant at Albany, told Johnston not to contact Cutter for advice about the arrangement of the *Catalog* until he heard from Putnam. On 9 September Putnam finally noticed that in an August letter Dewey had written of the classification scheme for the *Catalog* "as if settled." Putnam sensed trouble. He told Johnston sharply that the *Catalog* arrangement would not be determined "until passed on by the Publishing Board." On 29 September Johnston received a harsh lesson in Dewey persistence. The first two lines of a multipage letter were characteristically soft: "I am delighted to hear you say that you feel more optimistic about the catalog every day" and "I am sorry you could not have enjoyed the superb Library week. The weather was perfect." Then came harsh reality. "Your unfamiliarity with the previous history of the ALA Catalog has led you into an impossible position. I will try to get you straight on this matter." Dewey then recounted the development of the ALA *Catalog*. Since Johnston could not dispute Dewey's interpretation of the *Catalog*'s 25-year history, the New York State librarian was free to select any "tradition" he wished to reinforce his point of view.

Dewey especially emphasized *Catalog* arrangement. Johnston wanted to follow Hastings's advice, but Dewey was adamantly opposed. Because the New York State Board of Regents had already invested so much time and energy, he argued, the *Catalog* had to be "a class list and in DC order. . . . it is now too late to discuss radical changes for the edition." Johnston's response was terse. "We have forwarded your letter to the Librarian," he wrote. "If you desire to make an exhibit of the DC system, we shall be glad to do so, so far as expedient. This question the representatives of the Association, of whom you are one, will discuss and determine."[27]

Dewey then broadened his campaign. He complained to publishing board chairman Fletcher that Johnston was changing the rules in the middle of the game. Fletcher replied quickly, "So far as I can learn we of the Board are with you in your main contention of the matter." Reassured of his position, Dewey wrote Johnston that "no trifling with the matter will be tolerated. . . . I can rely on [the ALA Publishing Board] to stand loyally by me."

On 8 November Dewey wrote Putnam. He praised Johnston for cordiality, but informed Putnam he would not compromise. "As planned for years, the *Catalog* will be in DC order." Putnam had to acquiesce. He could not fight Dewey without support from the ALA publishing board, and since LC was committed to publishing the *Catalog* for ALA, he could not retreat. He neutralized the situation by proposing to relieve Johnston of any connection with the ALA *Catalog*, and by asking Dewey if Theresa West Elmendorf would be acceptable as a part-time replacement. She would serve as a liaison between the publishing board and the library, which would pay for her services. Dewey readily agreed, and Elmendorf willingly accepted Putnam's invitation. Johnston was out. Lane tried to console him by saying the publishing board thought his "Book-Notes" idea was good; "we ought to be able to think seriously of it by next fall."[28] The issue of *Catalog* arrangement had been resolved.

Lane's note to Johnston about a bibliographical periodical reflected an emerging consensus. At a joint meeting of the Pennsylvania Library Club and the New Jersey Library Association in March 1904, Fletcher outlined the work that the publishing board contemplated for the future. Among several possible projects he mentioned a bibliographical periodical. Dana, who had recently become director of the Newark Public Library, said that if the periodical also included ALA conference proceedings, it could become an ALA membership recruitment device and reach a wider audience than *Library Journal* and *Public Libraries*. It could also double as ALA's official journal. Dana did not think the bibliographical function could be absorbed into the *Library Journal* because it "was too strongly tinged with commercialism." Bowker reacted immediately. He said the new periodical would be too costly to produce, and he pleaded "not guilty" to Dana's charge of commercialism. *Public Libraries* protested a month later. "One cannot help wondering in reading the report of the discussion and the figures and statements made, if those making them know that there really is anything west of the Alleghenies. Even Mr. Dana seems to forget." Bowker suppressed his feelings and bowed to the inevitable. On 13 June he wrote Fletcher that the publishing board could use *Journal* office facilities free of charge "or at less cost than any other plan would involve" to publish a critical bibliographical periodical. But Fletcher had already modified his position.

I think we shall find it worthwhile to issue for the Publishing Board something in the way of an "appraisal of literature" applied to new books, in periodical form, and in so doing we are likely to add some other features, but all directly connected with the Board's work, and it would be my idea to turn over to the LJ and Public Libraries whatever periodical would care to take—I mean whatever feature might be suggested.[29]

Fletcher never mentioned Johnston's name.

While plans for a bibliographical periodical stagnated, a new dispute concerning the ALA *Catalog* materialized. On 31 March 1904 Dewey informed Putnam that "things are going on without your full knowledge in the direction of crippling the DC and booming the EC [Expansive Classification]" in the ALA *Catalog*. Putnam was piqued. Several days later, the publishing board voted to drop one index in the ALA *Catalog* which was to be arranged by DC. Dewey complained bitterly. He protested any implication the *Catalog* would promote the DC and he accused the board of late arrival in a project he had been working on for over 25 years. Since his staff was preparing the *Catalog* and the Library of Congress was publishing it, he did not see why the publishing board had any authority to determine its contents. "We want a dictionary catalog and a DC Catalog because most libraries use one or the other. It is no expression as to their merits, but a mere adoption of what is most used." By now Putnam had realized Dewey had not been open with all parties. He queried the publishing board whether the DC should be used in the ALA *Catalog* at all. When Dewey learned of Putnam's inquiry, he argued that most libraries used DC; the scheme was "natural" for the ALA *Catalog*.[30]

A second issue caused a minor skirmish. When Dewey drafted a title page for the *Catalog*, he identified the work as "Prepared by the New York State Library and the Library of Congress," but "under the auspices" of the ALA publishing board. Again, Putnam was suspicious. He sent a copy of the title page to Fletcher and asked if "it represents the decision and approval of the Publishing Board." Fletcher responded that the title page should read "under the direction of." In addition, the publishing board wanted a one-volume dictionary catalog. Wellman and Lane did not want it arranged by DC because they thought it tantamount to endorsing a particular classification scheme.

Dewey's response was equally quick. He had been working on the project for 27 years, he said. The New York State Board of Regents and the state library had invested countless hours and much money in the project. Just because the ALA publishing board contributed $1,200, and expended another $300 it had received from the Library of Congress for Elmendorf's services, the project was not "under the direction" of the board. Dewey said he was willing to be conciliatory, but pleaded for fairness. If Fletcher persisted, Dewey indicated the board of regents might entertain a request to return the $1,500 and publish the *Catalog* itself. In a second letter written later in the day he was more conciliatory with Putnam. He was willing to divide the *Catalog* into two parts, a DC list and a dictionary catalog. "The class list will have titles, notes and a subject index that will answer most purposes, and those who wish to determine about individual books will have to consult the dictionary catalog." He hoped the concession would satisfy "all concerned and that we may go through without losing more time in discussing proposed changes from the plan agreed on and which we have thought finally settled four or five times.[31]

Fletcher was disappointed with Dewey's attitude. ''The Publishing Board has been going on the assumption it had entire jurisdiction, by a majority vote, over the ALA *Catalog*,'' he wrote Putnam on May 24. ''Your communications . . . indicated that you had the same idea. Now Mr. Dewey claims for himself practically the ownership of the entire project and a right to direct as to its form, etc.'' Although Fletcher proposed a meeting with Dewey, Lane, and Wellman to resolve the problem and to avoid further delays, Dewey wrote board members that he would not compromise beyond the concession he had outlined to Putnam. Ultimately the board was forced to acquiesce if it wanted the *Catalog* published at all.[32] Dewey won, but it was a Pyrrhic victory. In order to save the DC he had used arguments and tactics similar to his justification for mixing ALA and Readers and Writers Economy Company funds in 1880, for using the Library Bureau to start a rival publication to LJ in 1896, and for manipulating the election of Winsor's successor as ALA president in 1897. In the process Dewey had alienated the members of the ALA publishing board and the Librarian of Congress. He had also unjustifiably manipulated one of Putnam's subordinates. Putnam, Lane, Fletcher, Wellman and Johnston had experienced the same Dewey intransigence that Winsor, Bowker and Poole had witnessed decades before. After 1904 they all became much more cautious of the New York State librarian.

By the time Dewey had won his way with the *Catalog*, plans for the St. Louis conference were almost complete. The executive board had decided at its 26 January meeting that the program would provide for only one general session per day, and only brief business meetings for each section. All papers were to address ''the present status of libraries and library work in this country,'' and deemphasize the practical approach so evident in the 1893 Chicago conference. The new edition of the *Catalog* seemed certain, and towards the end of the summer Fletcher appeared more optimistic about starting a bibliographical periodical. He asked Bowker to provide a prospectus, and wrote Johnston on 29 September, ''Just now I am in correspondence with one whom we hope to secure as editor.''[33] He did not elaborate.

Still, ALA leaders would have one more issue to consider. In February Dewey wrote Putnam ''I grow more and more impatient . . . that a very small minority of the ALA doubt the wisdom of increasing its membership and talk about getting unwieldy.'' He thought a natural solution was a ''library century, league or academy, strictly limited to 100 to do the work of a smaller body.'' He promised to bring the idea before the ALA council in St. Louis.[34]

The activity between the Niagara and St. Louis conferences had been busy, controversial, and taxing. No one knew that better than ALA President Herbert Putnam, who welcomed 577 registrants when he opened the conference on 17 October 1904; 284 came from Great Lakes states, 130 came from North Atlantic states; 392 attendees were women. Thirty foreign librarians from 16 different countries also registered. All wore white identification buttons. Although many disliked the badges, the *Library Journal* reported, "they seem to have been accepted as a necessary evil." By Putnam's direction, the conference was structured "to give an adequate record of things recently accomplished." Papers addressed state-of-the-art reviews of various areas of librarianship. Putnam scheduled six general sessions on successive mornings to enable conferees to enjoy the St. Louis exposition during the afternoons and evenings.

For his presidential address Putnam took a sweeping international look at the progress the profession had made over recent years. Secretary Wyer reported that the association had approximately 1,400 members. Although establishing a permanent headquarters and a paid secretary would undoubtedly accelerate growth, Wyer cautioned that results "will not be startling." Treasurer Jones reported a balance of $1,920.06, and Charles Soule noted that interest on the endowment fund had generated $5,700 for the publishing board, and $1,150 for general purposes.

Putnam assigned most ALA committees to report at the second general session. Among others, the library administration committee identified a schedule of statistics common to most libraries, and J. L. Harrison noted in his report on gifts and bequests that Carnegie's annual donations had dropped to $970,100 during the past year. The philanthropist was clearly donating less money for library purposes. Fletcher reported for the publishing board that the new ALA *Catalog* was in two parts "for greater convenience: the first part containing the classified and annotated list, the second the dictionary catalog of the same books." Fletcher also noted progress on the *Portrait Index*, and indicated the board would soon publish a recommended list of children's books prepared by the children's librarians section. Finally, he cited the need for "a periodical issue of selected and annotated titles of new books, prompt enough to be of service in the selection of books for purchase," and said that the board was considering an arrangement with Bowker and LJ to issue a purchase list "in combination with a monthly index to leading periodicals." Hopefully, annotations could be added subsequently.

At the fifth session Fletcher recounted the "annotation" movement, and concluded the association ought to proceed in four directions: (1) a list of books with descriptive annotations; (2) introductory essays to these lists which summarized the literature on the subject; (3) a bibliographical periodical "especially for the benefit of the smaller libraries" which would identify the best new books; and (4) a series of subject catalog cards which would identify the best books on a particular subject. He noted that Iles's scheme always "had in view the supplementing of the resources for judging books of even the largest and best supplied library." His suggestions, however, had "been directed rather to doing for the numerous small popular libraries what the larger libraries habitually do for themselves."

Although Mary S. Cutler Fairchild's paper on "Women in Libraries" was noted, but not read, at the final session, it still merits careful summary. At its beginning she said "there is practically no discrimination with regard to sex in the American Library Association," and attributed this to "the broadminded attitude of the men who have been leaders in the library movement from 1876 to the present day.'' She reported that 19 of the 21 largest libraries were directed by men, all of whom were paid between $3,000 and $7,000. The highest salary paid a woman was $2,100. She concluded weakly that because of ''natural sex limitations, and also actual weakness in the work of many women as well as because of conservatism and prejudice, many gates are at present closed to women.'' She generally ignored the sexism rife in the profession and society as a whole at the turn of the century.

Conferees spent considerably more time discussing the revision of cataloging rules by the United Kingdom's Library Association. Wyer then announced the election of new officers: E. C. Richardson as president; William E. Foster as first vice president; Theresa West Elmendorf as second vice president; Wyer as secretary; Jones as treasurer, and Haines as recorder. New council members included William Henry, A. H. Hopkins, J. C. Rowell, Anne Wallace and Hiller Wellman. Thereafter the conference adjourned.

Although Putnam determined that sections should not hold substantive meetings during the St. Louis conference, the state library commission section had other ideas. Based upon the successes of the 12 August 1903 Chicago meeting of the Wisconsin, Minnesota, and Iowa library commissions, and upon a survey compiled by a committee between that meeting and the St. Louis conference, Alice Tyler urged that the library commissions form a new organization to facilitate cooperation and minimize duplication of effort. She made three recommendations she considered to be essential to the organization's success: (1) a representative board consisting of one member from each cooperating library commission which would select an editor for bibliographic lists; (2) financial guarantees from each cooperating commission; and (3) a bimonthly buying list for recent books, a new handbook of library organization, and a manual describing the work and methods of the cooperating library commissions. She made no mention of Fletcher's report on the prospect of a bibliographical periodical. Section members then enjoyed a ''spirited discussion on ways and means for cooperative work,'' and thereafter voted to establish a League of Library Commissions to be ''affiliated'' with ALA. Melvil Dewey became president; Lutie Stearns, secretary. Members present also voted to continue the state library commissions section within the association.

The Bibliographical Society of America held its first annual meeting on 18 October, and elected William C. Lane president. Members present approved a constitution which cited the association's mission—''to promote bibliographical research and to issue bibliographical publications.'' In a subsequent discussion Lane noted that publications in ''certain bibliographical fields are already provided for.'' The Carnegie Institution had revived the *Index Medicus*, the ALA publishing board had issued various bibliographical aids, and certain professional societies had issued subject bibliographies. ''There is one field that remains open,'' he suggested; ''a bibliographical periodical is possible.'' The society also voted to continue preparing and circulating printed catalog cards for bibliographical series, and for the time being decided to meet annually with ALA. The new organization was off to an inauspicious beginning. Members sensed a need to organize to a common purpose, but were still unsure exactly what that purpose was.

The National Association of State Librarians held two uneasy meetings during the St. Louis conference. After NASL President Johnson Brigham pointed out the association had no money in its treasury, Dewey suggested "the time had come for some change to be made in the name, and also that it would be better to become a section of A.L.A." At a second meeting he was more explicit. "I have always felt that it was unwise to multiply associations." He did not mention that in two days he would become president of another new association, just one more in a long lineup which included NASL, the New York Library Club, and the New York Library Association. Others agreed, however hypocritical Dewey's own example really was. Members voted a name change to the National Association of State Libraries and requested that ALA council "substitute in its several publications the name 'National Association of State Libraries' for said State Librarians' Section." State librarians were now back under the ALA umbrella.

The executive board met only once during the conference to vote the continuation of section officers and to make new committee appointments. The council met three times. After approving the slate of nominees and deciding to hold the next national conference in Portland, Oregon, council members heard the report of the committee on permanent headquarters. They appointed a standing committee of five to consider the question further, and a parallel committee consisting of the publishing board chairman, the ALA secretary and three ALA ex-secretaries to consider hiring a permanent secretary who would work out of publishing board offices. When Dewey introduced his idea for an ALA academy, the council delayed action by appointing another committee of five to report at the next meeting.[35]

Like the 1893 Chicago conference, the 1904 St. Louis conference was a watershed in ALA history. It passively observed the birth of a League of Library Commissions which was dominated by midwesterners dedicated to the cause of small, rural libraries. It also witnessed the first annual meeting of the Bibliographical Society of America, which effectively diverted the interests of bibliographic scholars away from ALA. The association also committed itself to establishing a permanent headquarters with a paid executive just as soon as financially feasible, and adopted an organizational structure to support the move. Dewey got his way on the ALA *Catalog*, but paid a high price for his victory by losing the goodwill of Herbert Putnam and the ALA publishing board. His star continued to descend on the ALA horizon. Finally, most ALA leaders agreed that the profession needed a bibliographical periodical, but no one seemed sure how to get one. The coming year promised to be interesting.

Four days after the conference adjourned Johnson Brigham wrote Henry Legler, "Well, we shook them up pretty thoroughly at the SLC [state library commission] conference! Dewey said to me afterwards, 'You people are all right; and our Publishing Board is all wrong—too slow—too self-centered.' " The League of Library Commissions had definite ideas about a publishing program to serve its needs. If the ALA publishing board would not help, the league was prepared to move forward on its own. Legler wrote Brigham on 25 October, "We did shake them up a bit, but a little storm of that kind usually clarifies the atmosphere. I fear that the eastern people, with some notable exceptions, do not enter very heartily into the hustling spirit of the middlewest." He reminded Brigham the league had authorized appointment of a subcommittee to draft a plan on cooperative publications, and that as a member of that committee he would "negotiate" with the publishing board. "But if they fail to give satisfactory assurances of prompt work, the committee will undoubtedly proceed along independent lines." [36] The gauntlet was thrown down.

On 27 October Legler wrote publishing board secretary Lane. After saying he welcomed an opportunity to work with the board, he informed Lane that "the bi-monthly buying list of current books constitutes the immediate and urgent need of the Free Library Commissions." The small libraries whose interests the commissions served needed recommended lists to make best use of limited funds. "Promptness of publication would be the essential consideration. Frankly, the impression prevails that the machinery of the Publishing Board does not permit expeditious work." The utility of the bibliographical periodical would be enhanced by the addition of annotations, but the commissions considered speed of publication more important. Legler asked Lane if the board wished to undertake the project for the commissions.

Lane liked the idea. He sent a copy of Legler's letter to board chairman Fletcher of 31 October and wrote that "this is just the opportunity we have been waiting for." Guaranteed subscriptions by library commissions made the proposal more attractive than Bowker's and opened new possibilities for the annotative work "we have wanted to issue." To Legler he wrote, "The Publishing Board has long wanted to issue a periodical containing titles of select books with annotations, and I do not see why this should not be usefully combined with the buying lists such as the Wisconsin Commission has been issuing heretofore." He assured Legler that promptness was no problem. Fletcher wrote a similar note, but he was more defensive. Hurt that Legler had accused the board of slowness, he asked board treasurer Soule if this reflected a general impression throughout the association. Soule reassured him that it was not, but suggested a meeting at the coming ALA conference to discuss it. "Most criticisms could undoubtedly be explained in the course of an hour's general rough and tumble discussion in full meeting of the Association." Until then, Soule counseled patience. [37]

Legler moved quickly. He told several league members of his "preliminary correspondence" with the publishing board, and wrote Fletcher that the "cordial tone" of Lane's and Fletcher's letters "is a source of much satisfaction to the membership of the commission." Since the league's executive committee would

meet in Chicago on 28 November, he asked Fletcher for a more "definite
proposition" which the committee could discuss. The league wanted to know
what "price per hundred" the board would charge for subscriptions. In the past
the Wisconsin Free Library Commission had prepared book lists under Oregon
Public Library Commissioner Cornelia Marvin's direction and with the help of
University of Wisconsin faculty members. If the publishing board assumed control of publication, Wisconsin wished to withdraw from any responsibility for
preparation. Other commissions shared these sentiments. Legler concluded by
reemphasizing a point midwestern library commissions returned to repeatedly:
" . . . the great value of these lists lies in their availability for the small libraries,
and that with the Commissions in the middlewest this term embraces libraries
having from 500 to 1500 volumes." The propensity to reiterate this point to the
New England-dominated ALA publishing board suggests that midwestern library
commissioners were skeptical the board accurately understood their needs.[38]

On November 16 Dewey informed Bowker that the publishing board had
decided "to start the buying list." He said he had "fought hard to keep the
commissions from starting an organ of their own out west" because he wanted
ALA to control the publication. He hoped commissions would guarantee 80
percent of the cost of production. The board would pick up the remaining 20
percent from the Carnegie fund, but in order to minimize costs he suggested that
the board accept Bowker's offer to use LJ facilities. Bowker reiterated his offer,
but misinterpreted the purpose of the bibliographical periodical. He thought the
board wanted only monthly lists of recommended books which would eventually
cumulate into a new edition of the ALA *Catalog*, and carry the lists in a periodical
index he wanted to publish. Neither Dewey nor Fletcher bothered to correct
Bowker's impression.[39]

When the league's executive board met in Chicago on 28 November, members
mentioned only the joint efforts with the publishing board to publish a "cooperative issue . . . of selective buying lists." They made no mention of Bowker's
plan on the ALA *Catalog*; they may also have been unaware that Dewey and
Fletcher were planning to use *Library Journal* offices. The board also passed a
series of resolutions, one of which directed the ALA publishing board to secure
an editor for the buying lists who was "acceptable to the League." At first
Fletcher was upset that the resolutions "seem somewhat dictatorial," but he did
not press the issue. Instead, he indicated the publishing board wanted Theresa
West Elmendorf, former Milwaukee public librarian, as editor. League members
were delighted with his choice, but when Fletcher contacted Elmendorf she
declined because of her husband's poor health. To replace her, Fletcher named
Caroline Garland, director of the Dover (New Hampshire) Public Library.

Legler immediately protested that the selection had been made without consulting the league. Fletcher became perplexed. Although he retained Garland as
editor he complained to Dewey that the league viewed the publishing board as
"not much more than a printing agency for them." He could not understand
why league members "regard us as recalcitrant." Perhaps they had not realized

the bibliographical periodical "is something of our own in which they come in ... as supporters and patrons." League members decided to withhold support of the buying list periodical, which was two weeks away from publishing its first issue, until they could discuss it with the publishing board at the Portland conference. The two groups could not work together harmoniously; their relationship quickly deteriorated because of diverse interests. To demonstrate its own authority the publishing board reserved the right to name the new periodical. Some wanted "Cooperative Book Lists," others "Public Librarian Monthly," but Nina Browne and Dewey suggested that "A.L.A. Booklist" was more descriptively accurate.

Up to mid-February Bowker continued to believe that the publishing board wanted to marry the league's need for a periodical buying list with his own desire to issue a periodical index. He anticipated the move by dropping the "Literary Index" section from *Journal* pages. This also enabled him to reduce LJ's subscription price by 20 percent to counter criticisms that the periodical was too expensive for smaller libraries. But on 20 February, after he heard of the forthcoming ALA *Booklist*, he asked Fletcher if the board "changed its plans." Fletcher admitted to Bowker: "I'm put in a somewhat embarrassing position." On the one hand, the league had specific intentions for a booklist which the publishing board felt compelled to honor. He did not mention league control of subscriptions. On the other hand, Fletcher had not discouraged Bowker's plans for a joint periodical index/buying list. Fletcher saw no resolution to the problem except two separate publications.

Bowker was understandably upset. While the publishing board had made no formal commitment, he felt betrayed by eleventh-hour arrangements which ignored his interests. Despite his feelings, however, he gave *Booklist* a favorable review in LJ and welcomed its arrival in an editorial. *Public Libraries* was not so kind when Bowker's own *Library Index* appeared without a section evaluating new books. "Whence came the call for another index devoted to periodical literature?" its editor asked.[40] By this time Bowker probably had misgivings about fair play by midwestern library interests.

The *Booklist* issued its first number in February 1905. For individuals, subscriptions were $0.50 for eight issues per year; for state library commissions, the price was $2 per 100 copies for each number. As expected, the league committee which Legler chaired screened it very carefully. Within a week he responded. "We are very much pleased with the general form and appearance of the publication," but "disappointed ... in some particulars." First, he complained that 27 titles had already appeared in a recent list issued by the Wisconsin, Iowa, Minnesota and Indiana library commissions. Legler thought the duplication wasted librarians' time. Second, *Booklist* editors did not "grade" the selections. Because many of the selections were "too expensive" or of "limited interest" to small libraries with meager book budgets, the lack of a discriminating grading system prevented these libraries "from using the list as a guide in their purchases." Third, although the list arrived in mid-February, it included no selections published after Christmas. "Would it not be possible to include the latest books in this list?"

Although Legler concluded his letter by saying "we trust you will accept our criticism in the same friendly spirit which prompts it," his message was clear. The league had specific objectives for a buying list which it insisted the publishing board fulfill. If the board would not comply, state library commissions would cancel subscriptions. Fletcher was forced to be diplomatic. He thanked Legler for the cordial welcome the *Booklist* had received, and then addressed Legler's specific complaints. Duplication occurred because the "western commissions" had issued a December buying list too late for *Booklist* to make corrections. Because of "delays incident to the beginning of a new publication," the editors were not as prompt as they would be in the future. Finally, Lane and Browne thought the annotations made a grading system unnecessary. Lane especially "didn't see how it could be satisfactorily done." Fletcher promised Legler he would "look into it further with a view to a possible change in this respect."

Although the two men feigned cordiality, the tone of both letters was ice cold and businesslike. Dewey wrote Fletcher a month later that he was worried. "We must handle those western commission people carefully or we shall have a rival publishing board at full blast soon." The Portland conference was crucial. "I favor giving power to such of our board as go to close arrangements and keep them in line." Lane was so worried that he wanted the board to pay Browne's travel expenses to Portland, "since much depends upon our getting into good personal relations with the western commissions." Both Dewey and Lane had reason to worry. In June, just one month before the conference, the league issued a 58-page pamphlet entitled *Suggestive List of Books for a Small Library*. Cornelia Marvin had compiled this list of 1,200 titles, arranged it by DC, and included ordering information and an LC catalog card number.[41]

Although *Booklist* got off to a shaky beginning, the new edition of the ALA *Catalog* was a smashing success. By 1 January 1905, 20,000 copies had been distributed and a second printing ordered. Bowker was especially pleased that the bibliography "meant a great deal for the development of the usefulness of the smaller libraries." Progress on the *Portrait Index* did not go as well. In order to get the manuscript published at all, Putnam offered to issue it under an LC imprint. The league showed little interest in sponsoring such publications.[42]

Dewey charged ahead with his "library academy" scheme. He admonished peers to sell the idea to colleagues because "it can do no harm and may do large good." At an ALA council meeting on 1 April, he convinced the council to consider the matter and have him report at Portland. The *Library Journal* objected to his project. An editorial said it would create a separate body independent of the association which would eventually usurp some of its powers. In addition, it would tend to retain older members and retard the recruitment of new, countering the welcome trend which the ALA constitution inaugurated by making council members ineligible to succeed themselves. A better move, the *Journal* advised, would be to extend more power to the executive board and allow council more time "for the promulgation of library wisdom. . . . The library profession is, to our minds, facing the grave danger of overorganization and too many meetings." The *Journal* also called for the National Association of State Libraries and the League of Library Commissions to reenter "into organic relation" with ALA as sections. "One national organization, with departments sufficiently independent to do their own work, is more desirable than a number of associations imperfectly geared together."[43]

While ALA members debated the merits of Dewey's scheme, the New York State librarian found himself embroiled in the stickiest controversy of his professional career. Always the entrepreneur, Dewey had purchased lakefront acreage in Lake Placid, New York, a few years after he moved to Albany in 1889. Because of chronic hay fever problems, he spent summers there, and over the next several years had acquired enough additional acreage to begin a private club. He and his wife always maintained majority stock. Librarians were frequently invited. State library aasociations met there with some frequency, and Dewey sponsored an annual "Library Week" in the fall, at which various ALA committees, sections, and boards would meet between conferences. While librarians were encouraged to come, others were not. The clubhouse and hotel on the Lake Placid grounds excluded Jews. In early 1905 several prominent New York City Jews petitioned the New York State Board of Regents to remove Dewey from state employment, but the regents balked. They could neither demand that a private club correct its anti-Semitic practices (even though it was run by a public official under their employ), nor could they argue that Dewey was devoting too much time to a private enterprise and neglecting his job. They chose an awkward compromise. They simply reprimanded Dewey, and for a short time the controversy quieted. Although the library press and many ALA members cited Dewey's professional accomplishments and successes in defending him, Dewey's reputation was permanently tarnished. Librarians became more reluctant to defer to a man who had caused the profession national embarrassment. Dewey had already alienated important librarians in his private, behind-the-scenes machinations. Now he was alienating even more through his public activities.[44]

The council and executive boards met several times between conferences. At a 1 April meeting, the board mostly conducted routine business, but council discussed heavier issues. Dewey argued the association had to grow, but it needed a "manageable body" like an ALA academy to discuss library problems. Richardson polled the council to discern whether ALA business should be conducted by a smaller body; members responded "yes" almost unanimously. The council also considered Soule's report on the possible relationship between the publishing board and ALA headquarters. Soule suggested that ALA needed a paid executive for correspondence and management of the association's business. If the council would consent to naming the publishing board office as ALA "headquarters," the board would pay part of that executive's salary. The association would have to cover the remainder. The council welcomed Soule's suggestions and followed his recommendations. Members voted to establish a headquarters at publishing board offices in Boston, and directed the executive board to appoint an assistant secretary to take charge. The new employee would be paid from the accumulated interest of the endowment fund (but not including the Carnegie money) and from the profits generated by the publishing board.[45] Everyone understood it was an experiment, a feeble beginning which would last only as long as ALA could afford it, but the association had no other alternative if it wanted a headquarters. No one seemed willing to donate the money necessary to establish it in more grandiose style. Council members hoped a full-time, salaried executive could solicit enough funds to keep headquarters alive.

On April 11 Wyer reminded Bowker that the council's action did not suggest that headquarters should always be in Boston, but was merely a step to take advantage of a temporary situation. Dewey was more excited. He wrote Fletcher that "the supreme thing now is the headquarters," and he called for the appointment of a supervisory headquarters board. ALA President Richardson was less impressed with Dewey's suggestion, but he promised to consider it when the executive board met again on 22 April. By mutual agreement the executive and the publishing boards divided responsibility equally for the assistant secretary's salary. The executive board then gave E. Clarence Hovey a temporary appointment as assistant secretary until his appointment could be confirmed at the Portland conference.

Hovey's selection was hardly spontaneous. He carried the correct credentials for a financially strapped association whose executive and publishing boards were largely centered in New England. He had joined the association as a life member in 1890 when he was a trustee of the Brookline Public Library, and he had been instrumental in establishing the ALA endowment fund. Since 1895 he had been active in private business in Boston and New York. His contacts with the philanthropic world were believed to be excellent. LJ pronounced him "a man capable of doing just what the Association needs." Surprisingly, PL echoed these sentiments, but admitted not knowing Hovey well.[46]

Hovey would have a rough baptism as ALA's first paid officer. He immediately had to struggle with complex problems between the publishing board and the League of Library Commissions. On the train to the Portland conference, league members drew up a new constitution and established a committee on publications which would "secure and prepare material to be submitted to the Publishing Board of the ALA. Such publications as this latter body is not in a position to undertake will be issued at the expense and with the imprint of the League." Nina Browne later reported to Lane, "On the train it came to light that the Commission was furious with the Board and ready to slaughter the outgoing members that they might put on two western people." She told Lane the league was extremely displeased with what it called Fletcher's uncooperative, noncommunicative manner, and felt Wellman was "no more interested in board matters than he is in those of the Council." The league especially wanted to replace Fletcher with Legler, but Browne wondered how a chairman located in Wisconsin could run an office located in Boston. "Mr. Hovey and I poured oil as best we could and we think quite successfully, though the determination still remains to make a change." Browne was understandably apprehensive about the forthcoming conference.[47]

How much of this Richardson knew when he opened the Portland conference on 4 July is uncertain. LJ noticed that "state library commissions were strongly in evidence in informal conferences." The ALA president welcomed 359 registrants, 267 of whom were women; 131 attended from Pacific states, 95 from North Central states, and 95 from North Atlantic states. Richardson quickly deferred to ALA Secretary James I. Wyer, who reported that the association now boasted 1,228 members. He also predicted that the paid assistant secretary and the establishment of a permanent headquarters promised a brighter future "somewhat similar to that enjoyed by the National Education Association." Treasurer Jones reported a balance of $1,628.17, and Wyer read Soule's report for the endowment fund trustees, which indicated the Carnegie fund had contributed $3,050 to ALA publishing board activities. Wyer then read verbatim the proceedings of the 1 April council meeting. He carefully explained that decisions made at that meeting had direct bearing on the business of the conference. No discussion followed; instead, Richardson introduced a series of committee reports.

Fletcher's report for the publishing board was especially interesting. Wyer read it in his absence. The board chairman noted "slight" progress in board activities, and cited Hovey's appointment as one manifestation. He acknowledged that although the move had already relieved elected board members of much detail work, it was still too early to judge the results of the appointment. He admitted that the board's preoccupation with the ALA *Portrait Index* had delayed other projects; only after Putnam offered to publish the work under an LC imprint could the board turn its attention and financial resources to other projects, one of which was *Booklist*. He explained very carefully that once the board had found funds for the project it became unnecessary to accept Bowker's offer to launch a similar project through *Library Journal* offices. At the time of the report he noted that *Booklist* was reaching 3,000 libraries; Massachusetts and Wisconsin had standing orders for 500 copies of every issue, Minnesota 350, Indiana, Iowa, Pennsylvania and Vermont 200, Ohio 150, Colorado, Nebraska, New York, and Washington, 100 each. John Cotton Dana's Newark Public Library also subscribed 100 copies of each issue.

Fletcher lamented that the sale of board publications was "slower than it would be if the libraries generally were fully alive to their value." He noted that Lutie Stearns had added *Essentials in Library Administration* to the tracts series, and that Theresa Hitchler was preparing another on the subject of "cataloging for small libraries." He concluded his report by addressing the relationship between the publishing board and the League of Library Commissions, and chose his words carefully. At St. Louis the previous year "there seemed to be a mutual readiness to cooperate, and considerable correspondence was had later looking to an effective co-working." Unfortunately, "we have not succeeded as yet in settling the details of our mutual relations." Finally, he noted, "the League expresses the hope that these relations may be drawn closer at the Portland conference, a hope which is earnestly shared by the Board." No discussion followed the report.

Richardson saved his presidential address on "The National Library Problem Today" for the second general session the next morning. He noted the library's dual role: to provide information to individuals who want to advance knowledge; "to tempt the multitude to read readable books." He admitted the public library was "a maker of good citizens," and understood the institution's capacity to hasten the assimilation of foreign populations, "even the assimilation of the most unlike, the Orientals." He closed by reciting the benefits and necessity of a permanent headquarters for the association, and then addressed "the burning question" of a permanent location. "Shall it be the capitol of the nation or the metropolis of the nation?" Richardson preferred the former. He mentioned no other specific possibilities.

Wyer read the report on gifts and bequests which noted that during the previous year Carnegie had donated only $725,000 for public library buildings. Wyer hinted the philanthropist might be more receptive to requests for college and university library construction in the future. Dana gave a report for the committee on bookbuying which explained the committee's regular bulletins: "We have been conducting an elementary correspondence school on book purchasing in which the object had been to teach small libraries to get books to fit their own conditions and their own constituencies." In the first six months of 1905 the committee had issued 33,000 copies of the bulletins, 11,000 of which went to libraries from a *Public Libraries* list, 12,500 of which were distributed through state library commissions.

The fourth general session demonstrated what LJ called Richardson's "sympathetic recognition of the varied interests represented at the meeting." The ALA president had scheduled the entire session for state library commissions to discuss their work and concerns. Legler drew a clear distinction between library commissions in New England and the Midwest. The former gave direct aid to libraries with little supervision. The latter laid heavy emphasis on field and instructional work, encouraging the creation of new libraries and the revitalization or reorganization of old ones. "Instructional publications, such as book lists, bulletins, circulars of information are also made important channels of usefulness." In the former, "where libraries are older . . . a collection of 5,000 volumes is a small library." In the latter, "the library of from 200 to 2,000 volumes is termed small." In the Midwest, more than half the population had no access to libraries. Finally, Legler turned to the subject of publishing. He announced that "plans have been formulated for material extension of the publishing enterprises undertaken by the League of Library Commissions." He noted the need to cooperate and systematize routine tasks to reduce expenditures, but he made no mention of cooperation with the ALA publishing board.

At the sixth general session Dewey pushed his idea for an American Library Institute. Since the council did not have enough members present to take action, Dewey asked the association itself for approval. Conferees voted to sanction an institute to consist of "100 persons chosen from English-speaking America" and stipulated that "the ex-presidents of the A.L.A. be the first members . . . with power to add to their number, to organize and adopt needed rules." Dewey was thus successful in gaining association approval for an elite body to which members would have access only by selection. Its purpose was vague, but its existence was a compliment to Dewey's persistence in the face of some opposition and much indifference. Later in the session Dewey spoke on "Unity and Co-operation in Library Work." He still hoped the association could tap Carnegie for a donation.

I should like an opportunity to prove to any millionaire that he cannot put a million dollars into any university or hospital that will be so far-reaching in its influence as it would be if given to the A.L.A. or its representation to organize a permanent headquarters that shall undertake the work that belongs to librarianship. Do you forget what librarianship means—that civilization itself is simply the accumulation of the wisdom and the experience of all the world as preserved in books, that the book is the most wonderful thing that has been evolved in all the history of the race?

Dewey's rhetoric was obviously exaggerated, but perhaps it was no coincidence that University of Michigan Library Director Theodore W. Koch followed him with a talk on the successes of "Carnegie Library Buildings." Before adjourning, conferees elected a slate of new officers which duplicated the list of nominees the council had presented at the beginning of the conference: for president, Frank P. Hill; first vice president, Clement W. Andrews; second vice president, Caroline H. Garland; treasurer, Gardner M. Jones; and recorder, Helen E. Haines. Wyer remained ALA secretary while new council members included Crunden, Linda Eastman of the Cleveland Public Library, Mary Isom of the Library Association of Portland, Oregon, W. C. Kimball of the New Jersey Library Commission, and George T. Clark of the Stanford University Library.

Each ALA section held at least one meeting, but sessions of the state library commissions section won the most attention. Legler's report for the League of Library Commissions addressed the testy relationship between the league and the ALA publishing board. He noted that cooperation with the board would relieve the league of financial responsibilities for publishing material; at the same time the league could still solicit and prepare necessary manuscripts and provide the board with an adequate financial base by subscribing to its publications in large numbers. Unfortunately, however, the two groups could not agree on a unified publishing program. *Booklist* represented their only success, and even there the league felt it should have been given "an opportunity to approve the selection of an editor." As a result of these problems, the league decided to pursue the remainder of its publication program on its own. Alice Tyler's motion that the section request council to recognize the league's authority for its own programs and interests carried unanimously. Legler then indicated the league executive committee had already decided to join the section and affiliate with ALA, if council approved.

The council met three times during the conference. At its first two meetings council members opposed locating the next conference at Asheville, North Carolina, because people from the Mid- and Far West wanted to meet "nearer the eastern centers of library interests." Members also recommended to the executive board that the "experiment" of employing Hovey as assistant secretary be tried "for a year or so long as funds shall be available." Council then prepared for the eventual "closer affiliation" with the league and NASL by adopting two constitutional amendments to be ratified at the next conference. The first provided for affiliation on approval of two-thirds of council, the second gave affiliated organizations authority to use the association to publish "so much of the program, notices, circulars and proceedings . . . as it may deem advisable." At its third meeting, members approved the recommendations from the league and state library commissions section that they merge, thereby eliminating the latter as an ALA section.

The executive board met twice during the conference for routine business. They voted to allow NASL proceedings to become part of the ALA conference proceedings, to affiliate with the League of Library Commissions, and to abolish the state library commission section. Finally, they directed Assistant Secretary Hovey to prepare a circular to solicit new ALA members. After the conference adjourned, the board met twice more on the postconference trip. At their first meeting they directed ALA ex-presidents to draft a constitution and define an organization for ALI. At the second meeting they filled vacant appointments. The two vacancies on the ALA publishing board went to Henry Legler and the director of Cleveland's Western Reserve Library School, Electra C. Doren. The "westerners" had finally penetrated the publishing board.

Three other groups met during the conference. Attendance at the Bibliographical Society of America (BSA) meeting was negligible. The society had planned to meet in Chicago when the train carrying easterners linked up with another from the Midwest, but scheduling conflicts did not permit a stop. Papers scheduled for that meeting were read by title and accepted for printing. The Pacific Coast Library Association met to hear papers on library problems unique to their section of the country, while the National Association of State Libraries held its conference in two successful, well-attended sessions. At the second session, NASL adopted a constitution which mentioned ALA only once.[48]

The 1905 conference was one of ALA's frequent missionary sojourns to awaken an interest in libraries in less developed sections of the country. Although attendance was sparse, Pacific Coast librarians used the meeting to spark regional interest in library matters. Something else occurred at the conference, however, that proved to be more important. ALA had discovered an effective way to expand its structure in order to retain groups which threatened to break away from the association. By offering to cover the publishing needs of only officially affiliated organizations, ALA retained some very influential purse power. And it was this power which kept the league close. Members of the league had come to the conference dissatisfied with the treatment the ALA publishing board accorded them; they left the conference having filled the board's only two vacancies. For the first time in its history the publishing board had members who were employed by library agencies located west of the Alleghenies.

Patterned Accommodation: 1905–1909

Shortly after returning home Legler wrote Cornelia Marvin that "ALA responded to the wishes of the western commissions by giving us representation upon the Publishing Board to the fullest extent that was possible at the time." It was now incumbent upon the league "to frankly and fully state to the Publishing Board where they have failed in the past to meet the needs of the western commissions, and how they can supply these needs at the present time." To define that statement Legler appointed Marvin, Merica Hoagland of the Indiana Library Commission and Clara Baldwin of the Minnesota Library Commission to a league publications committee. He directed them to identify "the public issues which the ALA Publishing Board should undertake as soon as practicable." While the western contingent on the publishing board maintained its assertive stance, the eastern members demonstrated more conciliation. Nina Browne wrote Lane that "Wellman was dropped simply to ease Mr. Fletcher's fall, and not make it seem so hard." Bowker wrote Fletcher he was "sorry" Fletcher had stepped down because it broke up "the geographical contiguity which we had always thought important for business-like administration." He predicted that future board work would be "very difficult to administer" and perhaps much less effective.[49] He underestimated the resolve of western library commissions.

Legler continued his aggressive stand. He asked Hoagland on 29 August "to write me fully your views as to the value of publications which the ALA Board has underway, and also your suggestions as to new publications which ought to be undertaken to meet the need of the field workers in the middle-west." He made no secret of his loyalties. "Rest assured that as far as I am concerned there will be a vigorous presentation of the claims of our commissions among the Publishing Board activities." Dewey sensed trouble and called a meeting at Lake Placid during "library week." Soule became angry because he, Lane and Browne had not been consulted. He wanted Legler and Doren to come to 10½ Beacon Street before the board was forced to make decisions about future activities. Therefore, he argued, the first board meeting should be conducted in Boston. But the decision had already been made; Legler and Doren were on their way to Lake Placid, and both were considering whether to call for Garland's dismissal as *Booklist* editor. Alice Tyler also worried. If Legler and Doren pushed too hard, relations between *Booklist* and the library commissions would inevitably deteriorate. She proposed that Garland be invited to attend conferences of midwestern state library associations at the state associations' expense. "It seems to me the connection is very evident," she told Legler.[50]

When the publishing board met on 28 September, members elected Lane chairman, Soule treasurer, and Browne secretary. They passed a resolution complimenting Fletcher on his successes as a former board chairman, and directed Lane to settle all details relative to publishing the *Portrait Index*. Members also agreed to transact board business by mail between meetings, but "in voting by correspondence two adverse votes on the resubmission of the question shall prevent action." A copy of *Booklist* would be sent free to all ALA members, as the executive board has requested. Legler then convinced the board to give priority in *Booklist* for current buying lists for small rather than large libraries, for official news and announcements of ALA committees and affiliated organizations, for special bibliographies and topic lists which could also be distributed separately, and for the bulletins of the committee on bookbuying. The board discussed the possibility of another editor, but decided to continue Garland at $75 per issue. Finally, the board agreed that tracts would be sold at cost, and that the series itself was "ready to accept and print any manuscript submitted by the League of Library Commissions by unanimous vote of its Council for inclusion in this series." The vote effectively allowed Marvin, Hoagland, and Baldwin to dictate the direction of the tracts series.

The board met again in Boston three days later. After Browne explained the board's operations and methods, members took several routine actions concerning financial reports, and decided to issue a second series of publications in the future—handbooks. They also agreed to continue the annotated lists of American and English history.

Tyler, Marvin, and Ahern were delighted with Legler's accomplishments. Tyler was "especially pleased with the approved plans for the ALA *Booklist*," and again suggested that Garland "should visit the middle west and learn from personal observation the conditions of the small libraries." Before the month was out the board had issued Tract No. 6, Lutie Stearns's *Essentials in Library Administration*, No. 7, Theresa Hitchler's *Cataloging for Small Libraries*, and No. 8, Mary A. Tarbell's *A Village Library in Massachusetts: The Story of Its Upbuilding*. ALA publishing board activities had definitely taken a new direction. John Cotton Dana was less enthused. "I appreciate the difficulty of the situation just now," he told Lane, but "it looks as though (if I may venture to suggest) the Association needs somewhere a center of gravity!"[51]

In December the league publications committee issued its first report. The committee wanted a leaflet series containing "matter . . . interesting, attractive, journalistic, something which newspapers will print willingly," a handbook series outlining basic information on library commission work, and a bookmark series with elementary information for users of small libraries. Regarding existing board publications, the committee minced no words. "So many of the libraries do not have the books included in the A.L.A. *Portrait Index* that it is of no service to them." The *Booklist* was a "good beginning," but the editor needed to make it "a more thorough review of the field, including more western publications." The committee also advocated wider use of specialists. "We suggest the University of Wisconsin departments of history and economics as a beginning." Committee members also called for a new edition of the list of subject headings, placing citations in the ALA *Index* on cards, and wider circulation of Hewins's *Books for Boys and Girls*. Kroeger's *Guide to Reference Books* was "too long to be of the best use to the smaller libraries," while past numbers of the ALA tracts series contained "too much literary material and not enough journalistic extracts." On 19 December, Legler reminded Browne to include bulletin no. 19 of the ALA committee on bookbuying in the next issue of *Booklist*. "This is a matter of some financial importance to the Commissions . . . separate publication means a considerable amount of additional postage."[52]

On 26 December chairman Lane sent a lengthy letter to the publishing board. Should the board change the title of its bibliographical periodical to "the ALA Bulletin and Booklist?" Distributing it free through the mails at second class rates was illegal unless the association could prove *Booklist* was the informational organ of a professional society. Should the board retain Garland as editor at $75 per issue? She had requested $100 per issue as more just compensation for the amount of work demanded. Lane recommended that the board employ her at least through the May number, even if it later decided against her retention. "Should we encourage Miss Garland to make a visit to the west this spring for the sake of getting into better touch with the western needs?" Lane wanted to know who would pay expenses. He then informed the board the *Portrait Index* was near completion, and that the board would continue to cooperate with Dana's ALA publicity committee in printing circulars soliciting potential association members.

By spring, publishing board members had become more comfortable with each other, although Legler continued to be cautious and Lane showed special sensitivity to his needs. The league publications committee began to prepare a pamphlet on small library architecture for the tracts series. At the end of January 1906, Dewey asked Putnam if LC would do another edition of the ALA *Catalog*, and Lane forewarned the publishing board the ALA executive board would call for a report on the relationship between the board and ALA headquarters at a forthcoming meeting. When the publishing board met on 9 March, members suggested the board's office and administrative expenses should be carried by the new headquarters, although "the Board is willing to contribute temporarily, if need be." Lane indicated the board wanted to retain its entire income for the preparation and publication of manuscripts.[53]

Lane's response to the ALA executive board was conditioned by the activities of the permanent headquarters committee. The Portland conference had resolved little about a permanent headquarters except to continue the existing temporary arrangement. Wyer at first misinterpreted a directive from the executive board and appointed five more members to the committee. Besides Andrews, Billings, Bowker and Hopkins, Chairman Putnam also had to welcome Crunden, Dewey,

Lane, Wyer and Toronto Public Librarian James Bain. Since seven members of the committee were present at Lake Placid's "library week," Putnam called for a meeting between the publishing board and headquarters committee on 26 September to discuss "definite plans." Hovey explained his ideas to collect money to fund a new headquarters, and recommended locating it in Washington, New York City or Brooklyn. After Lane said the publishing board needed enough room for two workers and a large desk, Andrews suggested that the John Crerar Library in Chicago, still in temporary quarters, might have space for ALA headquarters in a new building it was planning, and Hopkins indicated the Carnegie Library in Pittsburgh might make a similar offer when its building was completed. The committee thanked them for their suggestions, but voted to recommend that the executive board extend the Boston headquarters experiment another year. The committee also urged the association to establish its permanent headquarters in New York as soon as financially feasible.

Two days later the headquarters committee held a joint meeting with the ALA executive board. Together, they appointed Bowker and Canfield as a special committee to locate a suitable place for headquarters in Manhattan near the Astor and Mercantile libraries. The two groups also took steps to prepare for a reorganization of the association which they felt would be necessary to insure headquarters success. They directed Wyer to develop several plans "for the reorganization of existing boards and committees of the Association," and circulate them for comment. Wyer noted the plans would have three common features: (1) a holding body which would control all ALA funds, and perhaps merge the trustees of the endowment fund, the finance committee, and the ALA treasurer's office; (2) an executive body which would have charge of all association administrative offices and merge the functions of the executive and publishing boards; and (3) a full-time secretary responsible to the executive body. "To establish any of these plans an extensive constitutional revision, perhaps even a new constitution, will be necessary," he said. The executive board also appointed E. C. Hovey chairman of a ways and means committee to find new sources of revenue to fund the new headquarters.[54]

Bowker was angry. "The committee on Headquarters is not charged with the problem of reorganizing the ALA," he wrote Dewey. Besides, one man always seemed to be introducing "additional wheels of organization. As Nathan said unto David, 'thou art the man!' " Dewey did not like Bowker's tone. "You wait a little before you 'Thou art the man' me," he responded. If Bowker studied the situation more closely, Dewey chided, "you will find yourself in accord with me." He did not elaborate. But Bowker did not stop with Dewey. In December he wrote Wyer that the headquarters committee was exceeding its authority when it talked of "radical" reorganization and the creation of new boards. "It would be an impertinence to the Association for that committee to annex 'the whole earth.' " Bowker's argument may have been persuasive. The headquarters committee spent no more time discussing reorganization. Part of the reason the committee so quickly abandoned the topic may also be traced to

Dewey's declining influence within ALA. In January 1906 he was forced out of office as New York State librarian. His explanations of Lake Placid's anti-Semitic practices were shallow, and as he became more of an embarrassment to the profession, he gradually withdrew from library affairs.

Bowker and Canfield did find a room in the New York Mercantile Library building suitable for ALA headquarters, but the association could not afford to lease it. By June 1906 Hovey and his ways and means committee admitted they had not found ways and means to fund a permanent headquarters. "I felt strongly last year that we were going faster than we were justified," Dewey told Putnam. Although the Librarian of Congress must have chuckled at the incredibility of Dewey's statement, perhaps Dewey was right to suggest the association consider offers from Andrews and Hopkins. Soule suggested Brooklyn instead of New York City because rents there were cheaper. On the eve of the ALA conference he wrote with more conviction. "I am firmly of the belief that we ought to do something with this and not wait for a possible gift from Carnegie, or anyone else. If we do not take immediate action," he wrote Bowker, "the national association will be weakened . . . at the expense of local clubs all over the country which are increasing in activity and influence. They need right now correlation and guidance. We ought to have as soon as possible a national headquarters, and a paid executive."[55] His letter reflected a sense of urgency not apparent in previous correspondence among headquarters committee members.

ALA members felt much less urgency about the American Library Institute. "There seems to be a mixed feeling regarding it," Browne told Lane shortly after the Portland conference. "Mr. Hovey has no respect whatever for Mr. Dewey." Dewey himself recognized a lack of enthusiasm. He wrote Putnam, "Others like you are not so much attracted by it." Hill had the problem pinpointed. "As you know, Dewey is rather inclined to go ahead with matters of this sort," he told Putnam, "and the only thing for us to do is to see that he doesn't go ahead too fast." When Dewey resigned his position in Albany, the institute's fortunes fell with him. During the winter ALI organized and adopted a constitution, and issued a list of 70 elected fellows. Dewey served as president of a board which also included Crunden, Canfield, Dana and Hill. Carr was elected secretary. As the summer ALA conference approached, Dewey recognized he probably would not attend and began encouraging Canfield to assume a leadership role in ALI.[56]

Part of ALI's early problems can be found in Bowker's concern with over-organization and Soule's concern about correlating and guiding the efforts of numerous library associations. The ALA executive board shared Soule's feelings. On 5 September 1905 Secretary Wyer issued a circular to the officers of state library associations and library clubs "to encourage more active cooperation." He suggested three approaches: (1) promptly exchanging all printed matter; (2) increasing ALA membership by promising a free subscription to the ALA *Booklist*; and (3) including all state and local library association officers in the new ALA handbook. Still the proliferation did not stop. In December 1905 the

Tennessee Library Association president proposed a Southern Library Association because ALA was "a mutual admiration society and junketing party, a northern organization unable to discuss or handle the problem" of the South. Many southern librarians disagreed openly, and LJ recommended "to defer any further steps toward the organization of a Southern Library Association until after the [ALA] meeting in the South . . . which is almost sure to be brought about for 1907." ALA conference location now became more than a missionary endeavor; it might also suffocate potentially fractious library association movements.[57]

Hovey continued to work hard with his ways and means committee to solicit more ALA members, raise more money, and strengthen the financial foundation of the association. Members looked to his office for measurable success and awaited a progress report on his efforts. On 11 January 1906 the executive board determined it was "inexpedient" to establish a permanent headquarters in New York until the association generated $5,000 net after Hovey's salary and traveling expenses were deducted. On 10 March the board advised council to raise the dues of first-time members from $2 to $3. Soule said the publishing board was ready to move to New York at any time, and would contribute either half the rent for headquarters or the entire cost of secretarial work for headquarters correspondence and clerical duties. The board decided to fund Hovey's job through 1 August if sufficient funds were available to guarantee it for a year. The council met later that day and approved the board's recommendation to raise membership dues.[58]

Anticipation more than apprehension characterized the Narragansett Pier conference when ALA President Frank P. Hill opened it on 30 June 1906. Unlike its predecessor, which witnessed a struggle between the League of Library Commissions and the ALA publishing board for control of the association's publishing program, the 1906 conference awaited good news about the establishment of a permanent association headquarters. Hill greeted 891 registrants; 647 came from Atlantic states, 134 from the North Central states, only 21 from the South; 611 registrants were women. The conference started out innocently enough. In his presidential address Hill concentrated on the changing nature of librarianship, exemplified in what he saw as a professional trend towards efficiency manager and away from expert bookman. In his secretary's report, Wyer read the two amendments passed at the previous conference, and recommended ratification because ALA could not act on applications for affiliation status by the League of Library Commissions and the National Association of State Libraries at the present conference until the amendments were ratified. "Should the Bibliographical Society of America be disposed to make similar overtures for affiliation," he said, "the relation will assuredly be welcomed." Wyer also explained the proposed introductory dues increase, and noted that ALA membership had climbed to 1,841, the association's largest enrollment ever. He attributed the increase to five causes: (1) the efforts of the ways and means committee to solicit a larger membership; (2) locating the 1906 conference in the East; (3) the executive board's 1 June recommendation for an entrance fee of $1; (4) closer attention to the membership list; and (5) a free subscription to *Booklist* for all members. Wyer ended his report by pressing for the establishment of a permanent headquarters. The association should not wait for a "gift sufficient to inaugurate the ideal plan," but move ahead on its own as best it could. Treasurer Jones reported a balance of $4,783.72, and Soule announced an endowment fund balance of $108,591.97. Bostwick reported that the committee on bookbuying continued to issue bulletins, which were now being printed in *Booklist*. The group requested standing committee status.

At the third session, the association voted to ratify amendments providing for affiliate status which allowed ALA to include proceedings of accepted affiliates in ALA's annual volume of papers. Thereafter, Lane gave a lengthy report for the ALA publishing board. He indicated that much of the board's time during the previous year had been devoted to publishing the *Portrait Index*, which cost the board more than twice the amount allocated to the newest edition of the ALA *Catalog*. He reported that the addition of Legler and Doren to the board "brought us new strength by making more close our connection with the library commissions and the library needs of the West." Sales records showed the board made $590 more than it spent during the past year. *Booklist* progressed satisfactorily. Editorial changes mandated by the September 1905 publishing board meeting would become more evident as new issues went to press. The board also decided to pull two numbers from its "tracts" series in order to inaugurate a new "handbooks" series. Hitchler's *Cataloging for Small Libraries* and Stearns's *Essentials in Library Administration* would represent the first issues. Lane concluded by saying that the board "stands ready to print . . . whatever the League asks," and expressed keen interest in the association's decision about establishing a permanent headquarters.

At the fourth general session Hovey delivered the report of the committee on ways and means. He noted that his committee was assigned two functions: to increase membership, and to raise funds to establish a permanent headquarters. On the first he cited success. ALA had increased by 603 members since the ways and means committee had assumed its duties. On the second, he was less exuberant. Although his committee had collected only $5,950, he concluded, "There is no reason why the American Library Association should not be self-supporting or largely so." In the discussion which followed Hovey demonstrated the same excitable character and optimistic attitude he had displayed at the 1894 conference. If ALA sported 3,000 members by 1907, an additional $2,500 to $3,000 could be applied to sustaining headquarters. Several members of the audience rose to make additional pledges, and by the time conferees moved to another topic, the association felt confident its executive board would act favorably on the ways and means committee report.

At the final general session, Hill reported that the executive board decided "American Library Association headquarters will be opened as soon after the 1st of September as it is possible to secure adequate quarters, and that Mr. E.

C. Hovey has been selected to be in charge of the headquarters (Applause)."
Officers for the new year would be C. W. Andrews of the Crerar as president,
E. H. Anderson of the New York State Library as first vice president, and
Katharine L. Sharp of the University of Illinois Library and Library School as
second vice president. Washington, D.C., Public Library Director George Bowerman would be the new ALA treasurer, while Helen Haines remained as recorder, and Wyer continued for the final third of his three-year term as ALA
secretary. New council members included Alice Tyler, Purd Wright, Putnam,
George Godard and T. W. Koch.

Four ALA sections met during the conference, while several law librarians
met informally to discuss the organization of an ALA law librarians section.
They had already agreed to organize themselves into an independent American
Association of Law Librarians, but to affiliate with ALA. The League of Library
Commissions met in two sessions. At the second, the league's publication committee reported on cooperation with the ALA publishing board. The National
Association of State Libraries and the Bibliographical Society of America both
held separate meetings, heard papers, and elected new officers. Proceedings for
the former were lost in the mail after the conference, so they were not included
with other affiliated organization conference proceedings.

On the surface the 1906 conference appeared to exhibit an optimistic, antic-
ipatory attitude towards the future. The executive board met four times during
the conference. Among several actions, the board directed the *Booklist* editor to
print annually a list of the officers of state library associations and commissions
and local library clubs. Board members spent much time considering the permanent headquarters, and finally decided to establish a permanent headquarters
in Boston if the first year's budget did not exceed $5,000. Hovey would be
retained as assistant secretary. The board also accepted Electra Doren's resignation from the publishing board due to ill health, and named Wellman to fill
the vacancy two days later.

Council met three times during the conference. At the first meeting several
people pushed Mary Ahern as nominee for first vice president. Andrews, who
had already received the nomination for president, objected that the first vice
president (who generally succeeded to the presidency the following year) should
not come from the same section of the country as the president. If Ahern was
nominated, he would withdraw his name. Others argued that Ahern was still on
the council, that precedent dictated a woman should get the second vice president's spot, and that no one with a purely commercial interest should ever succeed
to the ALA presidency. The opposition was too formidable; the move failed.
Sharp, who got the nomination as second vice president, wrote Annie Dewey,
"I never imagined that so much dirty politics could develop in the ALA." Ahern
left the session in a bitter mood, and the treatment accorded her became the
subject of much cloakroom conversation. In other action, the council selected
Asheville, North Carolina, as the site of its next meeting, decided to delay the
imposition of an additional entrance fee on new members until the ALA treasurer

could study it further, and approved the idea that librarians of the Southwest gather for a regional meeting.

A second topic of cloakroom discourse placed Melvil Dewey at the storm center for the last time at an ALA meeting. Dewey had already been discredited in New York for his anti-Semitism. In spring 1906, rumors began to circulate which accused him of sexual improprieties with several women at the 1905 ALA conference and postconference trip. While existing evidence cannot prove or disprove the charge, it does indicate that Isabel Ely Lord, director of Brooklyn's Pratt Institute Free Library, was the chief accuser. Although Dewey's wife, Annie, wrote Lord that the accusations were false and that she had the utmost trust in her husband, several friends advised Dewey to stay away from the 1906 conference. Why Dewey uncharacteristically chose to accept the advice is uncertain, but several close associates in attendance reported back with frequency and great detail. Canfield told Dewey "the older and better known members . . . were simply annoyed and repelled."[59]

Canfield's choice of words is revealing. Dewey had been controversial enough since becoming a member of the ALA in 1876, but "old stagers" also recognized how valuable his energy had been for the association and were willing to tolerate his frequent excesses. Mostly, the latter were privately handled. In 1905 and 1906, however, Dewey had become a public embarrassment for the American Library Association. New ALA members who had not witnessed Dewey's library activities over the previous 30 years had less reason to feel forgiving. Lord's accusations may have found a more receptive audience among younger professionals who had been reading the New York newspapers over the past years. Whatever the reason, however, Dewey's power and influence in the association had plummeted. He had lost his New York position, and with it the foundation for his ALA activities. Partly because of his own mistakes, partly because librarians from smaller communities found new, more effective leaders with untarnished reputations to carry their fight to the ALA executive and publishing boards, Dewey was never again a serious factor in ALA politics. And he knew it.

One more significant event occurred towards the end of the conference. Since Garland did not want to continue as *Booklist* editor without a salary increase, publishing board members considered alternatives. Dewey pushed for Theresa Elmendorf as a compromise candidate acceptable to East and Midwest. Legler pushed for Katharine MacDonald, an employee at the Wisconsin Free Library Commission. He promised to pay half her salary if the board would agree to move all editorial work to Madison. He pointed out that MacDonald already had a good working relationship with several University of Wisconsin professors who had annotated books for the league's published bibliographies in the past. But the publishing board's choice was predetermined. Elmendorf refused to be considered because her husband was gravely ill. Since Legler's idea promised that *Booklist* would maintain, perhaps even increase, quality at less cost, the board decided to accept his offer. MacDonald became the *Booklist*'s new editor.[60]

This arrangement may have made Wellman's appointment to the board more palatable to Legler and the League of Library Commissions.

Because the executive board decided for financial reasons to keep ALA headquarters in Boston, Hovey had to find more spacious quarters than were available at the Boston Athenaeum. He finally settled for two floors of a building at 34 Newbury Street, not far from the Boston Public Library, and only three doors away from the American Academy of Arts and Sciences headquarters. The mere existence of a headquarters suggested the growth and maturity of the association, and headquarters quickly came to symbolize the profession's emerging self-esteem. Shortly after the *Library Journal* introduced its August 1906 issue with pictures of the new quarters, monitoring the progress of the venture preoccupied the association's attention for the rest of the year. By prearrangement the ALA publishing board shared space in the building, and because of several new publishing ventures, tied its fortunes inextricably to those of headquarters. The history of ALA between the Narragansett Pier and Asheville conferences is largely a recounting of the activities at 34 Newbury Street, Boston, with an occasional reference to Madison, Wisconsin.

Despite the public approval of E. C. Hovey's appointment at the 1906 conference, not everyone was satisfied with the executive board's selection of the assistant secretary. Helen Haines did not like his methods for raising funds, and Bowker considered him less than "effective." Haines also noticed "there is considerable criticism concerning him in the Association—largely from the middle west." She was especially concerned with a plan to redistribute responsibilities which Hovey submitted to the executive board on 14 July. Wyer polled the board, then responded to Hovey on 10 August. As the association's permanent full-time executive secretary, he could assume duties formerly exercised by several other ALA officers. The board authorized him to collect dues and notify delinquent members, to compile and distribute all announcements and membership lists, and to keep the books for the trustees of the endowment fund and the publishing board. The board also authorized Hovey to work with the ALA committee on architecture to develop a collection of library architectural drawings, and to begin a headquarters library collection "only so far as it can be done without expense." Finally, the board directed all requests for expert library advice to appropriate ALA committees, and appointed a committee consisting of Gardner Jones, C. C. Soule, and D. P. Corey—all from Boston—"to provide constant supervision and assistance."[61]

Haines foresaw that the powers allocated to Hovey would have a significant impact on the relationship between LJ and ALA. She recommended to Bowker that she resign as ALA recorder, and that the *Journal* relinquish responsibility for the conference proceedings, since both tasks ought to be routinely assumed by the new ALA headquarters. Bowker agreed. He wrote Wyer on 15 August that "the Association must now face the question of selective publication and of doing the work independently of the *Library Journal* office." An LJ editorial echoed these sentiments. "The Proceedings, with the growth of the Association and related organizations, have come to be so voluminous as to make it questionable whether they can be in the future issued as a regular number of the *Journal*."[62] The implication was clear. ALA had to take full financial responsibility for its own publications; Bowker did not want to subsidize them anymore, although he expected LJ would remain ALA's official organ.

If ALA was going to publish its own proceedings, then the task would naturally fall to the publishing board, which met in late October. Its published minutes showed an additional alternative had been proposed. "The issue of a second publication as a bulletin of the Association was discussed, the sentiment of the Board being that it would be advisable, if a way could be found for accomplishing it." Bowker's move had backfired. By forcing the board to consider publishing its own proceedings, Bowker unwittingly sparked the creation of yet another library periodical. Board consensus concluded that as long as ALA had to publish its own proceedings, it might as well do so in its own official organ.

On 10 November Lane wrote a lengthy letter to executive board members. He noted that *Booklist* was not meeting expenses because the executive board had recently ruled all ALA members were entitled to a free subscription, and he suggested that the board might have to raise subscription rates. Then he recommended an alternative the publishing board may have discussed two weeks earlier. What did the board think of starting an ALA *Bulletin*, including the conference proceedings as one of its numbers, and soliciting advertisers to cover part or all of the publication costs? Wyer asked for a correspondence vote from the board. Response was mixed. While no one opposed a new bulletin, all wondered how the ALA could afford it, and several pointed out that accepting any advertising at all ran counter to general association policy. All agreed the issue ought to be discussed at the next meeting. In a letter to Sharp, Wyer concluded, "If, in the meantime, the Publishing Board decides to issue a Bulletin without including advertising, I take it that the consent of the Executive Board will not be required any more than to any other publishing enterprise."[63] On 6 December Wyer summarized the issue for the ALA executive board by asking three questions: (1) Since the publishing board would not start a *Bulletin* on its own, should the executive board underwrite it? (2) If the ALA started its own *Bulletin*, should it stop sending all members free copies of *Booklist*? (3) Should the new *Bulletin* include advertisements?

Dewey saw another opening. Since he was in the last of his three-year term on the publishing board, he routinely received copies of all its correspondence. And because Katharine Sharp, a former student who remained personally close to him, was a member of the ALA executive board, Dewey also received copies of executive board correspondence. On 26 November he wrote Wyer: "I am in favor of the publication of a bulletin and of restricting the *Booklist* to its original purpose." He reported much dissatisfaction that the *Library Journal*, a commercial venture, acted as the association's official organ, and indicated that creating a *Bulletin* would eliminate the need to furnish *Booklist* free to all members. It would also force libraries to join the association in order to obtain the proceedings. He urged quick action so the publishing board could announce the new bulletin in the next issue of *Booklist*. With fellow members of the publishing board he took a different approach. Why not consolidate *Public Libraries*, *Library Journal*, and the new *Bulletin* into one periodical controlled entirely by the association? He predicted that both Davidson and Bowker would acquiesce, then reversed a position he identified to Wyer less than a week before. "I . . . vote to send the *Booklist* to every ALA member." Two days later he wrote Bowker, included a copy of his letter to the ALA publishing board, and said, "I hope you will agree with this plan. I have opposed the *ALA Bulletin* idea, but they are bound to have it and for the first time I have consented to it." The duplicity in Dewey's efforts was unusually transparent; unfortunately Bowker's response is unknown.[64]

On 6 December Dewey wrote Legler that he had just returned from New England, where he had talked with Lane, Wellman, and Wyer. He told Legler he was not in favor of the "Boston experiment," especially under Hovey's direction. "You seem to be the only man on which we can agree to take charge of headquarters." The remainder of his letter was liberally spiced with first person plural pronouns which implied a fictitious consensus on Dewey's ideas. "Please write me in confidence whether with our loyal support you would take up this work. . . . We have been looking here for several years and think you are the man for the place." He also suggested that Ahern would be the strongest and most experienced person to edit the new consolidated journal. He urged her to consider a consolidated journal, and to move temporarily to Boston with Legler to take over the headquarters. In the meantime, however, "Stir up some Chicago man to give a house or endowment on condition that headquarters be established there. Hovey had this scheme in hand for Boston." To Hovey he wrote: "I will help you all I possibly can and club anyone else to do the same."

Whatever Dewey's reason for scheming and lying, his efforts failed when Legler forwarded a copy of Dewey's 6 December letter to Lane. In a marvelous understatement the Harvard librarian wrote Dewey: "I read your letter . . . with a good deal of surprise." He said Dewey's letter made it sound as if the publishing board wanted Legler to replace Hovey as ALA executive secretary. "So far as the publishing board is concerned, this is certainly not the case." He also doubted whether Dewey spoke for the ALA executive board because Soule, a member of the committee charged to monitor progress of ALA headquarters, felt "Hovey is doing admirable work for us, and it would be a distinct mistake, at least at the present time, to displace him." He also disagreed with Dewey's suggestion about Ahern. "I should very much doubt if she were the right person to put into the headquarters as editor and advisor." Finally, he requested Dewey to write Legler and explain that "you are speaking altogether for yourself, and not on behalf of the Board. I will delay writing him myself a few days, until I hear from you again."

Later Lane learned that Hovey had seen Dewey's letter to Legler. He quickly advised the ALA executive secretary to "dismiss the matter from your mind, and accept my assurance that Mr. Dewey wrote entirely on his own responsibility.'' Dewey's reply was feeble. ''My letter to Legler was intended to be confidential. There is no good talking outside about this thing.'' He concluded, ''I will certainly help Hovey all I can . . . but someday we must get a strong *library* man in there also, keeping Hovey if it seems best for the kind of work he can do.''[65] Dewey had committed his final blunder in ALA. He had embarrassed and alienated the ALA's executive secretary, the editors of *Public Libraries* and *Library Journal*, the most influential person in the League of Library Commissions, the committee assigned to supervise ALA headquarters, and the entire ALA publishing board. Except for past graduates of the New York State Library School, he no longer boasted a loyal constituency among ALA members. Reaction to Dewey's inept meddling demonstrated that he had ceased to be an influence in ALA politics.

On 22 December 1906 the ALA executive board met at the Park Avenue Hotel in New York City. Among other actions, the board accepted a report from the advisory committee on headquarters. Hovey was given a glowing review. ''We cannot too highly commend his intelligence, zeal, and devotion to the interests of the Association.'' Headquarters was keeping to the budget, but needed an additional $500 to manage the architectural plans ''which are coming in so fast as to embarrass us,'' and another $500 for travel so Hovey could solicit more funds. The board consented to the former, but only authorized Hovey to transfer unexpected balances from one budget item to another to cover his travel costs. Then, after hearing the treasurer's report, the board decided to consolidate the headquarters budget with the ALA's general funds ''and that in the future all receipts be credited to a single fund and all appropriations be charged against this fund.'' At the time board members did not explain their move.

One other item which drew action but was not reported in the public minutes concerned the ALA *Bulletin*. The board decided to authorize it partly to cut costs, partly to attract new members. The first issue appeared in January 1907. Lane announced it would be issued five or six times a year to all ALA members, that it would carry reports of executive board, council, and standing committee meetings, announcements of publishing board plans and publications, notices of association meetings and travel arrangements, and information about affiliated societies. In short, the new ALA *Bulletin* would publish news items which had been creeping into the *Booklist*, the same information which went free to non-ALA members because many state library commissions bought large quantities of *Booklist* and distributed copies free to public libraries within their respective states. The next step was only a matter of time. In March the *Bulletin* announced the association would discontinue its policy of distributing *Booklist* free to all ALA members.[66]

On 21 April 1907 Wyer explained the ramifications of the new distribution policy in a circular to *Bulletin* readers. The conference proceedings would no longer be included in the *Library Journal*. Copies of the *Booklist* went only to subscribers. However, libraries which paid a regular subscription rate would receive the *Booklist*, the *Bulletin*, and the proceedings. (Wyer regarded this practice as an inducement to trustees to have their libraries subscribe.) Although Wyer did not elaborate, the executive board's full plan now became clear. Cut the drain on the budget by sending *Booklist* to subscribers only; use the *Bulletin* as the only means of communication to which ALA members were entitled; devise a new fee structure to encourage more library memberships and generate more revenue for the association.[67]

Two more issues which arose between conferences concerned the publishing board; both pointed to trouble at the Asheville meeting. First, on 20 March Legler wrote Lutie Stearns that the editorial responsibilities for *Booklist* were consuming all of MacDonald's time. He intended to ask the board to employ her full-time at the Asheville conference. Second, a rumor began to circulate that Lane wanted to quit the publishing board after the conference. When Wellman found out it was true, he advised Lane against resignation. "Even if you did not do a single thing but lend the weight of your name and personality, I think such service alone would justify your continuing on the Board." Wellman was especially concerned with timing. "It seems to me a rather critical time, with the personnel of the Board changing, the relationship to headquarters to be adjusted, the possible criticism, etc." If Lane persisted, however, Wellman recommended Gardner Jones to replace him as chairman.[68]

Both the executive board and the council met in March. The board passed the entire question of what to do with the publication of the conference proceedings to the council. Members then proposed that the publishing board send a copy of *Booklist* to every member of ALA who asked in writing, but the executive board promised to reimburse the publishing board ten cents for each subscription. The executive board also decided to pay the expenses of a delegate to a meeting of Southwest librarians from ALA's general funds. Council met the next day, granted affiliate status to the American Association of Law Libraries, and expressed a unanimous opinion that the association should publish its own proceedings. President Andrews also announced a nominating committee for the forthcoming conference: Richardson, Hill, and Countryman.[69]

In April Wyer and Hovey got into a disagreement about affiliated organizations. Routinely, ALA members had in the past relied upon the ALA secretary to obtain the most favorable discount travel rates to conferences. Non-ALA members, many of whom belonged to affiliated organizations and traveled to the same conferences, also took advantage of the cheaper schedules. When Frederick O. Poole, president of the newly affiliated American Association of Law Libraries (AALL), and Louis Round Wilson, secretary-treasurer of the North Carolina Library Association (NCLA), requested similar privileges, Hovey refused to validate the tickets for discount rates unless AALL and NCLA members also joined ALA. Hovey hoped this position would increase ALA membership. Wyer's anger flashed when Poole reported Hovey's action. The ALA secretary explained to Hovey very carefully that "the American Association of Law Libraries is affiliated with the ALA, is an organization national in scope; we welcome affiliations, would hate to have such organizations break away from us and meet apart, and we are anxious to promote the most cordial relations with these and the state associations." He then wrote Poole and Wilson that members of their organization would indeed qualify for traveler's discounts, and informed other members of the executive board of his action. At the bottom of her copy of Wyer's letter (which she loyally forwarded to Dewey) Katharine Sharp wrote, "JI Wyer entirely right. ECH's plan is mere money grabbing."[70]

Other ominous clouds began to loom on the ALA horizon. Through Ahern, Legler learned that Lane wanted to resign as chairman of the publishing board. He also learned that Lane and Soule were pushing Gardner Jones as his replacement. In addition, Ahern reported that several people had organized to oppose her nomination to any ALA executive board position. Finally, she told Legler of a rumor that Hovey would be elected a member of the executive board at the Asheville conference. Legler was unalterably opposed to such a move. "Seems to me contrary to all public policy to vest in any official the right to . . . aid in determining by his vote the amount of his own compensation." He deplored the secrecy surrounding these moves and promised to monitor them carefully at the forthcoming conference. In an unrelated move, E. H. Anderson, Dewey's replacement at the New York State Library, asked Bowker to write to J. N. Larned, who was scheduled for the Asheville program. Anderson was concerned that Larned had not kept current on library affairs and would use his time to "champion Mr. Dewey's cause. . . . It will be a serious blow to decency," Anderson opined, but he also suggested that older members of the association "might be able to put Mr. Larned right."[71] Whether Bowker wrote Larned is uncertain, but Anderson's concerns proved unnecessary. Larned did not champion Dewey's cause at Asheville. He did not even attend.

The ALA conference which took place 23–29 May 1907, in Asheville, North Carolina, was hardly harmonious. ALA President Andrews had designed the program to concentrate on two topics: the library movement in the South and "the use of books." In addition, he wanted to provide time within general sessions for joint meetings with each of ALA's affiliated organizations. His efforts resulted in a tightly packed program which depended on strict adherence to schedule commitments. He failed to get cooperation. This problem, together with the most controversial election in ALA history, made the atmosphere of the Asheville conference testy. But the looming difficulties were not evident at first. LJ noticed attendance "was more proportionately representative of the different sections of the country than has been the case in larger meetings." Of 478 people registered, North Atlantic states sent 158 people; South Atlantic and North Central states sent 133 each; 310 registrants were women.[72]

The changing representation at Asheville paralleled shifts in ALA leadership over the previous decade, and comparing executive board members who held office from 1903 to 1907 with those who held office between 1892 and 1896 demonstrates change and continuity. The two groups shared common characteristics which clearly established their socioeconomic stature in the dominant culture. Nine out of ten members in both half-decade periods came from families who had lived in the United States for four generations or more. Three out of four traced their ancestors to Northwest Europe, and about the same proportion in both groups were Protestant, and not politically active. One in five was a declared Republican, one in 20 a declared Democrat; 98 percent were employed in library-related professional positions at the time they held an executive board position, and four of five were chief executives. The social profile of the ALA leadership had not changed much since 1876.

Changes were more subtle, and cumulative. In the 1892–1896 period, three of four had been born in the Northeast; only 15 percent in the Midwest. Eleven years later 71 percent were born in the Northeast; 29 percent in the Midwest. The latter percentage had nearly doubled. Although fewer men were serving on the board in the latter half-decade (80 to 71 percent) and more women (20 to 29 percent), the change is not significant because of the unwritten rule to award the second vice presidency to a female. Ahern had tried to challenge that tradition at the previous conference, and failed. Fewer board members were married in the latter half-decade (80 to 57 percent), although most of this change is attributable to the increase in women, all of whom were single. Noticeable changes had occurred in fathers' occupations, though. The managerial ranks dropped from 45 to 29 percent, while the professional ranks increased from 15 to 43 percent, nearly threefold. Board members also held slightly more earned degrees in the latter half-decade, although the distribution of the schools from which they had obtained their degrees changed very little. Those possessing library science degrees increased from 10 to 20 percent, reflecting the strength of the New York State Library School, which had graduated over one-third of the executive board members by the last half-decade.

More striking changes were evident in the types of libraries at which these executive board members held their positions. Less than half as many came from public libraries (60 to 29 percent), while more than four times as many came from state libraries and state library commissions (5 to 22 percent) and three times as many were library educators (5 to 14 percent). Noticeable changes also occurred in geographical location. While the Midwest was equally represented in both half-decades, representation from the Northeast declined (65 to 50 percent) while the South (including Washington, D.C., and its Library of Congress) increased from 0 to 14 percent. In sum, the ALA executive board members holding office between 1903 and 1907 continued to demonstrate characteristics common to the dominant political, social, and religious control groups of their times, but they assumed more diversity within their own profession.[73] It was also obvious that the dominance of the Northeast among the ALA leadership was eroding.

On 23 May ALA President Clement W. Andrews endured the first of several unpleasant council meetings. First order of business was the report of the nominating committee, ordinarily a routine matter. Previous nominating committees honored three traditional but unwritten rules: (1) nominate the first vice president for president; (2) nominate a woman for second vice president; (3) pass the presidency to an eastern librarian one year, a western librarian the next. The latter tradition dated from the late 1880s; the other two from the late 1890s. The process seemed simple enough. President Andrews, from Chicago's Crerar Library, would finish his term at the end of the Asheville conference. First Vice President Anderson, of the New York State Library, would succeed, thereby fulfilling rules (1) and (2). Helen Haines would be nominated to succeed Katharine Sharp as second vice president, thereby fulfilling rule (3) and opening for another the recorder's position, a post Haines no longer wanted.

The nominating committee, consisting of Richardson (chair), Hill, and Countryman, had no trouble with Haines and at first did not have to convince Anderson to accept the presidential nomination. But Soule, Wellman, Richardson, Lane, Jones and Horace Wadlin of the Boston Public Library had pressed the committee to nominate Hovey as ALA treasurer. Only Countryman objected, so the nomination carried. When Anderson heard it, he withdrew his name from consideration. He did not believe Hovey should be a member of an executive board which controlled his salary. The committee subsequently nominated N. D. C. Hodges of the Cincinnati Public Library to replace Anderson on the ballot, but easterners then complained the ALA presidency would go to two western men in succession. They strongly suspected that midwesterners generally disliked Hovey and were uncomfortable about locating headquarters in Boston, and they worried that noneastern groups within ALA wanted to terminate the headquarters experiment. But the nominating committee forged ahead and Richardson read the list of final nominees to the council: for president, Hodges; for first vice president, C. H. Gould of Montreal's McGill University; for second vice president, Haines; for secretary, J. I. Wyer; for treasurer, E. C. Hovey; and for recorder, Lutie Stearns.

Countryman then delivered a minority report. She objected to Hovey's nomination for two reasons: (1) the association's executive officer "should not be a member of the board which elects him"; it was "questionable business propriety" to place "the collection of the revenues of the Association fully into the hands of the office which spends the larger part of them." Anderson moved to amend the nominating committee report by substituting the name of A. H. Hopkins, director of Pittsburgh's Carnegie Free Public Library, for Hovey's. Before allowing action on Anderson's motion, Andrews read a letter from Soule complimenting Hovey on his administration of ALA headquarters. His tactic failed to persuade the council, however; Anderson's motion carried.

The removal of Hovey's name from the ballot alarmed eastern librarians who were convinced that ALA had to give the headquarters experiment a fair chance in an eastern city near the nation's library and publishing centers. Only two easterners remained on the slate of nominees; Haines, who hardly represented eastern library interests; and Wyer, a transplanted Nebraskan who had already had an unpleasant altercation with Hovey, and probably could not be counted on to support the ALA executive officer. For the time being, however, they took no concrete action.

In other action, council approved Lake Minnetonka, Minnesota, as the site for the 1908 ALA conference and accepted Bowker's resignation of the *Library Journal* as ALA's official organ. In addition, the council approved a report from a committee composed of Anderson, Sharp, and Wyer which stated that "members of affiliated organizations . . . and no others shall be entitled to all privileges in the way of railroad and hotel rates and conference hospitalities that are enjoyed by members of the ALA." Their message to Hovey was clear.[74]

The conference began in earnest the following day. In his presidential address on "The Use of Books," Andrews referred to the constant diversity among librarians. The 28 preceding conferences had not identified a "deadening uniformity of methods, nor even absolute identity of aims." He did not mention the common goal—"the best reading"—everyone took for granted. Wyer followed by summarizing the council's activities of 23 May, and then gave his secretary's report. ALA now sported a membership of 2,019. New provisions in the ALA constitution had given affiliate status to the National Association for State Libraries and the League of Library Commissions, but Wyer also noted "there are still two similar bodies, the Bibliographical Society of America and the American Association of Medical Libraries [sic], which we would be glad to see related to us in the same way." He cited progress at ALA headquarters, but emphasized it was "scarcely beyond the initial and somewhat experimental state." Finally, he noted steps which the association was taking to insure closer cooperation with state and local library associations, including attempts "to fix the dates of six state library meetings in the central part of the country at such consecutive times as shall permit the visit to each meeting of a single speaker." The treasurer's and endowment trustees' fund reports were submitted, but not read because Bowerman was ill and Soule was absent from the country. Yale University Reference Librarian Andrew Keogh concluded the session with a paper on "Bibliography," which Andrews carefully noted served two purposes: it fit his theme on "The Use of Books"; it served as the BSA "representative" on the general program.

Deloraine P. Corey, Massachusetts Free Library Commission member, opened the second general session on the next morning by giving a report from the committee on headquarters for fellow members C. C. Soule and Gardner Jones. He noted two of headquarters' most obvious successes, the systematization of business procedures and the acquisition of library architecture plans. The committee also complimented Hovey on his "zeal, intelligent work, and constant application" and expressed the hope "that the Association will be able to continue and enlarge the work so well begun, and that Mr. Hovey can be retained in its charge." Lane followed with a lengthy report from the ALA publishing board. Since the last annual conference the board had met twice in Boston (because it was "more convenient") and had taken in $486.23 more than it spent. Lane quickly pointed out that the figure hid a $1,056.41 loss incurred by *Booklist*. The chairman was pleased to report the cooperative arrangement with ALA headquarters, although he looked forward to the time when the publishing board would no longer have to contribute $500 annually for rental. The ALA *Portrait Index* was finally out—1,700 pages available for $3. In three months the Library of Congress had sold 640 copies.

The emergence of the *Bulletin* and its connection with *Booklist* required lengthier explanation. Lane said that when the former was established it became clear to the publishing board that the latter should no longer be distributed *gratis* to ALA members, but paid for like other board publications. Although the executive board thought free distribution to members who specifically requested it "desirable," the publishing board maintained its position. If it resumed free distribution, subscriptions would drop and "we should again have to raise the price of the *Booklist* as sold to Commissions, a measure which the Board would extremely regret." Legler's hand was evident in the action. Lane further reported progress on the compilation of an ALA list of subject headings and catalog rules, and although the board had issued no new tracts or handbooks since its last report, three were near completion: Edna Bullock's "The Management of Traveling Libraries," Cornelia Marvin's "Library Buildings," and Mary Plummer's "Library Training." Lane also reported progress on a children's list, several foreign lists "which may be helpful to librarians in communities where there is a considerable foreign population," a guide to nature study, and Adelaide Hasse's index to economic materials contained in state documents.

The third session began ominously when Bernard C. Steiner proposed a constitutional amendment to merge the ALA secretary, treasurer, and recorder into one office to be occupied by the ALA executive officer. Conferees successfully avoided open discussion of the issue by unanimously agreeing to forward the proposal to the council.[75] A potential explosion had been postponed to another day and another forum.

That evening the executive board met in executive session in Andrews's hotel room. Anderson moved to discontinue the headquarters experiment for financial reasons and to fire Hovey as executive secretary for inefficient management. He was obviously still upset about efforts to win Hovey a spot on the executive board, and he had never agreed with the positive reports on Hovey's effectiveness. Wyer supported Anderson, but Andrews opposed them both. The outgoing board had no "right to so embarrass the incoming board," he stated. After the meeting broke up, Andrews informed Hovey of Anderson's recommendation. Hovey then went straight to Lane, Corey, Jones, Richardson and Wadlin for advice. The five men quickly called a secret meeting—without Hovey present—and decided to see Anderson. What they discussed with him is unknown, but later that evening Richardson asked Hovey if he would, under a "gentleman's agreement," place his resignation in the hands of the executive board should Anderson force the issue. After consulting with other members of Richardson's committee, Hovey agreed. In fact, eastern librarians decided to follow Dana's recommendation and submit a separate slate of nominees because they were convinced Hovey had little chance to remain under the new board which the nominating committee proposed, and because they wanted to maintain headquarters on the East Coast. Hovey's fate and perhaps the fate of headquarters itself hinged on the results of the election of new executive board members. The election would become a litmus test of Hovey's strength within the association at large.[76]

The strategy created bad feelings which surfaced during the fourth general session. After Hovey read his "Report of the Executive Officer," Dana took the floor. "I understand that there have been objections on the part of some members of the Association to the action of the Council in establishing the Headquarters and appointing to administer the same an Executive Officer." He disagreed with the objections, and moved a resolution approving headquarters and the executive officer. Andrews objected; resolutions had to go through the council, he said. When Bowker pointed out that a similar resolution had already passed the council, Andrews withdrew his objection, and called the question. Ahern quickly interjected: "I think it is pretty well understood what my position is on the Headquarters question from the first." She asked Dana to consider an amendment which added "two words" to his motion, "and that is for establishing Headquarters at Boston 'at present.' " Dana agreed, and after Andrews said he had "held that opinion for a long time," and Bowker suggested "the results at Boston will be proof of the desirability of permanent Headquarters, whether they be located at Boston or Chicago, or even some minor city like New York," the amended motion passed unanimously.

Shortly thereafter the polls opened and the rift that had developed in private became readily apparent in the list of nominees. Against the list the nominating committee had passed and the council approved, eastern librarians added four people. They nominated Beatrice Winser, Dana's first assistant at the Newark Public Library, to oppose Stearns for recorder; Drew B. Hall, librarian of the Millicent Library in Fairhaven, Massachusetts, to oppose Hopkins for treasurer; B. C. Steiner of Baltimore's Enoch Pratt Free Library to oppose Wyer for secretary; and Arthur E. Bostwick, Chief of the Circulating Department of the New York Public Library, to oppose Hodges for president. Never before had association members been asked to choose between opposing factions in an open election. LJ described the scene nervously: " . . . while a general feeling of friendliness prevailed, there were strong cross currents of agreement and disagreement on the conduct of headquarters . . . and a regrettable amount of 'corralling' of uninformed delegates."[77] ALA "politics" had become public.

Despite the "electioneering and wirepulling" that LJ said went on in hallways and cloakrooms, most conferees were probably unaware of the deeper significance of ALA's first contested election. They likely did not suspect that Hovey's job and the continuance of the Boston headquarters depended on the election's outcome. Nonetheless, the final session was full of suspense. Andrews may have deliberately delayed the announcement until the final minutes before adjournment to minimize the ripples of dissatisfaction bound to spread no matter which way the election went. After four committee reports and eight short papers, Andrews asked the tellers to report the election. University of Texas Library Director Phineas Windsor responded: for recorder, Lutie Stearns, 277, Beatrice Winser, 35; for treasurer, Anderson Hopkins, 197, Drew Hall, 139; for secretary, James I. Wyer, 186, B. C. Steiner, 151; and for president, Arthur Bostwick, 181, N. D. C. Hodges, 157. Except for the all-important presidential office, the independent ticket had failed. Anderson decided not to press any action to fire Hovey since Wyer was still on the executive board, and still able to check any excesses. As a result, Richardson did not have to invoke the "gentleman's agreement." Because the election was a mixed success for both sides, the issues which separated them once more went back to hotel hallways and cloakrooms to emerge at yet another conference. Andrews adjourned the conference moments later.

The split evident in the two tickets preoccupied ALA members and distracted attention from the other meetings during the conference. All ALA sections held meetings, many taking two sessions, including the newly constituted catalog section. All three affiliated associations also met. A. J. Small, president of the new American Association of Law Libraries, reminded his audience that the AALL wanted its independence first, but welcomed ALA's constitutional change outlining an affiliated status extending "the advantages of advertising, rates, etc." The League of Library Commissions elected as its new president Chalmers Hadley, recently appointed secretary of the Indiana State Library Commission. The National Association of State Libraries concentrated its two sessions on noncontroversial matters. Finally, the unaffiliated Bibliographical Society of America also met; papers delivered addressed the history of printing in the South, bibliographical work in state libraries, and the development of a handbook of special collections in American libraries.

On 29 May the newly elected board met to fill committee vacancies. Bostwick wanted an opportunity "of smoothing down ruffled feathers" before the new board departed from the North Carolina meeting harboring too many hostile feelings. Theresa West Elmendorf replaced Dewey on the publishing board, and joined reappointees Lane, Legler, Soule, and Wellman. Legler became the new publishing board chairman. The executive board also requested that the publishing board issue the *Bulletin* bimonthly, with the *Handbook* and the *Proceedings* occupying an issue each. After Hovey excused himself from the meeting (the minutes specifically recorded this for obvious reasons) First Vice President Gould moved that arrangements for carrying on headquarters and employing Hovey be extended through 1 January 1908, and that Hovey be requested to report by 15 September 1907 "regarding the prospect of securing further practical support for carrying on Headquarters." Gould's motion carried unanimously.[78]

At no time since 1892–1893 had the association been so divided. Although Dewey was no longer around to champion their cause, small/rural/western library interests had found new leaders in Mary Ahern, Henry Legler and Gratia Countryman, and associations like the League of Library Commissions. Legler would

carefully control *Booklist* editorial offices from Madison and from his new position as chairman of the publishing board. Although his group did not want to
end the headquarters experiment, they were determined it would not be permanently located in Boston, where representatives of large/urban/eastern library
interests held most power. People like Lane, Richardson, Wellman and Hovey
interpreted Legler's position as anti-Hovey and anti-headquarters. They were
right about the former, wrong about the latter, and it was their misinterpretation
of the latter which motivated them to force an alternative slate of candidates at
the 1907 conference. The antagonistic feelings that this move caused were never
entirely eliminated, and the suspicions which arose from it clouded the atmosphere until the association did establish a permanent headquarters in Chicago.

After ALA members returned home, several people tried to give perspective
to the stormy conference in order to justify their individual actions. Wellman
suggested that the controversy had erupted because the "past Executive Board
had not cooperated as cordially with the Executive Officer as was reasonable
and that he had not had a fair chance to show what he could do." Hovey took
a similar approach in writing Bowker, but he emphasized that Anderson and
Wyer were the "prime movers." He also pointed out that when council members
replaced him with Hopkins as nominee for treasurer, they substituted the name
"of one who has shown enmity to me." Bowker said he thought Wyer and
Hopkins had opposed Hovey and not headquarters, but he encouraged the ALA
executive officer to accept the move in a spirit "of friendly criticism." Andrews
was less charitable, even though he supported Hovey throughout the conference.
"The fight should have been made strictly on the secretaryship, and have not
brought in an innocent third party. I cannot feel as well disposed towards Mr.
Hovey as I did in view of his action in the matter." Bowker did an admirable
job of explaining the election-headquarters-Hovey controversy in a June LJ
editorial, but criticized Hovey for "recent utterances" which tactlessly emphasized that the association "was to be made self-supporting and not to go a-
begging." Ahern spent most of her description assuring PL readers that western
ALA members did not want to abolish headquarters. She said nothing of Hovey.[79]

It was predictable that ALA leaders would focus most of their attention between
conferences on headquarters and Hovey. But they restricted their observations
to private correspondence; on the surface ALA activities appeared calm. State
library associations in the Midwest scheduled their annual fall conferences in
quick succession so ALA President Bostwick could visit them all in one circuitous
trip. *Public Libraries* applauded the cooperation manifest in such scheduling.
Ahern forewarned readers once again against "the mistaken notion of a few of
the leading members . . . that the Association is already too large and that its
membership would better be restricted than increased." While Bostwick took
his goodwill tour, however, ALA headquarters and Hovey were already in trouble.

In late July Bostwick decided he did not have the unilateral authority to renew
the headquarters lease at 34 Newbury Street. Hovey told Lane, who asked the
ALA president for clarification. Lane apparently thought Bostwick might have

another motive in mind and so informed him that "the question should not be confused with an entirely different one,—whether or not Mr. Hovey is to be continued as Executive Officer." Lane reminded him that "the maintenance of headquarters and the employment of any particular individual are two different subjects, one of which ought not to block the other." Bostwick replied he would renew the lease only if the entire executive board unanimously authorized him to sign it. He may have been especially sensitive about the issue because of the controversy surrounding the location of headquarters which had surfaced at the last conference. Bostwick then asked Legler if the publishing board would pay another full month's rent for the Newbury Street rooms until the executive board could clear up the problem at its September meeting. Legler later wrote Lane, "it seems to me there is no option left except to agree to his suggestion." He and ALA Recorder Lutie Stearns quickly cancelled previous commitments in order to attend the forthcoming publishing board meeting. But circumstances worked against them. The building's owner refused to extend the lease on a monthly basis. Bostwick had no choice but to poll board members by mail as quickly as possible. Not all board members responded, but the vote for renewing was unanimous among those who did. Bostwick and Wyer decided their only option was to renew the lease and get full, formal board approval at the forthcoming meeting.[80]

In the meantime, ALA Treasurer Hopkins was trying to determine the fiscal status of the association. His predecessor, George F. Bowerman, who had been ill most of 1907, had relinquished much of the routine accounting to Hovey. As Hopkins perused Hovey's figures he became more and more alarmed. Ultimately he was forced to conclude the executive officer was not a very careful bookkeeper. As he reworked Hovey's calculations to conform to a realistic expectation of income, Hopkins realized that ALA could not afford headquarters beyond 1 January 1908. He quickly informed the finance committee of the association's fiscal plight. Committee Chairman George A. MacBeth, a trustee of the Carnegie Free Public Library in Pittsburgh, expressed surprise, then promised aid, although he did not elaborate.

The executive board met the last week in September. Bostwick, Gould, Wyer, Hopkins, Andrews, Stearns, and Hovey attended. Andrews reported that the publishing board had agreed to contribute $500 to cover Hovey's salary through 1 January 1908. The board then discussed allocations for expenditures through the first of the year. After Hopkins presented his calculations, Hovey offered to resign effective 1 January 1908. The board then accepted his resignation. The ALA treasurer formally reminded the finance committee that Hovey still retained a balance of $600, a sum from which his salary could be drawn. The board then confirmed action by Bostwick and Wyer in renewing the headquarters lease, but "requested to ascertain on what terms it may be possible to terminate the occupancy of said quarters prior to the expiration of the lease." Finally, when Hopkins noted that Hovey had mistakenly placed $136 received for the *Proceedings* in the publishing board treasury, the board directed Hovey to prepare "a detailed statement of receipts and expenditures of Headquarters" for its next meeting, scheduled for Pittsburgh on 19 October.[81]

Because Legler had stopped at the board meeting on his way to Boston for a publishing board meeting scheduled for 1 October, he had the opportunity for several long talks with Hopkins and MacBeth about ALA's financial plight and Hovey's poor management of ALA funds. MacBeth told him that Pittsburgh's Carnegie Free Public Library would soon offer ALA rooms for its headquarters free of charge. He asked Legler to send a publishing board representative to the 19 October executive board meeting to inspect the premises and submit an opinion. Legler took this news to Boston, where publishing board members discussed it for two days. They finally decided to send Legler and Lane to the meeting, but their consensus hardly favored Pittsburgh. They acknowledged that publishing board offices should be in ALA headquarters, but only "if the latter are in New York or Chicago." Pittsburgh had four disadvantages: (1) it would necessitate the appointment of a new secretary; (2) it would force a change in board personnel because present board members were "too far removed" from Pittsburgh; (3) no publishing concern should change its location as a temporary expedient; and (4) the publishing board offices had to be located near a large library center to be able to draw on local professionals for consultation and membership.[82]

When the executive board met in Pittsburgh on 19 October, Bostwick, Gould, Wyer, Hopkins and Andrews were present; Hovey was not. By invitation MacBeth and Brett also represented the finance committee, and Legler represented the publishing board. Wyer and Bostwick reported that the terms of the lease at 34 Newbury Street did not prevent ALA from subletting its rooms, if necessary. Bostwick read Hovey's statement that it was impossible for him from data at his command "to furnish a detailed statement of the receipts and expenditures of headquarters." MacBeth said his committee had "great difficulty" preparing a budget because of the "uncertain condition [of] the association finances." He recommended three steps to correct the problem, the last one of which read: "That in future all bills be paid by and through the treasurer of the association and not through executive officers."

MacBeth then spoke for Pittsburgh's Carnegie Library, and offered the association 2,200 square feet of space "without expense and for an indefinite length of time" for headquarters and publishing board activities. The executive board thanked him, then inspected the building. When members reassembled, Legler presented the collective opinion of the publishing board identified at its 2 October meeting. The executive board discussed the opinion at length before coming to a decision. Because the "financial condition of the association renders it impossible further to maintain headquarters under present arrangements," the board recommended unanimously that council accept Pittsburgh's offer "to take effect as soon as possible." Board members also urged the council to meet in Pittsburgh on 9 December to decide the issue "unless the correspondence vote sent out herewith shall be unanimous,'' or unless the council relinquished responsibility for action to the executive board by majority vote.[83]

Legler was not satisfied. He circulated a summary of the executive board meeting to publishing board members and expressed ''purely a personal opinion'' that transferring the publishing board to Pittsburgh would be ''unwise.'' He admitted that the space and facilities there were ''excellent,'' but he disliked its location. As an alternative he recommended staying at 34 Newbury Street, and renting only one floor for $500 or less. That would allow the board to defer a decision on relocation until the Lake Minnetonka conference. He then appointed Lane and Soule as a committee to explore his alternative and he forwarded copies of his circular to ALA executive board and finance committee members.

The following day Brett wrote Legler confidentially that trustees of the Cleveland Public Library were also willing to provide space for ALA headquarters and the publishing board. Brett said he had welcomed his board's offer as ''very generous'' and potentially ''advantageous'' to both groups, but he believed the association ought to respond to Pittsburgh first. Gould hoped that publishing board offices would not separate from headquarters. ''You know how important it seems that the whole ALA should be represented in the Pittsburgh Library for a time at least.'' Legler was unconvinced. He wrote Lane that although the publishing board had not been asked to attend the 9 December executive board meeting, he wanted Lane to present the publishing board's case.[84]

While Legler jockeyed for position, Wyer received responses from 22 of the 25 council members. The results were far from unanimous. Thirteen favored accepting, six opposed, and three abstained. Eighteen had also voted against calling a special meeting. Wyer advised Bostwick that the ''opposition is so considerable and strenuous as to make it out of the question for the Executive Board to decide the matter.'' The association would not be able to decide on the Pittsburgh offer until next summer. What to do for the immediate future? ''It is my personal opinion that the course recommended by you and Mr. Andrews at Pittsburgh seems the wiser one, of letting the matter hold over till the Minnetonka meeting, providing a clerk to look after the necessary matters in Boston, from January to July.'' Privately Lane told Legler he was ''relieved'' that the question had been postponed. Lane had already contacted Bolton about moving the publishing board back to the Boston Athenaeum, but Bolton said he had no room.[85]

The postponement of a final decision on the Pittsburgh offer allowed other people time to maneuver. Hovey left office on 1 January 1908, and the following day the League of Library Commissions opened its annual midwinter conference at the Chicago Public Library, where members informally discussed the relocation of ALA headquarters. Andrews summarized the status quo, while Lutie Stearns recounted the history of its development. Largely at Mary Ahern's urging, the league passed a resolution. Because ''headquarters ought to be located with special reference to the extension of library interests in those sections of the country where efforts promised the greatest possibilities," the ALA executive board should consider "the advisability of selecting Chicago as the location for the ALA headquarters, in the event that suitable arrangements can be effected for the necessary quarters required." The headquarters question had received a new twist.

Two days later Ahern wrote to the trustees of the Newberry Library. As president of the Illinois Library Association, she asked them to "graciously permit the use of occupied space in the Newberry Library of Chicago for the Executive Offices of the American Library Association." She reminded them how important Poole had been to ALA. "It would be the most fitting thing, it seems to me, if the library to which he gave so much thought and devotion would open its doors as a home for the work of the Association." Stroking was not her only tactic. Ahern also got the Chicago Library Club and the library committee of the City Club of Chicago to write similar letters. Bowker soon got wind of Ahern's scheme: "ALA matters are rather mixed, and it does seem as though there was more pulling apart than pulling together," he lamented to Helen Haines. " 'The old order changes'—and let us hope the new order will work out alright, even if we have less part in it."[86]

At the publishing board meeting in Boston in February, Legler told committee members about a possible Chicago offer. Wellman worried. He wrote Bostwick that "New York is on the whole preferable to Chicago," and asked the ALA president if quarters might be found in the main NYPL building when completed, or lacking that, at least in a branch. Bostwick replied that he regretted the library did not have available space, but "I agree with you that New York is the best place for headquarters."

Ahern worked fast. When the Newberry trustees turned her down, she expanded her search to commercial firms dealing in library supplies and services. Since she knew the Crerar would provide space when its new building was completed in a few years, all she needed was temporary quarters. One firm in particular, the A. C. McClurg Company, showed active interest. On 10 March company secretary O. T. McClurg wrote Wyer that since the Crerar was still not ready for occupancy, "we might be in a position to help you out." The company was moving its wholesale department to another building, but the terms of its lease did not permit subletting. "No one, however, could prevent our giving space away," and for security's sake the company preferred to have it occupied rather than vacant through the end of the lease on 1 May 1914. McClurg also indicated that the company would be willing to wait for a decision until the Minnetonka conference.[87] Unfortunately, McClurg's letter did not reach Wyer's office until after he had left for an executive board meeting on 14 March, and thus an opportunity for quick response was lost.

Ahern broadened her campaign to other midwestern librarians. She wrote Legler on 16 March, "Why can't we include a wider circle than just Chicago in bringing the headquarters here?" Nine days later she invited Legler to Chicago to demonstrate to the McClurg Company board of directors the advantages of relocating publishing board offices to Chicago. When Wyer finally read Mc-Clurg's letter he composed a careful response. "Your informant has very much overstated the present situation" by saying the association was "seriously considering" moving to Chicago, he said. Chicago had been informally discussed as a possibility, but not seriously since no one had extended a definite proposition. With McClurg's offer, however, the situation had changed, and Wyer indicated that the association would gladly consider it at the Minnetonka conference.[88]

But Ahern kept pressing. *Public Libraries* editorialized in April that "Chicago, in the great valley which is the center of library activity in the United States, seems to be the logical place to put the headquarters of any Association whose membership reaches from the Atlantic to the Pacific." On 3 April she wrote Legler that she had promises from two other locations if McClurg's was not acceptable. The board of the Field Museum of Natural History would open space to ALA, and the Chicago Association of Commerce would be willing to offer "the top stories of some high buildings in the loop district." Finally, she told Legler, the Chicago Library Club was going to turn its 9 April meeting into "an ALA rally." She invited Legler to speak to the club because Chicago's library leaders were not generally supporting her efforts. Newberry Library Director John Vance Cheney did not associate much with fellow librarians, Chicago Public Library Director Frederick Hild harbored hostile feelings towards the ALA dating back to 1893, and Andrews of the Crerar "has some kind of queer notion that because he was on the original committee that provided for headquarters, it would be unbecoming for him to take any part at all." Although Legler was unable to attend, the "rally" went on without him. Ahern made the other two offers public, and noted that the Chicago Chamber of Commerce had secured an option on four locations, including space in the Chicago offices of the Library Bureau. In describing the meeting, PL concluded, "It hardly seems possible that the advantage of Chicago in location can be overlooked in making a decision."[89]

As the Minnetonka conference approached, opposing factions continued to compete for position. Deloraine Corey wrote Bostwick on behalf of the endowment fund trustees that the association should keep its money in Massachusetts banks. Because ALA was incorporated in the Bay State and under Massachusetts law considered a benevolent association, ALA funds were not taxed. "If there is any prospect of a removal," he told Bostwick, "an inquiry as to the possibility of taxation in the new locus would be desirable." He also said that the composition of the endowment fund committee would have to change if headquarters was moved.

Those in favor of Chicago were undeterred, however. Legler visited the McClurg building and was "very much impressed." He wrote Gould that the publishing board would contribute $1,500 per annum to maintaining headquarters in Chicago, "assuming that the right kind of person is selected" as executive secretary. He already had someone in mind, a compromise candidate who had remained above the controversy during the past two years. On 5 June he asked Theresa

West Elmendorf, who became vice-librarian at the Buffalo Public Library after the death of her husband, to consider the job if ALA could regroup the headquarters idea in Chicago. He also assured her that she would not "become involved in the politics of the Association, which have been at such red heat for the past few years." But Elmendorf balked. "I do not think that I can possibly allow the attempt to give me this position to be made," she said. She did not want to "displace" Nina Browne, and she was not sure that ALA could afford another executive secretary. And she did not want to give up her Buffalo position "for the sake of what will be, at the best, an experiment."[90]

Although the controversy surrounding the location of headquarters preoccupied ALA leaders between conferences, two other significant developments emerged. Dewey still wanted to promote the American Library Institute from afar. In January he asked the 50 ALI fellows to identify a sense of direction for the institute. The response was not encouraging. Lane wrote, "I should really dread to see it take up active work because that would mean one more demand on my time and thought." Gardner Jones stated, "I've never understood the necessity for this association." Putnam was no less sanguine about Dewey's effort, and Stearns thought the ALI "undemocratic." Any movement to push it threatened the whole ALA. "The Hovey fiasco . . . engendered bitter feelings," she said. "I believe the ALA members must try to pull together, shoulder to shoulder, to bring about the old-time harmony and unity." Hodges wrote, "To be perfectly frank, I am one of those who think the ALI should be given a decent burial." Only Bostwick supported ALI, and recommended Dana become its president and give it a sense of direction. Characteristically, Dewey refused to admit defeat. He recommended that the ALI board only schedule an informal session at Atlantic City in March and wait for a more propitious moment to plan for the future. No one argued.[91]

A second development surrounded the ALA constitution. Most ALA members recognized that the creation of the position of executive secretary made the existing constitution outdated because the duties it assigned to specific officers no longer conformed to functional reality. Part of Hovey's difficulties could be traced to the constitution's shortcomings. With the high probability that ALA would soon relocate headquarters and hire a new executive secretary, revising the constitution became increasingly important. Ahern was especially concerned. She offered the columns of *Public Libraries* for a symposium on the subject, and several librarians responded. Legler wanted a full-time, salaried executive secretary to manage the business affairs of the association *and* the publishing board. Dana preferred that the association be managed by an executive board of three, one of whom would be the executive officer.

At the Atlantic City executive board meeting in March, a constitutional revision committee drafted a list of recommendations. The executive board would consist of the president, two vice presidents and six other members, elected two each year for a three-year term. The council would consist of the ex officio members of the executive board, all ex-presidents, and 50 elected members, ten of whom would be elected each year for a five-year term. The executive board would conduct the business affairs of the association, while the council would "consider and discuss" questions which involved association "policy." The offices of secretary and treasurer would not be merged, and one member of the executive board would be designated chairman of the publishing board. These steps were specifically intended to eliminate the confusion about responsibilities between the executive board and the council over the past several years. The revision committee also addressed problems evident in the 1907 elections. Members recommended that voting privileges for new ALA members be limited during their first year of membership so elections would not be unduly affected by sectional allegiances. In addition, a nominating committee charged to assemble an "official ticket" would be appointed by the executive board; no board member could serve on the committee.[92]

Besides streamlining and centralizing authority and responsibility in the hands of the executive board, the revision committee's suggestions also had direct bearing on ALI. Dewey had wanted an institute for "considering and discussing" library matters. Since the revised constitution proposed to do the same thing with the council, some wondered if ALI was necessary at all. Several ALA members recognized this immediately. Dana reported to Wellman that "ALI can and will resolve itself into the Council of the ALA," but until the constitutional changes were made ALI should "continue to exist." It was in this environment that ALI held its "informal" Atlantic City meeting. For the first time ALI members perceived a purpose for meeting: their actions and procedures would serve as precedents to the ALA Council under a revised constitution. Finally, ALI seemed to have a *raison d'être* more acceptable than Dewey's persistence.

As the Minnetonka conference drew near, the three major library periodicals focused their attention on the revision of the constitution and the location of headquarters. LJ wanted the council to absorb the institute, and the executive board to have more power. Headquarters should be in New York. PL cautioned against giving the board too much power, and pushed for headquarters in Chicago. The *Bulletin* equivocated. "These are matters of great moment which can scarcely be rightly determined from personal or even sectional considerations."[93]

Unlike its predecessor, the 1908 ALA conference at Lake Minnetonka featured a surprisingly amiable spirit. Part of the reason may have come from the non-controversial conference theme Bostwick had chosen—"The Use and Value of Books." Probably more important was the geographic distribution of conferees. With 664 total registrants, the Minnetonka conference ranked third in size in ALA's 34-year history. Of the total, 444 came from North Central states, 106 from the North Atlantic states; 488 were women. The conference was clearly dominated by midwestern librarians, and the manifestations of this dominance surfaced frequently. The H. W. Wilson Company, a new but growing concern based in Minnesota, issued a conference paper entitled the *Daily Cumulative*.

The executive board and the council met before Bostwick had even opened the first general session on 22 June. The former heard Wyer read Nina Browne's letter recommending that endowment fund trustees be bonded. Wyer then read Corey's letter regarding the potential loss of tax advantages if the association moved its money out of Massachusetts. Finally, Wyer read his exchange of correspondence with George MacBeth of Pittsburgh and the A. C. McClurg Company of Chicago. "After discussion these letters and the whole question of location of Headquarters was referred to the Council."

Of 19 members present at the council meeting later that afternoon, only five came from North Atlantic states. Item one on the agenda was the location of headquarters. Andrews described offers from MacBeth and McClurg, and three other offers from Chicago. Curiously, council voted to relinquish responsibility for the entire matter to the new executive board, but expressed a hope that the publishing board chairman would have one vote on the question. When council polled itself on the most desirable location, the result proved lopsided: Chicago, 16; Washington, 2 (the ALA president did not vote). After hearing Bostwick's account of his trip to midwestern state library association meetings in October 1907, Andrews spoke for the committee on the issue of constitutional revision. He pointed out that the committee's recommendations encompassed three important changes: (1) enlarging and reconstituting the executive board; (2) greatly enlarging and reconstituting the council; and (3) explicitly identifying and distinguishing between the duties and the functions of the council and the executive board. Council voted that "the general scheme be approved and that its discussion in detail be made a special order of business at the next meeting of the Council."

Before adjourning, council accepted the nominating committee's slate of officers: for president, C. H. Gould; for first vice president, N. D. C. Hodges; for second vice president, Theresa W. Elmendorf; for treasurer, Purd B. Wright of St. Joseph, Missouri; and for recorder, Mary Ahern. Wyer was entering the second year of his second three-year term as secretary. If elected, the new executive board would have no one from the Northeast except ex-president Bostwick. The makeup of this slate of nominees may explain why the council had earlier been so willing to pass responsibility for relocating headquarters to a new executive board which would likely enjoy expanded powers under a revised constitution. Perhaps the struggle was over before it began. At Minnetonka, a rival slate of nominees would be impossible to carry given the large majority of midwestern librarians present. Northeastern librarians had to reconcile themselves to the impending shift. After 34 years, ALA was no longer in their control.

All of this may not have been obvious when Bostwick delivered his presidential address on "The Librarian as Censor" that evening. Bostwick contended librarians had to select the best books to justify their existence. Wyer followed with his secretary's report, which noted that ALA boasted 1,950 members, a drop from the previous year which had witnessed an increase in library memberships. He also read Hopkins's treasurer's report, which showed a balance of $2,775.83. Hopkins especially mentioned that since the beginning of the year "an entire new set of books was opened and a voucher system introduced."

Legler followed with a lengthy report from the publishing board. He emphasized the importance of locating headquarters and the publishing board in the same building for "mutual convenience and effective business administration," and he read a board resolution expressing a preference for New York or Chicago. He then gave an item-by-item progress report on ALA publications, both published and in process, and announced two new tracts, Mary Plummer's *Training for Librarianship*, and Chalmers Hadley's *Material for a Public Library Campaign*.

At the third session Bostwick introduced the headquarters issue. Hill quickly moved that " . . . headquarters should preferably be placed in a library building as soon as possible and shall not be located in connection with a commercial house having library interests." Steiner seconded. Hill later explained that he did not want the association "to lend its influence or its name to any commercial enterprise." Andrews disagreed with Hill's motion. He argued that it would not be "right to tie up the incoming Executive Board with an expression which will be interpreted by them as an instruction to refuse arrangements." Bostwick called for a rising vote and counted 81 for Hill's motion, 41 against. The motion lacked the three-fourths majority the old constitution required to bind the executive board. Conferees did, however, pass Hill's suggestion to refer the proposed motion to the council for consideration (but Hill's motion lost there also). At the fourth and final general session, Wyer read council reports and a draft of the revised constitution. Andrews moved its acceptance, Thwaites seconded, and the association adopted it unanimously. To take effect the new constitution needed another vote at the subsequent conference. Tellers then reported the results of the election, which duplicated exactly the slate of nominees presented to the council. No one challenged it. After passing the gavel to Gould, his successor, Bostwick adjourned the conference.

The new executive board met on 27 June to decide the headquarters question and to fill vacant committee positions. Legler joined them in voting unanimously to locate headquarters in Chicago, but he is not recorded as saying anything when they agreed with Hill's motion not to associate with a commercial house having library interests. The executive board then appointed Andrews, Legler and Ahern to a "committee on location of headquarters" in Chicago "with instructions to report to the Executive Board," and further voted that if headquarters could not be secured in Chicago by 15 August, the president was authorized to renew the Boston lease at 34 Newbury Street for six months. Committee appointments followed. Putnam, Andrews, Carr, Hill and Lane retained their spots on the constitutional revision committee, but the publishing board assumed a new geographic profile. Legler retained the chairmanship, but other members included Wellman, Elmendorf, Andrews, and MacDonald. Two years earlier the publishing board had four from New England, one from the Midwest; now the proportion was almost exactly reversed.

Each of the ALA sections held at least one meeting during the conference; most held two. Affiliated organizations met in multiple sessions. The American Association of Law Libraries took six sessions to conduct its business, while the League of Library Commissions devoted each of its three sessions to a particular topic. The National Association of State Libraries used only two sessions, but taken together they took more time than the other two organizations combined. In fact, NASL *Proceedings* cumulated to 44 pages as compared with 12 for the League and five for AALL. And since ALA funded the publication of the proceedings of all affiliated organizations, several people began to voice concern.[94]

From start to finish the Minnetonka conference was a midwestern dominated library affair. The constitutional revision and the headquarters issues easily passed the membership, council and executive board because midwesterners held a majority. In addition, the new executive and publishing boards no longer reflected northeastern majorities. Minnetonka manifested a geographic shift in the control of the ALA from Boston to Chicago. And it was in Chicago that the association would now try to relocate its headquarters.

The new committee had to move quickly. On 11 July, Andrews sent Gould a status report on all site offers. The committee recommended against the Field Museum of Natural History because it was too distant from the center of the city. In addition, the Library Bureau had already withdrawn its offer, and because efforts to locate space at the University of Chicago proved futile, the committee had only one recommendation—accept the proposal from the Chicago Chamber of Commerce. Andrews further explained that the rooms which the chamber offered had been donated by the A. C. McClurg Company. ''If this is satisfactory to you, the Committee will proceed immediately with the necessary arrangements,'' Andrews concluded. ''If not, they see no further use to the Association of their services in this connection and beg to be relieved of further responsibility in the matter.''[95]

At this point the situation became confusing. Because members of the executive board and the committee on the relocation of headquarters communicated by letter, messages often crossed in the mail. Therefore, it was difficult not only to coordinate efforts, but also to agree on just what action should be taken. Elmendorf and Ahern recommended that ALA accept the Chicago offer immediately, and Andrews assured Gould on 13 July that Legler would also approve. Wright objected, however, and Bailey and Hill reminded Gould of the association's recent vote against any connection with a commercial house. Hill was especially adamant—''hold aloof from entangling alliances'' and give up headquarters altogether rather than join McClurg, he urged. Next day Gould thanked Hill for his note and said that he agreed ''that the ALA should not be placed under any obligation to commercial houses, and I think the present Executive Board, as a whole, has the same feeling.'' On 15 July Wyer informed the executive board that ALA would be unable to renew its Boston lease for less than a year.[96]

On 18 July Gould wrote Andrews a lengthy formal note to explain his position. The ALA president said he did not yet have a copy of the board minutes for verification, but he did recall a resolution saying it was ''undesirable'' to associate with a commercial house. Since Andrews's committee had recommended accepting the same rooms McClurg had offered several months earlier, "the Chicago Association of Commerce must be intervening in name only." Gould regarded this arrangement as unacceptable in light of the board's resolution. "The headquarters question has been . . . dividing the Association for some time. Can we not manage to dispose of it now in such a manner that it will cease to be a burning question?" In an attached less formal note meant for Andrews's eyes only Gould expressed puzzlement. "There has been some misunderstanding of the position of the Executive Board, something which with Miss Ahern on your committee, I did not suppose would be possible." That same day Gould explained his position to Elmendorf and cautioned her against casting a hasty vote. "Do not let our appreciation of individuals lead us to place the ALA in a false position," he advised. "The need for immediate action is rather in Boston than Chicago" because the proprietor of 34 Newbury Street wanted to commit quarters for the forthcoming year.[97]

Next day Gould telegraphed Wyer for minutes of the 27 June executive board meeting. He wanted to make sure of his position, and to reexamine the committee's charge. "As I recollected," he wrote Wyer the following day, Andrews, Ahern and Legler were appointed "not to make recommendations concerning headquarters, but to see if any rooms other than those which had been under discussion could be obtained in Chicago." Wyer sent the minutes on 20 July, along with a note from Bostwick, indicating that he had voted to renew the Boston lease because "there seems to be so much feeling" against any connection with the McClurg company. Nonetheless, he would not "persist . . . in case I should be the only one on the Board voting in this way." Elmendorf felt the same way. She told Gould that she had voted for the offer because an affirmative vote would not hold up progress, while one negative vote would kill any further action. Still, she had reservations. "I don't know that I am altogether firmly convinced that Chicago is the ideal place." She also thought the association had misplaced priorities. "I think the question as to who is to manage headquarters . . . is much more vital. It isn't place; it is policy and intelligence and good feeling that matter, it seems to me."[98]

Although he had support, Gould recognized his position would be questioned. Andrews wrote him on 20 July, "Your recollection of the position of the members at the Board meeting and their action is very different from that of Miss Ahern," Andrews said; "Mr. Wright's and Mr. Wyer's letters to me confirm her view. From them it would seem that you are the only one who did not directly or indirectly express themselves [sic] in favor of the McClurg offer if [the committee] can do no better." But Gould would not retreat. Next day he wrote Wright, Ahern, and Legler that the Chicago Association of Commerce's intervention had not changed the issue. In his opinion ALA would still be associated with a commercial organization, a situation clearly prohibited by a resolution passed at the Minnetonka conference. Gould was especially careful with Legler. "I think we should not resort to a subterfuge to get ourselves out of a difficulty."

To Elmendorf he wrote, "We can really do nothing until every one of us is supplied with the minutes." Since Gould had already seen a copy, he felt certain of his position.[99]

Wyer was his strongest supporter. "The Chicago people are trying to force the McClurg proposal on us in a slightly different guise," he wrote Gould on 22 July, "and the tone of Mr. Andrews' letter is just a little pettish—as much as to say 'this or nothing.' " Bostwick also agreed with Gould's interpretation of the board's decision; Ahern and Andrews did not. "We have rather an interesting psychological study in the situation," Ahern wrote Gould. The executive board had voted unanimously for Chicago, she said, and reminded him that she had originally objected to Hill's motion "because it would remove all possibility of having headquarters in Chicago." The motion was changed "at my suggestion, to the approval of the *spirit* of the resolution. I am positive about these facts." She disclaimed any personal desire in the question except to see the association's best interests served, and she wondered why Gould had not been more vocal and articulate in his opinions at the executive board meeting which everyone was now misinterpreting. To Legler she wrote, "I am tired of the ALA controversy." She felt her position was sound and Gould "is now saying a lot of things that he should have said in Minnetonka. I have written him today to count me out in further discussion in the matter. I am willing to work, but I am not willing to quarrel."

Ahern was losing her resolve. So was Andrews. "I have been expecting a telegram reversing your previous decision and so relieving a position which is no credit to the Association." Andrews rendered his interpretation of the council and executive board action, and reminded Gould that the ALA owed the Chicago Association of Commerce a decision. If the executive board did not accept the committee's "recommendation," he would resign from the committee and the publishing board, since he would be too distant from the latter to provide adequate service.[100] Andrews was clearly embarrassed by Gould's intransigence on the issue, but Gould was determined not to act hastily. He speculated that the wrong move might split the entire association.

Pressure and confusion continued. Lane wrote Legler on 23 July that ALA had to decide quickly or the publishing board would have no official home. Browne told Gould the same thing. W. H. Manss of the Chicago Association of Commerce wrote Mary Ahern on 24 July that his organization deserved an answer. Because the offer "was not only published in our own paper, but was given publicity in all of the papers of Chicago and favorable comment was made in the editorials of the Chicago press," he told Ahern, "the people of Chicago are wondering what location has been decided upon." Ahern forwarded a copy of Manss's letter to Gould, reminded him that the offer had been given generous publicity, and forewarned him that several trustees of the John Crerar Library, who had promised the association space when their building was completed, were irritated with the association's lack of action. Since the offer from the commerce association afforded ALA a temporary solution until the Crerar was finished, she again advised Gould to accept it. Andrews again castigated Gould for opposing a plan "which has the approval of the Council and the Executive Board and is opposed, so far as I am aware, only by sectional and trade interest." To Legler he wrote that Gould's position "promises to block and nullify all our efforts to secure headquarters here." He suggested that Legler remind the ALA president of publishing board needs.[101]

On 24 July Legler wrote Gould a lengthy letter attempting to summarize the situation as he understood it. The committee favored the McClurg building, he told Gould, "but you declined to accept them as being in contravention with the wishes of the Association." And since the committee had no other possibilities and continuation of headquarters at 34 Newbury Street seemed impossible, the association had two alternatives: (1) rent headquarters "on a modest scale" in either Chicago or Boston for a year; or (2) rent a room in Boston which the publishing board could use temporarily, and transfer all other ALA business to the ALA secretary. He recommended the second option because Nina Browne was "not at all fitted to conduct the business of the association in a suitable manner." Legler did not clearly see where any acceptance of the proposition could result in any "material benefit to McClurg," but he was willing to accede to executive board wishes. In a letter to fellow members of the publishing board, he asked what arrangements the board should make to meet the future. Next day he wrote Andrews: "I appreciate fully the embarrassment which results from Mr. Gould's disinclination to join with the other members of the Board in accepting the McClurg quarters." He said that he would also resign if headquarters remained in the East. He even admitted to Lane on 26 July that the "necessity for having the members of the board locate near headquarters is borne upon me more forcefully than I am frank to say was formerly the case."[102]

On 25 July Gould sent a dispirited letter to Andrews. He quoted minutes of the executive board meeting in their entirety. The resolutions were clear, he said. ALA headquarters "should not be located in connection with a commercial house having library interests." That was a direct quote, Gould said. If the executive board favored McClurg, he asked, why did it appoint a Chicago committee? The offer was already in ALA hands, but since the board did not accept it at that time, "it is clear that your committee was asked to try to find other quarters than any which had been offered." He was not the only board member to disapprove the McClurg offer. In fact, only two people were unequivocally for it. Ahern had always supported the idea and Wright had only recently reversed his position. All others changed their minds when they read the minutes of the 24 June board meeting. He told Andrews: "I think the chief difficulty in regard to this whole matter has arisen because your Committee and one or two members of the Board have taken an approval of Chicago as synonymous with approval of accepting McClurg's offer." Although he did not directly accuse Andrews of overstepping his authority by attempting to negotiate for the association, evidence demonstrates that he certainly felt the Chicago committee had exceeded its charge. Despite his feeling, however, he asked

Andrews not to resign from any committees. Elmendorf and Wyer agreed. Gould later reflected on the committee's authority. "I had expected a report on what they had been able to accomplish, not a recommendation of the sort they sent in." On 28 July he asked the ALA executive board if the association should now try to rent new quarters, and if so, how much could it afford.[103]

The publishing board was also affected by the impasse because it needed a decision in order to plan for the coming year. Lane suggested that *Booklist* editorial offices remain in Madison, and he recommended F. W. Faxon as the next ALA executive secretary, when the association could afford it. Legler passed Lane's suggestion to Gould, and added his own opinion: "A mere makeshift arrangement [in Chicago] would . . . be a great mistake." It would be better to "worry along in Boston with inadequate arrangements" at 34 Newbury Street.[104] Gould agreed. Andrews wrote on 2 August. "I have transmitted your message to the Chicago Association of Commerce and with this action conclude my services to the Association." Gould asked Wyer to poll the executive board to determine ALA's next step, but before Wyer could draft a letter Legler felt compelled to take action. He instructed Browne to renew the publishing board's lease at 34 Newbury Street.[105]

The fight over the headquarters issue left a residue of bitterness among ALA leaders. Much of the animosity was cast in sectionalist feelings, but the competition between small and large library interests which had preoccupied ALA for the past few years served as an equally steady stimulant to perpetuation of discord. Everyone recognized the inadvisability of splitting the association, and in the end that attitude forced consensus on renewing the Boston lease. The most reluctant member of the board, however, remained Mary Ahern. As editor of *Public Libraries*, she could easily publicize the discord which had been kept private. On 3 September she wrote Gould that "an explanation from you of the entirely new and unexpected situation in regard to ALA headquarters will be expected by the librarians of the country." She offered the columns of *Public Libraries* for his explanation. Gould said he would refer her offer to the executive board. Within two weeks she resigned as ALA recorder. "Circumstances make it impossible for me to serve as I should like to do." Gould accepted her resignation four days later.[106]

The executive board met on 25 September. In addition to routine matters, the board appointed Alice B. Kroeger to replace Mary Ahern as ALA recorder. Wyer read Andrews's 11 July letter to Gould, after which the board discharged the committee. Wyer then announced that the board had unanimously agreed to renew the lease for 34 Newbury Street. A publishing board report also indicated that Elva Bascom of the Wisconsin Free Library Commission had replaced Katharine MacDonald as editor of *Booklist*. During the executive session members showed they were still interested in the Windy City by inviting Legler and Wellman of the publishing board to discuss the possibility of financing headquarters in Chicago. Each board agreed to contribute $1,500 towards the salary of an executive officer. Both also agreed to consult on the composition of the publishing board under the new constitution.[107]

On 1 October 1908, Mary Ahern entitled an editorial in *Public Libraries* "How A.L.A. Headquarters Were Lost to Chicago." She recounted her interpretation of events by suggesting that her committee believed that Hill's resolution "did not voice the feelings of a large part of the A.L.A.," and certainly "was not pertinent" to the Chicago Association of Commerce offer. She further explained that every member of the executive board voted to adopt the report, except Gould, who insisted that accepting the offer would violate Hill's resolution. "Subsequent correspondence failed to change his decision." When further consultation failed to produce a unanimous vote, Gould renewed the Newbury Street lease for one year. Ahern said she had invited Gould to explain his action in *Public Libraries*, then quoted from his letter explaining that he would refer her request to the executive board. The board never answered.

Neither Gould nor the ALA executive board replied to Ahern's editorial in print, but several castigated her in their private correspondence with the ALA president. "One member of the board has no right to take advantage of her position of editor to give a one-sided statement," Gardner Jones wrote. "All your friends will feel indignant at these absurd editorials. They are so puerile," Mabel Haines comforted Gould. But proponents of a Chicago ALA headquarters had not given up. When Legler addressed the Chicago Library Club on 8 October 1908, he assured club members "that headquarters would be in Chicago by September, 1909."[108]

For a short time the controversy subsided. Wyer privately addressed Ahern's interpretation of events, but did not convince her. Ahern then asked Legler for advice. He recognized the futility of persisting, and although he sympathized "with the annoyance which the matter has caused you," he counseled Ahern "there is nothing to be gained in continuing the controversy." In January Wyer asked Bowker if the new Engineers Building in New York City might be available, since "Chicago is not moving in the matter." He was concerned that the association would find itself in the same predicament as the previous summer if it did not act.[109]

Two months later Wyer became even more anxious. On 11 March he asked Gould to contact Legler because he sensed renewed efforts to locate headquarters space in Chicago. He was right. On 18 March Robert P. Walker of the Chicago Association of Commerce offered Gould 1,800 square feet of office space in the Ohio Building at a rate of one dollar per square foot. Two days later Ahern told Legler about the offer. Then, on 26 March, Wyer informed the executive board that "an early meeting will be necessary" to decide upon continuing executive offices in Boston "as it seems likely to be affected by a probable readjustment of the work of the Publishing Board." He suggested the meeting take place in either Cleveland or Buffalo on 15 April. Wyer did not send a copy of the circular to Legler.

The "readjustment" to which Wyer referred concerned negotiations between Andrews, who was still on the publishing board, and the H. W. Wilson Company of Minneapolis to transfer the publishing board's routine clerical and sales work to Minneapolis. Wilson had made the offer, and because the chances of relocating in Chicago continued to look dim, Andrews and Legler thought the move might save enough money to allow the publishing board to expand its contribution and bring headquarters to Chicago anyway. On 3 April, Gould told Legler about the Chicago Association of Commerce's new offer, but made no mention of the executive board meeting which was tentatively scheduled for 15 April. On 6 April Gould asked Andrews for a memo summarizing the status of negotiations with Wilson. On 9 April, Wyer told Gould that he had arranged an executive board meeting for Buffalo on 15 April. "I am sending no notices of the meeting to any but the members of the *Executive Board* presuming that Mrs. Elmendorf will be able to speak for the Publishing Board." Wyer wanted to restrict knowledge of the meeting as much as possible, perhaps to prevent a recurrence of the unpleasant activities of the previous summer. ALA Treasurer Purd Wright wrote Gould that he could not make the meeting, but he added that ALA could never establish headquarters without the financial contribution of the publishing board.[110]

About this time two other seemingly unrelated incidents took place which had tremendous impact upon the headquarters question. On 12 April, trustees of the Chicago Public Library asked for director Frederick Hild's resignation because of his "conservatism and lack of enterprise as an executive." When Hild ignored their request, the board fired him, effective 30 April. On 26 March Legler complained to Gould that Wyer had levied unfair criticism about a Wisconsin Free Library Commission publication in the ALA *Bulletin*. Legler decried the ALA secretary's "impropriety of using the official organ of the Association for the expression of what must be at best a personal view." Although Gould tried to temper Legler by agreeing with him, reassuring him "Mr. Wyer now takes the same view as you do," Legler became more and more suspicious of the ALA secretary and wondered whose interests he had at heart.

These suspicions mushroomed when Legler "unofficially, and wholly by accident" found out about the executive board meeting scheduled for 15 April. He wrote Gould on 12 April that he could not leave Madison "on such short notice," but he wanted the executive board to know about progress in negotiations with the Wilson Company. Should Wilson assume publishing board business functions and the ALA discontinue its Boston headquarters, Legler recommended the association use its remaining resources to hire a full-time secretary. The following day he showed more irritation at not being invited, especially since the publishing board's contribution to headquarters would undoubtedly play a large part in the executive board's final decision. Legler was already suspicious of Wyer; now he wondered about Gould.[111]

Although the primary purpose for calling the Buffalo meeting was the headquarters issue, the published minutes do not indicate it was even discussed. LJ's account noted all members of the board were present except Wright, that they considered the forthcoming conference program, discussed an invitation to an international library conference, and heard reports from the NEA cooperation committee and Wright's prepared statement on association finances. Whoever sent LJ a copy of the minutes, however, did not include everything. The meeting remained in session. After reviewing Wright's report, Gould suggested the "probability" that the publishing board would soon make arrangements "which will make it inexpedient for the Board to continue its present financial cooperation in maintaining executive offices." Based on that premise, the executive board recommended to its successor that Boston headquarters be discontinued. Wyer read Robert Walker's 18 March letter, but the board decided "the Association is not at present in a position to consider the offer."[112] Once again Chicago was spurned.

On 17 April Gould apologized to Legler for not inviting him to the executive board meeting. The ALA president explained he remembered Legler had indicated in mid-March he could not attend an April meeting. Gould said he then told Wyer, who subsequently decided not even to send Legler an invitation to the Buffalo meeting. Legler reluctantly accepted Gould's explanation, but stated, "I am deeply interested in the outcome of the meeting, and hope to get an early reply concerning your deliberations and conclusions." On 20 April Wright told Gould that he "was surprised to hear that Mr. Legler was not notified of the Buffalo meeting. He has a vote on headquarters." He forwarded a copy of his letter to Legler, who responded three days later that he was not offended, but he did want to know what happened at Buffalo. "Just as soon as we hear what action was taken there we shall decide upon our recommendations to the Publishing Board." On 27 April Wyer sent Legler an incomplete copy of the board minutes. He did not include a record of the discussion and vote on discontinuing headquarters, but told Legler that Gould would write him in more detail later.[113]

The secrecy surrounding the Buffalo meeting aroused suspicions. On 26 April Ahern asked Legler if he had heard any news. He responded: "I am densely ignorant as to what was done and there does not seem to be any disposition to enlighten me." He had just seen Brett, who had "quizzed Kroeger," but the latter said she was not in a position to reveal the substance of the meeting. Legler was frustrated. "I take it that it was sort of a secret social conclave which gathered at Buffalo and the rest of us are not to know the precious things in store for us until they are ready to tell us." Wright wrote Legler on 29 April that he still did not know the "actual business done" at Buffalo.

On 30 April, however, Wyer sent Wright an unofficial and private summary of the board's decision. After reading it, Wright became tense. His suspicions were fed by the secrecy surrounding the Buffalo meeting, and he immediately jumped to conclusions. If the publishing board gave Wilson control of its business functions, he speculated, and if ALA discontinued headquarters, ALA members could easily conclude that the publishing board had abandoned headquarters and forced its closing by withdrawing support. And since the end result would kill an eastern location (Boston) and resurrect a midwestern location (Minneapolis), the entire action could be interpreted as a political move to consolidate control of the association in the hands of midwestern librarians. Wright was incensed. He quickly cabled Legler, "An intimation just received indicates that the Publishing Board is to be made a scapegoat for somebody—or some idea." Legler was still angry that he had received no word about the substance of the 15 April board meeting. Now with Wright's cable in hand, he could come to only one conclusion. "The omission of an invitation [to Buffalo] was premeditated. I must say frankly that I am greatly surprised." Ahern wrote that she had been sent a copy of the board's minutes for *Public Libraries*, but noticed several pages missing. Did Legler know anything about them?[114]

On 1 May Gould finally sent Legler a copy of the elusive minutes, along with an explanation of the rationale behind the executive board's action. Gould said the board had essentially three choices. First, it could continue its minimum effort at Boston. Neither the association nor the council appeared to favor that option by their actions at the previous ALA conference. Second, it could provide adequate funding. That would require a commitment of $5,500 per year, and the association could afford only $2,500. Third, the board could follow the plan Legler suggested in his 12 April letter: move publishing board business functions to Minneapolis and reallocate the money saved to hire a full-time secretary. The board wanted to take Legler's advice, Gould explained, but members stressed the importance of hiring the right man (no one connected with the issue ever used the word "woman") and allowing him adequate clerical assistance. Gould also explained that the executive board's decision would only take effect when the publishing board acted on Wilson's offer.

Although Gould had been reasonable and logical in his explanations, Legler suspected Wright's conclusions were closer to the truth. If the publishing board accepted Wilson's offer, the board would be expected to increase its contribution to an experiment over which it would have little control. If the publishing board rejected Wilson's offer, headquarters would close and the situation would continue to deteriorate. Either way, the publishing board could not win. Legler also wondered whether Wyer was maneuvering to become ALA executive secretary. Wright recognized the publishing board's dilemma. After reading his complete copy of the board minutes he wrote Legler, "I cannot help wondering what became of three or four other propositions from Chicago which I happen to know were submitted direct." Next day he vented his anger about Wyer. "Is his desire to absolutely dominate the ALA so overpowering that he loses sight of the fitness of things?" On 3 May Ahern told Legler that she had just found out the Chicago Association of Commerce extended "half a dozen tenders" to ALA. The minutes indicated the executive board considered only one. "Strikes me as being a little high-handed and lacking somewhat in consideration for the Publishing Board," she said. Hastily penned at the bottom of her typewritten letter she added: "I have just been talking with C.P.L. authorities and *they are interested*." She did not elaborate.[115]

Legler's response to Gould was considerably tempered. He said he understood the executive board's predicament, but he could make no reply until Andrews reported progress on negotiations with the Wilson Company. He did point out, however, that if ALA's editorial and business offices separated, "the financial ability of the Publishing Board will be increased, but the necessity for appropriating its funds for the purpose mentioned will be materially lessened." Legler's words gave Gould little comfort. On 5 May he asked E. H. Anderson and John Shaw Billings to approach Carnegie about a donation. Anderson refused. The headquarters issue "has been a bone of contention in the ALA" for years, he said, and because of the constant turmoil, "I have lost interest in the whole idea." He said Billings agreed with him.

Just at the time when it appeared that ALA headquarters was doomed, however, Ahern hinted to Legler that a new development was surfacing in Chicago. She could not be more specific, but "by the action of less than ten people the whole situation has gone to the antipodes of the expressed opinion of the members of the association at Minnetonka." She warned Legler not to allow the publishing board or the executive board to make any "permanent arrangements" until she had more details. Legler was elated and promised Ahern that he would wait.[116]

The news finally broke late in the evening of 13 May. At its monthly meeting, the board of directors of the Chicago Public Library voted to offer ALA free space for its headquarters. The next morning Ahern cabled Legler. "Public library Board voted space for Headquarters. Glory Hallelujah." Legler quickly related the news to Gould, and added: "This seems to meet in every way the conditions imposed at Minnetonka, and for which you have contended so stoutly." Ahern later explained to Gould why the Chicago Public Library (CPL) had not come forward sooner. In April 1908 the Chicago Library Club asked Hild to approach his trustees about the headquarters matter. Several months later Hild reported that the CPL trustees had acted upon the suggestion "unfavorably," but it was not until after Hild was fired that the club found out he had never even brought the subject to the trustees' attention. Ahern intimated strongly that this was one of the reasons for Hild's dismissal. Andrews was even more specific. He wrote Legler on 15 May that Hild had opposed locating headquarters in the library from the beginning, and because he retained several friends on the board, they prevented the question from ever coming up.[117]

On 17 May, H. G. Wilson, secretary of the CPL board of trustees, officially extended the library's offer to ALA. The ALA president quickly thanked Wilson, but asked more specific information on the size and condition of the space offered. In the meantime Legler journeyed to Chicago to inspect the premises, and the Chicago Library Club formed a committee to offer its services to ease ALA's move from Boston. Executive board members Elmendorf, Wright, and Hodges declared for the Chicago offer, and Legler issued a positive report for the publishing board on the space the library offered.[118]

Now matters moved quickly. On 29 May Gould wrote the executive board— and Legler—forecasting how association finances would fare if headquarters moved to Chicago. The same day Ahern wrote Legler that she had convinced

Chalmers Hadley, secretary of the Indiana Library Commission, to apply for the new executive secretary's position which would inevitably develop from the Chicago offer. The animosity which had surfaced with such frequency since the Minnetonka conference the previous summer was quickly dissipating. As ALA members prepared for another conference, it appeared the headquarters issue would finally reach a satisfactory resolution.[119]

If ALA relocated headquarters in Chicago under a full-time executive secretary with adequate clerical assistance, the duties and responsibilities falling to that individual would render the ALA constitution obsolete. Theresa West Elmendorf noted problems with the constitution frequently in a speaking tour to midwestern state library associations. The American Library Institute, whose existence was actually threatened by the revised constitution, used most of its December 1908 meeting to discuss implications of the revisions. Many had already decided ALI was "a fifth wheel." "One of the Older Time" wrote in *Public Libraries* that ALI members "wished to eliminate absolutely from A.L.A. meetings the political element so annoying in recent years. The best members," he continued, "are thoroughly tired of the small but active and pernicious minority who go to A.L.A. meetings . . . to promote the fancied interests of themselves or some of their particular friends." Dana was more succinct. He thought the association did not need a constitution. "We have enmeshed ourselves long enough in rules and regulations. Let us have a board of directors, who, under certain general restrictions, shall run the institution."[120]

William F. Yust, director of the Louisville (Kentucky) Free Public Library, also did not agree with the proposed constitutional revisions. He expressed his views in a letter to *Public Libraries* which Ahern entitled, "Shall the ALA Remain Democratic?" Yust may have been prejudiced against ALA because the association had recently voted to switch its 1909 conference site from Louisville to Bretton Woods, New Hampshire. He had been unable to obtain favorable rail and hotel rates, and could not guarantee sufficient space. Rather than risk a light turnout, and possibly to answer complaints that New England deserved another turn, the association decided to cancel Louisville and reconsider it in the future. Whether the embarrassment piqued Yust's anger or not is unclear, but he did question council representation under the proposed constitution. The council would be too bulky at 75 members, only 25 of whom would be elected by the membership. Others would be selected by the council or merit membership either by holding office on the executive board, in affiliated organizations, or as ALA ex-presidents. Yust suggested it would be better not to have a council at all. Privately Legler agreed. He argued that the method of selecting the council would be "wholly undemocratic and subversive of the very principle underlying the creation of a council whose membership shall stand as sponsors on all library questions of public and professional interest." Although Legler felt strongly, he was unwilling to push his views too hard for fear of threatening the establishment of ALA headquarters at Chicago, an event he assigned a much higher priority.

He would support Yust at Bretton Woods, but he would not champion Yust's cause.[121]

On the eve of the Bretton Woods conference, the American Library Association had achieved a moderate state of equilibrium. It had come through a turbulent period in its history still intact. The developments which had occurred since the Waukesha conference of 1901 threatened to splinter the association on numerous occasions, but ALA always proved flexible enough to meet the challenges. No longer did directors of large libraries in the East control the association. ALA leadership was now more geographically and professionally representative. The new constitution promised to return responsibility for the association to a small group, but that group would be drawn from every constituency among the membership, except women. The publishing board not only reflected a broader geographic distribution, its publishing program sought to address more directly the needs of libraries small and large, rural and urban. The success of the *Booklist* was only one manifestation. ALA had accepted into its fold several affiliated organizations, attracting each by arranging discounted travel and hotel rates if they met coterminously with ALA, and promising to publish their proceedings. The headquarters question, the issue that provoked the bitterest debate within this eight-year period, turned in favor of the group which felt strongest about it. (Ironically, had it not been for the way Dewey and several of his cohorts had treated Hild at the 1893 Chicago conference, the issue may never have arisen at all.) Still, the headquarters "experiment" had to stumble in the East for eastern librarians to permit its relocation in the West.

The association also had grown large enough to afford its own salaried officer and staff. Carnegie's millions probably had as much to do with this growth as any internal factors. Each of the hundreds of library buildings he donated needed staff. While not all libraries hired trained professionals, employees still had needs which were conditioned by their work environment. ALA sought to meet these needs, and benefited accordingly. In summary, ALA had achieved a degree of independence which allowed it to enter the second decade of the twentieth century with confidence and excitement. The association was helping the profession to forge an identity which reflected the enduring values of the socioeconomic classes from which its leaders came. Its leaders would not argue over goals; ALA promoted libraries which collected "the best reading," however ill-defined the criteria was for determining that literature. They would argue over means, however; ALA members used their association as a forum to debate what was "the largest number" and how to provide adequate services "at the least cost." That was the professional identity ALA won for the profession it served, and the years 1901–1909 witnessed the struggle to achieve this identity. The next seven years would be spent consolidating gains made.

6   Consolidating Professional Gains, 1909–1917

In the fall of 1916, Matthew Dudgeon, who had succeeded Henry Legler as Secretary of the Wisconsin Free Library Commission in late 1909 when Legler became director of the Chicago Public Library, asked numerous authors to contribute to the December issue of the *Wisconsin Library Bulletin*. Dudgeon recognized that 40 years had passed since the Philadelphia conference, and to commemorate that milestone, he wanted the *Wisconsin Library Bulletin* to publish a series of articles summarizing ALA's progress. To Hiller Wellman, who had just completed his term as ALA president, Dudgeon wrote: "The central purpose of your article would be, as I see it, to inform library school students and newer members of the profession as to what the functions of the ALA are."

Wellman titled his lead article "What the American Library Association Has Become." He believed the most "obvious feature" for the majority of members was the annual ALA conference, which provided a forum for discussing current problems. In earlier years ALA had devoted most of its attention to problems of cataloging, classification, and "other details of library machinery," he said, but more recently the association concentrated on enlarging services and expanding the library's influence over specific clienteles like children, "the working man," the blind, foreigners, and prison and asylum inmates. ALA also provided the superstructure for a number of groups whose interests focused upon specific activities or types of libraries, including sections on cataloging, children's libraries, professional training, agricultural and school libraries, trustees, and the oldest, college and reference. In addition, several affiliated societies met coterminously with ALA at annual conferences, including the National Association of State Libraries, the League of Libraries Commissions, the American Association of Law Libraries and the Special Libraries Association. Other special interests within the profession were covered by numerous "roundtables."

Wellman suggested that "much of the real work" of the ALA was done at headquarters in Chicago, which was still housed in the Chicago Public Library at no cost to the association. George B. Utley, the ALA executive secretary who had succeeded Chalmers Hadley in 1911, provided aid and advice to the profession, and continued to collect library plans and statistics. The ALA publishing board used the same offices to issue its indexes, lists, and guides, and continued to publish *Booklist* "without advertisements and free from every commercial consideration." Other standing committees devoted attention to international relations, cooperation with the National Education Association, methods of library administration, standards for library training, relations with the book trade, bookbuying, binding, and government documents. Special committees discussed a code of rules for cataloging, problems with deteriorating newsprint, compiling "a comprehensive manual of library economy," and library ventilation, lighting and insurance rates. Wellman concluded his article by saying that ALA's most important contribution to the profession was fostering an *esprit de corps* which cultivated "standards of work and of professional conduct that are none the less observed for not being embodied in a written code." The professional spirit which ALA engendered, he said, allowed the association to "command loyalty and support."

Perpetual malcontent John Cotton Dana wrote a second article, entitled "What the A.L.A. Might Do." He argued sharply that the association had to have a briefer, broader constitution which vested more control in the hands of the executive board. In subsequent articles, George Utley explained the functions of ALA headquarters in Chicago, Katharine MacDonald Jones gave an abbreviated historical account of *Booklist* (whose editorial offices were now located in Chicago), and *Booklist* editor May Massee concluded the series by discussing the periodical's plans for the future.[1]

The mix of authors Dudgeon chose reflects the considerably calmer state of affairs which ALA matters had reached by 1916. Wellman was born, raised and employed in New England from birth to death. He adamantly supported ALA headquarters in Chicago, and was reasonably satisfied with the direction ALA was taking. Dana was born and raised in New England, but spent his first professional years in the West. He had come to Newark via Springfield, Massachusetts, and was persistently dissatisfied with ALA. Although he still wanted headquarters in New York, he echoed a minority position. George Utley was born and raised in New England, became director of the Jacksonville (Florida) Public Library in 1905, and moved to become executive secretary at ALA's Chicago headquarters in 1911. He proved to be the quintessential organization man, acceptable to all factions of the association. Katharine MacDonald Jones and May Massee were both midwestern women who regularly occupied subordinate positions within the ALA structure. They willingly assumed the tedious detail work necessary to publish *Booklist*, and accepted their lot without complaint. Dudgeon may not have chosen this mix deliberately, but his willingness to tap such a diverse group for a series of articles in the *Wisconsin Library Bulletin* reflects a state of equilibrium in the association which had been absent in the first decade of the twentieth century.

In fact, the most controversial issue confronting the association in late 1916 was locating the 1917 conference. ALA President Walter Brown, director of Buffalo (New York) Public Library, wrote Dudgeon on 25 September: "I certainly do not wish to consider anything anywhere else but the middlewest until the middlewest has a chance to help us out." Unfortunately, midwestern librarians could not agree on a site. Utley even wrote a circular asking them to hurry their decision. Dudgeon suggested Chicago to Brown because "we must bring the meeting nearer to the people of the middlewest. . . . the average librarian feels that the ALA convention is for the select few rather than for all." Brown later told Dudgeon that "recent developments" might eliminate Chicago from "consideration." He did not explain.[2]

ALA held a meeting in Chicago in December to resolve the problem. The council met, but made no decision on a site. The ALA constitution, which was passed at the 1909 conference, no longer forced them to decide. Instead, the executive board heard invitations from Cincinnati, Louisville and Mackinac Island. When board members could not agree, they asked the council for a referendum on the issue. Council members finally recommended Louisville, and the executive board set the conference dates for 21–27 June 1917. In other action the executive board reflected its concern about the association's national image by requesting its publicity committee to inquire about the cost of hiring a publicity expert.[3] With that "major" problem solved, ALA leaders returned home to plan the conference, which appeared would have most of the humdrum trappings of the previous four or five conferences. Wellman raised some ire when he advocated Bowker for ALA president, but he quickly retreated. Thomas L. Montgomery of the Pennsylvania State Library would get the nomination instead.[4]

By March 1917 it looked as if the association would travel to Louisville with a membership exceeding 3,300 and an annual budget of $24,000. Its leadership had not changed significantly in the previous ten years.[5] Several suggested that the lack of change manifested in its leadership proved that ALA was stagnating. Burton Stevenson, successful novelist/librarian from Ohio who had been observing ALA affairs for more than a decade, concluded:

The American Library Association was merely a humdrum professional organization, wrapped round with tradition, settled in its habits of thought, and chiefly occupied with matters of technical detail. Its members were quiet, inoffensive, well-behaved people, cherishing the same hobby and agreeing upon everything except whether a large circulation was a merit or a disparage.[6]

Previous chapters have shown that Stevenson's observations cannot be generalized to ALA's experiences since 1876. They do, however, accurately characterize the period from 1909 to the winter of 1917. In spring, external events changed all that. For nearly three years ALA had ignored the Great European War which began in August 1914. Except for a committee charged to discover ways to obtain German and Austrian publications held up by the British blockade, the association openly adhered to President Woodrow Wilson's request to remain neutral in thought as well as in deed. But Wilson's stance changed as the war progressed, and when Germany decided in January 1917 to resume the policy of unrestricted submarine warfare it had suspended because of American pressure in June 1916, Wilson decided to ask for a declaration of war to "make the world safe for democracy." Congress granted it on 5 April 1917.

This act had a profound effect on ALA, and gave the association a mission which preoccupied it for the next two and half years. After hearing of the war declaration, Frank Hill immediately advised ALA to cancel the Louisville conference. Bowker was more perceptive. "It seems to me that we should rather emphasize the binding forces of the nation such as the ALA." He recommended the annual conference take place as scheduled, but that the program be changed to formulate ways and means for the association to serve its country during a time of war. Others agreed. The Louisville conference program was changed, the association did formulate a plan of action, and ALA did make a significant contribution to its country's fighting forces. As Arthur Young has so ably demonstrated, the association's participation in World War I opened up exciting new areas for professional endeavor. It also signaled the end of the association's formative stages, and the opening of a new chapter in ALA history.[7] Without the relatively quiet, generally peaceful period during which the association could consolidate gains it had made up to 1909, however, ALA may not have been ready to contribute significantly to America's war effort.

Surprisingly, the Minnetonka conference and the opening of ALA headquarters in Chicago on 1 September 1909 had a unifying effect on the national library community. The revised constitution strangled what little influence the American Library Institute had had. The number of library professionals who questioned its very existence increased. "I hope that the Institute will quietly disband," William Coolidge Lane wrote ALI Secretary Henry J. Carr on 7 December 1909. John Shaw Billings simply resigned his membership. Only 17 members attended the ALI meeting in Chicago on 6 January 1910, which ran coterminously with ALA's now regularly scheduled midwinter session.

The new constitution exerted variant pressures on affiliated organizations. On the one hand, Bibliographical Society of America members Lane and Johnston reacted by suggesting that BSA membership should become "a very exclusive thing,—the names to be very selective and passed upon by a very exclusive committee." Advocates of this idea came from large East Coast libraries. Midwesterners closer to ALA headquarters were less enchanted with the scheme. For example, Oberlin's Azariah Root wrote Aksel Josephson of the Crerar, "This is not my idea at all." On the other hand, the League of Library Commissions manifested a much less suspicious attitude towards ALA. A unified movement to address the problem of library commissions seemed less urgent now that control of ALA and *Booklist* was in the Midwest. Only the infant Special Libraries Association (SLA) maintained its distance from ALA. SLA Secretary George Winthrop Lee wrote Boston Athenaeum Director Charles K. Bolton that SLA wished to classify institutions like the Athenaeum as special libraries. He encouraged Bolton to join the new association. Lee's efforts manifested an accelerated competition among related library and bibliographical associations to increase their membership rolls.[8]

One reason why the adjustments after ALA headquarters moved to Chicago progressed so smoothly can be traced to the new director of Chicago Public Library. Several months after Hild had been relieved of his duties, and the association had relocated its headquarters at the CPL, an examination committee appointed by the Chicago Civil Service Committee (and consisting of Herbert Putnam, Clement Andrews, and Frank Hill) recommended Henry Legler as Hild's successor. Politically, it was a brilliant move. Trustees wanted the library to expand services beyond the central building. Legler already enjoyed a national reputation for innovative methods of extending library services. The board also wanted someone sympathetic to ALA. Except for Ahern, no one had worked harder to bring association headquarters to Chicago. By making the appointment, the CPL board won the favor of ALA, the League of Library Commissions, the Midwest, and especially the Chicago library community. The board had also provided an excellent means to foster good relations between the ALA and CPL staffs. Legler had a vested interest in insuring headquarter's success.[9]

"Adjustment" ably characterizes ALA activity between conferences. Disturbances which surfaced occasionally were minor. On 25 October Edith Tobitt of the Omaha Public Library defied an established tradition and openly advocated Theresa West Elmendorf for ALA president. Dana quickly supported the move. He wrote Gould on 6 December, "Will you join me in suggesting that Mrs. Elmendorf be the next president of the ALA?" His motives were less than altruistic, however. He hoped Elmendorf's candidacy would enable the association to avoid an unpleasant contest which might mirror the divisive 1907 Asheville conference. Because ALA tradition dictated that the first vice president succeed to the presidency, because James I. Wyer occupied that office in 1909, and because many people thought Wyer had mishandled negotiations concerning ALA headquarters during the previous two years, Dana anticipated that his presidential candidacy would meet "strong opposition." He told Gould that Wyer's administration as ALA secretary was not "notably effective," nor did it "promote harmony."[10]

Publicly, ALA matters ran smoothly. In October, the Chicago Library Club gave new ALA Executive Secretary Chalmers Hadley an informal reception. In fact, *Public Libraries* noted that "the feeling of uneasiness as to the wisdom of A.L.A. headquarters in Chicago seemed to disappear like dew before the morning sun." The executive board, which met on 10 January, decided to locate the 1910 conference at Mackinac Island. In other action board members accepted Purd Wright's resignation as ALA treasurer. In his place they appointed Carl B. Roden, Legler's assistant at the Chicago Public Library. Control of ALA continued its swing towards the Windy City.

The ALA publishing board also met in January, and, among other actions, formally accepted an invitation from the League of Library Commissions to take over league publications "in order that the sale of all publications relating to library economy may be centralized." The relationship between the league and the ALA publishing board had clearly changed since 1903. The council met on 5 January, and after members asked the executive board to appoint a committee to explore ways to affiliate state library associations with ALA, President Hodges appointed Alice Tyler as chairman. Gould submitted a report from the committee on sections, which made three specific recommendations. First, petitions for establishing sections should only be circulated by 20 to 25 members "actively engaged" in beginning the section. Second, sections which had outlived their "usefulness" should be discharged by the council. Third, the general program committee should exercise tighter control over the amount of conference time section programs could take. After much discussion, council members voted to accept the first and second recommendations, but to reject the third. The association still exhibited a reluctance to impose restrictions on any groups which might break away from the parent organization.[11]

The association's continuing fear of runaway offspring manifested itself in other areas as well. On 21 February Hadley wrote Bostwick that Pacific Northwest librarians exhibited "a feeling of resentment against the ALA" because the association did not meet on the Pacific Coast more frequently. "Some have gone so far as to intimate that the Pacific Coast librarians should have an organization independent of the ALA," Hadley said. He thought the situation could be ameliorated "if a representative could be sent from the Association who will increase their interest and loyalty to the ALA." He named Judson T. Jennings, director of the Seattle Public Library, as his choice.[12]

On 9 April 1910, Hadley summarized his perceptions of ALA's Chicago headquarters to John Cotton Dana. He did not think the connection between the association and libraries across the nation was "as vital as it should be," and he wanted something closer to the camaraderie evident in the League of Library Commissions. He had hoped the executive offices would act as "a sort of crowbar with which library work could be pried out of obscurity and librarians out of isolation"; but realistically, he admitted, headquarters acted more like "a cake of yeast." Growth and improvement would be gradual and often not easily discernible. "We are like a board of health which cannot always enumerate the cases of typhoid it has prevented." Hadley also listed his routine duties, his efforts to publicize the association nationally, and measures he had taken to increase ALA membership. "I do not believe the A.L.A. Executive office can revolutionize everything in the library field," he concluded, "but I do believe that it can be a center for the Association, bring more library workers and activities in touch with that center, and help bring library work in touch with other agencies."[13]

The association commenced its annual conference in good spirits, with minor exceptions. Several members of the catalog section were angry that its meetings had been cancelled because section officers thought they discussed "unnecessary and uninteresting topics,'' but most of the remaining 532 delegates enjoyed the ''hazy, fog-filled week'' beginning 1 July 1910 on Mackinac Island. When ALA President N. D. C. Hodges called the first general session to order, he introduced a program on the ''specialization of interests'' which LJ noted ''becomes more and more characteristic of library development.'' Members spent their first general session singing songs of Michigan and listening to papers on Michigan history. In his presidential address, Hodges defended recreational reading as a necessary and beneficial library service.

The following morning Secretary Hadley gave a brief account of the establishment of ALA headquarters and his ideas for its future direction. After thanking the Chicago Library Club, the Chicago Public Library and especially Henry Legler for assistance, he noted that ALA membership had climbed over 2,000, including 53 new institutional members since August 1909. Hadley surmised that this increase had resulted from his massive letter-writing campaign to trustees of libraries not previously enrolled as ALA members.

The remainder of the conference passed smoothly. Between the first and second general sessions, meetings were held by the professional training section, the American Association of Law Libraries, the agricultural libraries roundtable, the catalog section, the trustees section, the children's librarians section, the college and reference section, the League of Library Commissions, the Special Libraries Association, the National Association of State Libraries, the Bibliographical Society of America, and the American Library Institute. In addition, the Wisconsin, Western Reserve, Pratt Institute, and Drexel Institute Library School alumni associations each hosted a dinner and reunion, as did the Pittsburgh Carnegie Library training school for children's librarians. The New York State Library School was conspicuous by its absence.

At the fourth general session on 6 July tellers reported the results of elections. Compromise was evident. Wyer became president, Elmendorf first vice president, and Johnston second vice president. Herbert Putnam and Purd Wright were elected to the remaining openings on the executive board, and new council members included Iowa State Librarian Johnson Brigham, Ottawa Public Library Director Lawrence J. Burpee, Indianapolis Public Librarian Eliza G. Browning, Director of Atlanta's Carnegie Library Training School Julia T. Rankin, and St. Louis Public Library Chief Cataloger Sula Wagner. As always, council members represented a variety of geographic regions, types of libraries, and types of library work. If history was any teacher, Elmendorf would succeed Wyer in 1911 to become the association's first female president. Critics had been effectively silenced. After brief remarks, Hodges closed the conference.

The council met three times during the conference. After Alice Tyler submitted her report on affiliation of ALA with state library associations at the first meeting, council members debated methods to draw the two groups closer together, but finally voted to continue Tyler's committee to further deliberate on the matter. By unanimous vote the council added five people to Tyler's committee: District of Columbia Public Library Director George F. Bowerman, Newberry Library

Director W. N. C. Carlton, Cleveland Public Library First Assistant Linda Eastman, Portland Library Association Director Mary F. Isom, and Seattle Public Library Director Judson T. Jennings. The ALA umbrella effectively reached the Pacific Northwest in an attempt to hold a restless constituency. In other matters, council members appointed a committee to consider the Special Libraries Association's request to affiliate with ALA. At executive board meetings members discussed at considerable length a request from the committee on library training to appropriate $500 for travel expenses to library schools. The board decided the money was not available, directed the secretary to disclaim any ALA endorsement of specific library schools in his correspondence, and not to print any list of library schools in the ALA handbook. The board also adopted a change in association bylaws which gave the council more control over establishing or discontinuing ALA sections.[14]

The Mackinac conference was mainly significant for its cooperative and compromising spirit. Wyer's election had been handled deftly, and Dana's biting wit had been deflected by making Elmendorf heir apparent. Hadley negotiated the conference persuasively. He demonstrated how smoothly the Chicago office was running, and offered concrete evidence by citing increased membership rolls in order to show the benefits of maintaining the new headquarters. The 1910 conference may have passed into ALA history quietly, but it served as a sharp contrast to many of its predecessors during the first decade of the twentieth century.

Between conferences the American Library Institute limped along. Edmund Lester Pearson often poked fun at the Institute in his column "The Librarian," which appeared regularly in the *Boston Evening Transcript*. Pearson complimented the Institute for having at least a few worthwhile papers at the Mackinac conference, but he wondered why these library immortals had not yet adopted an "official costume" and assumed "heraldic bearings." ALI members became increasingly embarrassed at its absence of purpose. Lane suggested "the institute ought to be wound up and come to an end" because of the reconstituted ALA council. Bostwick was less generous. He accused ALI of being "too lazy to commit suicide." By the spring of 1911 Putnam and Bowker were working on a proposal to dissolve ALI at the next conference.[15]

The League of Library Commissions wrestled with two problems between conferences. First, league officials recognized that their constitution needed revision in order to accommodate members from all sections of the country. Matthew Dudgeon suggested that the league pass a constitutional amendment providing for three vice presidents, each representing a different section of the country. Vice presidents could conduct midwinter sectional meetings. Second, the league's publications committee wanted to transfer all of its clerical work to the ALA publishing board, and restrict its own activities to soliciting and approving manuscripts. Since Legler was chairman of the publishing board, no one resisted the move, and the board agreed to take whatever the league approved. Despite the agreement, however, subsurface rumblings continued. Dudgeon complained to Tyler on 17 February that "the Booklist as well as the Association itself is run in the interest of the large libraries rather than in the interest of the small library." He conceded that the situation was natural because directors of large libraries had generally been ALA members for several decades. Nonetheless, "small library interests ought to have a representative on the Publishing Board." Tyler agreed.[16] Surprisingly, neither one appeared to think of Legler as a champion of small library interests. Times had changed; Legler now directed one of the nation's major urban libraries.

Other ALA matters met temporary obstacles. On 11 November 1910 Wyer reminded Gould that he was a member of a committee with Andrews and Bostwick to report to council on the Special Libraries Association's request for affiliation with ALA. He also told Gould that the agricultural librarians would soon petition for a section. The committee on library training had a more difficult task. Chairman Azariah S. Root had argued for several years that the committee needed travel money to inspect library schools. To be effective, inspections had to be systematic. Committee members agreed. Bostwick wanted the committee to accomplish for library education what Abraham Flexner's committee had done for medical education. Most people recognized the merits of Root's request, but the executive board still believed ALA could not afford it.[17] Board priorities obviously did not include a major commitment either to establish standardized library training or to institutionalize a credentialing process similar to those of other emerging professions.

In November, *Public Libraries* lamented Hadley's inadequate salary for the level of work which he was asked to perform. While she did not say so in print, Mary Ahern knew Hadley had recently been interviewed for the position of director of the Denver Public Library. She probably feared he would accept, unless ALA raised his salary. Her suggestion fell on deaf ears. She announced in her December issue that Hadley had agreed to accept Denver's offer. ALA headquarters would lose an ally from the Midwest. Selecting Hadley's successor promised to make the midwinter meeting in Chicago interesting.[18]

At the meeting the publishing board considered Legler's motion to remove *Booklist* offices from Madison to Chicago in an effort to consolidate control of all publishing board activities. Bostwick, Elmendorf, Andrews, and Roden agreed, but Elva Bascom, *Booklist* editor in Madison, vehemently opposed the proposed move. Board members deferred action until the next meeting, perhaps because they knew the League of Library Commissions would report the next day that it had agreed to allow the publishing board to issue all league publications from ALA headquarters. Still, Bascom would not give up; for the moment she had successfully turned back Legler's effort to relocate *Booklist* offices in Chicago.

Despite his loss to Bascom, however, Legler was generally satisfied with Chicago's progress. Dana was not. He had never approved moving headquarters to Chicago; he still preferred New York. On 3 January he wrote Frank Hill that within a five-hour train ride from New York one could find 1,000 libraries and 6,000 library workers. Within a five-hour ride from Chicago one could find only

300 libraries and 2,000 library workers. "I fancy you have found more library jobs for people outside your own library than Hadley says he has." He suggested the possibility of writing out "a scheme for the advancement of the things here in the East," and wondered if Hill would help.[19]

Council met on 6 January to consider two delicate matters. The first concerned affiliation with the Special Libraries Association. Gould reported that his committee "would, as a rule, prefer the formation of a Section of the American Library Association, rather than of a separate organization, when it is a question of one or the other." His committee conceded that the "formation of the Special Libraries Association has been justified by the results," and recommended granting SLA's petition to affiliate. But council deliberations showed no clear consensus. A majority decided to defer action on this issue until the next meeting. Council members did ask the program committee to provide space and time for SLA at the next ALA conference.

The second matter concerned affiliation with state library associations. Grand Rapids (Michigan) Public Library Director Samuel Ranck reported the results of Alice Tyler's poll of state library associations primarily from the Midwest. Library associations contacted agreed they ought to appoint official state delegates to ALA conferences and that ALA ought "in some way" to recognize them. Tyler's committee recommended that delegates be invited to attend council meetings, and perhaps share concerns at a roundtable meeting. The committee equivocated on membership fees, however. It could not decide whether to charge a flat fee per state library association or a fee proportionate to the number of state library association members. The council took no action, but extended the committee and promised to discuss the issue again at the forthcoming conference.

The executive board met on 5 January. Among other matters, it accepted Chalmers Hadley's resignation as ALA secretary, and unanimously voted to appoint George Burwell Utley to succeed him. Wyer, Elmendorf, Putnam, Andrews and Wright had stepped carefully in selecting Hadley's successor. While Utley shared many similarities with his predecessor, his background apparently was sufficiently different to appease critics from the East. Born to a Yankee family in Hartford, Connecticut, in 1876, he had graduated from Brown in 1899. Thereafter he became an assistant at the Watkinson Library in Hartford, and in 1901 transferred to the Maryland Diocesan Library of the Episcopal Church in Baltimore. In 1905 he became director of the Jacksonville (Florida) Public Library. By asking him to become executive secretary, board members could argue they appointed a librarian from the South with roots in the East. And since Utley was identified as a progressive librarian who advocated Sunday and holiday openings and extended borrowing privileges to children under 12, midwesterners found him much more palatable. Besides, midwestern librarians seemed less intense about the appointment now that ALA headquarters was comfortably settled in the Chicago Public Library.[20]

Dana persisted. On 4 January he wrote ALA President Wyer, "There seems to be a little feeling in the East that the ALA has not lived up to its Chicago opportunities the past year-and-a-half. The proper place for the headquarters of our organization, of course, is New York.'' He complained especially that the proceedings from the last conference still had not been disseminated to the membership and he lamented that the Chicago group had not lived up to the promises to raise funds to strengthen and improve headquarters. He informed Wyer of a rumor that ''an association of eastern librarians may be established in the near future.''

Dana forwarded a copy of his letter to Ahern, who promptly castigated him for several ''erroneous ideas.'' ALA headquarters in Chicago was in much better shape than it had been in Boston, she said. Midwestern libraries and librarians had benefited directly from its proximity, and eastern librarians had not noticed because they had not taken advantage of many new opportunities. For example, she noted, ALA officers and the ALA secretary received many speaking invitations from southern, midwestern and western library associations, but none from eastern library associations. She recalled ''a splendid campaign of newspaper publicity'' on behalf of libraries, and noted midwestern librarians had raised $1,000 to furnish ALA headquarters. ''Frankly, I think it is time for you to turn your glasses the other end around.'' She accused him of lobbying for SLA and working against ALA efforts to fuse a national library movement. ''Your threat of an Eastern association of librarians is not worthy of you,'' she scolded, and wondered if Bowker was ''the animating source of this present onslaught.'' She urged Dana not to conspire with him to damage ALA further. Elmendorf agreed. She wrote Dana on 17 January that ''a general 'slam' doesn't help,'' and asked for specific complaints about ALA.

Hill was delighted at the scuffle. ''Evidently she cannot see a great many miles around Chicago owing to the smoke,'' he wrote Dana, and urged him to continue to keep things ''stirred up, and that may bring a little more life into the association.'' He did note, however, that the ''new secretary, Utley of Florida, ought to be an improvement over Hadley.'' Dana responded to Ahern on 16 January, and although he did not address most of Ahern's criticisms, he did dispute her accusation about his befriending SLA at the expense of ALA. He argued that ALA had not supported the birth and development of SLA, and because it had ignored the interest of special librarians for so long, the latter felt compelled to form a separate group. Edmund Lester Pearson could not resist an opportunity for public comment. Writing as ''The Librarian,'' he teased that ''librarians themselves had become so accustomed to the dull, grey tone of these meetings that they become alarmed at anything else.''[21]

On 10 April Dana responded to Elmendorf. He accused the council of being ''clumsy and ineffective,'' and the publishing board of being ''slow'' and narrow-minded, especially regarding a restricted vision for *Booklist*, which he thought should address the public at large. ALA should schedule more conferences in eastern cities near larger population centers. One need only cite comparative conference attendance figures to demonstrate the wisdom of this suggestion, Dana argued. Because the ALA administration had not ''laid sufficient stress'' on activity between conferences, they had little real knowledge of the quality of papers scheduled for the annual conference. As a result, long reports are read to "weary audiences" who could more profitably read the reports in their spare time. Finally, Dana reiterated his position on ALA headquarters in Chicago, so far from the library, book trade and publishing centers of the nation. "Time will show that it is even a greater mistake than those who now disapprove of it yet realize."

Elmendorf responded a week later. ALA could not adopt a constitution acceptable to businessmen because their aims were different. The latter sought profit, the former sought social progress; the latter frequently needed quick, decisive action, the former frequently benefited from "prolonged discussion." Yes, Elmendorf admitted, the council was "clumsy," but because it was ineffective it could do "no harm. I am willing to let it live if it wants to. I do not need it." ALA had to move its conferences around the country in order to generate interest in ALA and to demonstrate the library movement was indeed national in scope. She agreed with Dana's criticisms about the lack of administrative work accomplished between conferences, the generally lackluster programs at ALA conferences, and the limited vision of *Booklist* editors. But she "distinctly" disagreed with him about the location of ALA headquarters, and the effectiveness of the publishing board.[22]

The ALA conference at Pasadena, California, in May 1911, was a disappointment. Attendance was good—582, 300 of whom were Californians—but most of the executive board members were unable to attend. LJ suggested that ALA was in a "sadly acephalous condition" at the conference. Although the least experienced of ALA officers, Secretary Utley, had to monitor the program, LJ later praised his "tactful energy" which "saved the meeting from any disastrous consequences." His secretary's report noted that ALA membership had grown to a record 2,118 members, 284 of which were institutions. Legler reported for the publishing board that any significant alteration of *Booklist* would, in the board's opinion, constitute a violation of Carnegie's gift. His words aimed at Dana's recommendation that *Booklist* should be more directed at the public. The ALA treasury showed receipts of $6,629.78 and expenditures of $2,134.03. The association was fiscally sound.

At the second session Andrews announced nominees for the forthcoming year: for president, Theresa W. Elmendorf; for first vice president, Henry Legler; and for second vice president, Mary Plummer, who had recently been appointed director of the New York Public Library Training School. Nominees to the executive board included Andrews and Eastman. Librarians nominated for council seats reflected some new faces and an increased geographical distribution: Denver Public Librarian Chalmers Hadley, Washington County (Maryland) Free Library Director Mary Titcomb, New Jersey Library Commission Organizer Sarah B. Askew, Oberlin College Library Director Azariah S. Root, and Los Angeles Public Library Cataloger Minnie Oakley. All were subsequently elected. In 1911, ALA had elected its first female president; it had also continued efforts to counter moves within the national library community to form splinter groups by absorbing potential dissidents into the governing structure.

At the last general session Mary Ahern moved a constitutional amendment. To enable state and special interest library associations to affiliate more easily with ALA, she wanted to restructure council by striking its authority to elect 25 of its own members, and instead to allow the association to add other members "under such conditions as the Association may determine by resolution adopted at any annual conference. . . ." Her intention was clear. Reduce the council's potential for perpetuating its own membership and expand it to include leaders of state and other special interest library associations. Ahern wanted to prevent groups like the Special Libraries Association from proliferating. Legler seconded, and discussion followed.

Hill objected that the amendment would eventually allow all ALA members to become members of council. Andrews begged a postponement because an ALA committee was already considering the issue; he did not want to preempt its recommendations. Legler thought Ahern's amendment would make ALA more democratic. Ranck agreed, and as a member of the committee which Andrews spoke of earlier, he endorsed the amendment. Lane objected on principle, but after an attempt to refer the entire matter of the executive board failed, Tyler called the question. The motion needed a three-fourths majority to pass. Although members cast 50 total votes, some voted twice, once as a personal member, the second time as representative of an institutional member. Ahern's amendment received only 36 votes, two votes shy of the necessary three-fourths. When the final tally was announced, Ahern was incensed. Many in the minority had exercised their two-vote prerogative, and Ahern later claimed that those in favor of the amendment actually outnumbered the opposition seven to one if second votes had not been counted. She would have to await a more propitious moment to push the amendment; unlike Minnetonka, not enough midwesterners were present to provide the votes necessary to carry her motion.

At the council meeting Alice Tyler presented the findings of her committee on affiliation with state library associations. She had two recommendations: (1) continue the committee through the midwinter meeting to study the subject further; (2) schedule a roundtable meeting at the next annual conference between representative state and regional library associations to discuss mutual problems. Council members agreed with both recommendations, and LJ later noted a consensus: "There should be such geographical distribution of members of the Council as to strengthen both the ALA and state associations." The council then discussed the touchy subject of affiliation with the Special Libraries Association, which had been carried over from the midwinter meeting. After extensive discussion, members voted to affiliate, but only subject to conditions outlined by a committee of three (Putnam, Isom, and Andrews) appointed to determine requirements for affiliation with ALA for all except state, local, and provincial associations. Council members may have intended this move as a warning against special interest librarians who wished to use ALA offices to form their own library associations. Affiliation would no longer be automatic.[23]

In August 1911 a familiar concern surfaced once again in private correspondence. Margaret Brown, director of the Iowa Library Commission's Traveling Library section, complained to Dudgeon that *Booklist* no longer served the needs of small libraries. Dudgeon worried. He wrote Minnesota Public Library Commissioner Clara Baldwin in spring, "If . . . Booklist fails to list many books which you after personal examination find suitable for traveling libraries, you have very seriously impeached [its] value."[24] Although midwestern library commission employees shared these sentiments, no one seemed inclined to push the issue into the open.

Most between-conference activity focused on the structure and composition of the council. Ahern used *Public Libraries* to keep the issue before the attention of the national library community. In July she complained of this "undemocratic condition." She was especially concerned with the question of affiliation. She also called upon ALA to clarify voting privileges for institutional members. "Who is empowered to cast the vote of an institution?" she asked. What if three or more officers from the same institution were present at the same time? "All are questions for which no answer is given in the document 'so carefully worked out' in 1908–9." Her persistence irritated library leaders in the East. Henry Carr complained to Dana that Ahern ought to temper her words, "but what's the use?"[25]

While Ahern worried about ALA affiliation with library associations, Frank Hill worried about their proliferation. In a presidential address to the New York Library Association on 5 September 1911, Hill noted "a tendency in recent years among those interested in special phases of library work to drift apart from the general organization, form their own association or section, and discuss their own problems." Their activities led to much duplication of effort, and dissipated the free time of librarians committed to the interests of several professional groups. "No wonder meetings lose their zest and that enthusiasm flags," he observed. He hoped that the "multiplication of associations will cease." With the council question threatening to precipitate a spirited debate at the midwinter meeting, Elmendorf realized she had better attend.[26]

The executive board met on 3 January and accepted the finance committee report showing actual income for 1911 at $18,764, up from the $16,850 estimated. The committee also estimated ALA income for 1912 at $19,450. The board agreed to operate on that budget, and increase the ALA secretary's salary from $2,100 to $2,400. Elmendorf appointed a committee to draft a bylaw identifying who could cast institutional votes and the board agreed to authorize $200 of the $500 requested by the committee on library training.

The council met two days later. Tyler and Ranck issued a majority report for the committee on the relation of ALA and state library associations, which noted that state library associations wished changes in the ALA constitution to accommodate more official representation. Tyler then recommended two constitutional amendments. The first would provide room in the council for a representative of each state or regional library association which met conditions set in ALA bylaws. The second would define the financial responsibilities of each association to ALA. Associations with fewer than 50 members would pay $5 annually. Those with more than 50 members would contribute ten cents per capita. Hill, the third member of the committee, agreed with the report, but dissented from recommendations to change the constitution.

The committee report occasioned extensive discussion. Some suggested that a per capita fee would penalize state library associations attempting to increase their membership. Others pointed out that many ALA members allowed their membership to lapse between conferences held outside their geographic areas. Still others worried over lack of continuity in the council, which might "tend to disarrange continued policies" if the council annually experienced a significant influx of new members. Ultimately council members refused to force a consensus. Instead, they voted to send the report back to the committee, and asked that it be printed in the *Bulletin*. The ALA secretary was also directed to find out how many state library association members also belonged to ALA.

LJ welcomed the procrastination. An editorial quoted "many experienced members of the ALA" who worried that "a wise continuity of policy" would be threatened if "leaders of library progress" were "accidentally omitted" by the new amendment. Ahern, on the other hand, railed once more against a constitution which allowed "this undemocratic and unwise principle of self-perpetuation." She predicted the amendment would be offered again at the forthcoming Ottawa conference, and she hoped "the specious technical interposition which prevailed at Pasadena ought not again prevail to defeat the will of the great majority."[27]

For the most part, the six general sessions of the thirty-fourth ALA annual meeting were harmonious and uneventful. Of the 750 people who attended the Ottawa conference, not more than one-sixth came from Canada. New York, Massachusetts, Pennsylvania, Illinois and Ohio were especially well represented among the remainder. At the first general session, ALA Secretary Utley forecast a rosy future for the association. He reported current membership at 2,360, up 314 from the previous year. Since 1909, income from membership fees had grown from $4,557.50 to an expected $5,800 in 1912. Between 1 November 1911 and 31 May 1912 headquarters dispatched 11,818 pieces of first-class mail, many of which assisted in the organization of libraries and library commissions in various states. During that time, headquarters had also helped place 12 persons in library posts. Utley also estimated that he spent one-fourth of his time on publishing board activities.

The harmony exhibited in the first general session was reflected in the remaining general sessions and in other meetings. The executive board met on 27 June. First order of business was the report of the nominating committee. When the board saw that the committee had nominated Anderson for the post of second vice president and Wellman for first vice president, Putnam moved that the slate be returned to the committee "with request that the precedent of nominating a woman for Second Vice-President be followed."

Since committee members really wanted Anderson to succeed to the ALA presidency the following year, they welcomed Putnam's motion in order to press Anderson to accept. When he acquiesced, the nominating committee acted quickly and returned the revised slate to the executive board, which approved the list: for president, Legler; first vice president, Anderson; second vice president, Isom; members of the executive board, Wellman and Koch. The board also accepted the committee's slate of nominees for council: Walter, Margaret Mann, chief cataloger at Pittsburgh's Carnegie Library, William Warner Bishop of the Library of Congress, Los Angeles Public Library Director E. R. Perry, and Cleveland Public Library Children's Librarian Caroline Burnite. All nominees were subsequently elected.

Legler reported for an ad hoc committee to determine voting privileges for institutional members. The board accepted the committee's recommendation to award the vote to the institution's "duly designated representative whose credentials are filed with the secretary." With equal speed the board dispatched the affiliation question by compromise. Andrews moved that ALA amend its constitution to allow council to elect 25 of its own members, but also to provide for "one member from each state, provincial and territorial library association (or any association covering two or more such geographical divisions) which complies with the conditions for such representation set forth in the by-laws." Bylaws were quickly adjusted to include representation for any library association with 15 members or more. Minimum annual dues for an affiliated society would be $5, plus ten cents per additional capita for associations with more than 50 members.

The Ottawa conference progressed smoothly, partly because pressing issues were handled diplomatically, partly because geographic representation at the conference was so even, partly because no one wanted to disturb the ALA's first female president. Shortly after the conference concluded, Elmendorf wrote Putnam, "Many good friends were kindly watching out that this year's course should not run onto rocks or shoals or into any untoward currents." ALA's bright future, and prospects for increased growth, also minimized the dissent within the association which had been so evident the decade before. Complaints about the conference were minor. LJ decried duplication evident in programs of affiliated associations; PL complained that many problems had been put off until the last session, when most ALA members were preoccupied with other things.[28]

But matters did not run so smoothly between conferences. Elva Bascom finished the ALA *Catalog* supplement of 3,000 titles, which appeared shortly after the conclusion of the Ottawa conference. The supplement sold well, and by the end of November it boosted sales for the publishing board from $8,500 in 1911 to an expected $15,000 for 1912. But the supplement's success contrasted sharply with private criticism of the board. Miriam E. Carey of the Minnesota Public

Library Commission asked Dudgeon on 19 November 1912 if the league would
consider publishing a recommended list of books for the insane which the Iowa,
Nebraska, Massachusetts, and Minnesota library commissions were preparing.
"We would like to see this list in print, naturally," she said, "but have been
told so much about the inability of the ALA Publishing Board to undertake
anything which may not have a large scale, that we are turning to you in the
hope that you may be willing to help us."[29] Carey suspected ALA publishing
board chairman Henry Legler no longer championed the interests of small libraries. Nor had the removal of ALA headquarters to Chicago stifled sectionalist
feelings west of the Appalachians. In past years ALA committee chairpersons
worried about appeasing the Midwest, but with the ALA "empire centering in
Chicago," as LJ described it, other sections began to grumble about underre-
presentation. Frank Walter's efforts to fill a committee on publicity was a case
in point. After suggesting Matthew Dudgeon, Josephine Rathbone of the Pratt
Institute Library School, and Carl Milam of the Indiana Public Library Commission as possible appointments, Walter reminded Dudgeon that the committee
composition represented an eastern and a western school and a secretary of a
library commission. Was it not "advisable to put someone on the Pacific slope
as well?" Dudgeon suggested that Walter also spread his committee representation among types of libraries in which his members were employed. His advice
implicitly acknowledged problems the increased specialization in the profession
was causing ALA. It occurred to neither man, however, to include women in
proportion to their numbers within ALA.[30]

The American Library Institute continued its lethargic course. Ahern tried to
inject some life into the group when she became secretary, but Dana advised
against efforts doomed to failure. "An organization with a pretentious name and
with a membership made up of people with considerable prominence appears
ridiculous in the eyes of the discerning if it does not do something worthy of
its name and membership," he told Ahern. "The Institute never has. It is a
joke. Let it do or die."[31]

The January meeting seemed almost innocuous. Financially, the association
had never been healthier. The publishing board increased its appropriation for
headquarters from $2,000 to $2,500, and the executive board in turn increased
the salary of the executive secretary to $3,000 for 1913. The publishing board
also voted to ask the league if it wanted a certain number of *Booklist* citations
starred as recommended for purchase. The council meetings were uneventful.[32]

Dudgeon was not happy with the publishing board's midwinter action. He
told Alice Tyler in confidence, "the Booklist has been gradually becoming a
tool for the big libraries rather than the small libraries." He suspected Legler
would soon renew efforts to move *Booklist* editorial offices out of Madison. "I
cannot but feel," he told Tyler, "that if this step is taken the library commissions
who are anxious to serve a constituency for small libraries must undertake
something of their own entirely distinct from the ALA Booklist." If *Booklist*
was moved to Chicago, he predicted, Bascom would resign as editor. Tyler

remembered that as part of its agreement with the board, the league "insisted" on a representative to protect the interests of the small libraries. "In looking over the list of the Publishing Board as it is now constituted I find there is no such representation, and that the large library point of view is absolutely dominant." She was less concerned about geographical representation.

Dudgeon reminded Tyler that Legler was originally placed on the board as the league's representative, but added, "He not only no longer represents it, but seems now to be inclined to disregard it." At the midwinter meeting Dudgeon heard rumors that Legler had said "the best that could be done was to prepare a suitable list of books for the large library, and let the small library get what they [sic] could out of it." Yet despite his opposition, Dudgeon stood ready to compromise. He suggested to Carl Milam that the league would probably not object to moving *Booklist*'s editorial offices to Chicago if the publishing board would guarantee one member who would represent the interests of small libraries.[33]

In the meantime Bascom had already decided to resign as *Booklist* editor. When Dudgeon assigned her new duties before she made her resignation public, Elmendorf criticized him for taking Bascom away from the periodical. Dudgeon shunned any blame. Bascom had already determined to leave, he said, in part because her efforts in compiling the *Catalog* supplement had not been adequately recognized. The board ascribed the supplement's success "entirely to Mr. Utley's publicity methods," he stated. "Miss Bascom probably put in literally an extra hour outside of regular hours of labor . . . for every minute that Mr. Utley gave to the publicity."[34]

As Dudgeon fretted about *Booklist* from Madison, Ahern plotted to shake up ALA from Chicago. Shortly after the midwinter meeting, she asked several ALA members for contributions to a symposium on ALA's future direction. Koch was immediately suspicious. "It looks to me like a journalistic method of getting spicy copy," he told Utley. "If I have any criticisms to make on the administration of the ALA, it will be made at the meetings of the Board."[35] But because others were less cautious, Ahern collected enough papers to publish a symposium in her June issue. Worcester (Massachusetts) Public Library Director Robert Shaw suggested increasing cooperation. Legler said that ALA should consolidate its funds under a "strong committee of small membership." George T. Little recommended a set of common library statistics. Frank K. Walter wanted a national publicity campaign to promote public library use. E. C. Richardson argued that ALA ought to promote the library as a means for "social betterment." Indiana State Librarian Demarchus Brown wanted ALA to instruct the public in good literature.

John Cotton Dana was less cautious, more specific. He said the ALA executive committee should get copies of all papers to be presented at the conference three weeks in advance, appoint a press agent to advertise ALA to the public, publish conference proceedings in parts to facilitate dissemination to interested audiences, and change the name and form of *Booklist*. In addition, he thought ALA should "proceed to lessen the dominance of library schools and their graduates," meet more often in large cities, and consider removing ALA headquarters to New York. Dana's recommendations hardly served as a foundation for quiet discussion at the ALA conference in the Catskill Mountains later that month.[36]

Over 900 attended the conference in the mountain resort, one-third of whom came from New York, another third from New England states. Legler planned the program around five general sessions, all scheduled for mornings. The 25 special sessions in the afternoons and evenings would appeal to "every phase of library activity." The nominating committee presented a slate of nominees, all of whom were unanimously elected for the coming year, including President E. H. Anderson, New York Public Library director; First Vice President Hiller C. Wellman, Springfield (Mass.) City Library director; Second Vice President Gratia Countryman, Minneapolis Public Library director; and executive board members Herbert Putnam and Harrison W. Craver, director of Pittsburgh's Carnegie Library. Public librarians would be running ALA for the next 12 months.[37] The remainder of the conference ran smoothly. Legler had carefully structured programs to create a minimum of friction between the various library associations, sections, and roundtables. To the outside world, the American Library Association looked like a cohesive group dedicated to a unified professional purpose.

Postconference irritations also remained minor. Ahern complained in an October PL editorial that the library profession had too many meetings. Azariah Root complained: "The destiny of the ALA are [sic] determined by a small group of the library profession mostly identified with large libraries; it is unlikely that the small libraries will receive very great consideration." A major obstacle to change was the constitution. "Poor Constitution! It has never ceased to be amended since I became a member [1889]," he said. "We have been in the circle of being run by a clique, going over to a democracy, and evolving a Council to take care of things and then deliberately putting ourselves in the hands of a clique again." Federation, he argued, represented the most equitable solution to the problem. Despite Root's criticisms, however, 12 state library associations chose to affiliate with ALA under the new constitutional provision at the midwinter meeting.[38]

Dana and Ahern continued to prod ALA's relative tranquillity. Dana told a friend on 9 August that because ALA would not expand *Booklist*'s utility to a wider audience, he had approached the American Booksellers Association for support of a new periodical. They seemed interested, he said, and suggested the entire operation might be run through the Special Libraries Association. Koch protested to Utley that Ahern's PL symposia were divisive. He told the ALA secretary that he had communicated his displeasure to Ahern, but she responded with a "stinging" letter. "It severed diplomatic relations between her office and mine for the time being."[39]

At council's midwinter meeting on 1 January 1914, Dana deliberately made his complaints public by requesting Utley to read them aloud. After the secretary finished, Hill immediately spoke in favor of Dana's suggestion about *Booklist*.

Legler objected. He said Dana criticized everything about *Booklist*, "except perhaps the quality of the paper." Ahern then attempted to interpret Dana's ideas. Make *Booklist* the same size as *Harper's Weekly*, give it an attractive newscover, hire people with national reputations to write columns, and distribute it from newsstands across the country. Profits realized from such a venture would allow ALA to distribute free copies to libraries. Hill then moved that the subject of changing *Booklist* be referred to the publishing board. The motion carried. After the meeting one council member suggested privately that perhaps the ALA ought to appoint a committee to report on "What is the matter with Dana?"[40]

Dana persisted, so Utley asked him to join a committee of three to study publicity for ALA. The Newark librarian refused. He complained that he had been a member of a committee with a similar purpose eight years earlier, but the association ignored its 11 recommendations because the administrative staff would not accept responsibility. "I think we have fooled away time enough on this," he told Utley. "Years go by and our association seemingly takes no advantage of the opportunities that are afforded."[41]

Ahern also persisted. In February 1914 she complained that smaller associations should not be bound by ALA regulations, and special library associations could easily survive as sections within ALA rather than as affiliates to the parent body. The results of affiliation made council an "unwieldy" body "dominated by a few strong personalities." She promised to propose a constitutional amendment to correct this inequity at the forthcoming annual meeting. Privately, Ahern assured Anderson and Wellman that she had ALA's best interests at heart. Similarly, Dana assured Utley that his criticisms "are not born of antagonism to anyone."[42]

Spring brought an uneasy quiet as Dana and Ahern became less vocal. Utley kept things running smoothly and attempted to anticipate problems before they arose. In February he asked Dudgeon about reading lists for foreign-speaking people living in rural areas. If the league compiled them, the publishing board would print them. Utley worked hard to minimize complaints that ALA favored large library interests. In March he moved forward on another front. He pressed librarians from New England to participate in the program of the forthcoming conference. Although Utley always pushed for more geographical balance among participants, his overtures to the East may also have been motivated by a desire to offset rumored attempts to start a regional library organization in the New England states.[43]

Most of the 1,366 people who registered for the ALA conference in Washington, D.C., on 25 May 1914 probably recognized the general pattern that conference schedules had assumed over the past several years. General sessions held for the entire membership were once again deliberately programmed to discuss various themes of general interest. But most ALA work took place in the meetings of various sections, the council and the executive and publishing boards. Ahern proposed her constitutional amendment at the third general session. She argued that the council was not "a deliberative body" because membership was too large, and she recommended that council composition be changed to include only members of the executive board, all ALA ex-presidents, and representatives of affiliated associations. Her motion that a committee of five be appointed to study the matter passed.

At the publishing board meeting the committee appointed to consider Dana's suggestion to change *Booklist*'s name recommended against him. Committee members argued the title aptly described the periodical's intent and carefully conformed to requirements of the original Carnegie grant. The board also considered supplementing *Booklist* with extra lists "suitable to the smallest libraries, the number not to exceed approximately 120 titles a year." Board members referred the matter to Massee and Legler, with power to act. At the council meeting Andrews announced his findings as chairman of the "Committee on Affiliation with Other than State, Provincial or Local Library Associations." Using statistics compiled from the Catskills conference, he noted that only 70 conferees were not ALA members. Of the 70, only 14 belonged to the Special Libraries Association, nine to the American Association of Law Libraries. He concluded that charging more for non-ALA members who came to ALA conferences to attend meetings of affiliated organizations would have resulted in additional revenue of only $35 to $40.

The newly elected executive board—consisting of President Hiller Wellman, First Vice President W. N. C. Carlton, Second Vice President Mary Titcomb, and executive board members Mary Plummer, Harrison Craver, Herbert Putnam and Judson Jennings—met on 29 May. Besides routine matters, the board asked Wellman's committee (Ahern, Hodges, Tyler, Jones, and Gould) to consider the "desirability of making any amendments to the constitution" and to report to the executive board at the midwinter meeting. The board also appointed Carlton to chair a committee to investigate the ALA's committee structure, and voted to accept Berkeley's invitation to host the 1915 ALA conference in California.[44] Once the executive board adjourned, the Washington conference faded quietly into ALA history.

Between conferences the publishing section happily announced it expected to earn over $16,000 in 1915. Legler especially complimented *Booklist* on "its tradition of unbiased evaluation of current publications and well-formulated policy of serving particularly the smaller and medium sized libraries." At a middle west section meeting of the League of Library Commissions, attendees pondered the question: "Is there any way in which small libraries can be warned against buying unsuitable books?" Andrews responded that libraries should "not buy books not included in the Booklist unless they were known to be good."[45] No one echoed concerns about the latent threat such practice presented to freedom of thought, learning and science that Richard Ely had identified at the 1901 ALA conference in Waukesha, Wisconsin; nor did anyone acknowledge the prior censorship potential of *Booklist*'s undefined selection criteria.

Except for Ahern, the committee to consider amending the ALA constitution seemed hesitant about its task. Chairman Hodges discouraged any attempt to contact the membership, "as it might lead to a demand for an entire reconstruction." Gardner Jones agreed, but Ahern was determined. She used *Public Libraries* to keep the issue alive, and concluded "it would be too bad if the opportunity to remedy the defects in the constitution . . . is allowed to go by without effort for the lack of attention." Gould was unimpressed with her logic. "I have thought very carefully over the Constitution," he wrote Hodges, "and I must confess that I have little to suggest by way of improving it." The committee held no meetings prior to the midwinter ALA conference.[46]

Other matters continued apace. Wellman pushed Charles Bolton to address the council's midwinter meeting on a library code of ethics. He also appointed a committee to consider establishing an ALA section for school librarians, but urged Utley not to expand the number of meetings scheduled for the Berkeley conference. Utley wrote Dudgeon that the executive board wanted to drop section meetings, but would not tamper with affiliated bodies like the league, SLA, AALL, or AASL. On the eve of the midwinter conference, the *Bulletin* proudly predicted that ALA membership would top 3,000 in 1915. The association's future continued to look bright.[47]

At the executive board's January meeting Second Vice President Plummer complained about the manner in which committee appointments were made. She claimed that either they were done hurriedly at the executive board's final meeting during the annual conference, or power to appoint was routinely delegated to the president and the secretary. To alleviate this problem the executive board decided to request that the people nominated for president, first vice president and the executive board at the annual conference get together 24 hours before their election and draw up a list of committee appointments. The board made no attempt to cloak its decision in democratic rhetoric. In ALA, nominations were still tantamount to election. At the council's January meetings members took no action on Wellman's suggestion that ALA formulate a formal code of ethics. Like establishing standardized library training or institutionalizing a credentialing process, the issue of formulating a code of ethics did not spark an excited consensus among the ALA leadership.

The report of the committee to consider revising the ALA constitution took more time. Only three members of the committee attended the midwinter session, and since they had not met previous to the midwinter meeting, they found it necessary to identify a consensus from deliberations held 24 hours before reporting to council. Naturally, the document which they developed reflected the committee's composition. Tyler and Ahern favored restructuring the council; Hodges, Jones and Gould did not. Since Gould and Jones did not attend the midwinter meeting, the committee's minority actually became a majority, thus enabling Tyler and Ahern to recommend that ALA eliminate the constitutional provision allowing council to elect 25 of its own members, and that it consider biennial meetings. Tyler and Ahern also called for a reexamination of the unwritten tradition allowing the first vice president to succeed to the presidency the next year. In his "minority" report, Hodges argued that the present constitution had not yet received a fair trial, and he complained that Jones and Gould had no chance to comment upon the preliminary report.

When the floor opened for discussion, Legler speculated that agitation within ALA would continue until all members of the ALA could vote for council members. Bostwick argued that council should retain its present construction, especially if the American Library Institute died, but Tyler suggested that the council had nothing to do with the Institute. Richardson recommended that all council members should be elected by the membership, but council size should not be reduced. Dudgeon agreed. Council members quickly accepted both reports, then postponed discussion until the next meeting.

Although Ahern and Tyler were discouraged at the council's action, Utley took a more optimistic view. He suggested to Dana on 14 January that had the Newark Librarian attended the meeting "to hear the very able and well prepared discussion you would not have felt that the criticisms you make were needed." LJ was equally impressed with the debate, but discouraged any move to change the council structure. "The organization of the library interests is now so well worked out that it seems a pity to begin changes in a retrogressive direction at the very moment that full organization has been achieved." PL remained as acerbic as its editor. "As the chairman of the committee announces himself as unalterably opposed to any 'tinkering' with the constitution, it is hardly likely that anything will come of the matter." Despite the criticism, however, Ahern gradually reconciled to majority opinion.[48]

The midwinter meeting produced yet another library organization. The Association of American Library Schools (AALS) was created by a resolution of the faculties of library schools. LJ welcomed it, as long as the ALA section on professional training was disbanded and AALS drawn into ALA as an affiliate body. PL was less sanguine. "It is to be hoped that the association will not develop into a mutual admiration society." The editor again expressed a preference for "one strong national body with various sections devoted to the particular problems."[49]

Compared to conferences in the first decade of the twentieth century, the 1915 conference at Berkeley passed by uneventfully. The 779 registrants spent much time touring the bay and its environs. Wellman chaired general sessions at which few issues were argued forcefully. Both Dana and Ahern were unable to push their individual projects before the membership. Ahern later complained, "The request for the consideration of a revision of the Constitution was again ignored by the Executive Board and the Council." Wellman's presidential address was synthetic. "We as librarians should prize and cherish the things of the mind and of the spirit." he said. "Only those gifted by God can hope for the supreme joy of feeding the pure, white flame that lights man's pathway through the ages." The remainder of the conference concentrated so much on noncontroversial practical matters that Edmund Lester Pearson observed that librarians "confuse tediousness with scholarship." The election of officers did feature one surprise, however. For the second time in its history, ALA elected a female as president—

Mary Wright Plummer. Walter Brown became first vice president, Chalmers Hadley second vice president, and Dudgeon and Ranck new members of an executive board already consisting of Craver, Putnam, Bostwick, and Jennings.[50]

Minor items occupied the attention of ALA officials between conferences. *Booklist* came under steady criticism, although most was privately communicated. Wellman told George Iles that publishing new editions of his bibliographies was unlikely because "the Board will want to experiment with more popular lists." Matthew Dudgeon complained that "the smaller librarian is not intensely interested in the ALA." The problem of adequately publicizing ALA in the nation's media forced more concentrated attention, however. Willis H. Kerr, chairman of the publicity committee, reported that the Berkeley conference had received 36 columns in local papers, 20 articles in national papers, and three reports in national magazines. *Public Libraries* suggested that ALA hire a permanent publicity officer who "would more than earn his salary" if publicity work was properly carried out. Dana reminded Utley once more of the recommendations his committee had made as early as 1906. Utley promised Dana that Kerr would study all previous reports on publicity and develop a coordinated program to better advertise ALA nationally. He suggested a news bulletin issued four or six times per year to newspapers and magazines.[51] One other issue which posed potential difficulties arose before the midwinter meeting. On 8 November 1915 Phineas Windsor, director of the University of Illinois Library, informed President Plummer that many people thought that council meetings ought to be open. Windsor disagreed. Council members represented constituencies, he said, and were expected to discuss library matters freely and frankly. Utley supported Windsor's position, but Plummer saw merit in the criticism.[52]

At the midwinter meeting, the executive board ordered the publicity committee to study all previous reports on publicity, and voted to locate the 1916 conference in Asbury Park, New Jersey. Plummer supported this vote by citing a survey which showed a large majority of midwestern librarians wanted an East coast meeting instead of a return to Mackinac. Council meetings were equally uneventful, but for the first time open to all ALA members. Apparently Plummer chose to heed the criticism Windsor identified the previous November. At a league meeting Henry Sanborn, director of the Bridgeport (Connecticut) Public Library, reported on a survey of Hoosiers directing small Indiana libraries about *Booklist*'s applicability to their institutions. The survey revealed that the periodical was "not perfect," but still represented "the best solution" and satisfied the needs of the small library "better than any other list." He asked library commissions to give *Booklist* more cooperation. Dudgeon explained that the independently issued Wisconsin Free Library Commission lists were only intended to supplement *Booklist* recommendations.

One other action at midwinter won Ahern's rare approval. The nominating committee decided to invite council members to suggest nominees for ALA offices. Ahern applauded the action as "more of a democratic action than has been customary," and suggested that the committee publish its list a month before the annual conference to give all ALA members an opportunity to study candidates. "As it has been decreed that the constitution must not be touched, perhaps a precedent might establish the custom." William Warner Bishop, who was on the nominating committee, felt the pressure. He told fellow committee member E. C. Richardson that responses to the request for nominations "have come in at a considerable number." Many wanted Root as president, but since Root was a member of the nominating committee, Bishop thought he was ineligible. "There seems to be a very definite feeling that Mr. Root's nomination was side-tracked a couple years ago in a manner not wholly ingenious and straightforward. One letter goes so far as to suggest that Root was put on the nominating committee particularly for the purpose of keeping him off the ballot."[53] Even in harmonious times ALA could not escape private accusations of politicking.

While the nominating committee wrestled with a slate of candidates, Utley announced that the ALA publicity committee intended to issue a quarterly entitled *American Library Press Bulletin* which would be sent to newspapers across the country. "This will be an attempt to interpret in news form all the good things being done by American and Canadian libraries." About the same time E. C. Richardson proposed to make ALI "an instrument for research and an inspiration for higher or specialized teaching within the library field." He argued that this change in direction would take ALI out of competition with the council, but still assign it a prestigious, vital role among library associations. *Library Journal* wished him success.[54]

One issue—the question of *Booklist*'s applicability to small public libraries—continued to crop up in private correspondence and threaten the ALA equilibrium which had been evident since 1910. Although Sanborn suggested reconciliation between library commissions and *Booklist*, Dudgeon resisted. He told Alice Tyler that *Booklist* was "becoming rather a check list for the larger libraries which do not need it." He asked her to contribute an article on the periodical for the July issue of the *Wisconsin Library Bulletin*, which he planned as a symposium on ALA. "My thought is that by stating some such facts we can assume an established standard which has been to a certain extent departed." Dudgeon also wrote to Legler that *Booklist* was recommending some fiction of questionable morality. "Possibly it is due to my Quaker and Methodist ancestry," he said, but he wanted Legler to know that many titles routinely acquired for a large public library collection were unsuitable for smaller libraries. Still Dudgeon was unsatisfied. He decided to invite Dana to contribute an article for his July issue tentatively entitled "What the American Library Association Might Be." He told Dana the association was in "danger of dropping into a conventionally conservative self-satisfied frame of mind which assumes that we are doing just what we ought to," and he wanted Dana to challenge the profession's passive disposition.[55]

Edmund Lester Pearson chose to satirize the peculiarities of ALA and other library associations in his 10 May 1916 *Boston Evening Transcript* column. He noted an increasing tendency to offer social activity to entice larger attendance at library association meetings, but he argued that three-fourths of the meetings had no *raison d'être*. "If all of them should do away with eighty percent of their futile discussions of usually unimportant and always uninteresting topics, it would work to the vast advantage of librarians and their work." National library meetings were especially "solemn farces." He then recounted "familiar sights"—young professionals hanging eagerly on every word of some boring speaker who discussed trivia; section meetings and subcommittee reports on the "Findings of the Ten Delegates who have proved the subject of pencil sharpeners to the utmost depth." Wise librarians went swimming, sailing, or played croquet, Pearson said, rather than waste time at meetings. Of course Pearson greatly exaggerated, but the seeds of truth were evident enough to provide a foundation for his satire.

As the conference approached, Ahern resumed her criticism of the methods of selecting ALA nominees to office. In June she reminded PL readers that the nominating committee had been invited to identify a slate of candidates one month before the conference. She thought the invitation a "good one," but was not confident it would be accepted. "Remembering the smothering process indulged in by authority last year—one cannot hope that democracy has returned so quickly to the conduct of A.L.A. affairs." She was right. On 2 June 1916, William Warner Bishop wrote other members of the nominating committee that "despite the urgence of 'Public Libraries,' " he had "not made public, and shall not make public, these results." He argued the committee's only responsibility was to the executive board, and that the latter would determine if it wanted to release the names of candidates early.[56]

The slate was elected exactly as nominated when ALA members gathered at Asbury Park. A record-setting 1,386 registrants cast their votes for Walter Brown as president, Harrison Craver as first vice president, George Locke of the Toronto Public Library as second vice president, and Josephine Rathbone and Arthur Bailey as new executive board members. The rest of the conference experienced little controversy. The executive board recommended that ALA publish a list of nominees a month before conferences. Plummer's presidential address, read in her absence due to illness, referred to a crisis abroad. Although the significance of events abroad might suggest "the littleness of things, the subserviency of technique" among librarians, she comforted her audience by saying "our profession has a not insignificant part to play in world matters." Conferees also listened to several speeches on immigration and Americanization. The council discussed similar subjects.[57]

Attention to these matters reflected a growing concern among librarians about the Great European War, at the time nearly two years old but still a continent away. Officially, ALA assumed a position of neutrality. On one occasion the association weakly requested that the British government not blockade library materials imported from Germany, but Great Britain politely refused. ALA did not protest. Library periodicals carefully avoided taking sides, although they did express the hope that it would soon be over and that all parties could resume normal relations. Privately, librarians probably mirrored the rest of the population and gradually leaned towards England. Bolton wrote to Bowker on 10 April 1915. "We had better undergo much more serious inconvenience, and delay or loss of current German publications," he said, "than in any way to cripple the effort of the allies to put down the arrogant and un-American ideals which seem to possess the leaders of modern Germany." Bowker agreed. "You and I do not differ as to our general feeling on the questions of war." Others worried about the war's impact on supplying materials to answer reading needs to patrons. The publishing board had to cancel plans for a Bohemian list because libraries could not get foreign titles. [58]

The association consistently approached the subject of the war with circumspect caution while the United States remained a neutral power. All of that changed on 4 April 1917, however. When Woodrow Wilson requested a declaration of war against the Central Powers, he inadvertently accelerated the development of the American Library Association. But that is yet another chapter in ALA history.

Epilogue

"This is a big world, Charlie. . . . There is a great dearth of skilled and competent librarians; character, dignity, deportment and worldly wisdom are as essential to success as knowledge of books." William Frederick Poole wrote these words to Charles Evans on 15 February 1871. On 1 June 1914 Matthew Dudgeon wrote E. C. Richardson that a "cultivated" person is "one who has a correct judgment as to what is worthwhile in work, in literature and in life," one who could "select those things which are most essential," and one who possesses "a keen appreciation of the virtue and beauty in those things which his judgment tells him are worthwhile and which he is able to select." By putting "cultivated" individuals in library positions, "have we not made out a strong case for the library?"[1]

Forty-three years separated these two letters, yet both concentrate more attention on the necessary "inherent" qualities that Poole and Evans thought individuals should bring to librarianship than on the specific skills they could learn. "Character" and "cultivation" were the words most frequently mentioned. Naturally, ALA members expected their leaders to possess both. An analysis of common socioeconomic and professional characteristics ALA leaders shared between 1876 and 1917 give even more definition to the social meaning of these words. Nothing in the collective profile reflected in Appendix I and II indicates that ALA executive board members differed substantially from other dominant control groups in the political, social, religious, and professional arenas in America during the Progressive era.[2] The board was composed largely of individuals whose ancestors had come from Northwestern Europe (i.e., Anglo-Saxon heritage) four or more generations previous. They tended to be Protestant, but did not identify with any particular political party. In fact, a cursory glance at the historical record demonstrates they generally shunned politics as a necessary evil outside their profession, and an unbecoming commodity within their profession which too often soiled the reputations of the institutions under their care. In addition, the overwhelming majority were white males about 50 years of age. Four out of five held the administrative rank of chief executive in libraries in which they were employed. From its beginnings, then, ALA was run largely by white Anglo-Saxon male library directors who had labored in the profession for about 20 years.

The ALA motto, "the best reading for the largest number at the least cost," serves as a useful outline for analyzing the change and continuity which characterized the association's embryonic years. By breaking the motto into three distinct parts for closer analysis, and juxtaposing these parts against the 41-year ALA history recounted in previous chapters, it becomes readily apparent that the association spent most of its time and energies adjusting to shifting pressures and influential power groups whose priorities aimed at achieving one of the last two components. At the same time, ALA rendered only occasional attention to the first component, which represented the primary goal towards which leaders directed ALA activities, and which bound the association together.

Between 1876 and 1917 ALA leaders were members of a highly homogeneous group who held convictions compatible with their own sociocultural "enduring" values. They shared a relatively closed definition of reality and believed a rational, informed electorate was essential to democracy. They also shared an abiding faith in the ability of acquired knowledge to solve all social and personal problems. "Is there any agency other than the printed page that can so well present to the human being the bird's eye view of all that there is in life?" Dudgeon asked Richardson in the 1914 letter quoted earlier. ALA leaders were convinced that good reading—or more appropriately "the best reading"—would improve character, and promote good behavior, material progress and cultural uplift; bad reading would debilitate character, promote bad behavior, retard material progress, and stagnate if not reverse cultural progress. "The best reading" was *the* goal, the "real library work" as Dewey called it, to which ALA leaders moved their libraries and their professional association. ALA leaders thought it was a goal upon which they all agreed and therefore it required no critical examination during their annual conferences. Because the reading of good literature would serve to induce society to reduce social conflict and insure social order, libraries would function as a means to channel the interests of the American people towards the dominant culture, of which ALA leaders were both members and supporters. They were convinced that the reading of good literature would correct social perspective and reinforce the socially sound values that they held in such high esteem. Stock "the best reading," they agreed, and the libraries under their care should serve a useful social function. By making it the cornerstone goal of their professional association, ALA leaders provided the binding thread which tied its members together.

That goal became the symbol which drew them to annual conferences. Behind it they maintained an *esprit de corps*, made their vocational sacrifices, and committed their professional lives. It enabled them to forge a consensus into a professional identity, and to give meaning and status to their work; it also helped distinguish their social contributions from the scores of other technical and

professional groups which attached themselves to new state-subsidized institutions and bureaucracies and organized into associations during these four decades.[3] Finally, the symbol was conveniently portable: it could be taken to any
site where ALA leaders thought a "missionary venture" would reap professional
benefits. During its formative years, ALA conferences were a necessity. They
gave the association a sense of function and purpose, and perpetuated a feeling
of permanence which did not solidify until ALA established a permanent headquarters in Chicago in 1909.

Very few people asked about the criteria for determining "the best reading."
Men (and later more and more women) of "character" and "cultivation" intuitively "knew" how to "make the proper selection of these things that are
worthwhile." Being members of a culturally homogeneous socioeconomic group,
they thought criteria for selecting "the best reading" came naturally. On rare
occasions, however, one issue surfaced as a painful reminder of a persistent
dilemma the association seldom addressed openly and never resolved—the fiction
question. Most ALA members agreed that their libraries should stock good fiction
and shun bad fiction, but when forced to determine the difference between the
two in order to settle "borderline" cases like Stephen Crane's *The Red Badge
of Courage*, association members could come to no agreement. By the end of
the period under study ALA leaders had recognized the divisive yet transitory
nature of the question; perhaps they also recognized they could not agree, and
in order to avoid accusations that the association equivocated on the specific
criteria centering on the very goal around which they rallied, it appears they
decided to keep their disagreements out of association activities as much as
possible. Arguments over what was quality fiction tended to polarize ALA members and threatened a closer analysis of the very goal which bound them together,
and upon which they thought people of cultivation and character agreed. Apparently, some things were better left unsaid.[4]

If the goal, that first element in the ALA motto, went relatively unquestioned,
the means toward that goal inherent in the other two elements did not. And it
was the differing means advocated for differing purposes by differing specialized
groups within the profession which forced most of the action in ALA. Advocates
of differing means mixed in various combinations and assumed a variety of
substantially different forms throughout the association's embryonic years.

The image which the profession projected to the world derived from a perception of the goal and the means to achieve it, and the association itself mirrored
this image. It presents a perplexing composite picture of the profession which
came to be both a strength and a weakness. Charles Knowles Bolton hinted at
this dilemma in a "Librarian's Canons of Ethics" which he published in *Public
Libraries* in 1909. Under Section XIX, "Bearing in Public," he argued, "A
librarian is a person of influence, and seeking the respect of all his fellow-
citizens, cannot carelessly choose his company, nor indulge in habits and tastes
that offend the social or moral sense." Under Section XX, "Use of His Name,"
Bolton said, "A librarian should stand on neutral ground and should be chary

of lending his name to a public controversy to add weight to the contention of a local faction, or to commercial enterprises, even those that have an educational or philanthropic motive."[5] Within the parameters defined by their "consensus" interpretation of "the best reading," then, librarians had to remain passively neutral where other emerging professions and groups in the Progressive era could take active visible advocacy roles.

Herbert Putnam struggled with this problem at an informal discussion session at the 1912 Ottawa conference. "Our profession," he said—but then he paused for a few seconds before resuming his address:

I use the term because it is current. We have assumed it, and no one has challenged it. There are grounds in which one might, I suppose, be challenged. . . . A profession should imply uniform standards in such qualifications; but the qualifications of persons accepted among us for library posts of importance,—even among persons who have made notable success in such posts,—vary extraordinarily in both kind and degree. A profession should imply a certain homogeneity in ideals, methods, and relations; while among us there is still a notable diversity. The final characteristic of a profession is its influence upon the community as such. Now, our lack of such an influence as a body is in part due to the lack of that homogeneity in ideal method and personnel—but in part also to the necessary limitations of our office. We are necessarily non-partisan. We are to furnish impartially the ammunition for both sides of every issue. The moment we become identified with a single side merely, we lose our influence and our authority. The result of this neutrality is an attitude which to the world at large must seem somewhat colorless; but also a habit of mind which insensibly in itself becomes neutral. We are content to be observers. We avoid becoming contestants. Such characteristics do not go to the solidification of opinion in a profession, nor to the assertion of it in an an aggressive way. The sum total of all of which (observations upon us) is that in spite of our numbers, in spite of the momentous aggregate that our "establishment" represents, in spite of the assured place which it occupies in the community and the social system, we are at present, and in many ways must continue to be, an aggregate of individuals, rather than a body politic.[6]

When Putnam finished, no one took issue with his words, nor did the library press feel compelled to comment upon them in print. Putnam had identified a professional consensus to which its members had reconciled themselves, for better or worse; elaboration apparently seemed unnecessary.

ALA leaders agreed upon (but did not precisely define) the goal of the association; they also acknowledged the institutions they served had to be passive advocates of the dominant culture. Libraries could not coerce Americans to "the best reading," but they could make those materials readily available. Librarians came to recognize they were exercising a social responsibility by making these materials available so individuals could help themselves to a better life. That concept (within the parameters defined above) became the library's strongest *raison d'être*, one to which leading members of the dominant culture in the Progressive era eagerly subscribed. ALA certainly supported the state that subsidized the institutions librarians sought to serve, and libraries benefited directly from the economic system which allowed a few aggressive individuals to amass huge fortunes, parts of which were sometimes given to libraries.[7] One of the most prominent members of this *nouveau riche*, Andrew Carnegie, made the library the target of his multimillion dollar benefactions precisely because it represented the one institution which fostered the rugged individualism upon which he believed the country was built. Others agreed; libraries proliferated (especially in the Midwest) and the American Library Association prospered accordingly.

Not once in his extemporaneous speech did Putnam identify "the best reading" as the profession's primary goal. That goal was so ingrained in the profession's collective conscience it needed little comment, much less a reminder. Putnam did, however, bemoan a "lack of homogeneity in ideal method and personnel" which he claimed retarded the profession's influence.[8] Unconsciously, he had hit upon the latter two elements in the ALA motto, and in the process had identified "a notable diversity." The history of the American Library Association between 1876 and 1917 must concentrate upon the diversity of methods as they played politics with the association's development. To understand the foundation for this diversity, one need only trace the changes in the collective profile of ALA executive board members between two samples of library leaders over this 41-year period.

Comparing a "typical" ALA executive board member holding office between 1882 and 1886 with a "typical" member occupying the same position between 1913 and 1917 illustrates changes in the leadership of the association during these four decades. In the former half-decade a board member was most likely a married 50-year-old white male librarian born in the Northeast. His father was a member of the managerial class. He possessed at least an undergraduate degree from a northeastern college or university, but had no formal library science education. He came to librarianship from the ranks of another profession, and he directed a public or privately endowed research library located in the Northeast. In the latter half-decade, a board member was still a 50-year-old white male librarian, but less likely to be married or born in the Northeast. His father was a professional instead of a manager. He possessed an undergraduate degree from a midwestern college or university and had nearly one chance in two of having some formal library science education. He was just as likely as not to have entered librarianship from the ranks of another profession, and he directed a public library in the Northeast, although the possibility of occupying a similar position in the Midwest or South was equally as great. He had also been a member of ALA for more than two decades.[9]

ALA leaders agreed on a goal and an overall service concept which ministered to that goal, but they could not always agree on the best means to achieve it, i.e., how to make that goal available "to the largest number at the least cost." The struggle to address these more practical problems by defining the appropriate means ("least cost") and identifying the appropriate groups ("largest number") occupied ALA's collective attention during its formative years, and occasioned

most of the political struggles which periodically threatened to tear its organizational fabric. And the attention which ALA gave to these matters served to
forge the profession's identity in the community of professions. ALA became
known not as a research organization, but as a practice organization; its members
did not constitute a community of inquiry, but a community of methodists.[10] As
professionals best able to determine the means to a commonly accepted goal,
they agreed that they deserved a position of authority. Already members of a
cultivated public, they were now a status group deserving social prestige just
like other emerging professions because they were practitioners in a specialized
field who, by virtue of their unique skills, knew the best, most efficient, and
quickest way to get at the information and knowledge contained in "the best
reading" which lined their library shelves. The dominant culture had already
determined that the acquisition of such information and knowledge was socially
beneficial; libraries were funded by tax dollars drawn from the American public.
Members of the ALA leadership had convinced themselves they were helping
to create "arsenals of a democratic culture" ready to wage war against ignorance.
But they did not realize they were also self-appointed "apostles of culture" (as
Dee Garrison has accurately labeled them) who were members of a patronizing
elite concerned over a perceived lack of domestic order caused by the pressures
of a pluralist society.[11]

From 1876 to 1886 the association was satisfied to rally around "the best
reading" as the professional purpose. ALA was monitored by "old stagers"
like Winsor and Poole who defended conventional librarianship. Beyond partic-
ipating in the compilation of a new edition of *Poole's Index*, the association
could boast little progress towards the goals Dewey outlined for it in 1876 and
1877. But the "old stagers" were not concerned with what Dewey perceived
as lack of progress. By its mere existence the association provided a means to
fill up on the "library spirit" once a year, and to display that missionary spirit
to the nation by locating the annual conference around the Northeast quadrant
of the country. For those reasons alone, they felt, ALA deserved to exist.

By 1893 the association had changed considerably. The "old stagers" no
longer controlled; they were replaced by a new breed of professionals, who,
although still generally centered in New England, were much more eager to
systematize library work and make it more efficient ("at the least cost") through
their professional association. Social problems occasioned by industrialization,
urbanization, immigration, and a frightening growth of mass culture products
forced new approaches in order to make "the best reading" more available "to
the largest number at the least cost." Led by Melvil Dewey, the association had
become more active. The ALA *Catalog* and a forthcoming handbook of library
economy were only two obvious manifestations of the change in ALA's direction.
More would come in the near future. Dewey's leadership position within ALA
was secured by allies on the executive board, by his control of the "Albany
Regency" and by the increasing number of Dewey library school students who

successfully completed his mechanistic curriculum and assumed numerous positions in libraries across the country.

The changes evident in the association by 1901 still related to method, not goal, but questions about reaching "the largest number" surfaced with more regularity as ALA began to manifest the numerous growing pains characteristic of organizational adolescence. Sections, roundtables, special interests, and other types of library groups jockeyed for places in the ALA structure to push their causes. Increasingly notable was a group which represented "western" library interests. They thought that ALA devoted too much attention to urban library interests, not enough to the isolated rural patron. Around the turn of the century they began to exert more pressure on the association to alter its direction, and privately lamented that their interests would never be adequately addressed as long as ALA control continued to reside in the Northeast.

In 1909 the association could boast a more tangible symbol of permanence. By opening a Chicago headquarters with a salaried executive officer and a paid staff, the association announced to the world it had reached professional maturity. Over the past ten years it had proved flexible enough to sometimes deflect, but most often to absorb, the development of splinter groups which challenged its position as the national voice of the American library community. Its governing groups demonstrated a collective profile which was more representative of every constituency within the membership, except women. The proliferation of sections, roundtables and affiliated organizations continued to focus attention on "the largest number," while the birth of *Booklist*, the ALA *Bulletin*, supplements to the ALA *Catalog*, cooperative cataloging schemes, and the publication of numerous indexes, self-help library tracts, and other library aids, insured that the "best reading" identified for the association could indeed reach those larger numbers "at the least cost." It was during this decade that the association forged the professional image it displayed to the world at large. That image was symbolized and solidified in the national conscience by the existence of and the activities generated by the Chicago headquarters.

On America's entry into World War I in 1917, the American Library Association had achieved a level of stability which allowed Burton Stevenson to characterize it fairly as "merely a humdrum professional organization, wrapped round with tradition, settled in its habits of thought, and chiefly occupied with matters of technical detail." ALA leaders continued to find relative consensus on "the best reading." Mechanisms were already in place to identify that reading "at the least cost," although technological innovations like the telephone and the automobile would force minor adjustments in the near future. The reforming spirit of the Progressive era had identified the "problem" groups in American society—the immigrants, the urban indigent, and criminal and insane, the remote rural dweller, the impressionable child, to name but a few—and the historical record shows that ALA had sponsored some activity or group which sought to address the socialization needs of each. Like society at large, however, ALA continued to ignore discrimination against blacks and women.[12] By 1917, it almost seemed as if the association had finally exhausted the potential client groups of libraries, and had come within reach of specifically measuring ''the largest number'' it could serve. But war came in April 1917, and the arena which contained the ''largest number'' suddenly expanded to worldwide dimensions which neither Woodrow Wilson's idealism nor ALA's restricted service definitions could at that time constructively comprehend.

Appendix I

Collective Profile— Constant Characteristics: American Library Association Executive Board Members, 1876– 1917

Variable Number	Variable Name	Frequency (73 of 86, or 84% of Total)[a]
1	Number of family generations in the U.S.	
	Unknown	4%
	Fourth or more	90%
	Third	2%
	Second	2%
	First	2%
2	Family's country of origin	
	Unknown	25%
	Northwest Europe	75%
3	Religion	
	Unknown or unaffiliated	35%
	Protestant	65%
4	Political affiliation	
	Unknown or not declared	72%
	Republican	18%
	Democrat	6%
	Independent	4%
5	Employed in library-related professional positions at the time during which an executive board position was held	
	Yes	98%
	No	2%
6	Rank of library position at the time during which an executive board position was held	
	Chief executive	80%
	Assistant	14%
	Other	6%

[a]Figures indicate in absolute numbers and percentages the proportion of the total population for whom sufficient information could be found.

Appendix II

Collective Profile—Changing Characteristics: American Library Association Executive Board Members, 1876–1917

Chronological Periods[a]

Variable Number	Variable Name	1876 (6 of 7 or 85% of Total)	1882–1886 (13 of 14 or 93% of Total)	1892–1896 (21 of 26 or 81% of Total)	1903–1907 (14 of 17 or 82% of Total)	1913–1917 (19 of 22 or 86% of Total)
7	Birthplace[b]					
	Northeast	100%	100%	75%	71%	50%
	Midwest	0	0	15%	29%	44%
	Other	0	0	10%	0	6%
8	Sex					
	Male	100%	100%	80%	71%	67%
	(excluding second vice president)	(0)	(0)	(100%)	(100%)	(n/a)
	Female	0	0	20%	29%	33%
	(excluding second vice president)	(0)	(0)	(0)	(0)	(n/a)
9	Marital status (all frequencies expressed as % of total)					
	Married	83%	92%	85%	57%	56%
	Male	(83%)	(92%)	(75%)	(57%)	(56%)
	Female	(0)	(0)	(10%)	(0)	(0)
	Single	17%	8%	15%	43%	44%
	Male	(17%)	(8%)	(15%)	(14%)	(11%)
	Female	(0)	(0)	(10%)	(29%)	(33%)

Variable Number	Variable Name	Chronological Periods[a]				
		1876 (6 of 7 or 85% of Total)	1882-1886 (13 of 14 or 93% of Total)	1892-1896 (21 of 26 or 81% of Total)	1903-1907 (14 of 17 or 82% of Total)	1913-1917 (19 of 22 or 86% of Total)
10	Father's occupation[c]					
	Unknown	17%	23%	25%	21%	28%
	Professional	17%	15%	15%	43%	50%
	Managerial	50%	55%	45%	29%	17%
	Other	16%	7%	15%	7%	5%
11	Highest earned degree					
	Grade school	0	0	5%	7%	0
	High school	33%	8%	20%	7%	17%
	Normal (or 2 years)	0	0	10%	14%	22%
	Undergraduate	33%	31%	25%	36%	33%
	Masters	17%	31%	20%	14%	17%
	Ph.D.	0	0	0	7%	6%
	Physician	0	0	0	0	0
	Law	0	8%	5%	0	6%
	Divinity	17%	22%	15%	14%	0
12	Schools at which under graduate degrees earned[b]					
	No higher education	33%	8%	25%	14%	16%
	Northeast	67%	85%	55%	57%	39%
	Midwest	0	7%	7%	20%	45%
	Other	0	0	0	7%	0

241

APPENDIX II, continued

Variable Number	Variable Name	1876 (6 of 7 or 85% of Total)	1882-1886 (13 of 14 or 93% of Total)	Chronological Periods[a] 1892-1896 (21 of 26 or 81% of Total)	1903-1907 (14 of 17 or 82% of Total)	1913-1917 (19 of 22 or 86% of Total)
13	Library science education					
	None	100%	100%	90%	64%	61%
	BLS program	0	0	10%	22%	17%
	Non-degree/ Certificate	0	0	0	14%	22%
14	Library science schools attended					
	None attended	100%	100%	90%	64%	61%
	NYSLS/Columbia	0	0	10%	36%	39%
15	Occupation prior to first library position[c] Library post					
	First position	17%	16%	25%	29%	44%
	Professional	66%	70%	60%	50%	44%
	Manager	0	7%	5%	14%	0
	Other	17%	7%	10%	5%	12%
16	Mean age at which office held	46	50	51	47	52
17	Mean date at which joined ALA	1876	1877	1881	1890	1896

APPENDIX II, continued

Variable Number	Variable Name	Chronological Periods[a]				
		1876 (6 of 7 or 85% of Total)	1882-1886 (13 of 14 or 93% of Total)	1892-1896 (21 of 26 or 81% of Total)	1903-1907 (14 of 17 or 82% of Total)	1913-1917 (19 of 22 or 86% of Total)
18	Mean number of years as member of ALA when executive office held	0	9	15	17	21
19	Type of library at which position held when serving as a member of the executive board					
	Public	50%	33%	60%	29%	61%
	Academic	0	17%	15%	14%	0
	State (including public library commission)	17%	8%	5%	22%	17%
	Library education	0	0	5%	14%	11%
	Privately endowed research	0	25%	10%	7%	6%
	Other	18%	17%	5%	14%	5%
20	Geographical location of position[b]					
	Northeast	50%	67%	65%	50%	44%
	Midwest	33%	17%	30%	29%	33%
	South (including Washington, D.C.)	17%	17%	0	14%	11%
	West	0	0	5%	0	6%
	Other	0	0	0	7%	6%

243

APPENDIX II, continued

[a] Figures given below chronological time period designations indicate in absolute numbers and percentages the proportion of the total population within each chronological period for whom sufficient information could be found.

[b] Geographical distributions adapted from the divisional composition of regions used by the Bureau of the Census throughout this time period. See U.S. Bureau of the Census, Historical Statistics of the United States, Colonial Times to 1957 (Washington, D.C.: Government Printing Office, 1960), 4.

[c] Occupational groupings adapted from David L. Kaplan and M. Claire Casey, Occupational Trends in the United States, 1900-1950 (Washington, D.C.: Bureau of the Census, Working Paper No. 5, 1958).

Appendix III

ALA Conference Locations, Presidents, and Attendance, 1876–1917

DATE	LOCATION	PRESIDENT	ATTENDANCE
1876	Philadelphia	Justin Winsor	103
1877	New York	Justin Winsor	66
1878	(no conference)	Justin Winsor	
1879	Boston	Justin Winsor	162
1880	(no conference)	Justin Winsor	
1881	Washington	Justin Winsor	70
1882	Cincinnati	Justin Winsor	47
1883	Buffalo	Justin Winsor	72
1884	(no conference)	Justin Winsor	
1885	Lake George, N. Y.	Justin Winsor	87
1886	Milwaukee	William Frederick Poole	133
1887	Thousand Islands, N. Y.	William Frederick Poole	186

DATE	LOCATION	PRESIDENT	ATTENDANCE
1888	(Kaaterskill Falls, N. Y.)[1]	Charles Ammi Cutter	(32)
1889	St. Louis	Charles Ammi Cutter	106
1890	White Mountains (Fabyans), N. H.	Frederick M. Crunden	242
1891	San Francisco	Melvil Dewey (to July 1891)[2]	
		Samuel Swett Green (July-Nov. 1891)	83
1892	Lakewood, N. J./Baltimore/ Washington	K. August Linderfelt (to April 1892)[3]	
		William Isaac Fletcher (May 1892)	260
1893	Chicago	Melvil Dewey	311
1894	Lake Placid, N. Y.	Josephus N. Larned	205
1895	Denver	Henry M. Utley	147

247

DATE	LOCATION	PRESIDENT	ATTENDANCE
1896	Cleveland	John Cotton Dana	363
1897	Philadelphia	William H. Brett	315
1898	Chautauqua, N. Y.	Justin Winsor (to Oct. 1897) [4]	
		Herbert Putnam (Jan.-Aug. 1898)	494
1899	Atlanta	William Coolidge Lane	215
1900	Montreal	Reuben G. Thwaites	452
1901	Waukesha, Wis.	Henry J. Carr	460
1902	Magnolia, Mass.	John Shaw Billings	1,018
1903	Niagara Falls	James K. Hosmer	684
1904	St. Louis	Herbert Putnam	577
1905	Portland, Ore.	Ernest C. Richardson	359

DATE	LOCATION	PRESIDENT	ATTENDANCE
1906	Narragansett Pier, R. I.	Frank P. Hill	891
1907	Asheville, N. C.	Clement W. Andrews	478
1908	Lake Minnetonka, Minn.	Arthur E. Bostwick	664
1909	Bretton Woods, N. H.	Charles H. Gould	620
1910	Mackinac Island, Mich.	N.D.C. Hodges	532
1911	Pasadena, Cal.	James I. Wyer[5]	582
1912	Ottawa, Canada	Theresa West Elmendorf	704
1913	Kaaterskill, N. Y.	Henry E. Legler	892
1914	Washington	Edward H. Anderson	1,366
1915	Berkeley, Cal.	Hiller C. Wellman	779
1916	Asbury Park, N. J.	Mary Wright Plummer[6]	1,386
1917	Louisville, Ky.	Walter L. Brown	824

1. Unofficial, informal conference.

2. Resigned for reason of health.

3. Resigned. Resignation accepted effective date of election.

4. Died October 22, 1897.

5. Absent from conference.

6. Died September 21, 1916. Conference sessions presided over by ALA vice president.

Abbreviations

AL	*American Libraries*
ALA Archives	American Library Association Archives, University of Illinois Library, Archives, Urbana, Illinois
ALJ	*American Library Journal*
Andrews Mss, MIT	Clement W. Andrews Papers, University Archives, Massachusetts Institute of Technology, Cambridge, Massachusetts
BALA	*Bulletin of the American Library Association*
Beer Mss, TU	William Beer Papers, Special Collections Division, Howard-Tilton Memorial Library, Tulane University, New Orleans, Louisiana
Billings Mss, NYPL	John Shaw Billings Papers, Special Collections, New York Public Library, New York City
Bishop Mss, UM	William Warner Bishop Papers, Bentley Historical Library, University of Michigan, Ann Arbor, Michigan
Blatchford Mss, Newberry	Eliphalet W. Blatchford Papers, Archives, Newberry Library, Chicago, Illinois
BAA	Boston Athenaeum Archives, Boston Athenaeum, Boston, Massachusetts
BPL Archives	Boston Public Library Archives, Boston Public Library, Boston, Massachusetts
Bowker Mss, NYPL	Richard R. Bowker Papers, Special Collections, New York Public Library, New York City
Brett Mss, CPL	William Howard Brett Papers, Archives, Cleveland Public Library, Cleveland, Ohio
Carlton Mss, Newberry	W.N.C. Carlton Papers, Archives, Newberry Library, Chicago, Illinois

Carr Mss, ALA Archives	Henry J. Carr Papers, American Library Association Archives, University of Illinois Library, Archives, Urbana, Illinois
Cheney Mss, LC	John Vance Cheney Papers, Manuscripts Division, Library of Congress, Washington, D.C.
CLC Minutes, CHS	Chicago Library Club, Minutes, Chicago Historical Society, Chicago, Illinois
Cole Mss, AAS	George Watson Cole Papers, American Antiquarian Society, Worcester, Massachusetts
Cole Mss, ALA Archives	George Watson Cole Papers, American Library Association Archives, University of Illinois Library, Archives, Urbana, Illinois
Countryman Mss, MinnHS	Gratia Countryman Papers, Division of Archives and Manuscripts, Minnesota Historical Society, St. Paul, Minnesota
Dana Mss, NPL	John Cotton Dana Papers, New Jersey Room, Newark Public Library, Newark, New Jersey
Dana Mss, SPL	John Cotton Dana Papers, Archives, Springfield Public Library, Springfield, Massachusetts
Davis Mss, UM	Raymond C. Davis Papers, Bentley Historical Library, University of Michigan, Ann Arbor, Michigan
Dewey Mss, CU	Melvil Dewey Papers, Special Collections, University Library, Columbia University, New York City
Director's File, DPL	Detroit Public Library Director's File, 1904–1919, Burton Historical Collections, Detroit Public Library, Detroit, Michigan
Dudgeon Mss, WSHS	Matthew S. Dudgeon Papers, Manuscripts Division, Wisconsin State Historical Society, Madison, Wisconsin
Evans Mss, UI	Charles Evans Papers, Rare Book Room, University of Illinois Library, Urbana, Illinois
FRVLA Records, UW-GB	Fox River Valley Library Association Records, 1898–1913, Special Collections, Library-Learning Center, University of Wisconsin—Green Bay, Green Bay, Wisconsin
Gould Mss, MU	Charles H. Gould Papers, University Archives, McLennon Library Building, McGill University, Montreal, Quebec, Canada
R. P. Hayes Mss, HL	Rutherford P. Hayes Papers, Rutherford B. Hayes Library, Fremont, Ohio
Hosmer Mss, MinnHS	James K. Hosmer Papers, Division of Archives and Manuscripts, Minnesota Historical Society, St. Paul, Minnesota
JLH	*Journal of Library History*

Johnston Mss, LC	W. Dawson Johnston Papers, Manuscripts Division, Library of Congress, Washington, D.C.
Koopman Mss, BU	H. L. Koopman Papers, Special Collections, John Hay Library, Brown University, Providence, Rhode Island
Lane Mss, HUA	William Coolidge Lane Papers, Harvard University Archives, Harvard University, Cambridge, Massachusetts
LC Archives	Library of Congress Archives, Central Services Division, Library of Congress, Washington, D.C.
LCE-NA	Letters Sent by the Commissioner of Education, 1870–1909. Records of the Bureau of Education. Department of Interior. Microcopy No. 635. National Archives, Washington, D.C.
LDO-UI Archives	Library Dean's Office: American Library Association Correspondence, 1909–1943, University of Illinois Library, Archives, Urbana, Illinois
Librarian's File, NPL	Newark Librarians - Letters (1888–1902), New Jersey Room, Newark Public Library, Newark, New Jersey
LJ	*Library Journal*
LQ	*Library Quarterly*
MLC Mss, MinnHS	Minutes (1899–1919), Minnesota Public Library Commission, Division of Archives and Manuscripts, Minnesota Historical Society, St. Paul, Minnesota
NOPL Archives	Library Archives, New Orleans Public Library, New Orleans, Louisiana
PL	*Public Libraries*
Poole Mss, Newberry	William Frederick Poole Papers, Archives, Newberry Library, Chicago, Illinois
Proceedings [date]	Proceedings of the annual American Library Association Conferences, 1876–1917. To 1907, bound into volumes of *Library Journal*; from 1907, bound into volumes of the *Bulletin of the American Library Association*.
PST Mss, ALA Archives	Publishing Services, Associate Executive Director, Treasurer's Correspondence, 1899–1901, American Library Association Archives, University of Illinois Library, Archives, Urbana, Illinois
Putnam Archives, CSD-LC	Herbert Putnam Papers, Library of Congress Archives, Central Services Division, Library of Congress, Washington, D.C.
Putnam Mss, LC	Herbert Putnam Papers, Manuscripts Division, Library of Congress, Washington, D.C.
PW	*Publisher's Weekly*
Reid Mss, LC	Whitelaw Reid Papers, Manuscripts Division, Library of Congress, Washington, D.C.

Richardson Mss, PU	Ernest Cushing Richardson Papers, Special Collections, Firestone Library, Princeton, New Jersey
Roden Mss, Newberry	Carl B. Roden Papers, Archives, Newberry Library, Chicago, Illinois
Roosevelt Mss, LC	Theodore Roosevelt Papers, Manuscripts Division, Library of Congress, Washington, D.C.
Root Mss, OCA	Azariah Smith Root Papers, Archives, Oberlin College Library, Oberlin, Ohio
SPL Archives	Springfield (Massachusetts) Public Library Archives, Director's Office, Springfield Public Library, Springfield, Massachusetts
StLPL Archives	St. Louis Public Library Archives, Archives and Rare Book Room, St. Louis Public Library, St. Louis, Missouri
Stevenson Mss, LC	Burton Egbert Stevenson Papers, Manuscripts Division, Library of Congress, Washington, D.C.
Swift Mss, HU	Lindsay Swift Papers, Houghton Library, Harvard University, Cambridge, Massachusetts
Thwaites Mss, WSHS	Reuben G. Thwaites Papers, Manuscripts Division, Wisconsin State Historical Society, Madison, Wisconsin
Trustees' Records, BPL	Minutes of the Board of Trustees, 1916–1920, Director's Office, Boston Public Library, Boston, Massachusetts
Utley Mss, DPL	Henry Munson Utley Papers, Burton Historical Collection, Detroit Public Library, Detroit, Michigan
Wellman Mss, SPL	Hiller C. Wellman Papers, Archives, Springfield Public Library, Springfield, Massachusetts
WFLC-WSHS	Records of the Wisconsin Free Library Commission, Manuscripts Division, Wisconsin State Historical Society, Madison, Wisconsin
Winsor Letters, LJ/RC	Justin Winsor Letters, bound into 1881 volume of *Library Journal*, and located in the Rosary College Library, River Forest, Illinois
Winsor Mss, HUA	Justin Winsor Papers, Harvard University Archives, Harvard University, Cambridge, Massachusetts
Winsor Mss, MHS	Justin Winsor Papers, Massachusetts Historical Society, Boston, Massachusetts
WLA Mss, WSHS	Wisconsin Library Association Papers, Manuscripts Division, Wisconsin State Historical Society, Madison, Wisconsin

Notes

For purposes of brevity the author has used the following citation patterns for (a.) published periodical articles, and (b.) unpublished manuscript materials:

a. Periodical title abbreviation, volume number, month number, last two digits of year, page.

e.g., ALJ 1 (11/76): 90.

b. Correspondents, day of month, month number, last two digits of year, location of materials (abbreviated).

e.g., Eaton to Winsor, 2/7/75, Superintendent's File, BPL Archives.

Preface

1. Dewey originally worded the motto "The best reading for the largest number at the least expense." See LJ 1 (3/77): 247. He later changed it. For a more complete account of the evolution of the motto, see Melvil Dewey, "Origin of the A.L.A. Motto," PL 11 (1906): 55.

2. Charles Rosenberg, "Toward an Ecology of Knowledge: On Discipline, Context and History," in *The Organization of Knowledge in Modern America, 1860–1920,* ed. Alexandra Oleson and John Voss (Baltimore: The Johns Hopkins University Press, 1979), 446, 448.

Chapter One: An Auspicious Beginning: The Philadelphia Conference of 1876

1. ALJ 1 (11/76): 90, 140. A year later *American Library Journal* changed its name to *Library Journal.*

2. The best account of this conference remains George Burwell Utley, *The Librarians' Conference of 1853: A Chapter in American Library History* (Chicago: American Library Association, 1951).

3. For a comprehensive account, see Francis Miksa, "The Making of the 1876 Special Report on Public Libraries," JLH 8 (1/73): 30–40.

4. Eaton to Winsor, 2/7/75, Superintendent's File, BPL Archives, cited in Edward

G. Holley, *Raking the Historic Coals: The A.L.A. Scrapbook of 1876* (Urbana, IL.: Beta Phi Mu, 1967), 7. The Williams-Eaton correspondence is cited in Miksa, "The Making of the 1876 Special Report," 40, footnote 56. See also Justin Winsor, "Report of the Superintendent," *Seventeenth Annual Report of the Trustees of the Public Library, 1869. City Document No. 115* (Boston: Alfred Mudge and Sons, 1869), 26.

5. See PW No. 223 (22/4/76): 528.

6. In reconstructing the chronology of events leading up to the conference I have relied heavily upon Holley, *Raking the Historic Coals*. Unless otherwise indicated all quotations and citations to correspondence related to conference' planning can be found there.

7. See Dewey memo dated 18/5/76, Dewey Mss, CU.

8. Poole probably forgot correspondence he had had with Dewey nearly three years earlier. See Poole to Dewey, 5/11/73, Dewey Mss, CU.

9. Eaton to Dewey, 22/7/76, LCE-NA. There is some evidence that Dewey and Leypoldt wanted to use both the bureau and the conference to promote the *Journal*. Dewey wrote Leypoldt: "You say in a p.s. 'by all means have the prospectus a part of the call and a part of the report.' . . . I fancied you would not want it to appear that we were too much interested in the conference on account of the Journal which we hoped to give strength by the meeting." Dewey to Leypoldt, n.d., Dewey Mss, CU. The note provides some evidence to justify Eaton's action and Poole's initial reaction to joining a conference call advocated by commercial publishers.

10. "Library and Bibliographical Notes," PW 10 (16/9/76): 476; Boston *Daily Advertiser*, 14/9/76.

11. ALJ 1 (9/76): 14.

12. ALJ 1 (9/76): 5–6.

13. See Dewey's statement in a conference session entitled, "In Memory of the Late William Frederick Poole, LL.D.," in *Proceedings, 1894*, 170.

14. Poole to Dewey, 15/6/76, quoted in Holley, *Raking the Historic Coals*, 61.

15. This cameo description of Winsor is taken from the published reminiscences of another, much younger conference participant. See William E. Foster, "Five Men of '76," BALA 20 (10/26): 313–314. See also Wayne Cutler and Michael Hope Harris, *Justin Winsor: Scholar Librarian* (Littleton, CO: Libraries Unlimited, Inc., 1980), 32–33; 48–49.

16. This picture was drawn from several sources. See Foster, "Five Men of '76," 314–316; James I. Wyer to Carl Roden, n.d., Roden Mss, Newberry; and an unpublished "Autobiography" by John V. Cheney in Cheney Mss, LC. See also *Proceedings, 1894*, 168; *1916*, 383; and William L. Williamson, *William Frederick Poole and the Modern Library Movement* (New York: Columbia University Press, 1963), 48–49.

17. Winsor was even more forceful two years later. "There is no way in which a librarian shows his catholicity so strongly as in his championing of trash, as it is called,— innocuous matter, I mean, for I am not considering vicious writing." Justin Winsor, "A Librarian's Catholicity," *Literary World* 9 (1/11/78): 94. See also Winsor's "Library Lectures and Other Helps," LJ 3 (5/78): 120.

18. For a more comprehensive argument on this point, see John Y. Cole, "Storehouses and Workshops: American Libraries and the Uses of Knowledge," in *The Organization of Knowledge in Modern America, 1860–1920*, 370. For a more comprehensive discussion of the ideology and background philosophy structuring librarians' attitudes towards read-

ing, see Francis L. Miksa (ed.), *Charles Ammi Cutter: Library Systematizer* (Littleton, CO: Libraries Unlimited, Inc., 1977), 29–43.

19. A large body of historical literature addressing the question of middle-class efforts to insure "social order" and maintain "social control" has appeared in the last 15 years. The seminal work which introduced this paradigm was Robert H. Wiebe, *The Search for Order, 1877–1920* (New York: Hill and Wang, 1967), especially Chap. 5. See also Mary O. Furner, *Advocacy and Objectivity: A Crisis in the Professionalization of American Social Science, 1865–1905* (Lexington, KY: University of Kentucky Press, 1975); Sally Gregory Kohlstedt, *The Formation of the American Scientific Community: The American Association for the Advancement of Science, 1848–1860* (Urbana, IL: University of Illinois Press, 1976); Burton J. Bledstein, *The Culture of Professionalism: The Middle Class and the Development of Higher Education in America* (New York: W. W. Norton & Co., 1976); Thomas L. Haskell, *The Emergence of Professional Social Science: The American Social Science Association and the Nineteenth Century Crisis of Authority* (Urbana, IL: University of Illinois Press, 1976); Paul Boyer, *Urban Masses and Moral Order in America, 1820–1920* (Cambridge, MA: Harvard University Press, 1978); T. Jackson Lears, *No Place of Grace: Antimodernism and the Transformation of American Culture, 1880–1920* (New York: Pantheon Books, 1981); and Alan Trachtenberg, *The Incorporation of America: Culture and Society in the Gilded Age* (New York: Hill and Wang, 1982).

20. Unless otherwise indicated, quotations and evidence on the conference of 1876 are taken from *Proceedings, 1876*. See especially 106, 134, 140 and 141.

21. In the past ten years American public library historians have struggled to address the "social control" thesis posited by Michael H. Harris in his *The Role of the Public Library in American Life: A Speculative Essay* (Urbana, IL: University of Illinois Graduate School of Library Science. Occasional Paper No. 117, 1975), and developed more fully by Dee Garrison in her *Apostles of Culture: The Public Librarian and American Society, 1876–1920* (New York: The Free Press, 1979). While this author will take exception to several of their conclusions and in future chapters will criticize their samples as too restricted, he is nonetheless indebted to these two scholars for introducing this provocative paradigm to the American library history community. For a fair assessment of Harris and Garrison which seeks to locate their ideas in the context of American public library history literature, see Francis L. Miksa, "An Interpretation of American Public Library History," in *Public Librarianship: A Reader*, ed. Jane Robbins-Carter (Littleton, CO: Libraries Unlimited, Inc., 1982), 73–90.

22. See Appendix I and II. This data is discussed in more detail in Wayne A. Wiegand, "American Library Association Executive Board Members, 1876–1917: A Collective Profile," *Libri* 31 (7/81): 22–35.

Chapter Two: Rallying around "The Best Reading": The Formative Stages, 1876–1886

1. *Proceedings, 1886*, 383.
2. *Proceedings, 1886*, 203.
3. *Proceedings, 1886*, 381.
4. *Proceedings, 1886*, 341–342.
5. *Proceedings, 1886*, 344.
6. *Proceedings, 1886*, 351. For a good summary of this debate, see John Phillip

Comaromi, *The Eighteen Editions of the Dewey Decimal Classification* (Albany, NY: Forest Press Division, Lake Placid Education Foundation, 1976), Chap. 5.

7. *Proceedings, 1886*, 376.

8. *Proceedings, 1886*, 381.

9. Kephart to Koopman, 11/7/86, Koopman Mss, BU.

10. The ramifications of this decision upon library graduate education and upon subsequent claims for a place for librarianship in the community of professions would not be felt seriously until the twentieth century. For a provocative analysis which demonstrates the function a theoretical body of knowledge performs for the historical development of a profession, see Magali Sarfatti Larson, *The Rise of Professionalism: A Sociological Analysis* (Berkeley, CA: University of California Press, 1977), especially Chap. 4.

11. "American Library Association," ALJ 1 (3/77): 253–254.

12. A signed copy of the contract can be found in Dewey Mss, CU.

13. Leypoldt to Dewey, 20/10/76, Dewey Mss, CU.

14. Dewey to Bowker, 20/11/76, Bowker Mss, NYPL.

15. Dewey to Billings, 26/5/77, Billings Mss, NYPL.

16. Circular found in Bowker Mss, NYPL.

17. ALJ 1 (7/77): 395. In part, the squabble over Winsor's salary was the result of Irish-American reaction to public institutions controlled by Boston Brahmins. See Cutler and Harris, *Winsor*, 28–30, for a more comprehensive analysis. Larson argues that the desire to depoliticize hiring practices for professional posts constitutes part of the drive towards professionalism. See Larson, *Rise of Professionalism*, 138–145.

18. *Proceedings, 1877*, 29.

19. ALJ 2 (9/77): 14.

20. New York *World*, 9/9/77, quoted in Holley, *Raking the Historic Coals*, 10–11.

21. Winsor to Mrs. Winsor, 9/9/77 and 6/10/77, Winsor Mss, HUA.

22. Samuel Swett Green, *The Public Library Movement in the United States, 1853–1893* (Boston: The Boston Book Company, 1913), 59.

23. *Ibid.*, 73; LJ 2 (10/77): 221.

24. Green to Winsor, 6/11/77, Winsor Mss, HUA.

25. Dewey to Bowker, 24/10/77, Bowker Mss, NYPL.

26. Contract attached to Bowker to Cutter, 13/1/79, Bowker Mss, NYPL, in which Bowker complains of the complex agreement.

27. LJ 3 (11/78): 330; (12/78): 385.

28. Bowker to Dewey, 9/1/79; Bowker to Cutter, 13/1/79; and Bowker to Winsor, 15/1/79, Bowker Mss, NYPL.

29. Bowker to Winsor, 16/6/79, Winsor Letters, LJ/RC. See also Leypoldt to Bowker, 1/7/79, Bowker Mss, NYPL.

30. LJ 3 (5/78): 113–115; (6/78): 144–147.

31. See Dewey circular, January 1879, found in Davis Mss, UM.

32. LJ 2 (8/77): 423–427; 3 (7/78): 186; (8/78): 222–223; (11/78): 331; 4 (5/79): 155–156.

33. LJ 3 (4/78): 43–44; (7/78): 186; PL 11 (3/06): 55.

34. Dewey to Winsor, 14/6/79, Winsor Letters, LJ/RC.

35. Direct quotes taken from *Proceedings, 1879*, 282, 286–287, 289, 300, and 303. Cutter's report to *The Nation* is reprinted in full in LJ 4 (7–8/79): 311–312. The transfer of ALA Supply Department stock to Dewey's Readers and Writers Economy Company is explored more fully in Francis L. Miksa, "Melvil Dewey and the Corporate Ideal,"

in *Melvil Dewey: The Man and the Classification*, ed. Gordon Stevenson and Judith Kramer-Greene (Albany, NY: Forest Press, 1983), 80–91.

36. LJ 4 (12/79): 443; 5 (11/12/80): 307–308.

37. Poole to Dewey, 8/11/80, Dewey Mss, CU.

38. LJ 4 (11/79): 404; 5 (1/80): 12; (3/80): 77; and Perkins to Dewey, 9/11/80, Dewey Mss, CU.

39. These events were reconstructed from the information contained in a series of letters between Dewey and Winsor. See Green to Dewey, 25/10/80; Dewey to Winsor, 13/12/80; Winsor to Dewey, 14, 20, 23 and 31/12/80; 14 and 25/1/81, Dewey Mss, CU. See also Green to Dewey, 14/1/81, Dewey Mss, CU; and LJ 5 (11–12/80): 303. For a more complete account of how Dewey became involved in the Readers and Writers Economy Company, see Dee Garrison, *Apostles of Culture: The Public Librarian and American Society, 1876–1926* (New York: The Free Press, 1979), 120–124.

40. See Bowker to Dewey, 1/10/79, Dewey Mss, CU; *Library Journal* "Circular," 10/1/80; and Bowker to Winsor, 20/1/80, Bowker Mss, NYPL.

41. See LJ 5 (6/80): 168; Jacob Schwartz to Dewey, 30/6/80; Foster to Dewey; Homes to Dewey; Edmonds to Dewey; Fletcher to Dewey; and Smith to Dewey, 1/7/80; Poole to Dewey, 2/7/80; and Crunden to Dewey, 3/7/80, Dewey Mss, CU. For information on the Poole-Bowker incident, see Bowker to Dewey, 6/10/80, Dewey Mss, CU.

42. LJ 5 (7–8/80): 207–208; (9–10/80): 248–249; Leypoldt to Bowker, 11/8/80; and Augusta Leypoldt to Bowker, 18/9/80, Bowker Mss, NYPL.

43. Leypoldt to Dewey, 4 and 7/10/80; 15 and 20/1/81; Cutter to Dewey, 14 and 16/1/81, Dewey Mss, CU; LJ 5 (11–12/80): 303.

44. Foster to Dewey, 15/1/81, Dewey Mss, CU.

45. *Proceedings, 1881*, 122, 131, 133, 135, and 140; LJ 6 (6/81): 181; Dewey to Bowker, 6/6/81, Bowker Mss, NYPL. For a discussion of attitudes towards politicians experienced by other groups of professionals, see Bruce Sinclair, *A Centennial History of the American Society of Mechanical Engineers, 1880–1980* (Toronto: University of Toronto Press, 1980), 42; and Barbara Gutmann Rosenkrantz, *Public Health and the State: Changing Views in Massachusetts, 1842–1936* (Cambridge, MA: Harvard University Press, 1972), 74.

46. LJ 6 (2/81): 23–24, 30. Hoyt's article is reprinted on page 30.

47. LJ 6 (6/81): 181; (11/81): 314; Dewey to Bowker, 6/6/81, Bowker Mss, NYPL.

48. See PL 19 (12/14): 450–451, for an autobiographical account of the meeting.

49. LJ 7 (1/82): 4; (2/82): 28–29. See also Poole to Davis, 1/4/82, Davis Mss, UM.

50. *Proceedings, 1882*, 192, 195, 197, 201, and 205.

51. LJ 7 (9/82): 226–228; (12/82): 290.

52. Larned to Davis, 22/5/83, Davis Mss, UM; Larned to Dewey, 31/7/83 and 3/8/83; and Whitney to Dewey, 10/6/83, Dewey Mss, CU.

53. Quotes taken from *Proceedings, 1883*, 225, 261, 263, 267, 288, 289, 293, 294, and 295. See also Cutter's summary of the conference in *The Nation* 23 (8/83): 157–158. Dewey had some indication of Poole's opposition to a formal library training school before the conference. See Poole to Dewey, 14/7/83, Dewey Mss, CU.

54. Poole to Dewey, 17/12/83; Dewey to Poole, 19/12/83; Poole to Dewey, 28/12/83; Dewey to Poole, 6/3/84; and Poole to Dewey, 13/3/84, Dewey Mss, CU.

55. See Bowker to Dewey, 19 and 24/1/85; 27/4/85; 18/5/85; 18 and 23/12/85; 4/3/86; Dewey to Bowker, 23/3/86; and Bowker to Dewey, 30/3/86, Dewey Mss, CU; Annie Dewey to Bowker, 2 and 10/4/86; and Dewey to Bowker, 15/4/86, Bowker Mss, NYPL.

56. LJ 9 (4/84): 69; C. Alex Nelson to H. L. Koopman, 25/7/84, Koopman Mss, BU. See also Eaton to Dewey, 21/7/85, LCE-NA.

57. For comments on the works by Hewins and Perkins, see LJ 7 (10/82): 249; and 10 (4/85): 91. See also Dewey to Rutherford P. Hayes, 19/1/83; and 10/12/84, R. P. Hayes Mss, HL.

58. Theresa West to Lucy Stevens (Librarian of the Toledo [Ohio] Public Library), 16/12/83, copy found in Dewey Mss, CU; Poole to Billings, 14/3/84, Billings Mss, NYPL; Eaton to Dewey, 10 and 16/10/84; and Eaton to Winsor, 23/10/84, LCE-NA.

59. Crunden to Dewey, 11/3/84; Winsor to Dewey, 20/2/85; Dewey to Winsor, 23/2/85; Dewey Mss, CU. Winsor's note about "figureheads" is penned in the margin of the last letter cited.

60. Reuben A. Guild to Dewey, 8/5/85; Foster to Dewey, 15/6/85; Dewey to Winsor, 5/8/85; Bowker to Dewey, 27/8/85; and Winsor to Dewey, 29/8/85, Dewey Mss, CU; Dewey to "Program Committee of the ALA," 11/8/85, Billings Mss, NYPL; and Dewey to Bowker, 11/8/85, Bowker Mss, NYPL.

61. Quotes taken from *Proceedings, 1885*, 296, 309, 310, 311, 333, and 342. See also Ernest C. Richardson, "Bibliothecal Science and Economy—Article II of the A.L.A. Constitution," LJ 10 (9/85): 244–245.

62. Poole to Dewey, 3/10/85, Dewey Mss, CU.

Chapter Three: Pushing for "The Least Cost": Dewey's Resurgence, 1885–1893

1. Frederick W. Faxon, "Times Past—Twenty-four ALA Conferences Recalled," *Proceedings, 1916*, 286–287. The most complete account of the exposition remains David F. Burg, *Chicago's White City at 1893* (Lexington, KY: University Press at Kentucky, 1976).

2. Quotes taken from *Proceedings, 1893*, 1, 9, 15, 18, 20, 55–56, 57, 58, 67, 75, and 79. See also George Iles to Bowker, 18/7/93, Bowker Mss, NYPL; *Nation* 57 (31/8/93): 150; Katharine L. Sharp, "The A.L.A. Library Exhibit at the World's Fair," LJ 18 (8/93): 280–284; and "Memorandum on the ALA Columbian Expo Exhibit," Johnston Mss, LC. Poole's comment on the "Albany Regency" is quoted from Carl Roden to W. L. Williamson, 1/1/53, Roden Mss, Newberry.

3. See Appendix I and II.

4. For an example of Dewey's "placement" activities, see Dewey to Eliphalet W. Blatchford (a trustee of the Walter Newberry estate, which would soon fund the erection of a major research library in Chicago bearing the benefactor's name), 14/3/87, Blatchford Mss, Newberry. See also N. H. R. Dawson (Commissioner of Education) to Dewey, 29/1/87, LCE-NA. Dewey's comments on the school are quoted from Sarah K. Vann, *Melvil Dewey: His Enduring Presence in Librarianship* (Littleton, CO: Libraries Unlimited, Inc., 1978), 113. See also Arthur Bostwick, *A Life with Men and Books* (New York: H.W. Wilson Co., 1939), 165, for Bostwick's second hand account of the library community's attitude towards the opening of Dewey's school.

5. LJ 12 (4/87): 164–165; Olan S. Davis (of the Library Bureau) to Dewey, 28/3/87, Dewey Mss, CU; and Dewey to John Shaw Billings, 27/5/87, Billings Mss, NYPL. See also a copy of the minutes of a committee meeting at the Library Company in Philadelphia which determined that "the arrangement and classification of Mr. Melvil Dewey is the best brought to our notice," as found in Dewey Mss, CU.

6. Fletcher to Bowker, 21/10/86; Tedder to Bowker, 19/11/86; and Augusta Leypoldt to Bowker, 9/12/86, Bowker Mss, NYPL; Dewey to Thomas, 20/1/87; Bowker to Dewey, 14/5/87; and Bowker to Dewey, 26/5/87, Dewey Mss, CU.

7. E.C. Richardson to Dewey, 4/1/87; Soldan to Dewey, 7/2/87, Dewey Mss, CU; LJ 11 (10/86): 404; (11/86): 442; and 12 (4/87): 152

8. *Proceedings, 1887*, 423, 427, 438, and 457; LJ 12 (8/87): 279; Evans to Poole, 30/12/87; Guild to Poole, 12/9/87, Poole Mss, Newberry.

9. Cutter to Dewey, 17/10/87, Dewey Mss, CU.

10. LJ 13 (1/88): 3; Richard Spamer to Poole, 17/2/88; Dewey to Poole, 22/9/87; and Evans to Poole, 8/4/88, Poole Mss, Newberry; Horace Kephart to Koopman, 24/9/87, Koopman Mss, BU.

11. Bowker to Dewey, 1 and 21/12/87, and 3/1/88; Bowker to H. E. Davidson, 16/1/88; Bowker to Dewey, 8 and 14/5/88; and H. M. Utley (Director of the Detroit Public Library) to Dewey, 24/5/88, Dewey Mss, CU; Mary W. Plummer to George Watson Cole, 1/6/88, Cole Mss, ALA Archives. While Dewey's spring may have looked gloomy on the surface, he was already working on obtaining a new position. See his letters to Whitelaw Reid (secretary of the Board of Regents of the University of the State of New York), 2/12/87; and 11 and 26/1/88, Reid Mss, LC.

12. *Proceedings, 1888*, 301 and 322.

13. C. Alex Nelson to Bowker, 31/12/88, Bowker Mss, NYPL. The full story behind Dewey's move from Columbia to Albany has yet to be told. For primary source material, see Dewey to Reid, 25/11/88; Dewey circular (and responses), 26/11/88; Dewey to Reid, 18/12/88, Reid Mss, LC. See also N. H. R. Dawson to Dewey, 12/12/88, LCE-NA; W. T. Peoples to G. W. Cole, 18/1/89; and Frank Patten to Cole, 4/5/89, Cole Mss, ALA Archives; and Bowker to Dewey, 8/12/88; and Dewey to Bowker, 20/12/88, Dewey Mss, CU.

14. Crunden to Dewey (marked "private and confidential"), 24/4/89, Dewey Mss, CU. See also Cutler to Dewey, 4/5/89, Dewey Mss, CU.

15. Quotes taken from *Proceedings, 1889*, 269, 273, 276, and 287. For comment on election of ALA officers, see J. N. Larned to Poole, 17/5/89, Poole Mss, Newberry.

16. Bowker to Dewey, 12/12/89, Dewey Mss, CU. See also Dewey to Bowker, 21/12/89; Bowker to Dewey, 28 and 31/12/89, Dewey Mss, CU, for further evidence of the hostility between the two men. See also Frank Patten to Cole, 14/6/89, Cole Mss, ALA Archives; Blatchford to Dewey, 30/1/90, Blatchford Mss, Newberry; and Carnegie to Dewey, 15/5/90, Dewey Mss, CU.

17. Root to Poole, 19/6/89, Poole Mss, Newberry; Cole to Dewey, 18/1/90, Dewey Mss, CU; Paul L. Ford to E. C. Richardson, 27/1/90, Richardson Mss, PU; Ford to Poole, 11/2/90; Foster to Poole, 30/1/90, Poole Mss, Newberry; Dewey to Cutter, 12/6/90, Dewey Mss, CU; and Bean to Evans, 10/8/90, Evans Mss, UI.

18. John V. Cheney to Dewey, 1/2/90; Crunden to Dewey, 21/2/90; Dewey to Crunden, 25/2/90; Crunden to Dewey, 8/3/90, Dewey Mss, CU; Minerva L. Sanders (of the Pawtucket, Rhode Island, Public Library) to Rutherford P. Hayes, 10/4/90, R. P. Hayes Mss, HL; and C. M. Hewins to Clement W. Andrews (director of the Massachusetts Institute of Technology Library), ?/6/90, Andrews Mss, MIT.

19. Dewey to Bowker, 15/7/90; Ada North (University of Iowa librarian) to Dewey, 5/9/90; William Coolidge Lane to Dewey, 15/1/90, Dewey Mss, CU; W. T. Harris to Cutter, 23/10/90; Harris to E. Clarence Hovey, 23/9/90, LCE-NA; LJ 15 (9/90): 276; J. P. Dunn to Dewey, 23/8/90, Dewey Mss, CU.

20. LJ 15 (12/90): 5; *Proceedings, 1890*, 87, 90, 94, 103, 105, 123, 129, 131, and 140. For reaction to Poole's speech, see J. L. Whitney to Boston Public Library Board of Trustees, 20/9/90, "Whitney Folder," BPL Archives; Henry Demarest Lloyd to Poole, 21/9/90, Poole Mss, Newberry; Hannah P. James to Dewey, 27/9/90, Dewey Mss, CU; and F. M. Crunden to Lindsay Swift, 15/4/91, Swift Mss, HU.

21. LJ 16 (1/91): 14–15. See also American Library Association, "Papers Prepared for the World's Library Congress," in U.S. Bureau of Education. *Report of the Commissioner of Education for the Year, 1892–93* (Washington: Government Printing Office, 1895), pts. I and II, Chap. ix, pp. 691–1014.

22. Chandler to Dewey, 10/4/91, Dewey Mss, CU; "Special Report on Public Documents" (10/91), "Bowker File," Putnam Archives, CSD-LC.

23. Tyler to Dewey, 31/10/90; Soule to Dewey, 17/1/91 and 14/3/91; Fletcher to Dewey, 18/3/91; Dewey to Soule, 29/6/91; Hill to Dewey, 27/7/91; and Dewey to Whelpley, 29/7/91, Dewey Mss, CU; Dewey to ALA Executive Board, 11/7/91, as found in LJ 16 (7/91): 200; Green to Poole, 22/7/91, Poole Mss, Newberry; Green to Billings, 28/7/91, Billings Mss, NYPL; Hill to George Watson Cole, 16/6/91, Cole Mss, AAS; LJ 16 (7/91): 199.

24. "Report of the Trustees of the Endowment Fund, August 30, 1891," *Proceedings, 1891*, 77–78; Glenn to Poole, 9/9/91; Hovey to Poole, 28/9/91, Miscellaneous Materials, Archives, Newberry.

25. Harris to Crunden, 3/3/91; Harris to Frank Hill, 3/3/91; Harris to F. T. Bickford (Secretary of the Board of Management of the Exhibits of the Government of the United States to the World's Columbian Exposition), 4/4/91; Harris to Hovey, 12/9/91, LCE-NA; LJ 16 (4/91): 135; (6/91): 167; and (8/91): 251–252.

26. R. C. Davis to H. M. Utley, 12/3/91, Director's File, DPL. See also Charles R. Dudley (librarian of the Mercantile Library of the Denver Chamber of Commerce) to Dewey, 4/7/91; Soule to Dewey, 17/10/90; and Cutter to Dewey, 19/11/90, Dewey Mss, CU; LJ 16 (1/91): 4 and 15.

27. *Proceedings, 1891*, 68, 74, 85, 111–112, 116–117, and 121.

28. LJ 16 (11/91): 327; *The Nation* 29 (10/91): 329–330.

29. LJ 17 (1/92): 25 and 27; Clarke to Cole, 28/2/92, Cole Mss, AAS.

30. LJ 17 (1/92): 3; Ames to George Watson Cole, 28/2/92, Cole Mss, AAS; Dunn to Dewey, 5/3/92, Dewey Mss, CU; Fletcher to Bowker, 15/1/92, Bowker Mss, NYPL; LJ 17 (1/92): 6.

31. Hild to Hill, 4/1/92, Librarians' File, NPL; James to Dewey, 11/1/92; Harris to Dewey, 1/2/92; ALA circular, 1/4/92; and Harris to Dewey, 5/5/92, Dewey Mss, CU; Harris to Secretary of the Interior Hoke Smith, 12/5/92, LCE-NA; Hill to Dewey, 11/4/92, Dewey Mss, CU; LJ 17 (6/92): 207–208. During the winter of 1892 Dewey was being considered for the post of director of the University of Chicago Library. While Soule thought Dewey should take it—"there is room [in Chicago] for a new impulse to work . . . on the whole Northwest"—Hill urged Dewey to remain in Albany. "It would have been interesting to have you and Dr. Poole in the same city; but we can forego that." Soule to Dewey, 30/1/92; Hill to Dewey, 19/2/92, Dewey Mss, CU. Winsor told Poole that Cutter had tipped him about the offer to Dewey. Winsor to Poole, 8/4/92, Poole Mss, Newberry. For a more complete account of Dewey's interaction with University of Chicago officials concerning the post of library director, see C. Haynes McMullen, "The Administration of the University of Chicago Library, 1892–1928" (Ph.D. diss., University of Chicago, 1949).

32. Hill to Dewey, 29/4/92, Dewey Mss, CU; Hill to Cole, 30/4/92, Cole Mss, ALA; Green to Poole, 2/5/92; Larned to Poole, 3/5/92; Winsor to Poole, 5/5/92; and Dewey to Poole, 5/5/92, Poole Mss, Newberry; Cutter to Dewey, 3/5/92; Hill to Dewey, 6/5/92, Dewey Mss, CU; Hill to Bowker, 10/5/92, Bowker Mss, NYPL. For a more complete account of the events surrounding this incident, see Wayne A. Wiegand, "The Wayward Bookman: The Decline, Fall and Historical Obliteration of an ALA President, Part I," AL 8 (3/77): 134–137; "Part II," AL 8 (4/77): 197–200.

33. *Proceedings, 1892,* 41, 42, 49, 51–60, 63, 66, 67, 70, 90, 184a–184b, and 281–282. A copy of the amended constitution can be found in the Blatchford Mss, Newberry. See also LJ 17 (6/92): 191; (9/92): 386; and Dewey to ALA vice presidents, 22/2/93, Poole Mss, Newberry.

34. James to Dewey, 16/6/92; Hill to Dewey, 16/6/92; Crunden to Dewey, 17/6/92; Cutter to Dewey, 19/6/92; Cutter to Dewey, 20/6/92; Dewey to "Members of the ALA Columbian Exposition Committee," 22/6/92; Crunden to Dewey, 26/6/92 and 5/7/92, Dewey Mss, CU; Cutter to C. Alex Nelson, n.d. (attached to letter dated 1/4/93), Poole Mss, Newberry.

35. Cutler to Wire, 8/7/92; Wire to Cutler, 12/7/92, quoted in Volume I, CLC Minutes, CHS, pp. 26 and 27; LJ 17 (7/92): 246; and (11/92): 457.

36. Hild to Dewey, 8 and 29/8/92; Dewey to "Standing Committee," 5/9/92; Dewey to Hild, 5/9/92; Hill to Dewey, 9/9/92; Crunden to Dewey, 12/9/92; and James to Dewey, 19/9/92, Dewey Mss, CU.

37. Document entitled "ALA Columbian Meeting, 1893, by Melvil Dewey," in Dewey Mss, CU. See also LJ 18 (2/93): 44–45.

38. Dewey to Cutler, 1/10/92; Cutter to Dewey, 14/10/92; and Cutler to Dewey, 29/10/92, Dewey Mss, CU; LJ 17 (12/92): 491–492; 18 (1/93): 41; and (4/93): 123–124; W. T. Harris to "Librarians," 21/1/93, LCE-NA; "Program for the A.L.A. Chicago Meetings," by Melvil Dewey, 21/2/93, Dewey Mss, CU; Dewey to Bowker, 8/3/93, Bowker Mss, NYPL.

39. Cutler to Harris, 22/2/93; Dewey to Harris, 24/4/93; Harris to Dewey, 26/4/93; Dewey to Harris, 26/4/93; Harris to Dewey, 29/4/93; Dewey to Harris, 6/6/93, Dewey Mss, CU.

40. Dewey "To members of the ALA," 20/5/93; Dewey "To the Editor," 1/6/93, Dewey Mss, CU; Dewey to ALA Standing Committee, 13/6/93, copy found in Lane Mss, HUA; Crunden to Dewey, 15/6/93; James to Dewey, 2/7/93; Dewey to Harris, 29/6/93, Dewey Mss, CU; Harris to Secretary of the Interior, 11/7/93, LCE-NA. Copy of the "ALA Yearbook, 1893," found in Dewey Mss, CU.

41. Superintendent of Documents John G. Ames to Dewey, 14/1/93; Dewey to Dunn, 28/4/93 and 29/6/93; Dewey to Fletcher, 1/10/92; Fletcher to Dewey, 3/10/92; Dewey to Fletcher, 14/11/92; Fletcher to Dewey, 30/11/92, Dewey Mss, CU; review of the "A.L.A. Index," LJ 18 (2/93): 50; Dewey to "ALA Council," 7/3/93, Poole Mss, Newberry; Bowker to Dewey, 7/3/93; James to Dewey, 14/3/93; Winsor to Dewey, 14/3/93; Dewey to Hovey, 31/3/93, Dewey Mss, CU; Tessa Kelso "To the Editor of the *Library Journal*," as found in LJ 17 (11/92): 444; and James to Dewey, 1/6/93, Dewey Mss, CU.

42. Cutter explained his situation in Cutter to Bowker, 2/3/93, Bowker Mss, NYPL. See also Winsor to Poole, 20/3/93, Poole Mss, Newberry. Newberry Library Trustee Franklin MacVeagh warned Poole of the board's attitude in MacVeagh to Poole, 27/3/

93, copy found in Winsor Mss, MHS. Edith E. Clarke, Poole's cataloger at Newberry, noted the library's internal problems in Clarke to Dewey, 5/7/93, Dewey Mss, CU.

Chapter Four: A Struggle to Identify "The Largest Number": The Pressures of Growing Factionalism, 1893–1901

1. Frank P. Hill to John Cotton Dana, 2/7/01, Dana Mss, SPL; LJ 26 (9/01): 402.

2. *Proceedings, 1901*, 88, 113, 120, and 121. See also Herbert Putnam to Charlotte Putnam (wife), 10/7/01, Putnam Mss, LC.

3. *Proceedings, 1901*, 131, 171, and 173. See also Putnam to Wife, 10/7/01, Putnam Mss, LC.

4. *Proceedings, 1901*, 173. See also Putnam to Wife, 10/7/01, Putnam Mss, LC; PL 6 (7/01): 296–297; Crunden to Billings, 6/7/01; Richardson to Billings, 12/7/01; Faxon to Billings, 20/7/01; and Billings to Faxon, 22/7/01, Billings Mss, NYPL; and Bowker to Billings 29/7/01, Bowker Mss, NYPL. See also Bostwick, *A Life with Men and Books*, 182, for Bostwick's observations of Billings's attitudes towards public libraries.

5. Carr to Cole, 11, 16 and 22/9/93, Cole Mss, AAS. See also Theresa West to Dewey, 24/10/94; and Dewey to West, 15/11/94, Dewey Mss, CU, for an allegation that part of ALA's financial difficulties could be traced to a mistake Carr made in handling funds.

6. Dewey to Macalister, 5/10/93; Dewey to Harris, 26/10/93; Dewey to Hill, 28/10/93; Dewey to Parks, 2/11/93, Dewey Mss, CU; LJ 18 (12/93): 513–514; copy of circular entitled "American Library Association World's Columbian Exposition Committee," dated Jan. 1894, found in Cole Mss, AAS.

7. For letters which demonstrate Larned's concern about duplication, see Larned to H. L. Koopman, 21/2/94, Koopman Mss, BU; Larned to Cole, 5/5/94, Cole Mss, AAS; Larned to William Beer, 2/6/94, Beer Mss,TU; and Henry Carr to Clement W. Andrews, 13/7/94, Andrews Mss, MIT. See also LJ 18 (12/93): 513–514; 19 (2/94): 52–57; (4/94): 119, 137–138; (6/94): 206–207; and (7/94): 237–238; George Iles to Dewey, 12/6/94, Dewey Mss, CU; and Fletcher to Lane, 20/4/94, BAA.

8. Fletcher to Dewey, 3/10/94, Dewey Mss, CU.

9. *Proceedings, 1894*, 145, 146, 153, and 175. See also LJ 19 (10/94): 327 and 347.

10. Dewey to Harris, 21/1/95; Harris to Dewey, 24/1/95; and Dewey to Harris, 28/1/95, Dewey Mss, CU.

11. Dewey to ALA Cooperation Committee, 8/3/95; Fletcher to Dewey, 18/3/95; Dewey to Lane, 26/3/95; Dewey to ALA Publishing Section Executive Board, 9/4/95, Dewey Mss, CU.

12. Massachusetts Library Club, "Circular: Monthly Lists of Selected Fiction, May 10, 1895," found in Dewey Mss, CU. See also Circular, ALA Committee on Public Documents "To Librarians," 12/12/94, Andrews Mss, MIT; Bowker to Cole, 11/6/95, Cole Mss, AAS; Brett to Andrews, 29/10/94, Andrews Mss, MIT; LJ 20 (3/95): 76; and (8/95): 282–283.

13. LJ 20 (7/95): 233; Utley to Lane, 22/7/95, Vol. 4, BAA; Hill to Cole, 29/7/95, Cole Mss, AAS; Dewey to Dana, 10/8/95, Dewey Mss, CU; *Proceedings, 1895*, 4, 36, 52, 59, 66, 67, 84, 85, 86, 88, and 89.

14. Elmendorf to Dewey, 2/9/95; Dana to Dewey, 4/9/95; Dewey to Dana, 10/9/95; and Dewey to Elmendorf, 12/9/95, Dewey Mss, CU.

15. LJ 21 (1/96): 3; (2/96): 70; (3/96): 107; and (4/96): 132, 153.

16. LJ 20 (11/95): 373, 387–388. See also Cole circular, 9/12/95, Cole Mss, AAS.

17. The chronology of events is reconstructed from the following:
West to Dewey, 23/4/96; Dewey to West, 31/1/96; Dewey to Meleney, 4/2/96; Stearns to Dewey, 20/2/96; Dana to Dewey, 4/3/96; and Ahern to Dewey, 16/3/96, Dewey Mss, CU. For evidence of the continuing feud between Dewey and Bowker over the origins of ALA and LJ, see Bowker to Dewey, 7/9/95; Bowker to Dewey, 23/1/96, Dewey Mss, CU; Dewey to Bowker, 9/3/96, Bowker Mss, NYPL; and Elmendorf to Brett, 22/10/95, Brett Mss, CPL. For an indication of how tightly Dewey controlled his Library Bureau stock, see William Parker (Library Bureau Treasurer) to George Watson Cole, 13/10/96, Cole Mss, AAS.

18. Tessa Kelso to Bowker, 4/2/96; Dewey to Bowker, 9/3/96; Bowker to Thwaites, 18 and 27/3/96; Bowker to Davidson, 20/3/96; Bowker to Elmendorf, 2/4/96; and Bowker to Dana, 2/4/96, Bowker Mss, NYPL; Bowker to Dewey, 7/3/96; Dana to Dewey, 11/3/96; Bowker to Dewey, 18/3/96; and Elmendorf to Dewey, 19/3/96, Dewey Mss, CU.

19. Dewey to Meleney, 3 and 10/4/96; Dewey to Ahern, 11/4/96; Dewey to West, 27/4/96; and Dana to Dewey, 14/5/96, Dewey Mss, CU; LJ 21 (5/96): 216; "Prospectus," PL 1 (5/96): 3. See also E. M. Fleming, *R. R. Bowker: Militant Liberal* (Norman, OK: University of Oklahoma Press, 1952), 190–191, for another point of view.

20. Larned to Dana, 13/1/96; document entitled "To the Honorable Board of Directors of the National Educational Association," 2/3/96; Bowker to Dewey, 8/3/96; Dana to Dewey, 20/7/96, Dewey Mss, CU; Bowker to Dana, 8/3/96; Bowker to Dewey, 8/3/96, Bowker Mss, NYPL; LJ 21 (4/96): 149–150; (6/96): 280; (7/96): 328; and "Editorial," PL 1 (6/96): 52–53.

21. LJ 21 (4/96): 157; (6/96): 280–282; Lane to Bowker, 2/6/96, Bowker Mss, NYPL; and Utley to Bowker, 4/12/95, Utley Mss, DPL.

22. Dana to Bowker, 15/1/96; Bowker to Dana, 19/6/96, Bowker Mss, NYPL; Dana and Elmendorf to Lane, 17/1/96, Vol. IV, BAA; Elmendorf to Brett, 9/5/96; Carr to Brett, 6/6/96; F. Richmond Fletcher (of Boston's Library Bureau office) to Brett, 1/8/96, Brett Mss, CPL; Dana to Dewey, 2/6/96; Dana to Dewey, 20/7/96; West to Dewey, 17/7/96, Dewey Mss, CU; LJ 21 (10/96): 440; "Editorial," PL 1 (7/96): 90–91; John Cotton Dana, "A.L.A. Organization," PL 1 (9/96): 178–179.

23. *Proceedings, 1896*, 1–5, 12, 103, 125, and 155. See also James to Brett, 28/9/96, Brett Mss, CPL; LJ 21 (9/96): 410–418; and Frederick W. Faxon, "Times Past— Twenty-four ALA Conferences Recalled," *Proceedings, 1916*, 287.

24. For a record of the proceedings of the joint commission, see U.S. Congress, Senate. *Conditions of the Library of Congress.* 54th Cong., 2d sess., no. 1573. Washington, D.C.: Government Printing Office, 1897. See also Clarke to Brett, 13/10/96, Brett Mss, CPL; Bowker to Lemuel Ely Quigg, 18/11/96; Bowker to ALA Secretary Rutherford P. Hayes, 24/11/96; Fletcher to Bowker, 28/11/96, Bowker Mss, NYPL; and Dewey to Billings, 9/12/96, Billings Mss, NYPL. Spofford was replaced by John R. Young as Librarian of Congress when William McKinley assumed the presidency the following year.

25. LJ 22 (11/97): 23; PL 2 (1/97): 20–21.

26. Bowker to Putnam, 24/12/96; Putnam to Bowker, 29/12/96, Bowker Mss, NYPL; Dewey to Brett, 11/12/96, Brett Mss, CPL; LJ 22 (11/97): 23.

27. Winsor to Dewey, 28/1/97, Dewey Mss, CU; copies of Dana's circular can be found in Brett Mss, CPL, and Carr Mss, ALA Archives; PL 2 (2/97): 56–57; Bowker to

Dewey, 4/2/97; Dewey to Bowker, 5/2/97; Dewey to Putnam 5/2/97; and W. R. Eastman to Dewey, 5/2/97, Dewey Mss, CU.

28. LJ 22 (2/97): 75, 91–93; (3/97): 128. Dana later criticized Brett and Hayes for not pushing for the $500 appropriation. See Dana to Brett, 9/4/97, Brett Mss, CPL.

29. LJ 22 (1/97): 6; Salender to Hutchins, 19/2/97, letter bound into the *Proceedings of the Wisconsin State Library Association, 1891–1911*, as found in Box 17, WLA Mss, WSHS.

30. PL 2 (3/97): 88–89, 94–95; Dana to Brett, 26/4/97 and 3/5/97, Brett Mss, CPL; PL 2 (4/97): 142–145; (5/97): 176–177; Wire to Brett, 5/5/97, Brett Mss, CPL.

31. LJ 22 (3/97): 201–202; Brett to Lane, 16/4/97, Vol. 6, BAA; LJ 21 (10/96): 440; 22 (1/97): 5, 21–22; 21 (11/96): 514; 22 (4/97): 211–212; (5/97): 253–254; Ahern to Brett, 7/4/97; Elmendorf to Brett, 21/4/97; Fletcher to Brett, 24/4/97; Dana to Brett, 29/4/97; and Elmendorf to Brett 30/4/97, Brett Mss, CPL. For the resolution to the tariff problem, see LJ 22 (8/97): 30.

32. *Proceedings, 1897*, 95, 99, 103, 155, 159, and 173. See also LJ 22 (7/97): 339; (11/97): 686; PL 2 (11/97): 448–449; Dewey "To the members of the A.L.A.," 30/6/97; and James to Hayes, 4/12/97, copy found in Dewey Mss, CU.

33. PL 2 (10/97): 400–401; Wire to Dewey, 26/10/97; Dewey to "Executive Board of the ALA," 12/11/97; Haines to "Executive Board of the ALA," 14/11/97; James to Dewey, 15/11/97; Hayes to Dewey, 15/11/97, Dewey Mss, CU.

34. Dewey to Hayes, 16/11/97; Dewey to ALA Executive Board, 16/11/97; Dewey to Executive Board, 23/11/97; James to Dewey, 26/11/97; Brett to Dewey, 26/11/97 (2 letters); and Haines to Dewey, 27/11/97, Dewey Mss, CU; Hayes to Brett, 20/11/97, Brett Mss, CPL.

35. Hayes to Dewey, 2/12/97; Crunden to Hayes, 3/12/97; Crunden to Dewey, 3/12/97; James to Hayes, 4/12/97; James to Dewey, 4/12/97; Dewey to Hayes, 8/12/97; Hayes to Dewey, 8/12/97, Dewey Mss, CU.

36. Brett to Hayes, 10/12/97; Brett to Dewey, 10/12/97, Brett Mss, CPL; Hayes to Dewey, 11/12/97, Dewey Mss, CU.

37. Dewey to Hayes, 14/12/97; Bowker to Dewey, 24/12/97; Haines to Dewey, 28/12/97, Dewey Mss, CU; LJ 22 (12/97): 735; Dewey to Bowker, 28/12/97; Dewey to Haines, 3/1/98; and Haines to Dewey, 5/1/98, Dewey Mss, CU.

38. Bowker to Dewey, 10/1/98; Haines to Dewey, 10/1/98; and 12/1/98; Dewey to Haines, 17/1/98; Dewey to Brett, 14/1/98; and 17/1/98; Dewey to Putnam, 18/1/98; and 28/1/98; and Putnam to Dewey, 26/1/98, Dewey Mss, CU. See also Haines to Brett, 17/1/98, Brett Mss, CPL; and LJ 23 (1/98): 22–23.

39. LJ 23 (2/98): 47; PL 3 (2/98): 46,47; Crunden to Carr, 16/1/98, Carr Mss, ALA Archives; and Ahern to Dewey, 13/1/98, Dewey Mss, CU.

40. Steiner to Dewey, 15/10/97; Dewey to Ahern, 22/1/98, Dewey Mss, CU; LJ 23 (3/98): 105–106; PL 3 (1/98): 10–11; Stearns to Dana, 17/3/98; Ahern to Dana, 13/4/98, Dana Mss, SPL.

41. Billings to McKinley, 18/11/97, Billings Mss, NYPL; Bowker to Young, 27/11/97, "Incoming Correspondence, 1897–99, Librarian of Congress," LC Archives; Roosevelt to Bowker, 29/11/97, Roosevelt Mss, LC; and Bowker to Henry Cabot Lodge, 8/2/98, Bowker Mss, NYPL.

42. LJ 22 (11/97): 696–697; 23 (1/98): 24–25; (2/98): 65; (5/98): 195, 200–201; (6/98): 227–228, 253–254; and (7/98): 295; Lane to Elmendorf, 6/1/98; W. E. Parker (of the Li-

brary Bureau) to Dana, 13/1/98, Dana Mss, SPL; Bowker to Lane, 15/6/98, Bowker Mss, NYPL; and Fairchild to Dewey, 10/1/98, Dewey Mss, CU.

43. Dewey to Haines, 17/1/98; Dewey to Young, 26/2/98; Dewey to Hazeltine, 4/5/98, Dewey Mss, CU; Dewey to Koopman, 30/3/98, Koopman Mss, BU; "Minutes, May 20, 1898," Trustees Records, BPL; Putnam to Dewey, 26/5/98, Dewey Mss, CU; Dewey "To the Speakers at the Lakewood Meeting," 15/6/98, Brett Mss, CPL; Bowker to Dewey, 16/6/98; Dewey to Bowker, 23/6/98; Bowker to Dewey, 28/6/98, Bowker Mss, NYPL.

44. LJ 23 (7/98): 271–272; 283–293; 293–294; *Proceedings, 1879,* 125–126, 137, and 154–156; Dana to Putnam, 12/7/98, Dana Mss, SPL; PL 3 (7/98): 242–243; 250; Carr to Lane, 14/1/99, Carr Mss, ALA Archives.

45. PL 3 (12/98): 388; LJ 23 (12/98): 671–672; Katharine L. Sharp to Brett, 7/3/99, Director's Letterbooks, LDO-UI Archives.

46. Dana to George P. Brown, 8/2/99; Hutchins to Dana, 27/2/99, Dana Mss, SPL; Beer to Bowker, 22/10/98, NOPL Archives; LJ 23 (9/98): 532–533; 24 (1/99): 111–112; Lane to Soule, 10/1/99, copy found in Dewey Mss, CU.

47. LJ 23 (10/98): 580; 24 (3/99): 122; PL 4 (1/99): 24–25; LJ 23 (12/98): 668–669; Merica Hoagland (secretary of the Library Legislation Committee of the Indiana Union of Literary Clubs) to Carr, 27/2/99, Carr Mss, ALA Archives; and "Minutes, April 19, 1899," FRVLA Records, UW-GB. See also Molly Catlin, "Club Room for Men," *Wisconsin Library Bulletin* 2 (2/06): 29–30.

48. Dana to Putnam, 19/9/98, Dana Mss, SPL; LJ 23 (9/98): 518; Thwaites to Crunden, 19/9/98; Hill to Crunden, 1/10/98; Carr to Crunden, 18/11/98; Crunden to Dana, 9/1/99, Dana Mss, SPL; PL 4 (4/99): 112–113, 144–145; Dana to "Members of the Revision Committee," 9/3/99, Dana Mss, SPL; R. R. Bowker, "Memorandum on Revision of the ALA Constitution," 11/3/99, Bowker Mss, NYPL.

49. Dana to Bowker, 14/3/99; Bowker to Dana, 16/3/99; Dana to Carr, 17/3/99; Dana to Bowker, 20/3/99; Carr to Dana, 24/3/99, Dana Mss, SPL; Dana to Carr 29/3/99, Carr Mss, ALA Archives.

50. Bowker to Solberg, 12/4/99, Bowker Mss, NYPL; Utley to Carr, 24/4/99, Carr Mss, ALA Archives; Dana to Bowker, 25/4/99, Dana Mss, SPL; copy of the proposed revised constitution in LJ 24 (4/99): 156.

51. This incident is covered in greater depth in Wayne A. Wiegand, "Herbert Putnam's Appointment As Librarian of Congress," LQ 49 (7/79): 255–282.

52. Beer to Wallace, 6/2/99, NOPL Archives; Wallace to Carr, 7/3/99; Lane to Carr, 26/3/99; Carr to Lane, 30/3/99; Wallace to Carr, 1/4/99; Carr to Wallace, 4/4/99; Lane to Carr, 15/4/99, Carr Mss, ALA Archives.

53. Putnam to Charlotte Putnam, 9 and 11/5/99, Putnam Mss, LC; Ahern to Charles H. Gould, 20/4/00, Gould Mss, MU.

54. *Proceedings, 1899,* 17, 94, 97, 99, 111, 120, 130–131, and 142; LJ 24 (4/99): 207–215; PL 4 (6/99): 252–253.

55. Utley to Carr, 27/5/99; Carr Mss, ALA Archives; PL 4 (6/99): 253; Dana to T. W. Elmendorf, 9/6/99, Dana Mss, SPL; LJ 24 (11/99): 627–628; PL 5 (2/00): 54–55; Thwaites to Haines, 7/12/99; Carr to Baltimore Badge and Novelty Company, 17/2/00, Carr Mss, ALA Archives.

56. Robert A. Kilbourne to Carr, 25/8/99; Carr to Nason, 10/10/99; Nason to Carr, 13/10/99; Carr to Nason, 14/11/99; Nason to Carr, 17/11/99; and Carr to Nason, 20/11/99, Carr Mss, ALA Archives.

57. Bowker to Hasse, 7/2/00; Bowker to Thomas C. Platt (Chairman, Senate Com-

mittee on Printing), 24/2/00, Bowker Mss, NYPL; Thwaites to Dana, 22/11/99; Hasse to Dana, 22/12/99; Kroeger to Dana, 2/1/00; Josephson to Dana, 11/5/00; Dana to Josephson, 17/5/00; Josephson to Dana, 22/5/00, Dana Mss, SPL; Carr to Faxon, 17/2/00, Carr Mss, ALA Archives.

58. Lane to Putnam, 6/12/99, "Harvard File," Putnam Mss, CSD-LC; Lane to "Robert," 7, 8, and 9/3/00, Lane Mss, HUA; Lane to Iles, 13/3/00, PST Mss, ALA Archives.

59. Dana to Ahern, 22/6/99, Dana Mss, SPL; LJ 24 (10/99): 585; PL 4 (7/99): 322–323; Lane to Bolton, 5/2/00, BAA; Harris to Crunden, 23/12/99, LCE-NA; Lane to Bowker, 19/2/00, PST Mss, ALA Archives; Bowker to Carnegie, 2/3/00, Bowker Mss, NYPL; Carr to Soule, 10/3/00; Soule to Carr, 21/3/00, Carr Mss, ALA Archives.

60. Lane to "Members of the A.L.A. Publishing Section," 12/2/00, PST Mss, ALA Archives; Thwaites to Carr, 10/4/00; Carr to Thwaites, 18/4/00; Thwaites to Carr, 21/4/00, Carr Mss, ALA Archives.

61. Dana to Josephson, 31/5/00, Dana Mss, SPL; Dewey to Ahern, 12/12/99, Dewey Mss, CU; Ahern to Dana, 19/2/00; Dana to Ahern, 24/2/00, Dana Mss, SPL; Carr to Dana, 10/10/99; Bishop to Carr, 11/10/99, Carr Mss, ALA Archives; PL 4 (12/99): 448–449.

62. *Proceedings, 1900*, 83, 122, and 143. See also Dana to Hasse, 22/6/00, Dana Mss, SPL; and Lane to Putnam, 21/6/00, "Harvard University File," Putnam Mss, CSD-LC.

63. Harris to Andrews, 30/6/00 and 6/7/00, LCE-NA; Oivind Hovde (ed.), *What Became of Jens? A Study in Americanization Based on Reminiscences of J.C.M. Hanson, 1864–1943* (Decorah, Iowa: Luther College Press, 1974), 172–173, 174–175; Bowker to Putnam, 26/11/00, "Bowker File," Putnam Mss, CSD-LC; Lane to Fletcher, 30/11/00, PST Mss, ALA Archives; LJ 25 (12/00): 727; 26 (1/01): 22–23; Bowker to Putnam, 18/3/01, Bowker Mss, NYPL; "Minutes, April 24, 1901," MLC Mss, MinnHS; Dana to Carr, 30/7/00, Carr Mss, ALA Archives; and Dana to Dewey, 18/4/01, Dana Mss, SPL.

64. Dana to Carr, 23/7/00, Dana Mss, SPL; Hill to Carr, 4/10/00; Carr to Dana, 24/10/00, Carr Mss, ALA Archives; Dana to Carr, 29/10/00, Dana Mss, SPL; Carr to Dana, 7/11/00; Dana to Carr, 20/11/00; Carr to Dana, 21/11/00, Carr Mss, ALA Archives; Dana to Brett, 24/11/00, Dana Mss, SPL; Carr to Dana, 27/11/00; Browning to Carr, 28/11/00; Carr to Browning, 30/11/00; Carr to Haines, 21/12/00; Carr to Dana, 27/12/00, Carr Mss, ALA Archives; Carr to Dana, 27/1/01; Dana to Kroeger, 22/1/01; Dana to Fairchild, 30/4/00; Dana to Anderson, 29/4/01, Dana Mss, SPL.

65. LJ 25 (12/00): 742; PL 6 (1/01): 12–13; J. L. Whitney to Johnston, 31/12/00; Winship to Johnston, 29/1/01, Johnston Mss, LC; Ahern to Dana, 2/1/01, Dana Mss, SPL; Davidson to Bowker, 17/5/01, Bowker Mss, NYPL.

66. LJ 25 (11/00): 675; Ahern to Carr, 15/11/00, Carr Mss, ALA Archives; PL 5 (12/00): 429; Thwaites to Carr, 19/12/01, Carr Mss, ALA Archives; Putnam to Bowker, 4/6/01; Putnam to Ahern, 10/6/01, Putnam Mss, CSD-LC; Ahern to Dana, 11/6/01; Dana to Ahern, 13/6/01; Green to Dana, 13/6/01; Dana to Green, 15/6/01, Dana Mss, SPL; Carr to Richardson, 22/6/01, Carr Mss, ALA Archives.

Chapter Five: Forging a Professional Identity: Adjustment and Accommodation, 1901–1909

1. John Cotton Dana, who had been instrumental in starting *Public Libraries*, remained disillusioned with the quality of the national library press. He wrote H. L. Koopman, "I have not given up the idea of a journal for grown-up people devoted to

the subject of printing of books, and to libraries." Dana to Koopman, 27/7/09, Koopman Mss, BU.

2. Legler to Wright, 1/6/09, WFLC-WSHS; and W. N. C. Carlton (director of the Newberry Library) to Newberry Board of Trustees, 30/11/09, Miscellaneous Correspondence File, Archives, Newberry Library, Chicago. See also Bowker to Gould, 15/7/09, Bowker Mss, NYPL, in which Bowker compliments Gould on his "careful desire to be fair to all" during the conference.

3. *Proceedings, 1909*, 129, 135, 136, 169, 170, 172, 176, and 177; LJ 34 (8/09): 355, 358. See also Bernard C. Steiner, "A Brief on the Proposed Changes of the Constitution of the American Library Association," 31/12/08, copy found in Billings Mss, NYPL.

4. A.G.S. Josephson to Legler, 8/6/09; Baldwin to Legler, 4/9/09, WFLC-WSHS; Ahern to Wellman, 12/6/09, Wellman Mss, SPL; LJ 34 (7/09): 308; (8/09): 385; BALA 3 (11/09): 463–464; LJ 35 (1/10): 22–23; Louis Bailey, "In Memory of Chalmers Hadley," *Guide Post* 33 (11/58): 10; Bowker to Fletcher, 19/7/09; Fletcher to Bowker, 15/12/09, Bowker Mss, NYPL.

5. See, for example, Adelaide Hasse to Dana, 2/8/01; Helen Haines to Dana, 16/8/01; and Ahern to Dana, 5/11/01, Dana Mss, SPL.

6. PL 6 (11/01): 536–537; LJ 26 (10/01): 756–757; Dana to Ahern, 17/11/01, Dana Mss, SPL.

7. Dewey to Members of the ALA Committee on the St. Louis Exhibit, 14/1/02, Dewey Mss, CU; Merrill to W. Dawson Johnston, 28/2/02; Johnston to Putnam, 11/6/02, Johnston Mss, LC; Billings to Merrill, 3/3/02; Billings to Josephson, 13/3/02, Root Mss, OCA; LJ 17 (3/02): 146.

8. LJ 26 (9/01): 689; (11/01): 800, 806; F. A. Hutchins to "Librarians and Directors of Wisconsin Libraries," 20/8/01, bound into *Wisconsin Free Library Commission Miscellaneous Publication, 2* and located in Library School Library, University of Wisconsin, Madison, Wisconsin. A review of the handbook appears in LJ 27 (8/02): 784, the same page on which Larned's *Literature of American History* is reviewed. The difference in coverage of the two works is striking, and suggestive. See also *Second Annual Report of the State Public Library Commission of Minnesota, 1901–1902* (Minneapolis: Lumber Exchange Printing, 1903), 6, 7.

9. LJ 26 (11/01): 789; 27 (3/02): 142; Harris to Dewey, 28/3/02, LCE-NA; Dewey to Putnam, 16/4/02, "Dewey File," Putnam Archives, CSD-LC.

10. Billings to Bowker, 22/11/01, Billings Mss, NYPL; Bowker to Billings, 25/11/01; Bowker to "Members of the ALA Publishing Board," 16/12/01; Lane to Bowker, 29/12/01, Bowker Mss, NYPL; Billings to Carnegie, 16/3/02; Billings to Fletcher, 30/5/02, Billings Mss, NYPL. For background information on the origins of the Carnegie Institution, see Howard S. Miller, *Dollars for Research: Science and Its Patrons in Nineteenth-Century America* (Seattle: University of Washington Press, 1970), 172–177.

11. *Nation* 75 (7/02): 7–8; *Proceedings, 1902*, 6, 9, 62, 84, 156, and 250; LJ 27 (8/02): 774–775; Billings to Putnam, 1/9/02, Putnam Mss, CSD-LC; LJ 28 (3/03): 118.

12. LJ 27 (8/02): 772–773; (9/02): 825–827, 839; 28 (1/03): 37; and circular announcing library meeting bound into *Proceedings of the Wisconsin State Library Association, 1891–1911,* as found in WLA Mss, WSHS; Thwaites to Seymour, 15/4/03, Thwaites Mss, WSHS.

13. Dewey to ALA Publishing Board, 3/7/02, Lane Mss, HUA; Fletcher to Bowker, 29/9/02; Dewey circular entitled "A.L.A. Catalog of 1904," 15/11/02, as found in

Bowker Mss, NYPL; Dewey to Wellman, 18/11/02, SPL Archives; LJ 27 (12/02): 989, 1016; and Dewey to Putnam, 1/12/02, "Dewey File," Putnam Mss, CSD-LC.

14. Johnston to Lane, 15/12/02; Lane to Johnston, 7 and 23/1/03; Putnam to Johnston, 17/1/03; Johnston Mss, LC; Putnam to Lane, 6/4/03; Putnam to Fletcher, 6/4/03, Putnam Mss, CSD-LC; Iles to Johnston, 25/4/03, Johnston Mss, LC.

15. Putnam to Dewey, 23/5/03; Dewey to Putnam, 8/6/03, "Dewey File," Putnam Mss, CSD-LC; Fletcher to Johnston, 26/5/03; Iles to Johnston, 13/6/03, Johnston Mss, LC.

16. Hosmer to Putnam, 9/9/02, "Minneapolis Public Library File"; Hill to Putnam, 18/10/02, "Brooklyn Public Library File"; Dewey to Putnam, 2/9/02; Putnam to Dewey, 22/10/02; Dewey to Putnam, 25/10/02; Putnam to Dewey, 27/10/02; Dewey to Putnam, 12/11/02, "Dewey File," Putnam Mss, CSD-LC; LJ 27 (12/02): 1016.

17. (Unpublished) "Autobiography," Hosmer Mss, MinnHS.

18. Hosmer to Putnam, 23/3/03, quoted in "Memorandum No. 12," Allen R. Boyd to Herbert Putnam, Putnam Mss, CSD-LC; Wellman to Bolton, 4 and 16/4/03; Wellman to Thompson, 16/4/03; Wellman to Montgomery, 16/4/03, SPL Archives; Wellman to Putnam, 16/4/03, "Springfield Public Library File," Putnam Mss, CSD-LC; Hosmer to Billings, 17/4/03, Billings Mss, NYPL; LJ 28 (6/03): 275.

19. *Proceedings, 1903*, 28, 109, 152, 165, 224, 225, and 226; LJ 28 (8/03): 608, 609–610; 618, and 619.

20. LJ 28 (8/03): 636; (9/03): 670, 681; 29 (9/04): 483, 498; Thwaites to Legler, 8/3/04, Thwaites Mss, WSHS. See also *Proceedings, 1904*, 247–248.

21. LJ 28 (1/04): 24–25; (6/04): 310; Bowker to Josephson, 20/1/04, Bowker Mss, NYPL.

22. Gardner Jones to Putnam, 18/7/03; Haines to Putnam, 18/7/03; Richardson to Putnam, 20/7/03; Hosmer to Putnam, 21/7/03; Wyer to Putnam, 24/7/03; and Dana to Putnam, 28/7/03; all quoted in A. R. Boyd to Putnam, 20, 24, and 29/7/03, Putnam Mss, CSD-LC.

23. Wellman to Bolton, 21/7/03, Wellman Mss, SPL; Wright to Putnam, 28/7/03; Jones to Putnam, 28/8/03; Haines to Putnam, 9/9/03; all quoted in memoranda from A. R. Boyd to Putnam, 4/8/03, 2 and 10/9/03, Putnam Mss, CSD-LC; Bowker to Bostwick, 27/11/03; Bostwick to Bowker, 22/1/04; Bowker to Bostwick, 25/1/04; Bostwick to Bowker, 27/1/04; Bowker to Bostwick, 29/1/04, Bowker Mss, NYPL.

24. Billings to Putnam, 1/7/03; Bowker to Putnam, 13/7/03, as quoted in memorandum from A. R. Boyd to Putnam, 21/7/03, Putnam Mss, CSD-LC; Putnam to Bowker, 15/7/03, Bowker Mss, NYPL; LJ 28 (8/03): 592; (11/03): 757–764. See also Dewey's "National Library Institute," PL 9 (1/04): 16–19.

25. Copy of minutes of the meeting found in Dewey Mss, CU; Billings to Putnam, 15/12/03, Billings Mss, NYPL; Bowker to Putnam, 16/12/03; Putnam to Bowker, 17/12/03; and Bowker to Putnam, 19/12/03, Bowker Mss, NYPL.

26. Putnam to Johnston, 10/7/03; Johnston to Dewey, 14/7/03; Hastings to Johnston, 16/7/03; Lane to Johnston, 17/7/03; Dewey to Johnston, 17/7/03, Johnston Mss, LC.

27. Seymour to Johnston, 17/8/03; Putnam to Boyd, 9/9/03, as quoted in Boyd to Johnston, 21/9/03; Dewey to Johnston, 29/9/03; Johnston to Dewey, 5/10/03, Johnston Mss, LC.

28. Fletcher to Dewey, 15/10/03; Dewey to Johnston, 17/10/03, Dewey Mss, CU; Dewey to Putnam, 8/11/03, copy in Johnston Mss, LC; Dewey to Theresa West Elmen-

dorf, 16/11/03, "Dewey File," Putnam Mss, CSD-LC; Lane to Johnston, 28/12/03, Johnston Mss, LC.

29. LJ 29 (4/04): 168, 184–186; (5/04): 227–228; Bowker to Putnam, 20/4/04, Bowker Mss, NYPL; PL 9 (5/04): 236–237, 239–241; Bowker to Haines, 5/5/04; Fletcher to Bowker, 31/5/04; Bowker to Fletcher, 3 and 13/6/04, Bowker Mss, NYPL.

30. Dewey to Putnam, 31/3/04; Dewey to Fletcher, 5/4/04; Dewey to Putnam, 6/4/04; Dewey to Putnam, 11/4/04, "Dewey File," Putnam Mss, CSD-LC.

31. Putnam to Fletcher, 19/5/04; Dewey to Fletcher, 21/5/04; Dewey to Putnam, 21/5/04, all quoted in Boyd to Putnam, 27/5/04, Putnam Mss, CSD-LC.

32. Fletcher to Putnam, 24/5/04, quoted in Boyd to Putnam, 26/5/04; Dewey to Fletcher, 24/5/04, quoted in Boyd to Putnam, 27/5/04, Putnam Mss, CSD-LC; Dewey to Wellman, 24/5/04, Wellman Mss, SPL; Fletcher to Putnam, 25/5/04, as quoted in Boyd to Putnam, 1/8/04, Putnam Mss, CSD-LC. See also Dewey to Putnam, 10/8/04 and 10/9/04, "Dewey File," Putnam Mss, CSD-LC, for evidence of some of the adverse ramifications Dewey experienced because of this "victory."

33. LJ 29 (2/04): 81; Putnam to Minneapolis Public Library Director Gratia Countryman, 16/5/04, Countryman Mss, MinnHS; Fletcher to Bowker, 19/8/04, Bowker Mss, NYPL; Fletcher to Johnston, 29/9/04, Johnston Mss, LC.

34. Dewey to Putnam, 3/2/04, "Dewey File," Putnam Mss, CSD-LC; PL 9 (5/04): 238; (6/04): 274–475; LJ 29 (6/04): 300.

35. *Proceedings, 1904*, 147, 158, 162, 170, 171, 195, 201, 203, 221, 239, 248, 252, and 257; LJ 29 (11/04): 589–602.

36. Brigham to Legler, 24/10/04; Legler to Brigham, 25/10/04, WFLC-WSHS.

37. Legler to Lane, 27/10/04, WFLC-WSHS; Lane to Fletcher, 31/10/04; Lane to Fletcher, 31/10/04; Soule to Fletcher, 1/11/04, copies found in Dewey Mss, CU.

38. Legler to Elizabeth C. Earl (of Indiana Public Library Commission), 4/11/04; Legler to Fletcher, 15/11/04, WFLC-WSHS.

39. Dewey to Bowker, 16/11/04; Bowker to Dewey, 26/11/04; Bowker to Fletcher, 26/11/04, Bowker Mss, NYPL.

40. LJ 30 (1/05): 4, 27; Fletcher to Dewey, 25/1/05; Browne to Dewey, 27/1/05, Dewey Mss, CU; Browne to Legler, 15/1/05, WFLC-WSHS; Bowker to Fletcher, 23/2/05; Fletcher to Bowker, 25/2/05, Bowker Mss, NYPL; LJ 30 (3/05): 135, 157, and 180; PL 10 (3/05): 126–127.

41. Legler to Fletcher, 7/3/05; Fletcher to Legler, 15/3/05, WFLC-WSHS; Dewey to Fletcher, 10/4/05; Lane to Dewey 23/5/05, Dewey Mss, CU; LJ 29 (5/05): 224–227; 31 (1/06): 45.

42. LJ 30 (1/05): 3–4, 24; Bowker to Putnam, 8/12/04; Bowker to Fletcher, 14/11/04, "Bowker File," Putnam Mss, CSD-LC.

43. Dewey to "Committee on the Library Academy," 4/2/05 and 2/3/05, Dewey Mss, CU; Dewey to "Committee on the Library Academy," 28/3/05, Thwaites Mss, WSHS; LJ 30 (5/05): 268.

44. The best account of the incident is Dee Garrison, *Apostles of Culture: The Public Librarian and American Society, 1876–1920* (New York: The Free Press, 1979), 149–153.

45. PL 10 (3/05): 140–143; LJ 30 (5/05): 289–291.

46. Wyer to Bowker, 11/4/05, Bowker Mss, NYPL; Dewey to Fletcher, 13/4/05; Richardson to Dewey, 20/4/05, Dewey Mss, CU; LJ 30 (5/05): 267, 291, and 310; PL

10 (6/05): 274; Wyer to Richardson, 8/6/05, as quoted in Boyd to Putnam, 12/6/05, Putnam Mss, CSD-LC.

47. Browne to Lane, 6/7/05, Lane Mss, HUA; summary of league meeting attached to Legler to Ahern, 7/9/05, WFLC-WSHS.

48. LJ 30 (8/05): 483–485; *Proceedings, 1905,* 4, 7, 41, 44, 45, 108, 124, 145, 181, 193, 195, and 198. See also Wyer to Legler, 18/7/05, WFLC-WSHS, for the announcement of Legler's and Doren's appointments to the ALA publishing board.

49. Legler to Marvin, 7/8/05, WFLC-WSHS; Browne to Lane, 8/8/05, Lane Mss, HUA; Bowker to Fletcher, 18/8/05, Bowker Mss, NYPL.

50. Legler to Hoagland, 29/8/05, WFLC-WSHS; Soule to Dewey, 15/9/05, Dewey Mss, CU; Tyler to Legler, 26/9/05, WFLC-WSHS.

51. "Minutes," ALA Publishing Board, as found in Lane Mss, HUA; LJ 30 (10/ 05): 803, 819, and 830; Lane to Johnston, 5/10/05, Johnston Mss, LC; Legler to Ahern, 28/10/05; Legler to Marvin, 2/11/05; and Tyler to Legler, 9/11/05, WFLC-WSHS; Dana to Lane, 9/11/05, as found in Dewey Mss, CU.

52. "Report of the League of Library Commissions Publication Committee, December, 1905," as found in Dudgeon Mss, WSHS; Legler to Browne, 19/12/05, WFLC-WSHS.

53. Lane to ALA Publishing Board, 26/12/05, Dewey Mss, CU; Circular, League of Library Commissions to Library Commissions and State Libraries, 29/11/06, Dudgeon Mss, WSHS; Dewey to Putnam, 26/2/06, "Dewey File," Putnam Mss, CSD-LC; Lane to Members of the ALA Publishing Board, 2/3/06; Minutes, ALA publishing board meeting, 9/3/06, copy found in Lane Mss, HUA.

54. Dewey to Putnam, 5/9/05, Dewey Mss, CU; Wyer to Members of the Committee on Permanent Headquarters, 7/9/05, Bowker Mss, NYPL; LJ 30 (11/05): 862–864, 864– 865; "Report—Committee on Permanent Headquarters, September 28, 1905," Bowker Mss, NYPL.

55. Dewey to Bowker, 11/11/05; Bowker to Dewey 18/11/05; Dewey to Bowker, 20/11/05; Bowker to Wyer, 10/12/05; Bowker to Putnam, 26/5/06, Bowker Mss, NYPL; Dewey to Putnam, 2/6/06, "Dewey File," Putnam Mss, CSD-LC; Dewey to Bowker, 2/6/06, Bowker Mss, NYPL; Soule to Bowker, 23/6/06, as quoted in Boyd to Putnam, 27/6/06, Putnam Mss, CSD-LC; Soule to Bowker, 23/6/06, Bowker Mss, NYPL.

56. Browne to Lane, 8/8/05, Lane Mss, HUA; Dewey to Putnam, 5/9/05, Dewey Mss, CU; Hill to Putnam, 5/9/05, as quoted in Boyd to Putnam, 6/9/05, Putnam Mss, CSD-LC; LJ 31 (2/06): 71–72; PL 11 (3/06): 108–109; Dewey to Carr, 28/6/06, Dewey Mss, CU.

57. Wyer to "Officers of State Library Associations and Library Clubs," 5/9/05, as found in WFLC-WSHS; Anne Wallace to Dewey, 12/12/05, Dewey Mss, CU; LJ 31 (2/ 06): 49.

58. "Work and Needs of the American Library Association," LJ 30 (11/05): 858– 860; 31 (2/06): 75; (4/06): 174–176.

59. *Proceedings, 1906,* 102, 154, 178, 183, 184, 215, 248, 279, and 280; LJ 31 (7/ 06): 301–302. For background information on the accusations made against Dewey, see Annie Dewey to Lord, 15/6/06; Sharp to Annie Dewey, 10/7/06; Canfield to Dewey, 5/ 7/06, Dewey Mss, CU.

60. Dewey to ALA Publishing Board, 13/6/06, Dewey Mss, CU; *Proceedings, 1907,* 54–55.

61. Haines to Bowker, 18/7/06, Bowker Mss, NYPL; Wyer to ALA executive board,

24/7/06; Wyer to Hovey, 10/8/06, Dewey Mss, CU. See also LJ 31 (9/06): 665–666; and "Headquarters Committee," BALA 1 (1/07): 6–7.

62. Haines to Bowker, 13/8/06; Bowker to Wyer, 15/8/06, Bowker Mss, NYPL; LJ 31 (9/06): 653.

63. LJ 31 (11/06): 774–775; "Minutes, ALA Publishing Board, October 23, 1906," as found in Lane Mss, HUA; Lane to "Members of the Executive Board," 10/11/06; Wyer to Sharp, 19 and 22/11/06; Wyer to ALA Executive Board, 6/12/06, as found in Dewey Mss, CU.

64. Dewey to Wyer, 26/11/06, Dewey Mss, CU; Dewey to "Publishing Board," 3/12/06; Dewey to Bowker, 5/12/06, Bowker Mss, NYPL.

65. Dewey to Legler, 6/12/06, as found in Lane Mss, HUA; Dewey to Ahern, 6/12/06, Dewey Mss, CU; Dewey to Hovey, 8/12/06; Lane to Dewey, 15/12/06; Lane to Hovey, 18/12/06; and Dewey to Lane, 19/12/06, Lane Mss, HUA.

66. LJ 32 (1/07): 26–29; (2/07): 75–76; Wyer to ALA executive board, 12/06, Dewey Mss, CU; BALA 1 (3/07): 7–8.

67. Wyer to "Readers of the ALA Bulletin," 21/4/07, copy found in Dewey Mss, CU. The plan proved successful for recruiting libraries as members. By May, their number increased 200 percent. PL 19 (5/07): 185.

68. Legler to Stearns, 20/3/07, WFLC-WSHS; Wellman to Lane, 3/5/07, Lane Mss, HUA.

69. LJ 32 (5/07): 216–218.

70. Wyer to Hovey, 1/4/07; Wyer to Poole, 1/4/07; Wyer to Sharp, 1/4/07, as found in Dewey Mss, CU.

71. Legler to Ahern, 7/5/07, WFLC-WSHS; Anderson to Bowker, 15/5/07, Bowker Mss, NYPL.

72. Andrews to Agnes Van Valkenburgh (ALA Cataloging Section Secretary), 14/1/07, as found in Lane Mss, HUA; LJ 32 (6/07): 266.

73. See Appendix I and II.

74. Information gathered from PL 12 (6/07): 261; Wellman to Drew Hall, 7/6/07, Wellman Mss, SPL; Hovey to Bowker, 14/6/07, Bowker Mss, NYPL; and *Proceedings, 1907*, 298.

75. *Proceedings, 1907*, 10, 13, 15, 52–53, 55, 56, 57, and 87.

76. Information gathered from Hovey to Bowker, 14/6/07, Bowker Mss, NYPL; Wellman to Hall, 7/6/07, Wellman Mss, SPL; Andrews to Bowker, 28/6/07, Bowker Mss, NYPL.

77. *Proceedings, 1907*, 117, 118, and 119; LJ 32 (6/07): 266, 271.

78. Bostwick, *A Life with Men and Books*, 194–195; *Proceedings, 1907*, 191, 249, 297, and 301.

79. Wellman to Hall, 7/6/07; Wellman to Ahern, 15/6/07, Wellman Mss, SPL; Bowker to Hovey, 13/6/07; Hovey to Bowker, 14/6/07; Bowker to Hovey, 19/6/07; Bowker to Andrews, 26/6/07; Andrews to Bowker, 28/6/07, Bowker Mss, NYPL; LJ 32 (6/07); 246–248; PL 12 (6/07): 260–261.

80. PL 12 (10/07): 310–311; Lane to Bostwick, 1/8/07; Bostwick to Lane, 5/8/07; Legler to Lane, 2/8/07, Lane Mss, HUA; Legler to Karen Jacobson (of the Minnesota Public Library Commission), 22/8/07; Stearns to Jacobson, 7/9/07, WFLC-WSHS; Circular, Wyer to ALA executive board members, 10/9/07, Gould Mss, MU.

81. BALA 1 (11/07): 2–5; LJ 32 (10/07): 454–456. Information about Hopkins and MacBeth obtained from "Confidential" copy of the minutes of the ALA publishing board,

1/10/07, as found in Lane Mss, HUA. See also Lane to Legler, 8/2/08; and Lane to Soule, 15/2/08, Lane Mss, HUA, for a more detailed account of Hovey's loose bookkeeping.

82. LJ 32 (10/07): 455–456; Minutes, ALA publishing board, 1 and 2/10/07, Lane Mss, HUA.

83. LJ 32 (11/07): 505–506. See also Circular, Wyer to Members of the ALA council, 21/10/07, copy found in Bowker Mss, NYPL; and Legler to Members of the ALA publishing board, 23/10/07, Gould Mss, MU.

84. Legler to Members of the ALA publishing board, 23/10/07, Gould Mss, MU; Brett to Legler, 24/10/07, WFLC-WSHS; Gould to Legler, 1/11/07, Gould Mss, MU; Legler to Lane, 2/11/07, Lane Mss, HUA.

85. Wyer to Bostwick, 8/11/07, copy found in Gould Mss, MU; Lane to Legler, 27/11/07, Lane Mss, HUA; LJ 32 (11/07): 567; Wyer to Members of the ALA executive board, 5/12/07, Gould Mss, MU; Legler to Browne, 30/12/07, Lane Mss, HUA.

86. LJ 33 (2/08): 59–60, 62; PL 13 (2/05): 48–53; Irene Warren (president of the Chicago Library Club) to trustees of the Newberry Library, 4/1/08; Ahern to trustees of the Newberry Library, 6/1/08; Charles H. Brown, Marcus P. Hatfield and George E. Hosher (of the Library Committee of the City Club of Chicago) to trustees of the Newberry Library, 7/1/08, "Miscellaneous Materials," Newberry Library Archives, Chicago; Bowker to Haines, 6/2/08, Bowker Mss, NYPL.

87. LJ 33 (3/08): 103–104; Wellman to Bostwick, 17/2/08; Bostwick to Wellman, 18/2/08, Wellman Mss, SPL; McClurg to Wyer, 10/3/08, as read into the Minutes of the ALA executive board meeting, 22/6/08, and found in *Proceedings, 1908*, 407.

88. LJ 33 (5/08): 190; Ahern to Legler, 16 and 25/3/08, WFLC-WSHS; Wyer to McClurg, 23/3/08, as read into the Minutes of the ALA executive board meeting, 22/6/08, and found in *Proceedings, 1908*, 407–408.

89. PL 13 (4/08): 130–133; Ahern to Legler, 3 and 6/4/08, WFLC-WSHS; LJ 33 (5/08): 194; and PL 13 (5/08): 170–171 and 188–191. See also "April 9, 1908," Volume II, 83–86, CLC Minutes, CHS.

90. Corey to Bostwick, 9/5/08, as read into the Minutes of the ALA executive board meeting, 22/6/08, and found in *Proceedings, 1908*, 406–407; Legler to Gould, 28/5/08, Gould Mss, MU; Legler to Elmendorf, 5/6/08; and Elmendorf to Legler, 9/6/08, WFLC-WSHS. Lane anticipated Elmendorf would accept. He had already sent an unsolicited letter to Brown University Librarian H. L. Koopman recommending Nina Browne for a vacant position in his library's cataloging department. See Lane to Koopman, 10/6/08, Koopman Mss, BU.

91. LJ 33 (1/08): 18; Lane to Dewey, 9/1/08; Jones to Dewey, 9/1/08; Putnam to Dewey, 10/1/08; Stearns to Dewey, 11/1/08; Hodges to Dewey, 11/1/08; Bostwick to Dewey, 10/1/08; Dewey to Canfield, 11/1/08; Dewey to ALI Board, 17/1/08, Dewey Mss, CU.

92. PL 12 (3/08): 88–89; (4/08): 130–133; Legler to Lane, 2/11/07, Lane Mss, HUA; Dana to Wellman, 27/12/07, Wellman Mss, SPL; BALA 2 (5/08): 37.

93. Dana to Wellman, 21/3/08, Wellman Mss, SPL; LJ 33 (4/08): 148; PL 13 (4/08): 134–139; LJ 33 (5/08): 160; PL 13 (6/08): 212–213; BALA 2 (5/08): 29.

94. LJ 33 (7/08): 255, 279–283; PL 13 (7/08): 250–253; F. W. Faxon, "Times Past—Twenty-Four ALA Conferences Recalled," *Proceedings, 1916*, 291; *Proceedings, 1908*, 126, 129, 194, 197, 408 and 411.

95. Legler to Andrews, 2/7/08; Legler to Ahern, 10/7/08, WFLC-WSHS; Browne to Lane, 7/7/08, Lane Mss, HUA; Andrews to Gould, 11/7/08, Gould Mss, MU.

96. Ahern to Gould, 17/7/08; Andrews to Gould, 13/7/08, Gould Mss, MU; Ahern to Legler, 17/7/08, WFLC-WSHS; Wright to Gould, 15/7/08; Elmendorf to Gould, 18/7/08; Bailey to Gould, 8/7/08; Hill to Gould, 17/7/08; Gould to Hill, 15/7/08; Wyer to members of the ALA executive board, 15/7/08, Gould Mss, MU.

97. Gould to Andrews, 18/7/08 (2); Gould to Elmendorf, 18/7/08, Gould Mss, MU.

98. Gould to Wyer, 20/7/08; Wyer to Gould, 20/7/08; Elmendorf to Gould, 20/7/08; Gould Mss, MU.

99. Andrews to Gould, 20/7/08; Gould to Wright, 21/7/08; Gould to Ahern, 21/7/08; Gould to Legler, 21/7/08; Gould to Elmendorf, 22/7/08, Gould Mss, MU.

100. Wyer to Gould, 22/7/08; Bostwick to Gould, 23/7/08; Ahern to Gould, 22/7/08; Andrews to Gould, 23/7/08, Gould Mss, MU; Ahern to Legler, 23/7/08, WFLC-WSHS.

101. Lane to Legler, 23/7/08, Lane Mss, HUA; Manss to Ahern, 24/7/08, copy found in Gould Mss, MU; Browne to Gould, 24/7/08; Andrews to Gould, 24/7/08; Ahern to Gould, 24/7/08, Gould Mss, MU; Andrews to Legler, 24/7/08, WFLC-WSHS.

102. Legler to Gould, 24/7/08, Gould Mss, MU; Legler to ALA publishing board, 24/7/08, Lane Mss, HUA; Legler to Andrews, 25/7/08, WFLC-WSHS; Legler to Lane 26/7/08, Lane Mss, HUA.

103. Gould to Andrews, 25/7/08; Elmendorf to Gould, 27/7/08; Gould to Wyer, 28/7/08; Gould to ALA executive board, 28/7/08, Gould Mss, MU. See also Wright to Gould, 28/7/08, Gould Mss, MU.

104. Lane to Legler, 28/7/08; Legler to Gould, 30/7/08, copy found in Lane Mss, HUA; Legler to Gould, 31/7/08, Gould Mss, MU.

105. Andrews to Gould, 2/8/08; Gould to Wyer, 6/8/09; Wyer to Gould, 8/8/08, Gould Mss, MU; Legler to Wright, 11/8/08, WFLC-WSHS; Wyer to Annie Sullivan, 12/8/08; Wyer to ALA executive board, 25/8/08, Gould Mss, MU.

106. Ahern to Gould, 3 and 15/9/08; Gould to Ahern, 19/9/08, Gould Mss, MU.

107. LJ 33 (10/08): 404–406; PL 13 (11/08): 364–365; "Minutes of the ALA Executive Board meeting, September 25, 1908," copy found in Gould Mss, MU.

108. PL 13 (10/08): 308–311; Jones to Gould, 5/10/08; Haines to Gould, 6/10/08, Gould Mss, MU; "October 8, 1908," Volume II, p. 90, CLC Minutes, CHS.

109. Wyer to Ahern, 21/10/08; Ahern to Legler, 24/10/08; Legler to Ahern, 27/10/08, WFLC-WSHS; PL 14 (1/09): 16–17; Wyer to Bowker, 4/1/09, Bowker Mss, NYPL.

110. Wyer to Gould, 11/3/09; Walker to Gould, 18/3/09, Gould Mss, MU; Ahern to Legler, 20/3/09, WFLC-WSHS; Wyer to ALA executive board, 26/3/09; Gould to Legler, 3/4/09; Gould to Andrews, 6/4/09; Wyer to Gould, 9/4/09; Wright to Gould, 10/4/09, Gould Mss, MU.

111. LJ 34 (5/09): 214; Legler to Gould, 26/3/09; Gould to Legler, 3/4/09; Legler to Gould, 12/4/09; Legler to Gould, 13/4/09, Gould Mss, MU.

112. LJ 34 (5/09): 222–223; Minutes, ALA executive board meeting, 15/4/09, copy found in Gould Mss, MU.

113. Gould to Legler, 17/4/09; Legler to Gould, 19/4/09; Wright to Gould, 20/4/09, Gould Mss, MU; Legler to Wright, 23/4/09, WFLC-WSHS; Wyer to Gould, 27/4/09, Gould Mss, MU.

114. Ahern to Legler, 26/4/09; Legler to Ahern, 27/4/09; Wright to Legler, 29 and 30/4/09; Legler to Wright, 30/4/09; Ahern to Legler, 30/4/09, WFLC-WSHS.

115. Gould to Legler, 29/4/09, Gould Mss, MU; Wright to Legler, 1 and 2/5/09; Ahern to Legler, 3/5/09, WFLC-WSHS.

116. Legler to Gould, 4/5/09; Anderson to Gould, 6/5/09, Gould Mss, MU; Ahern to Legler, 6/5/09; Legler to Ahern, 7/5/09, WFLC-WSHS.

117. Ahern to Legler, 14/5/09, WFLC-WSHS; Legler to Gould, 14/5/09; Ahern to Gould, 14/5/09, Gould Mss, MU; Andrews to Legler, 15/5/09, WFLC-WSHS.

118. Wilson to Gould, 17/5/09; Gould to Wright, 20/5/09; Hodges to Gould, 22/5/09, Gould Mss, MU; Legler to Gould, 20/5/09; Legler to Elmendorf, 20/5/09, WFLC-WSHS; "May 24, 1909," Volume II, p. 104, CLC Minutes, CHS.

119. Gould to ALA executive board members, 29/5/09, Gould Mss, MU; Ahern to Legler, 29/5/09, WFLC-WSHS; Memo "To the Members of the Executive Board," n.d., Gould Mss, MU; PL 14 (6/09); 220–221.

120. Carr (secretary of the ALI) to ALI members, 22/10/08, copy found in Billings Mss, NYPL; LJ 33 (11/07): 427; (12/07): 483; BALA 2 (11/08): 435; Carr to ALI Fellows, 21/12/08, copy found in Dewey Mss, CU; PL 14 (1/09): 52–55; (3/09): 98–99.

121. PL 14 (4/09): 132–133; Legler to Ahern, 15/5/09, WFLC-WSHS. For information on the problems with scheduling the conference in Louisville, see Dana to Gould, 6/8/08; Gould to Wyer, 8/1/09, Gould Mss, MU; and PL 14 (2/09): 56–57.

Chapter Six: Consolidating Gains, 1909–1917

1. Dudgeon to Wellman, 4/10/16, Wellman Mss, SPL; "American Libraries: XI; The American Library Association," *Wisconsin Library Bulletin* 12 (12/16): 426–436.

2. Brown to Dudgeon, 25/9/16, WFLC-WSHS; Utley "To the 'Middle West' Members of the A.L.A.," 28/9/16, Bishop Mss, UM; Dudgeon to Brown, 13/11/16; Brown to Dudgeon, 16/12/16, WFLC-WSHS.

3. LJ 42 (2/17): 113–119.

4. Wellman to Putnam, 2/2/17, Wellman Mss, SPL; Wellman to Gould, 13/3/17, Gould Mss, MU.

5. See Appendix I and II. Note especially Appendix II, the "1913–1917" column.

6. Burton E. Stevenson, "Introduction [to Theodore Koch's *Les Livres à la Guerre*, 1920]," 10/6/20, Stevenson Mss, LC.

7. Hill to Bowker, 6/4/17; Bowker to Hill, 9/4/17, Bowker Mss, NYPL. See also Arthur Young, *Books for Sammies: The American Library Association in World War I* (Pittsburgh: Beta Phi Mu, 1981).

8. Lane to Carr, 7/12/09, Lane Mss, HUA; Billings to Carr, 6/12/09, Billings Mss, NYPL; LJ 35 (2/10): 71–73; Root to Josephson, 16/9/09, Root Mss, OU; "Suggestions for Changes in the Constitution of the League of Library Commissions to Be Acted Upon at the Annual Meeting of the League in 1910," Dudgeon Mss, WSHS; Lee to Bolton, 9/4/10, BAA.

9. LJ 34 (10/09): 426, 448–449; PL 14 (10/09): 229, 295. See also Helen H. Horowitz, *Culture and the City: Cultural Philanthropy in Chicago from the 1880's to 1917* (Lexington, KY: University of Kentucky Press, 1976), 215–216, for a discussion of the CPL Board's motives for hiring Legler.

10. Tobitt to "Editor of *Public Libraries*," 25/10/09, PL 14 (12/09): 380–381; Dana to Gould, 6 and 13/12/09; and 5/1/10, Gould Mss, MU.

11. LJ 34 (12/09): 557–558; 35 (2/10): 73–76; PL 15 (2/10): 60–61. See also Alice Tyler to "Members of the State Library Association," n.d., copy found in Bishop Mss, UM.

12. Hadley to Bostwick, 21/2/10, StLPL Archives. See also Mary Francis Isom to

Hiller Wellman, 5/5/10, Wellman Mss, SPL. Isom noted indignantly, "Do you realize that it is six years since it has met in Canada? Don't you think the Northwest again has a claim?"

13. Hadley to Dana, 9/4/10, Dana Mss, NPL.

14. PL 15 (6/10): 232–233; Frederick W. Faxon, "Times Past—Twenty-four ALA Conferences Recalled," *Proceedings, 1916*, 291–292; LJ 35 (7/10): 320–329; ALA executive board minutes, 1/7/10, ALA Archives, UI.

15. "The Librarian," *Boston Evening Transcript*, 17/8/10; Lane to Carr, 19/11/10, Lane Mss, HUA; Bowker to Bostwick, 6/2/11, Bowker Mss, NYPL; Bowker to Putnam, 14/2/11; Putnam to Bowker, 25/3/11, "Bowker File," Putnam Mss, CSD-LC.

16. A. L. Bailey to Dudgeon, 29/7/10 and 31/10/10; Alice S. Tyler (Secretary of the Iowa Library Commission) to Dudgeon, 8/11/10; Robert Bliss to Mary Hazeltine, 27/9/10; Bliss to Dudgeon, 11/10/10, Dudgeon Mss, WSHS; Dudgeon to Tyler, 27/2/11; Tyler to Dudgeon, 21/3/11, WFLC-WSHS.

17. Wyer to Gould, 18/11/10, Gould Mss, MU; Root to Bostwick, 8/12/10; Bostwick to Root, 18/12/10; Adam J. Strohm (Trenton, New Jersey, Public Librarian) to Root, 21/12/10; Tyler to Root, 23/12/10, Root Mss, OU; "Minutes, 15 June 1911," Vol. 1, ALA executive board minutes, ALA Archives, UI.

18. PL 15 (11/10): 385; (12/10): 426–427.

19. "Minutes, 1909–35," Editorial Committee Secretary Series 67/2/1, ALA Archives, UI; LJ 36 (2/11): 81; Dana to Hill, 3/1/11, Dana Mss, NPL.

20. LJ 36 (2/11): 72–79; BALA 5 (1/11): 12, 13, and 15. For background information on Utley, see Ronald Blazek, "Utley, George Burwell (1896–1946)," *Dictionary of American Library Biography* (Littleton, CO: Libraries Unlimited, 1978), 525–527.

21. Dana to Wyer, 4/1/11; Ahern to Dana, 12/1/11; Elmendorf to Dana, 17/1/11; Hill to Dana, 18/1/11; Dana to Ahern, 16/1/11, Dana Mss, NPL; "The Librarian," *Boston Evening Transcript*, 8/2/11. See also Ahern's editorial, "Concentration," PL 16 (2/11): 58–59, for an open argument against fragmentation of the nation's library interests.

22. Dana to Elmendorf, 10/4/11; Elmendorf to Dana, 21/4/11, Dana Mss, NPL.

23. LJ 36 (7/11): 321–322, 353–357, and 366–367; *Proceedings, 1911*, 84–85, 188–192. See also PL 16 (7/11): 292–293, for Ahern's reaction to the vote on her amendment, and Charles F. Lummis to Dana, 26/5/11, Dana Mss, NPL.

24. Brown to Dudgeon, 7/8/11, Dudgeon Mss, WSHS; Dudgeon to Baldwin, 16/3/12, WFLC-WSHS.

25. PL 16 (7/11): 282–293; Carr to Dana, 7/12/11, Dana Mss, NPL.

26. Hill's speech was reported in both LJ 36 (10/11): 487–489, and PL 16 (11/11): 368–371. See also Elmendorf to Dudgeon, 13/12/11, WFLC-WSHS.

27. PL 17 (2/12): 50–53; (6/12): 214–215; LJ 37 (2/12): 57; 91–98; BALA 6 (1/12): 6, 10–11, 13. Utley had earlier advanced a questionnaire on the issue to council members so they could prepare their research. See Utley to ALA council, 15/12/11, copy found in Root Mss, OU.

28. LJ 37 (8/12): 438–443, 447–450, and 450–452; (9/12): 490; *Proceedings, 1912*, 60–66; Minutes, 27/6/12, ALA executive board, ALA Archives, UI; Elmendorf to Putnam, 9/7/12, Putnam Mss, LC; PL 17 (10/12): 308–309. For a more direct look at the nominating process, see Hadley to Gould, 8/4/12 and 14/5/12, Gould Mss, MU.

29. LJ 37 (11/12): 628–629; BALA 6 (11/12): 450; Carey to Dudgeon, 19/11/12, WFLC-WSHS.

30. LJ 36 (7/11): 321–322; Walter to Dudgeon, 6/8/12; Dudgeon to Walter, 9/8/12; Walter to Dudgeon, 13/8/12, WFLC-WSHS.

31. Ahern to Koopman, 25/11/12, Koopman Mss, BU; Dana to Ahern, 18/12/13, Secretary-Treasurer's Scrapbook, 1911–1933, American Library Institute, ALA Archives, UI. Pearson continued to parody ALI. See his poem, "To the Library Institute," *Boston Evening Transcript*, 6/3/12, and 29/1/13.

32. LJ 38 (2/13): 93–99; BALA 7 (1/13): 4.

33. Dudgeon to Tyler, 10/1/13; Tyler to Dudgeon, 18/1/13; Dudgeon to Tyler, 20/1/13; Tyler to Dudgeon, 31/1/13, and 12/2/13, WFLC-WSHS.

34. Dudgeon to Bascom, 3/4/13; Dudgeon to Elmendorf, 29/5/13, WLFC-WSHS.

35. PL 18 (3/13): 108–109; Ahern to Bolton, 28/2/13, BAA; Ahern to W. N. C. Carlton, 28/2/13, Carlton Mss, Newberry; Ahern to Lane, 3/3/13, Lane Mss, HUA; Ahern to Root, 4/3/13, Root Mss, OCA; Koch to Utley, 13/3/13; and Utley to Koch, 18/3/13, copies found in Bishop Mss, UM.

36. PL 18 (5/13): 190; (6/13): 242–249.

37. LJ 38 (8/13): 459–468; *Proceedings, 1913,* 105, 245.

38. PL 18 (10/13): 320–323; Root to Ahern, 20/10/13, Root Mss, OU; BALA 7 (11/13): 502; 8 (1/14): 26–27.

39. Dana to "Mr. Lapp," 9/8/13, Dana Mss, NPL; Koch to Utley, 20/8/13, copy found in Bishop Mss, UM.

40. BALA 8 (1/14): 6–7, 10–12, 13, and 15–17; LJ 39 (2/14): 119–120, 123–127. See also *Boston Evening Transcript*, 7/1/14, where Pearson gave support to Dana's ideas in a "Librarian" column; and Ranck to Dana, 10/2/14, Dana Mss, NPL, for Ranck's observations on council reaction to Dana's letter.

41. Dana to Ranck and Wright, 20/1/14, Dana Mss, NPL. Dana quoted his correspondence with Utley in this letter.

42. PL 19 (2/14): 50–51; Ahern to Anderson, 2/2/14; Ahern to Wellman, 6/2/14, Wellman Mss, SPL; Dana to Utley, 7/2/14, Dana Mss, NPL.

43. Utley to Dudgeon, 19/2/14; Dudgeon to Cornelia Marvin, 13/5/14, WFLC-WSHS; E. H. Anderson to C. K. Bolton, 10/3/14; Utley to Bolton, 13/3/14, BAA.

44. *Proceedings, 1914*, 98, 152–153, 195, and 215; LJ 39 (7/14): 530–535, 542.

45. LJ 39 (7/14): 540–541; BALA 9 (1/15): 41–42.

46. Utley to Hodges, 17/2/14; Hodges to Gould, 8/7/14; Gould to Hodges, 23/12/14, Gould Mss, MU; PL 19 (11/14): 394–395; (12/14): 434–437.

47. Wellman to Bolton, 11/11/14, BAA; Carlton to Wyer, 30/11/14, Archives, Newberry; Utley to Dudgeon, 3/10/14, WFLC-WSHS; BALA 9 (11/14): 503.

48. LJ 40 (2/15): 81, 116–122; BALA 9 (1/15): 10, 13, 22, and 24–27; PL 20 (2/15): 58–59; "Report to the Executive Board," by W. N. C. Carlton 31/12/14, copy found in W. W. Bishop Mss, UM; Utley to Dana, 14/1/15, Dana Mss, NPL.

49. LJ 40 (2/15): 81–82; PL 20 (3/15): 112–113. A comprehensive account of the origins of the AALS (now known as ALISE - the Association for Library and Information Science Education) can be found in Donald G. Davis, Jr., *The Association of American Library Schools, 1915–1968: An Analytical History* (Metuchen, NJ: The Scarecrow Press, 1974).

50. *Proceedings, 1915*, 90, 93, and 148; *Boston Evening Transcript*, 30/6/15; PL 21 (1/16): 14–15.

51. Utley to Bowker, 29/7/15, Bowker Mss, NYPL; Wellman to Iles, 15/10/15, Well-

man Mss, SPL; Dudgeon to Utley, 23/10/15, WFLC-WSHS; BALA 9 (11/15): 459–460; PL 21 (1/16): 12–13; Dana to Utley, 17/12/15; Utley to Dana, 8/1/16, Dana Mss, NPL.

52. Windsor to Plummer, 8/11/15; Utley to Windsor, 16/11/15; Plummer to Windsor, 19/11/15, LDO-UI Archives.

53. BALA 10 (1/16): 27–28, 31, 32, 42, 43, 56, and 57–58; LJ 41 (2/16): 81; PL 21 (2/16): 68–69; Bishop to Richardson, 4/2/16, Richardson Mss, Princeton.

54. Utley to "Friends of the American Library Association," 10/4/16, Director's Office Correspondence, Archives, NYPL; Richardson to Koopman, 2/3/16, Koopman Mss, BU; LJ 41 (3/16): 161; (4/16): 233–234.

55. Dudgeon to Tyler, 4/5/16; Dudgeon to Legler, 4/5/16, WFLC-WSHS; Dudgeon to Dana, 4/5/16, Dana Mss, NPL.

56. *Boston Evening Transcript*, 10/5/16; PL 21 (6/16): 264–267; Bishop to "Members of the ALA Nominating Committee," 2/6/16, Bishop Mss, UM.

57. *Proceedings, 1916*, 111, 381.

58. PL 19 (11/14): 394–395; 21 (4/16): 173; Bolton to Bowker, 10/4/15; Bowker to Bolton, 15/4/15, Bowker Mss, NYPL; Minutes of the ALA publishing board, 29/12/15, copy found in WFLC-WSHS; Minutes of the ALA publishing board, 29/12/15, ALA Archives, UI.

Chapter Seven: Epilogue

1. Poole to Evans, 15/2/71, Evans Mss, UI; Dudgeon to Richardson, 1/6/17, WFLC-WSHS.

2. See Appendix I. For evidence of the socioeconomic homogeneity of members of other emerging professional groups, see Robert L. Church, "Economists as Experts: The Rise of an Academic Profession in the United States, 1870–1920," in Lawrence Stone (ed.), *The University in Society, Vol. II* (Princeton, NJ: Princeton University Press, 1974), 571–609; Alan Creutz, "Social Access to the Professions: Late Nineteenth-Century Academics at the University of Michigan as a Case Study," *Journal of Social History* 15 (Fall 1981): 73–87; P.M.G. Harris, "The Social Origins of American Leaders: The Demographic Foundations," *Perspectives in American History*, 3 (1969): 157–344; Kenneth L. Kusmer, "The Social History of Cultural Institutions: The Upper Class Connections," *Journal of Interdisciplinary History* 10 (Summer 1979): 137–146; Robert A. McCaughey, "The Transformation of American Academic Life: Harvard University, 1821–1892," *Perspectives in American History*, 8 (1979): 239–332; and Dorothy Ross, "The Development of the Social Sciences," in Alexandra Oleson and John Voss (eds.), *The Organization of Knowledge in Modern America, 1860–1920* (Baltimore: The Johns Hopkins University Press, 1979), 107–138.

3. For scholarly analyses of these other groups, see authors and titles cited in note 19, Chapter One.

4. For a summary of the disputes over fiction which occasionally raged outside the association, see Paul S. Boyer, *Purity in Print: The Vice-Society Movement and Book Censorship in America* (New York: Scribner's,1968), especially 31–32. See also Esther Jane Carrier, *Fiction in Public Libraries, 1876–1900* (New York: The Scarecrow Press, 1963), and Dee Garrison, "Immoral Fiction in the Late Victorian Library," *American Quarterly* 28 (Spring 1976), 71–89. Unfortunately, Evelyn Geller's *Forbidden Books in American Public Libraries, 1876–1939: A Study in Cultural Change* (Westport, CT: Greenwood Press, 1984), came to the author's attention after completion of his analysis.

5. A copy of Bolton's "canons" can be found in pamphlet form in BAA.

6. *Proceedings, 1912*, 65.

7. The view that the Progressive era witnessed the seizure of the state by big business interests which were eager to control the economy and society through regulatory legislation and institutions is argued most forcefully in Gabriel Kolko, *The Triumph of Conservatism: A Reinterpretation of American History, 1900–1916* (New York: The Free Press, 1963) and James Weinstein, *The Corporate Ideal in the Liberal State, 1900–1918* (Boston: Beacon Press, 1968).

8. Without the strength inherent in "advocacy" institutions like schools and universities, ALA lacked the grounds to force a credentialing process which would have monitored access to the profession, added legitimacy to librarianship's claims for a place on the professional horizon, and minimized some of the status anxiety evident in Putnam's speech. For a persuasive argument which evaluates the impact of the credentialing process on the development of professions, see Magali Sarfatti Larson, *The Rise of Professionalism: A Sociological Analysis* (Berkeley, CA: University of California Press, 1977).

9. See Appendix II.

10. For a discussion of other professional organizations whose members deemed themselves communities of inquiry, see Haskell, *The Emergence of Professional Social Science* (1977), 187–188, and Furner, *Advocacy and Objectivity* (1975), 258–259.

11. It was Michael H. Harris who first introduced the American library history audience to ideas expressed in secondary literature written by revisionist historians, and particularly by revisionist educational historians like Michael B. Katz, *The Irony of Early School Reform: Educational Innovation in Mid-Nineteenth Century Massachusetts* (Boston: Beacon Press, 1968); Marvin Lazerson, *Origins of the Urban School: Public Education in Massachusetts, 1870–1915* (Cambridge, MA: Harvard University Press, 1971); and David Tyack, *The One Best System: A History of American Urban Education* (Cambridge, MA: Harvard University Press, 1974). See especially Harris's "The Purpose of the American Public Library: A Revisionist Interpretation of History," LJ 98 (15/9/73): 2509–2514. While Harris's ideas have remained tentative because they lack a sound, comprehensive research base, they have nonetheless permanently dented the roseate analysis of the late nineteenth-century public library movement offered by Jesse H. Shera, *Foundations of the Public Library: The Origins of the Public Library Movement in New England, 1629–1855* (Chicago: University of Chicago Press, 1949), and Sidney H. Ditzion, *Arsenals of a Democratic Culture: A Social History of the American Public Library Movement in New England and the Middle Atlantic States from 1850 to 1900* (Chicago: American Library Association, 1947), and have served as a forerunner to Dee Garrison's more substantial *Apostles of Culture: The Public Librarian and American Society, 1876–1920* (New York: The Free Press, 1979). A good summary and analysis of the historiography discussing the public library movement, 1850–1900, can be found in Francis Miksa, "An Interpretation of American Public Library History," in Jane Robbins-Carter (ed.), *Public Librarianship: A Reader* (Littleton, CO: Libraries Unlimited, Inc., 1982), 73–90.

12. A critical and scholarly historical analysis of the problems and progress of both these groups within the association is desperately needed. For an excellent general discussion of women in professions, see Barbara J. Harris, *Beyond Her Sphere: Women and the Professions in American History* (Westport, CT: Greenwood Press, 1978). For an abbreviated discussion of library services to blacks at the turn of the century, see John Hope Franklin, "Libraries in Pluralistic Society," in *Libraries and the Life of the Mind in America* (Chicago: American Library Association, 1977), 12–13.

Bibliography

I. Essay on Unpublished Primary Source Materials

For a study of the American Library Association, 1876–1917, certain manuscript collections (both personal and institutional) are essential, others helpful, and several useful to clarify minor details. The Melvil Dewey MSS in the Special Collections Department at Columbia University is an extensive collection which no one writing American library history from 1876 to 1905 can afford to neglect. In fact, the first nine boxes represent the ALA archives for the association's early years. They contain much more information on ALA activities to 1906 than the ALA Archives at the University of Illinois. In addition, eight boxes of Dewey's personal correspondence, one box of personal letterbooks and 20 boxes of materials and correspondence pertaining to the Library Bureau, *Public Libraries*, *Library Journal*, etc., are invaluable primary source materials.

The R. R. Bowker MSS, housed in the New York Public Library Annex, are contained in 29 letterbook volumes and 171 boxes. Especially helpful are the personal and private office letterbooks covering the years 1875–1913. Bowker's handwriting is often difficult to read, especially in the early letterbooks, but incoming correspondence is conveniently arranged alphabetically by folder. A register provides cross references to other folders containing relevant information. Like the Dewey collection, the Bowker MSS at NYPL represent an essential source of information on late nineteenth/early twentieth century American library history. Library historians will find a second Bowker collection in the Manuscripts Division of the Library of Congress only marginally helpful. Most of its contents deal with Bowker's nonlibrary activities.

Less essential than the Bowker and Dewey collections, but still important to this study, are the William Frederick Poole MSS at the Newberry Library in Chicago. In 26 boxes researchers will find Poole materials that cover the years 1858–1894, but concentrate mostly on the 1886–1894 period. Much of the collection is business correspondence, but a generous sampling of personal correspondence makes careful perusal necessary. The Henry J. Carr MSS in the ALA Archives at the University of Illinois are especially important for the years 1897–1901, when Carr was most active in ALA. Correspondence shows that Carr tried to remain neutral and noncommittal, but controversial issues constantly surface in his correspondence. The George Watson Cole MSS at the American

Antiquarian Society in Worcester, Massachusetts, represents an extensive collection vir-
tually untapped by previous researchers. In the collection's 66 manuscript boxes, and 92
octavo volumes (including 51 diaries written in shorthand), the library historian will find
much valuable material on ALA between 1888 and 1898, the decade during which Cole
was most active in the association. The remainder of the collection relates to Cole's
numerous bibliographic endeavors. Other Cole collections which are less helpful can be
found at the Sterling Memorial Library at Yale University (concentrating mostly on Cole's
bibliographical activities) and the ALA Archives. The latter contains one manila envelope
of miscellaneous correspondence, 1886–1906, focusing mostly on collecting ALA member dues.

A large collection of John Cotton Dana papers in the Springfield (Massachusetts) Public
Library Archives provides valuable information on the many important ALA committees
on which Dana served. Five lettercopy books (all indexed) yield information on the
committee on library training and several consecutive constitutional revision committees.
One box of correspondence contains information on Dana's participation on the committee
for cooperation with NEA, and ten boxes contain incoming correspondence on a variety
of ALA matters. The Dana MSS at the Newark Public Library are smaller, but do provide
about 700 letters criticizing ALA activities between 1911 and 1914, when Dana was most
caustic. The Denver Public Library archives contain one box of Dana materials, most of
which Chalmers Hadley accumulated for his biography of Dana.

An important source of information on the tense association politics surrounding the
relocation of ALA headquarters to Chicago is the Charles H. Gould MSS at McGill
University in Montreal. Thirteen boxes of incoming correspondence (including two concentrating almost exclusively on Gould's ALA activities), and 27 letterbooks provide
excellent material to reconstruct a history of the move. The William Coolidge Lane MSS
at Harvard can be found in four different collections, all housed in the University Archives.
One collection consists of Lane's journal for March 1900; a second collection is contained
in three boxes and houses especially valuable materials on the activities of the ALA
publishing board; a third collection isolates Lane's "Librarian's Files, 1897–1937"; a
fourth collection offers little on Lane's ALA activities, but does contain personal information concerning his extracurricular scholarly pursuits. The William Howard Brett MSS
in the Cleveland Public Library archives can be found in three vertical filing cabinet
drawers. Especially helpful for this study are the seven folders relating to ALA primarily
for the years 1895–1898, when Brett was most active in association matters. Like the
Dana MSS, the Hiller C. Wellman MSS in the Springfield Public Library are extensive.
In 140 boxes library historians will find a large volume of materials on Wellman's activities
from 1902 to 1948, both within and without the ALA. Unfortunately, however, they are
poorly arranged and difficult to search.

Although the Herbert Putnam collections are all housed in the Library of Congress,
they are scattered and hard to analyze. A personal correspondence collection, in 34
containers in the Manuscript Reading Room, contains materials on Putnam's private
affairs. Although this collection does not reveal much about Putnam's LC or ALA
activities, it does give insightful glimpses into Putnam the man, husband and father,
which in turn allows library historians to better understand Putnam the librarian. More
valuable for purposes of this study are the "Herbert Putnam Archives" located in LC's
Central Services Division. This large collection is arranged alphabetically in files. Relevant
correspondence can be retrieved by requesting files kept on principal agencies, institutions
and people. Exceptionally valuable files for this book include "ALA," "Melvil Dewey,"

"R. R. Bowker," "Harvard," and the "Minneapolis Public Library." The files of the Library of Congress are massive; the Herbert Putnam Archives occupies only a minor portion. The serious library historian must be prepared to spend hours pouring over LC archives. To cite but one example, the author found several valuable letters important to this study quoted in letters from Allan Boyd (Putnam's personal secretary) to Putnam, which were summarized in letterpress copybooks not included in the regular Putnam Archives. Institutional archives like these often require huge amounts of research time, but the bits and pieces one picks up often provide essential information to connect events and causes.

While the most important source of information on ALA's early history will always be the Dewey MSS at Columbia, library historians will nonetheless find the ALA Archives at the University of Illinois of some use for the years 1876–1917. Especially helpful is the ALA Publishing Services Treasurer's Correspondence, 1899–1901, which reflects the direction Lane wanted to take the publishing board, and the James I. Wyer Autograph Collection, which contains letters from most ALA presidents before 1925. An exceptionally valuable collection heretofore largely ignored by library historians is the records of the Wisconsin Free Library Commission, contained in over 200 boxes at the Wisconsin State Historical Society in Madison. Because Legler, Dudgeon and Stearns were all very active in bringing ALA headquarters to Chicago, and were extremely active in pressing the interests of the western librarians, this collection offers important information on ALA politics from 1895 to 1915. The National Archives in Washington, D.C., houses another helpful institutional collection. Contained in Records of the Bureau of Education is the correspondence of the Commissioner of Education, 1870–1909. Letters sent in response to inquiries from ALA members shed light on the cooperative efforts (and the resulting friction) between ALA and the bureau.

Collections helpful to this study also include the John Shaw Billings MSS at the New York Public Library Annex. Although contained in 80 boxes and 11 letterbooks, the paucity of materials on ALA reflects Billings's relative lack of concern with the most important association governing his profession. The William Warner Bishop MSS at the University of Michigan are housed in 28 boxes, most of which concentrate on years subsequent to the focus of this study. The Eliphalet Blatchford MSS at the Newberry Library in Chicago are contained in 17 boxes, and while most of its contents represent Blatchford's incoming business correspondence, the library historian will nonetheless find helpful information in letters to and from Brett, Crunden, Dewey, Larned, Poole and Putnam. Before her death, Gratia Countryman went through her papers, now housed at the Minnesota Historical Society in St. Paul. The six boxes contain notes in her own handwriting which she interfiled with the correspondence she chose to preserve. Box one was especially beneficial to this study. The Matthew S. Dudgeon MSS at the Wisconsin State Historical Society contain numerous letters relating to the League of Library Commissions and its publications committee. The Charles Evans MSS in the Rare Book Room at the University of Illinois Library concentrate on Evans's life, which was touched by ALA activities only infrequently. This collection is valuable, however, for the Poole correspondence it contains. Poole often shared his ideas about ALA with Evans, even though the latter took little part in association activities.

The James K. Hosmer MSS are located in three boxes at the Minnesota Historical Society. One box contains his typewritten but unpublished autobiography, curiously written in the third person. The W. Dawson Johnston MSS at the Library of Congress contain nine boxes of Johnston correspondence from 1900 to 1927, and provide much information on the Bibliographical Society of America, the development of ''Book Notes'' (later called *Booklist*) and Johnston's own temporary participation on the editorial board of the 1904 edition of the ALA *Catalog*. The Special Collections Department at Brown University recently acquired a 108-box collection of the papers of Henry Lyman Koopman. Although relatively little material concentrates on ALA, the remaining materials provide excellent background on the activities of the Massachusetts Library Club and Koopman's various professional endeavors. The extensive Whitelaw Reid MSS at the Library of Congress may seem an unlikely source for information on American library history, but Reid was a New York newspaper editor and diplomat who corresponded with many librarians because of his position on the Board of Regents of the University of the State of New York. The collection is especially convenient to use because of a detailed register which lists all of Reid's correspondents alphabetically by surname, and then locates the correspondence within the collection. Reid correspondents included Ahern, Andrews, Bowerman, Carnegie, Perkins, Putnam, Richardson, and Spofford, and are especially good for information on Dewey. The Azariah S. Root MSS at Oberlin College contain much material on ALA, especially on Root's participation on the committee on library training. Root's correspondence with Aksel G. S. Josephson is especially revealing.

The Justin Winsor Mss are housed in two separate collections. The massive collection at the Massachusetts Historical Society centers almost entirely on Winsor's historical pursuits, and contains little relating to his library endeavors. The collection in the Harvard University Archives, however, contains some letters on the New York and London conferences of 1877, and diaries for the years 1881–1883 and 1890–1897. A surprising ''find'' occurred on a trip to Rosary College in River Forest, Illinois, in 1975. While touring the college library, Sister Lauretta McCusker showed the author a set of letters bound into an 1881 volume of the *Library Journal* which Rosary had sitting on its shelves. A quick glance made it obvious the letters were in Winsor's hand. The letters proved especially helpful in identifying the details surrounding Dewey's problems and his resignation as ALA Treasurer in 1881.

Institutional archives housing materials helpful to this study include scrapbooks in the Boston Athenaeum Archives, which consist of incoming correspondence of Boston Athenaeum librarians. They are chronologically ''gathered'' (approximately one volume per year) and indexed. The Boston Public Library maintains the minutes of its Board meetings. Important to this study are two volumes dated 1916–1920. The BPL archives has several folders under the names of former directors who were important in ALA history, including Herbert Putnam, James L. Whitney, Mellon Chamberlain, and C. F. D. Beldon. Analysis of the three volumes of the minutes (1891–1923) of the Chicago Library Club, located at the Chicago Historical Society, makes the turn of the century split between western and eastern libraries obvious, and demonstrates the lengths to which Chicago librarians were willing to go to secure ALA headquarters.

The nine boxes of the Detroit Public Library Director's Files (1904–1919), located in the Burton Historical Collections, provide background information on the founding of the Michigan Library Association and illustrate how its founders felt about competition with ALA. Records of the Fox River Valley Library Association (1898–1931) in the Special Collections department of the University of Wisconsin-Green Bay Library show how midwestern librarians differentiated their needs from those of professional peers in the East. These problems are mirrored in the extensive collections of the Illinois State Library's Extension Service at the Illinois State Archives in Springfield. Series I and III of the University of Michigan Library Archives provided some information on interaction between Michigan's university librarians and ALA during the association's formative years. The Minnesota State Historical Society holds one box of materials that contains the minutes of the meetings of the Minnesota Public Library Commission. Like library commission records found elsewhere in the Midwest, these minutes demonstrate midwestern librarians' perception of their "unique" needs and a desire to have them addressed. Twenty-one letterbooks in the New Orleans Public Library archives which cover the years 1897–1915 contain some letters written between William Beer and ALA officials, while the Director's Office Correspondence at the New York Public Library Annex for the years under study reveal only scattered correspondence concerning the association. Ten boxes of Newark Librarians contain mostly incoming correspondence relating to internal library operations, but the collection has enough tidbits to justify the search and add detail to the history of ALA. The Archives and Rare Book Room at the St. Louis Public Library houses six boxes of Crunden/Bostwick materials of interest to this study. Besides the Dana and Wellman MSS already mentioned, the Springfield Public Library Archives also contains related correspondence in five boxes and one drawer, all located in the Director's Office. Librarians at the University of Illinois played prominent roles in ALA activities, and as a result, the archives of the University of Illinois are helpful for understanding parts of an ALA history. Especially valuable are the records of the Library Dean's office, and the Library Science Director's office.

Manuscript collections which aided the completion of research on this study include: the Cyrus Adler MSS, located in the American Jewish Archives on the Cincinnati Campus of Hebrew Union College; the Mary Ahern MSS in the American Library Association Archives; the Clement Andrews MSS at MIT; the William Beer MSS at Tulane University; the Charles Knowles Bolton MSS at the Massachusetts Historical Society; the Bolton-Stanwood Family Papers at the American Antiquarian Society; the W. N. C. Carlton MSS at the Newberry Library; the Andrew Carnegie MSS at the Library of Congress; the John Vance Cheney MSS at the Newberry Library and the Library of Congress; the Robert Clarke MSS at the Cincinnati Historical Society; the Raymond C. Davis MSS at the University of Michigan's Bentley Historical Library; the Julius Dexter MSS at the Cincinnati Historical Society; the Charles Dudley MSS at the Denver Public Library and the State Historical Society of Colorado in Denver; the Linda Eastman MSS in Radcliffe College's Schlesinger Library and in the Cleveland Public Library archives; the Charlotte Perkins Gilman MSS at Radcliffe College's Schlesinger Library (which contains several letters between Gilman and her father, Frederick Beecher Perkins); the Reuben A. Guild MSS at Brown University; the William Torrey Harris MSS at the Library of Congress; the Samuel Foster Haven MSS at the American Antiquarian Society; the Rutherford P. Hayes MSS at the Rutherford B. Hayes Library in Fremont, Ohio; the Frank Avery Hutchins MSS at the Wisconsin State Historical Society; the A. Alice Jones MSS at the New York Public Library; the Theodore Wesley Koch MSS at the University of Michigan's Bentley Historical Library; the David C. Mearns MSS at the Library of Congress; the William Stetson Merrill MSS at the Newberry Library; the Thomas J. Owen, Jr., MSS at the Alabama Department of Archives and History in Montgomery; the Ernest Cushing Richardson MSS at Princeton University; the Carl B. Roden MSS at the Newberry Library; the Katharine L. Sharp MSS at the University of Illinois Archives; the Thorvald Solberg MSS at the Library of Congress; the Burton Egbert Stevenson MSS at the Library of Congress; the Adam J. Strohm MSS in the Detroit Public Library's Burton Historical Collections; the Lindsay Swift MSS in Harvard's Houghton Library; the Reuben G. Thwaites MSS at the Wisconsin State Historical Society; the George B. Utley MSS at

the American Library Association Archives; the Henry M. Utley MSS at the Detroit
Public Library's Burton Historical Collection; the Addison Van Name MSS at Yale
University; the Frank K. Walter MSS at the University of Minnesota; the C. C. Williamson
MSS at Columbia; the papers of the Wisconsin Library Association at the Wisconsin
State Historical Society; and the Records of the Librarian at Yale University.

II. Published Primary Sources

Articles

Ahern, Mary E. "Educational Force of a Public Library," *Chautauquan* 37 (August
    1903): 487–490.
Billings, John Shaw. "The Public Library: Its Uses to the Municipality," *Library Journal*
    28 (June 1903): 293–294.
Bishop, William Warner. "The American Library Association: Fragments of Autobiog-
    raphy, Part I," *Library Quarterly* 19 (January 1949): 36–45; "Part II," 21 (January
    1951): 35–41.
———. "Some Chicago Librarians of the Nineties: Fragments of Autobiography,"
    Library Quarterly 13 (October 1944): 339–348.
Bowker, R. R. "Seed Time and Harvest—The Story of the ALA," *Bulletin of the
    American Library Association* 20 (October 1926): 303–309.
Crunden, Frederick M. "The Public Library and Civic Improvement," *Chautauquan* 43
    (June 1906): 335–344.
———. "Public Library: A Paying Investment," *Outlook* 73 (February 28, 1903): 494–
    499.
Cutter, Charles A. "Pernicious Reading in Our Public Libraries," *Nation* 33 (November
    10, 1881): 370–371.
Dana, John Cotton. "About Small Public Libraries," *American City* 9 (August 1913):
    132–134.
———."All-Year Schools," *Independent* 74 (January 16, 1913): 137–139.
———. "Fiction Readers and the Libraries," *Outlook* 74 (June 27, 1903): 512–515.
———. "Women in Library Work," *Independent* 71 (August 3, 1911): 244–250.
Dewey, Melvil. "The Library as an Educator," *Library Notes* 1 (June 1886): 1–5.
———. "What the A.L.A. Was Intended to Be and to Do," *Wisconsin Library Bulletin*
    13 (February 1917): 41–49.
Fletcher, William Isaac. "The Public Library Movement," *Cosmopolitan* 18 (1894): 99–
    106.
Foster, William E. "Five Men of '76," *Bulletin of the American Library Association* 20
    (October 1926): 312–323.
Haines, Helen Elizabeth. "The Place of the Public Library in the Community," *Dial* 50
    (June 16, 1911): 463–465.
Hazeltine, Mary Emogene. "Library in a Small City," *Outlook* 71 (May 24, 1902): 252–
    253.
———. "Opportunities for College Women in Library Work," *Bookman* 42 (February
    1916): 685–691.
Hewins, Caroline Maria. "The Development of the Public Library in Connecticut," *The
    Connecticut Magazine* 9 (1905): 161–184.

"History of the Wisconsin Library Commission," *Wisconsin Library Bulletin* 5 (September-October 1909): 73–76.

Hutchins, Frank Avery. "Unselfish Public Service," *Review of Reviews* 49 (March 1914): 275–276.

Kennedy, John Pendleton, Jr. "The Value of a State Library Commission," *South Atlantic Quarterly* 5 (July 1906): 275–287.

Lapp, John A., et al. "My Contribution to the Special Library Movement: A Symposium by Some of Our Founders," *Special Libraries*, 23 (May-June 1932): 209–214.

Legler, Henry Eduard. "Chicago—The Chief Library Extension Center," *Survey* 23 (October 9, 1909): 74–75.

Nourse, Henry Stedman. "The Massachusetts Library Commission," *Citizen* 1 (March 1895): 12–14.

"Public, Society and School Libraries in the United States of 1,000 Volumes and Over in 1900," in United States. Department of the Interior. Bureau of Education. *Report of the Commissioner of Education for the Years 1899–1900*. Vol. I (Washington: Government Printing Office, 1901), pp. 946–1165.

Putnam, Herbert. "What It Means to Be a Librarian," *Ladies' Home Journal* 17 (February 1900): 22.

Stearns, Lutie E. "My Seventy-Five Years: Part I, 1866–1914," *Wisconsin Magazine of History* 42 (Spring 1959): 211–218.

Stevenson, W. M. "Restriction of Fiction in Public Libraries," *Citizen* 3 (November 1897): 203–204.

Taylor, Graham. "Civil Service Success in Chicago Librarianship," *Survey* 23 (October 9, 1909): 71–73.

Utley, George B. "The American Library Institute: A Historical Sketch," *Library Quarterly* 16 (April 1946): 152–159.

Books and Pamphlets

Adams, Herbert Baxter. *Public Libraries and Popular Education*. Albany, NY: University of the State of New York, 1900.

Bixby, A. F., and Howell, A. *Historical Sketches of the Ladies Library Associations of the State of Michigan*. Adrian, MI: Times Expositor Steam Print, 1876.

Bacon, Corinne. *What Makes a Novel Immoral?* White Plains, NY: The H. W. Wilson Company, 1914.

Baldwin, Clara F., comp. *League of Library Commissions Handbook*. Chicago: League of Library Commissions, 1910.

Bolton, Charles Knowles. *American Library History*. Chicago: American Library Association Publishing Board, 1911.

Bostwick, Arthur Elmore. *The American Public Library*. New York: D. Appleton and Company, 1910.

———. *The Different West as Seen by a Transplanted Easterner*. Chicago: A.C. McClurg & Co., 1913.

———. *A Life with Men and Books*. New York: H.W. Wilson Company, 1939.

Bowerman, George Franklin. *Some Memories, 1868–1945*. Washington: Privately printed, 1956.

Columbia University. School of Library Service. *School of Library Economy of Columbia College, 1887–1889: Documents for a History*. New York: Columbia University School of Library Economy, 1937.

Compton, Charles H. *Fifty Years of Progress of the St. Louis Public Library, 1876–1926*. St. Louis: St. Louis Public Library, 1926.

Dana, John Cotton, ed. *Library Primer*. Chicago: Library Bureau, 1899.

———. *What State and Local Library Associations Can Do for Library Interests*. Boston: ALA Publishing Board, 1905.

Dewey, Melvil. *Librarianship as a Profession for College-Bred Women*. Boston: Library Bureau, 1886.

DeWitt, Benjamin Parke. *The Progressive Movement: A Non-Partisan, Comprehensive Discussion of Current Tendencies in American Politics*. New York: The Macmillan Company, 1915.

Durnell, Jane B., and Stevens, Norman D., eds. *The Librarian: Selections from the Column of that Name*. Metuchen, NJ: The Scarecrow Press, 1976.

Fletcher, William Isaac, ed. *A.L.A. Index to General Literature, Biographical, Historical and Literary Essays and Sketches, Reports and Publications of Boards and Societies Dealing with Education, Health, Labor, Charities and Corrections*. Boston: American Library Association Publishing Section, 1893.

———. *Public Libraries in America*. Boston: Roberts Brothers, 1894.

Freeman, Marilla Waite. *Library Administration on an Income of $1,000 to $5,000 a Year*. Boston: American Library Association Publishing Board, 1905.

Gilman, Daniel Coit. *Development of the Public Library in America*. Ithaca, NY: Cornell University, 1891.

Green, Samuel Swett. *The Public Library Movement in the United States, 1853–1893*. Boston: The Boston Book Company, 1913.

Hadley, Chalmers. *A.L.A. Material for a Public Library Campaign*. Boston: American Library Association Publishing Board, 1907.

Hasse, Adelaide R. *The Compensations of Librarianship*. New York: Privately Published, 1919.

Hewins, Caroline Maria, comp. *Books for Boys and Girls: A Selected List*. Boston: American Library Association Publishing Section, 1897.

———, comp. *Books for the Young: A Guide for Parents and Children*. New York: Leypoldt, 1882.

Holley, Edward G. *Raking the Historic Coals: The A.L.A. Scrapbook of 1876*. Pittsburgh: Beta Phi Mu, 1967.

Hovde, Oivind M., ed. *What Became of Jens? A Study in Americanization Based on the Reminiscences of J.C.M. Hanson, 1864–1943*. Decorah, IA: Luther College Press, 1974.

Hutchins, Frank Avery. *Suggestive List of Popular Books for a Small Library*. Madison: Wisconsin Free Library Commission, 1897.

———. *Traveling Libraries in Wisconsin*. Madison: Wisconsin Free Library Commission, 1896.

———. *Two Years' Progress of the Libraries in Wisconsin*. Madison: Democrat Printing Company, 1898.

Larned, Josephus Nelson. *Books, Culture and Character*. Boston: Houghton Mifflin, 1906.

Legler, Henry Eduard. *State Library Commissions*. Boston: American Library Association Publishing Board, 1905.

Leypoldt, Mrs. Augusta Harriet, and Iles, George, comp. *List of Books for Girls and Women and Their Clubs with Notes and a List of Periodicals and Hints for Girls' and Women's Clubs*. Boston: American Library Association Publishing Section, 1895.

Perkins, Frederick Beecher. *Best Reading: Hints on the Selection of Books, on the Formation of Libraries, Public and Private, on Courses of Reading, etc., with a Classified Bibliography for Easy Reference*. 4th ed. rev. and enl. New York: Putnam [c1877].

Plummer, Mary Wright. *Hints to Small Libraries*. Brooklyn: Pratt Institute Free Library, 1894.

Sargent, John Frederick, comp. *Reading for the Young: A Classified and Annotated Catalog with an Alphabetical Author Index*. Boston: Library Bureau, 1890.

Smith, Charles Wesley. *Library Conditions in the Northwest*. Boston: American Library Association Publishing Board, 1905.

United States Department of the Interior, Bureau of Education. *Public Libraries in the United States of America: Their History, Condition and Management. Special Report, Part I*. Washington: Government Printing Office, 1876.

United States Office of Education. *Statistics of Public, Society and School Libraries, 1923*. Washington: Government Printing Office, 1926.

Unpublished Dissertations and Master's Theses

Borome, Joseph Alfred. "The Life and Letters of Justin Winsor." Ph.D. diss., Columbia University, 1950.

Branscomb, Lewis Capers, Jr. "A Biobibliographic Study of Ernest Cushing Richardson, 1860–1939." Ph.D. diss., University of Chicago, 1954.

Collier, Francis G. "A History of the American Public Library Movement Through 1880." Ph.D. diss., Harvard University, 1953.

Colson, John. "The Public Library Movement in Wisconsin, 1836–1900." Ph.D. diss., University of Chicago, 1973.

Esterquest, Ralph T. "War Literature and Libraries: The Role of the American Library in Promoting Interest and Support of the European War, 1914–1918." Master's thesis, University of Illinois, 1940.

Foreman, Carolyn. "An Analysis of Publications Issued by the American Library Association, 1907–1957." Master's thesis, University of Texas, 1959.

Hale, Charles Edward. "The Origin and Development of the Association of College and Research Libraries, 1889–1960." Ph.D. diss., Indiana University, 1976.

Hanson, Eugene Russell. "Cataloging and the American Library Association, 1876–1956." Ph.D. diss., University of Pittsburgh, 1974.

Lee, Michael M. "Melvil Dewey (1851–1931): His Educational Contributions and Reforms." Ph.D. diss., Loyola University of Chicago, 1979.

Linderman, Winifred B. "The History of the Columbia University Library, 1876–1926," Ph.D. diss., Columbia University, 1959.

McMullen, C. Haynes. "The Administration of the University of Chicago Library, 1892–1928." Ph.D. diss., University of Chicago, 1949.

Maddox, Lucy Jane. "Trends and Issues in American Librarianship as Reflected in the Papers and Proceedings of the American Library Association, 1876–1885," Ph.D. diss., University of Michigan, 1958.

Miksa, Francis. "Charles Ammi Cutter: Nineteenth Century Systematizer of Libraries." Ph.D. diss., University of Chicago, 1974.

O'Loughlin, Sister M.A.J. "The Emergence of American Librarianship: A Study of Influences Evident in 1876." Ph.D. diss., Columbia University, 1971.

Scott, Edith. "J.C.M. Hanson and His Contributions to Twentieth Century Cataloging." Ph.D. diss., University of Chicago, 1970.

Sparks, Claude Glenn. "William Warner Bishop." Ph.D. diss., University of Michigan, 1967.

III. Secondary Sources

Articles

Bailey, Louis J. "In Memory of Chalmers Hadley," *Guide Post* 33 (November 1958): 9–10.

Ben-David, Joseph, and Collins, Randall. "Social Factors in the Origins of a New Science: The Case of Psychology," *American Sociological Review* 31 (August 1966): 451–474.

Bestor, Arthur E., Jr. "The Transformation of American Scholarship, 1875–1917," *Library Quarterly* 23 (July 1953): 164–179.

Bidlack, Russell E. "The Coming Catalogue of Melvil Dewey's Flying Machine: Being the Historical Background of the A.L.A. Catalog," *Library Quarterly* 27 (July 1957): 137–160.

Bloomfield, Maurice. "Fifty Years of Comparative Philology in America," American Philological Association, *Transactions* 50 (1919): 62–83.

Bobinski, George S. "William Isaac Fletcher: An Early American Library Leader," *Journal of Library History* 5 (April 1970): 101–118.

Borden, Arnold K. "The Sociological Beginnings of the Library Movement," *Library Quarterly* 1 (July 1931): 278–282.

Camfield, Thomas M. "The Professionalization of American Psychology, 1870–1917," *Journal of the History of the Behavioral Sciences* 9 (January 1973): 66–75.

Casey, Marion. "Charles McCarthy's 'Idea': A Library to Change Government," *Library Quarterly* 44 (January 1974): 29–41.

———. "Efficiency, Taylorism and Libraries in Progressive America," *Journal of Library History* 16 (Spring 1981): 265–279.

Cavallo, Dom. "Social Reform and the Movement to Organize Children's Play During the Progressive Era," *History of Childhood Quarterly* 3 (Spring 1976): 509–522.

Cawelti, John G. "America on Display: The World's Fairs of 1876, 1893, 1933." In *The Age of Industrialism in America: Essays in Social Structure and Cultural Values*, edited by Frederic Cople Jaher, 317–363. New York: The Free Press, 1965.

Church, Robert L. "Economists as Experts: The Rise of an Academic Profession in the United States, 1870–1920." In *The University in Society, Vol. II*, edited by Lawrence Stone, 571–609. Princeton, NJ: Princeton University Press, 1974.

Coats, A. W. "The First Two Decades of the American Economic Association," *The American Economic Review* 50 (September 1960): 555–574.

Cole, John Y. "LC and ALA, 1876–1901," *Library Journal* 98 (15 October 1973): 2965–2970.

———. "A National Monument for a National Library: Ainsworth Rand Spofford and the New Library of Congress, 1871–1897,'' *Records of the Columbia Historical Society of Washington, D.C., 1971–72*, 48 (1973): 468–507.

———. ''Storehouses and Workshops: American Libraries and the Uses of Knowledge.'' In *The Organization of Knowledge in Modern America, 1860–1920*, edited by Alexandra Oleson and John Voss, 364–385. Baltimore: The Johns Hopkins University Press, 1979.

Comaromi, John P. ''The Foundations of the Dewey Decimal Classification: The First Two Editions.'' In *Melvil Dewey: The Man and the Classification*, edited by Gordon Stevenson and Judith Kramer-Greene, 135–147. Albany, NY: Forest Press, 1983.

———. ''Knowledge Organized Is Knowledge Kept: The Dewey Decimal Classification, 1873–1976,'' *Quarterly Journal of the Library of Congress* 33 (October 1976): 311–331.

Conway, Jill. ''Women Reformers and American Culture, 1870–1930,'' *Journal of Social History* 5 (Winter 1971–72): 164–177.

Corwin, Margaret Ann. ''An Investigation of Female Leadership in Regional, State, and Local Library Associations, 1876–1923,'' *Library Quarterly* 44 (April 1974): 133–144.

Cravens, Hamilton. ''The Abandonment of Evolutionary Social Theory in America: The Impact of Academic Professionalization upon American Sociological Theory, 1890–1920,'' *American Studies* 12 (Fall 1971): 5–20.

Creutz, Alan. ''Social Access to the Professions: Late Nineteenth-Century Academics at the University of Michigan as a Case Study,'' *Journal of Social History* 15 (Fall 1981): 73–87.

Curti, Merle. ''America at the World Fairs, 1851–1893,'' *American Historical Review* 55 (July 1950): 833–56.

———; Green, Judith; and Nash, Roderick. ''Anatomy of Giving; Millionaires in the Late Nineteenth Century,'' *American Quarterly* 15 (Fall 1963): 416–435.

Dain, Phyllis. ''Ambivalence and Paradox: The Social Bonds of the Public Library,'' *Library Journal* 100 (1 February 1975): 261–266.

Dale, Doris C. ''A Nineteenth Century Cameo; Melvil Dewey in 1890,'' *The Journal of Library History* 13 (Winter 1973): 48–56.

Dane, Chase. ''A Chapter on the History of ALA: The Publishing Board,'' *Illinois Libraries* 36 (May 1954): 186–189.

Daniels, George H. ''The Process of Professionalization in American Science: The Emergent Period, 1820–1860,'' *Isis* 58 (Summer 1967): 151–166.

Ditzion, Sidney. ''The Anglo-American Library Scene: A Contribution to the Social History of the Library Movement,'' *Library Quarterly* 16 (October 1946): 281–301.

———. ''The Social Ideas of the Library Pioneer: Josephus Nelson Larned, 1836–1913,'' *Library Quarterly* 13 (April 1943): 113–131.

———. ''Social Reform, Education, and the Library, 1850–1900,'' *Library Quarterly* 9 (April 1939): 156–84.

Edlund, Paul. ''A Monster and a Miracle: The Cataloging Distribution of the Library of Congress, 1901–1976,'' *Quarterly Journal of the Library of Congress* 33 (October 1976): 383–421.

Fain, Elaine. ''Manners and Morals in the Public Library: A Glance at Some New History,'' *Journal of Library History* 10 (April 1975): 99–105.

———. "The Library and American Education: Education Through the Secondary School," *Library Trends* 27 (Winter 1979): 327–352.

Finkelman, Paul. "Class and Culture in Late Nineteenth-Century Chicago: The Founding of the Newberry Library," *American Studies* 16 (Spring 1975): 5–22.

Franklin, John Hope. "Libraries in a Pluralistic Society." In *Libraries and the Life of the Mind in America*, 3–15. Chicago: American Library Association, 1977.

Galambos, Louis. "The American Economy and the Reorganization of the Sources of Knowledge." In *The Organization of Knowledge in America, 1870–1920*, edited by Alexandra Oleson and John Voss, 269–282. Baltimore: The Johns Hopkins University Press, 1979.

Gambee, Budd L. " 'An Alien Body': Relationships Between the Public Library and the Public Schools, 1876–1920." *Ball State University Library Science Lectures*, First Series (1973): 1–23.

———. "The Great Junket: American Participation in the Conference of Librarians, London, 1877," *Journal of Library History* 22 (January 1967): 9–44.

———. "Best Foot Forward: Representation of American Librarianship at World's Fairs, 1853–1904." In *Library History Seminar Number 3*, edited by Martha Jane Zachert, 137–174. Tallahassee: *Journal of Library History*, 1968.

———. "The Role of American Librarians at the Second International Library Conference, London, 1897." In *Library History Seminar Number 4*, edited by Harold Goldstein and John Goudeau, 52–85. Tallahassee: Florida State University School of Library Science, 1972.

Garrison, Dee. "Cultural Custodians of the Gilded Age: The Public Librarian and Horatio Alger," *Journal of Library History* 6 (October 1971): 327–336.

———. "Dewey the Apostle." In *Melvil Dewey: The Man and the Classification*, edited by Gordon Stevenson and Judith Kramer-Greene, 29–47. Albany, NY: Forest Press, 1983.

———. "Immoral Fiction in the Late Victorian Library," *American Quarterly* 28 (Spring 1976): 71–89.

———. "The Tender Technicians: The Feminization of Public Librarianship, 1876–1905," *Journal of Social History* 6 (Winter 1973): 131–159.

Glasier, Gilson G. "History of the American Association of Law Libraries," *Law Library Journal* 49 (May 1956): 82–104.

Goode, William J. "Encroachment, Charlatanism, and the Emerging Profession: Psychology, Sociology, and Medicine," *American Sociological Review* 25 (December 1960): 902–914.

Goodwin, Jack. "A Preliminary Survey of Materials Available for the Study of American Library History in Washington, D.C." In *Proceedings of the Fourth Library History Seminar*, edited by Harold Goldstein and John Goudeau, 23–29. Tallahassee: Florida State University School of Library Science, 1972.

Griffen, Clyde. "Occupational Mobility in Nineteenth-Century America: Problems and Possibilities," *Journal of Social History* 5 (Spring 1972): 310–332.

Greenstein, Fred I. "New Light on Changing American Values: A Forgotten Body of Survey Data," *Social Forces* 42 (May 1964): 441–450.

Grotzinger, Laurel. "The Proto-Feminist Librarian at the Turn of the Century: Two Studies," *Journal of Library History* 10 (July 1975): 195–213.

Gutman, Herbert G. "Work, Culture and Society in Industrializing America, 1815–1919," *American Historical Review* 78 (June 1973): 531–588.

Harris, Neil. "Cultural Institutions and American Modernization," *Journal of Library History*, 16 (Winter 1981): 28–47.

Harris, Michael H. "An Idea in the Air: How the ALA Was Born," *Library Association Record* 78 (July 1976): 302–304.

———. "Portrait in Paradox: Commitment and Ambivalance in American Librarianship, 1876–1976," *Libri* 26 (December 1976): 281–301.

———. "Public Libraries and the Decline of the Democratic Dogma," *Library Journal* 101 (1 November 1976): 2225–2230.

———. "The Purpose of the American Public Library: A Revisionist Interpretation of History," *Library Journal*, 98 (15 September 1973): 2509–2514.

Harris, P.M.G. "The Social Origins of American Leaders: The Demographic Foundations," *Perspectives in American History* 3 (1969): 157–344.

Henderson, Kathryn Luther. " 'Treated with a Degree of Uniformity and Common Sense': Descriptive Cataloging in the United States—1876–1975," *Library Trends* 25 (July 1976): 227–271.

Hessey, T. M. "Early Catalog Code Development in the United States, 1876–1908," *Journal of Library History* 11 (July 1976): 218–248.

Hickey, Doralyn J. "Subject Analysis: An Interpretive Survey," *Library Trends* 25 (July 1976): 273–291.

Higham, John. "The Matrix of Specialization." In *The Organization of Knowledge in Modern America, 1860–1920*, edited by Alexandra Oleson and John Voss, 3–18. Baltimore: The Johns Hopkins University Press, 1979.

Holley, Edward G. "Academic Libraries in 1876," *College and Research Libraries* 37 (January 1976): 15–47.

———. "ALA at 100." In *ALA Yearbook*, edited by Robert Wedgeworth, 1–32. Chicago: American Library Association, 1976.

———. "Who We Were: Profiles of the American Librarian at the Birth of the Professional Association, 1876," *American Libraries* 7 (June 1976): 323–326.

Jackson, Sidney L. "Tax-Supported Library Service to the People: Why Was 1876–1877 the Nodal Point?" *International Library Review* 4 (October 1972): 417–421.

Jaher, Frederic Cople, "The Boston Brahmins in the Age of Industrial Capitalism." In *The Age of Industrialism in America: Essays in Social Structure and Culture Values*, edited by Frederic Cople Jaher, 188–262. New York: The Free Press, 1968.

———. "Nineteenth Century Elites in Boston and New York," *The Journal of Social History* 5 (Fall 1972): 32–77.

Jameson, J. Franklin. "The American Historical Association, 1884–1909," *American Historical Review* 15 (October 1909): 1–20.

Jelin, Victor. "The Instrumental Use of Libraries: A Study of the Intellectual Origins of the Modern Industrial Libraries in Nineteenth Century America," *Libri* 20 (January-March 1970): 15–28.

Kaser, David. "A Century of Academic Librarianship as Reflected in the Literature," *College and Research Libraries* 37 (May 1976): 110–127.

———. "The Dewey Era in American Librarianship." In *Melvil Dewey: The Man and the Classification*, edited by Gordon Stevenson and Judith Kramer-Greene, 9–24. Albany, NY: Forest Press, 1983.

Kirshner, Dan S. "The Ambiguous Legacy: Social Justice and Social Control in the Progressive Era," *Historical Reflections* 2 (Summer 1975): 69–88.

Kolko, Gabriel. "Brahmins and Business, 1870–1914: A Hypothesis on the Social Basis of Success in American History." In *The Critical Spirit: Essays in Honor of Herbert Marcuse*, edited by Kurt H. Wolff and Barrington Moore, Jr., 343–363. Boston: Beacon Press, 1967.

Kusmer, Kenneth L. "The Social History of Cultural Institutions: The Upper Class Connections," *Journal of Interdisciplinary History* 10 (Summer 1979): 137–146.

McCaughey, Robert A. "Four Academic Ambassadors: International Studies and the American University before the Second World War," *Perspectives in American History* 12 (1979): 561–607.

———. "The Transformation of American Academic Life: Harvard University, 1821–1892," *Perspectives in American History* 8 (1974): 239–332.

Magrath, Gabriella, BVM. "Library Conventions of 1853 and 1877," *Journal of Library History* 8 (April 1973): 52–69.

Markowitz, Gerald E., and Rosner, David Karl. "Doctors in Crisis: A Study of the Use of Medical Education Reform to Establish Modern Professional Elitism in Medicine," *American Quarterly* 25 (March 1973): 83–107.

Martin, Lowell. "The American Public Library as a Social Institution," *Library Quarterly* 7 (October 1937): 546–563.

Massman, Virgil F. "From Out of a Desk Drawer: The Beginnings of ALA Headquarters," *Bulletin of the American Library Association* 63 (April 1969): 475–481.

Maxwell, Margaret F. "The Genesis of the Anglo-American Cataloging Rules," *Libri* (September 1977): 238–262.

Menan, Nancy V. "Library History Resources in New York City." In *Proceedings of the Fourth Library History Seminar*, edited by Harold Goldstein and John Goudeau, 12–22. Tallahassee: Florida State University School of Library Science, 1972.

Mickelson, Peter. "American Society and the Public Library in the Thought of Andrew Carnegie," *Journal of Library History* 10 (April 1975): 117–138.

Miksa, Francis. "An Interpretation of American Public Library History." In *Public Librarianship: A Reader*, edited by Jane Robbins-Carter, 73–90. Littleton, CO: Libraries Unlimited, Inc., 1982.

———. "Melvil Dewey and the Corporate Ideal." In *Melvil Dewey: The Man and the Classification*, edited by Gordon Stevenson and Judith Kramer-Greene, 49–100. Albany, NY: Forest Press, 1983.

———. "The Making of the 1876 Special Report on Public Libraries." *Journal of Library History* 8 (January 1973): 30–40.

Moore, B. Lawrence. "The Spiritualist Medium: A Study of Female Professionalism in Victorian America," *American Quarterly* 27 (May 1975): 200–221.

Mumford, W. A. "The American Library Association and the Library Association: Retrospect, Problems and Prospects," *Advances in Librarianship* 7 (1977): 145–176.

Muraskin, William A. "The Social Control Theory in American History: A Critique," *Journal of Social History* 9 (June 1976): 559–569.

Newmeyer, Jody. "The Image Problem of the Librarian: Femininity and Social Control," *Journal of Library History* 11 (January 1976): 44–67.

Ollé, James G. "The Library Association and the American Library Association: Their First Fifty Years," *Journal of Librarianship* 9 (October 1977): 247–260.

Parrish, John B. "Rise of Economics as an Academic Discipline: The Formative Years to 1900," *Southern Economic Journal* 34 (July 1967): 1–16.

Rayward, W. Boyd. "Melvil Dewey and Education for Librarianship," *Journal of Library History* 3 (October 1968): 297–312.

Reingold, Nathan. "National Science Policy in a Private Foundation: The Carnegie Institution of Washington." In *The Organization of Knowledge in America, 1860–1920*, edited by Alexandra Oleson and John Voss, 313–341. Baltimore: The Johns Hopkins University Press, 1979.

Rogers, Daniel T. "Socializing Middle-Class Children: Institutions, Fables and Work Values in Nineteenth-Century America," *Journal of Social History* 13 (Spring 1980): 354–367.

Rodriguez, Robert D. "Classification and Subject Indication: Highlights of the Anglo-American Debate, 1850–1950," *Libri* 31 (December 1981): 322–340.

Rosenberg, Charles E. "The Bitter Fruit: Heredity, Disease and Social Thought in Nineteenth-Century America," *Perspectives in American History* 7 (1974): 189–235.

———. "Sexuality, Class and Role in Nineteenth-Century America," *American Quarterly* 25 (May 1973): 131–153.

———. "Social Class and Medical Care in Nineteenth-Century America: The Rise and Fall of the Dispensary," *Journal of the History of Medicine and Allied Sciences* 29 (January 1974): 32–54.

———. "Toward an Ecology of Knowledge: On Discipline, Context and History." In *The Organization of Knowledge in Modern America, 1860–1920*, edited by Alexandra Oleson and John Voss, 440–455. Baltimore: The Johns Hopkins University Press, 1979.

Rosencrantz, Barbara Gutman. "Cart before Horse: Theory, Practice and Professional Image in American Public Health, 1870–1920," *Journal of the History of Medicine and Allied Science* 29 (January 1974): 55–73.

Ross, Dorothy. "The Development of the Social Sciences." In *The Organization of Knowledge in Modern America, 1860–1920*, edited by Alexandra Oleson and John Voss, 107–138. Baltimore: The Johns Hopkins University Press, 1979.

———. "Socialism and American Liberalism: Academic Social Thought in the 1880s," *Perspectives in American History* 11 (1977–78): 5–79.

Rothstein, Samuel. "The Development of the Concept of Reference Service in American Libraries, 1850–1900," *Library Quarterly* 23 (January 1953): 1–15.

Rydell, Robert W. "The World's Columbian Exposition of 1893: Racist Underpinnings of a Utopian Artifact," *Journal of American Culture* 1 (Summer 1978): 253–275.

Saveth, Edward N. "The American Patrician Class: A Field for Research," *American Quarterly* 15 (Summer 1963): 235–252.

Scott, Edith. "The Evolution of Bibliographic Systems in the United States, 1876–1945," *Library Trends* 25 (July 1976): 293–310.

Shils, Edward. "The Order of Learning in the United States: The Ascendancy of the University." In *The Organization of Knowledge in Modern America, 1860–1920*, edited by Alexandra Oleson and John Voss, 19–47. Baltimore: The Johns Hopkins University Press, 1979.

Smith-Rosenberg, Carroll, and Rosenberg, Charles. "The Female Animal: Medical and Biological Views of Woman and Her Role in Nineteenth-Century America," *Journal of American History* 60 (September 1973): 332–356.

Stielow, Frederick J. "Censorship in the Early Professionalization of American Libraries, 1876–1923," *Journal of Library History* 18 (Winter 1983): 37–54.

Sullivan, Larry E. "Reading Habits of the Nineteenth-Century Baltimore Bourgeoisie: A Cross-Cultural Analysis," *Journal of Library History* 16 (Spring 1981): 227–240.

Tannenbaum, Earl. "The Library Career of Lutie Eugenia Stearns," *Wisconsin Magazine of History* 39 (Spring 1956): 159–165.

Thackray, Arnold, and Merton, Robert K. "On Discipline Building: The Paradoxes of George Sarton," *Isis* 63 (December 1972): 473–495.

Thomison, Dennis V. "The A.L.A. Goes West: The 1891 San Francisco Conference," *California Librarian* 37 (April 1976): 31–35.

———. "The A.L.A. and Its Missing Presidents," *Journal of Library History* 9 (October 1974): 362–367.

Tucker, John Mark. "Azariah Smith Root and Social Reform at Oberlin College," *Journal of Library History* 16 (Spring 1981): 280–292.

Van Hoesen, Henry B. "The Bibliographical Society of America—Its Leaders and Activities, 1904–1939," *Papers of the Bibliographical Society of America* 35 (1941): 177–202.

Vince, Thomas L. "The Legacy of Burton E. Stevenson," *Journal of Library History* 9 (January 1974): 73–82.

Veysey, Laurence. "The Plural Organized Worlds of the Humanities." In *The Organization of Knowledge in Modern America, 1860–1920*, edited by Alexandra Oleson and John Voss, 51–106. Baltimore: The Johns Hopkins University Press, 1979.

Weinberg, Daniel E. "The Ethnic Technician and the Foreign Born: Another Look at Americanization Ideology and Goals," *Societas* 7 (Summer 1977): 209–229.

Wiegand, Wayne A. "American Library Association Executive Board Members, 1876–1917: A Collective Profile," *Libri: International Library Review* 31 (August 1981): 22–35.

———. "Herbert Putnam's Appointment as Librarian of Congress," *Library Quarterly* 49 (July 1979): 255–282.

———. "The Lion and the Lady: Another Look at the Firing of Mary L. Jones as Los Angeles Public Librarian in 1905," *Library and Information Science Research*, 5 (Fall 1983): 273–290.

———. "Melvil Dewey and the American Library Association, 1876–1907." In *Melvil Dewey: The Man and the Classification*, edited by Gordon Stevenson and Judith Kramer-Greene, 101–128. Albany, NY: Forest Press, 1983.

———. "The Wayward Bookman: The Decline, Fall and Historical Obliteration of an ALA President, Part I," *American Libraries* 8 (March 1977): 134–137; "Part II," *American Libraries* 8 (April 1977): 197–200.

———. "The View from the Top: Changing Perspectives of Reference and Technical Service Departments by Library Administrators, 1890–1920," *The Reference Librarian*, 9 (Fall/Winter 1983): 11–27.

———, and Greenway, Geri. "A Comparative Analysis of the Socioeconomic and Professional Characteristics of American Library Association Executive Board and Council Members, 1876–1917," *Library Research: An International Journal* 2 (Winter 1981): 309–325.

Wilson, Daniel J. "Professionalization and Organized Discussion in the American Philosophical Association, 1900–1922,'' *Journal of the History of Philosophy* 17 (January 1979): 53–69.

Winger, Howard W., ed. "American Library History: 1876–1976," *Library Trends,* 25 (July 1976): entire issue.

Young, Arthur P. "Daniel Coit Gilman in the Formative Period of American Librarianship," *Library Quarterly* 45 (April 1975): 117–140.

Young, Betty. "Josephus Nelson Larned and the Public Library Movement," *Journal of Library History* 10 (July 1975): 323–340.

Books

Aaron, Daniel. *Men of Good Hope: A Story of American Progressives*. New York: Oxford University Press, 1951.

American Library Association. *Division of Cataloging and Classification in Retrospect: A History of the Division of Cataloging and Classification of the American Library Association, 1900–1950*. Chicago: American Library Association, 1950.

Anderson, Florence, comp. *Carnegie Corporation Library Program, 1911–1961*. New York: Carnegie Corporation, 1963.

Badger, Reid. *The Great American Fair: The World's Columbian Exposition and American Culture*. Chicago: Nelson-Hall, Inc., 1979.

Baker, Elizabeth F. *Technology and Women's Work*. New York: Columbia University Press, 1964.

Baltzell, E. Digby. *The Protestant Establishment: Aristocracy and Caste in America*. New York: Random House, 1964.

Barker-Benfield, G. J. *The Horrors of the Half-Known Life: Male Attitudes Towards Women and Sexuality in Nineteenth-Century America*. New York: Harper and Row, 1976.

Barth, Gunther. *City People: The Rise of Modern City Culture in Nineteenth Century America*. London: Oxford University Press, 1982.

Bay, J. Christian. *The John Crerar Library, 1895–1944: An Historical Report Prepared Under the Authority of the Board of Directors*. Chicago: The John Crerar Library, 1945.

Bender, Thomas. *Toward an Urban Vision: Ideas and Institutions in Nineteenth-Century America*. Lexington, KY: University Press of Kentucky, 1975.

Bergamini, John D. *The Hundredth Year: The United States in 1876*. New York: G. P. Putnam's Sons, 1976.

Berlant, Jeffrey L. *Professional and Monopoly: A Study of Medicine in the United States and Great Britain*. Berkeley, CA: University of California Press, 1975.

Bernard, Luther Lee and Jessie. *Origins of American Sociology: The Social Science Movement in the United States*. New York: Russell and Russell, 1943.

Bestwick, Jay W. *The Work of Frederick Leypoldt: Bibliographer and Publisher*. New York: R. R. Bowker, 1942.

Bishop, William Warner, and Keogh, Andrew, eds. *Essays Offered to Herbert Putnam by his Colleagues and Friends on his Thirtieth Anniversary as Librarian of Congress, 5 April 1929*. New Haven: Yale University Press, 1929.

Blair, Karen J. *The Clubwoman as Feminist: True Womanhood Redefined, 1868–1914*. New York: Holmes and Meier Publishers, Inc., 1980.

Bledstein, Burton J. *The Culture of Professionalism: The Middle Class and the Devel-*

opment of Higher Education in America. New York: W. W. Norton & Co., Inc., 1976.

Bobinski, George S. *Carnegie Libraries: Their History and Impact on American Public Library Development*. Chicago: American Library Association, 1969.

Boller, Paul F., Jr. *American Thought in Transition: The Impact of Evolutionary Naturalism, 1865–1900*. Chicago: Rand McNally, 1969.

Boorstin, Daniel Joseph. *The Americans: The Democratic Experience*. New York: Random House, 1973.

Boyer, Paul S. *Purity in Print: The Vice-Society Movement and Book Censorship in America*. New York: Scribner's, 1968.

———. *Urban Masses and Moral Order in America, 1820–1920*. Cambridge, MA: Harvard University Press, 1978.

Bramley, G. A. *A History of Library Education*. Hamden, CT: Archon, 1969.

Brandes, Stuart D. *American Welfare Capitalism, 1880–1940*. Chicago: University of Chicago Press, 1976.

Bremner, Robert Hamlett. *American Philanthropy*. Chicago: University of Chicago Press, 1960.

Brough, Kenneth J. *Scholar's Workshop: Evolving Conceptions of Library Service*. Urbana, IL: University of Illinois Press, 1953.

Bruno, Frank John. *Trends in Social Work, 1874–1956: A History Based on the Proceedings of the National Conference of Social Work*. New York: Columbia University Press, 1948.

Bryan, Alice I. *The Public Librarian*. New York: Columbia University Press, 1952.

Burg, David F. *Chicago's White City of 1893*. Lexington, KY: University Press of Kentucky, 1976.

Calvert, Monte. *The Mechanical Engineer in America, 1830–1910: The Professional Cultures in Conflict*. Baltimore: Johns Hopkins University Press, 1967.

Carrier, Esther Jane. *Fiction in Public Libraries, 1876–1900*. New York: The Scarecrow Press, 1965.

Casey, Marion. *Charles McCarthy: Librarianship and Reform*. Chicago: American Library Association, 1981.

Cawelti, John G. *Apostles of the Self-Made Man*. Chicago: University of Chicago Press, 1965.

Chandler, Alfred Dupont. *The Invisible Hand: The Managerial Revolution in American Business*. Cambridge, MA: The Belknap Press, 1977.

Churchwell, Charles D. *The Shaping of American Library Education*. Chicago: American Library Association, 1975.

Clark, Robert Judsen, ed. *The Arts and Crafts Movement in America, 1876–1916*. Princeton University Press, 1972.

Colburn, David R., and Pozzetta, George E., eds. *Reform and Reformers in the Progressive Era*. Westport, CT: Greenwood Press, 1983.

Cole, George Watson. *Early Library Development in New York State (1800–1900)*. New York: New York Public Library, 1927.

Cole, John Y., ed. *Ainsworth Rand Spofford: Bookman and Librarian*. Littleton, CO: Libraries Unlimited, 1975.

Colorado State Library. *Colorado's Century of Public Libraries*. Denver: Colorado State Library, 1959.

Comaromi, John Phillip. *The Eighteen Editions of the Dewey Decimal Classification*. Albany, NY: Forest Press Division, Lake Placid Education Foundation, 1976.

Compton, Charles Herrick. *Fifty Years of Progress of the St. Louis Public Library, 1876–1926*. St. Louis: St. Louis Public Library, 1926.

———. *Memories of a Librarian*. St. Louis: St. Louis Public Library, 1954.

Conner, Martha. *Outline of the History of the Development of the American Public Library*. Chicago: American Library Association, 1931.

Constantine, J. Robert. *The Role of Libraries in the Cultural History of Indiana*. Bloomington, IN: Indiana State Library, 1970.

Cramer, Clarence Henley. *Open Shelves and Open Minds: A History of the Cleveland Public Library*. Cleveland: The Press of Case Western Reserve University, 1972.

Crunden, Robert M. *Ministers of Reform: The Progressives' Achievement in American Civilization, 1889–1920*. New York: Basic Books, Inc., 1982.

Cutler, Wayne, and Harris, Michael H., eds. *Justin Winsor: Scholar Librarian*. Littleton, CO: Libraries Unlimited, Inc., 1980.

Dain, Phyllis. *The New York Public Library: A History of Its Founding and Early Years*. New York: The New York Public Library, Astor, Lenox and Tilden Foundations, 1972.

Danton, Emily Miller, ed. *Pioneering Leaders in Librarianship*. Chicago: American Library Association, 1953.

Davies, Donald William. *Public Libraries as Culture and Social Centers: The Origin of the Concept*. Metuchen, NJ: The Scarecrow Press, 1979.

Davis, Allen Freeman. *Spearheads for Reform: The Social Settlements and the Progressive Movement, 1890–1914*. New York: Oxford University Press, 1967.

Davis, Donald Gordon, Jr. *The Association of American Library Schools, 1915–1968: An Analytical History*. Metuchen, NJ: The Scarecrow Press, 1974.

Dawe, Grosvenor. *Melvil Dewey: Seer, Inspirer, Doer, 1851–1931*. Lake Placid, NY: Lake Placid Club, 1932.

Ditzion, Sidney Herbert. *Arsenals of a Democratic Culture: A Social History of the American Public Library Movement in New England and the Middle Atlantic States from 1850–1900*. Chicago: American Library Association, 1947.

Douglas, Ann. *The Feminization of American Culture*. New York: Alfred A. Knopf, 1977.

Du Mont, Rosemary Ruhig. *Reform and Reaction: The Big City Public Library in American Life*. Westport, CT: Greenwood Press, 1977.

Eastman, Linda Anne. *Portrait of a Librarian: William Howard Brett*. Chicago: American Library Association, 1940.

Faulkner, Harold Underwood. *The Quest for Social Justice, 1898–1914*. New York: The Macmillan Company, 1937.

Fishbein, Morris. *A History of the American Medical Association, 1847–1947*. Philadelphia: W. B. Saunders Company, 1947.

Fitzpatrick, Edward Augustus. *McCarthy of Wisconsin*. New York: Columbia University Press, 1944.

Fleming, Edward McClung. *R. R. Bowker: Militant Liberal*. Norman, OK: University of Oklahoma Press, 1952.

Frankfort, Roberta. *Collegiate Women: Domesticity and Career in Turn-of-the-Century America*. New York: New York University Press, 1977.

Furner, Mary O. *Advocacy & Objectivity: A Crisis in the Professionalization of American*

Social Science, 1865–1905. Lexington, KY: The University Press of Kentucky, 1975.

Gabriel, Ralph H. *The Course of American Democratic Thought: An Intellectual History Since 1815*. New York: The Ronald Press Co., 1940.

Garceau, Oliver. *The Public Library in the Political Process*. New York: Columbia University Press, 1949.

Garrison, Dee. *Apostles of Culture: The Public Librarian and American Society, 1876–1920*. New York: The Free Press, 1979.

Geller, Evelyn. *Forbidden Books in American Public Libraries, 1876–1939: A Study in Cultural Change*. Westport, CT: Greenwood Press, 1984.

Ginger, Ray. *Age of Excess: The United States from 1877 to 1914*. New York: The Macmillan Company, 1965.

——. *Altgeld's America*. Chicago: Quadrangle Books, 1965.

Goldman, Eric Frederick. *Rendezvous with Destiny: A History of Modern American Reform*. New York: Alfred A. Knopf, 1952.

Goldstein, Harold, ed. *Milestones to the Present: Papers from Library History Seminar V*. Syracuse, NY: Gaylord Professional Publications, 1978.

Gorham, Deborah. *The Victorian Girl and the Feminine Ideal*. Bloomington, IN: Indiana University Press, 1982.

Gould, Joseph Edward. *The Chautauqua Movement: An Episode in the Continuing American Revolution*. Albany, NY: State University of New York Press, 1972.

Greer, Colin, ed. *Divided Society: The Ethnic Experience in America*. New York: Basic Books, 1974.

Grob, Gerald N. *Workers and Utopia: A Study of Ideological Conflict in the American Labor Movement, 1865–1900*. Chicago: Quadrangle Books, 1969.

Grotzinger, Laurel Ann. *The Power and the Dignity: Librarianship and Katharine Sharp*. Metuchen, NJ: The Scarecrow Press, 1965.

Gusfield, Joseph R. *Symbolic Crusade: Status Politics and the American Temperance Movement*. Urbana, IL: University of Illinois Press, 1963.

Guttman, Allen. *The Conservative Tradition in America*. New York: Oxford University Press, 1967.

Haber, Samuel. *Efficiency and Uplift: Scientific Management in the Progressive Era, 1890–1920*. Chicago: University of Chicago Press, 1964.

Hadley, Chalmers. *John Cotton Dana: A Sketch*. Chicago: American Library Association, 1943.

Hall, Peter D. *The Organization of American Culture, 1700–1900: Private Institutions, Elites, and the Origins of American Nationality*. New York: New York University Press, 1982.

Haller, John S. *American Medicine in Transition, 1840–1910*. Urbana IL: University of Illinois Press, 1981.

——. *Outcasts from Evolution: Scientific Attitudes of Racial Inferiority, 1859–1900*. Urbana, IL: University of Illinois Press, 1971.

——. *The Physician and Sexuality in Victorian America*. Urbana, IL: University of Illinois Press, 1974.

Halttunen, Karen. *Confidence Men and Painted Women: A Study of Middle-Class Culture in America, 1830–1870*. New Haven, CT: Yale University Press, 1983.

Hamlin, Arthur T. *The University Library in the United States: Its Origins and Development*. Philadelphia: University of Pennsylvania Press, 1981.

Hardy, Stephen. *How Boston Played: Sport, Recreation, and Community, 1865–1915.* Boston: Northeastern University Press, 1982.

Hareven, Tamara K., ed. *Anonymous Americans: Explorations in Nineteenth-Century Social History.* Englewood Cliffs, NJ: Prentice-Hall, 1971.

Harris, Barbara J. *Beyond Her Sphere: Women and the Professions in American History.* Westport, CT: Greenwood Press, 1978.

Harris, Michael H. *A Guide to Research in American Library History.* Metuchen, NJ: The Scarecrow Press, 1974.

———, and Davis, Donald G., Jr., comp. *American Library History: A Bibliography.* Austin: University of Texas Press, 1978.

Harris, Michael H. *The Role of the Public Library in American Life: A Speculative Essay.* Urbana, IL: University of Illinois Graduate School of Library Science. Occasional Paper No. 117. 1975.

Harris, Neil. *The Land of Contrasts, 1880–1901.* New York: George Braxillier, 1970.

Hart, James David. *The Popular Book: A History of America's Literary Taste.* New York: Oxford University Press, 1950.

Haskell, Thomas L. *The Emergence of Professional Social Science: The American Social Science Association and the Nineteenth-Century Crisis of Authority.* Urbana, IL: University of Illinois Press, 1977.

Hays, Samuel P. *Conservation and the Gospel of Efficiency: The Progressive Conservation Movement, 1890–1920.* Cambridge, MA: Harvard University Press, 1959.

———. *The Response to Industrialism: 1885–1914.* Chicago: University of Chicago Press, 1957.

Hicks, John D. *The Populist Revolt: A History of the Farmers' Alliance and the People's Party.* Minneapolis: The University of Minnesota Press, 1931.

Higham, John. *History: Professional Scholarship in America.* New York: Prentice-Hall, Inc., 1965.

———. *Strangers in the Land: Patterns of American Nativism 1860–1925.* New York: Atheneum Books, 1972.

———, and Conkin, Paul K., eds. *New Directions in American Intellectual History.* Baltimore: The Johns Hopkins University Press, 1979.

Hofstadter, Richard. *The Age of Reform: From Bryan to F.D.R.* New York: Random House, 1955.

———. *Social Darwinism in American Thought.* Boston: Beacon Press, 1955.

Holley, Edward G. *Charles Evans: American Bibliographer.* Urbana, IL: University of Illinois Press, 1963.

Hoogenboom, Ari. *Outlawing the Spoils: A History of the Civil Service Reform Movement, 1865–1883.* Urbana, IL: University of Illinois Press, 1961.

Horowitz, Helen Lefkowitz. *Culture and the City: Cultural Philanthropy in Chicago from the 1880s to 1917.* Lexington, KY: University Press of Kentucky, 1976.

Houser, Lloyd J. and Schrader, Alvin M. *The Search for a Scientific Profession: Library Science Education in the U.S. and Canada.* Metuchen, NJ: The Scarecrow Press, 1978.

Jackson, Sidney J., Herling, Eleanor B., and Josey, E.J., eds. *A Century of Service: Librarianship in the United States and Canada.* Chicago: American Library Association, 1976.

Jensen, Richard. *The Winning of the Midwest: Social and Political Conflict, 1888–1896.* Chicago: University of Chicago Press, 1971.

Joeckl, Carleton Brums. *The Government of the American Public Library*. Chicago: University of Chicago Press, 1935.

Johnson, William R. *Schooled Lawyers: A Study in the Clash of Professional Cultures*. New York: New York University Press, 1978.

Kalisch, Phillip Arthur. *The Enoch Pratt Free Library: A Social History*. Metuchen, NJ: The Scarecrow Press, Inc., 1969.

Kammen, Michael. *People of Paradox: An Inquiry Concerning the Origins of American Civilization*. New York: Alfred A. Knopf, 1975.

Kaplan, Louis. *The Growth of Reference Service in the United States from 1876–1893*. Chicago: Association of College and Research Libraries, 1952.

Kaser, David. *A Book for a Sixpence: The Circulating Library in America*. Pittsburgh: Beta Phi Mu, 1980.

Katz, Michael B. *The Irony of Early School Reform: Educational Innovation in Mid-Nineteenth Century Massachusetts*. Boston: Beacon Press, 1968.

Kaufman, Martin. *American Medical Education: The Formative Years, 1765–1910*. Westport, CT: Greenwood Press, 1976.

Keller, Martin. *Affairs of State: Public Life in Late Nineteenth-Century America*. Cambridge, MA: Harvard University Press, 1977.

Kennedy, David M., ed. *Progressivism: The Critical Issues*. Boston: Little, Brown, 1971.

Kett, Joseph F. *The Formation of the American Medical Profession: The Role of Institutions, 1780–1860*. New Haven, CT: Yale University Press, 1968.

Kirkland, Edward Chase. *Industry Comes of Age: Business, Labor and Public Policy, 1860–1897*. New York: Holt, Rinehart and Winston, 1961.

Koch, Theodore Wesley. *A Book of Carnegie Libraries*. White Plains, NY: H. W. Wilson Co., 1917.

Kohlstedt, Sally Gregory. *The Formation of the American Scientific Community: The American Association for the Advancement of Science, 1848–1860*. Urbana, IL: University of Illinois Press, 1976.

Kolko, Gabriel. *The Triumph of Conservation: A Reinterpretation of American History, 1900–1916*. Chicago: Quadrangle Books, 1967.

Kraditor, Aileen S. *The Idea of the Woman Suffrage Movement, 1890–1920*. New York: Columbia University Press, 1965.

Kraus, Joe Walker. *William Beer and the New Orleans Libraries, 1891–1927*. Chicago: Association of College and Research Libraries, 1952.

Kruzas, Anthony Thomas. *Business and Industrial Libraries in the United States, 1820–1940*. New York: Special Libraries Association, 1965.

Kuklick, Bruce. *The Rise of American Philosophy, Cambridge, Massachusetts, 1860–1930*. New Haven, CT: Yale University Press, 1977.

Lagemann, Ellen Condliffe. *A Generation of Women: Education in the Lives of Progressive Reformers*. Cambridge, MA: Harvard University Press, 1979.

Larson, Magali Sarfatti. *The Rise of Professionalism: A Sociological Analysis*. Berkeley, CA: University of California Press, 1977.

Lasch, Christopher. *The Culture of Narcissism: American Life in an Age of Diminishing Expectations*. New York: W. W. Norton & Co., Inc., 1978.

———. *The New Radicalism in America, 1889–1963: The Intellectual as a Social Type*. New York: Alfred A. Knopf, 1965.

Lawler, John. *The H. W. Wilson Company: Half a Century of Bibliographic Publishing.* Minneapolis: University of Minnesota Press, 1950.

Lazerson, Marvin. *Origins of the Urban School: Public Education in Massachusetts, 1870–1915.* Cambridge, MA: Harvard University Press, 1971.

Learned, William S. *The American Public Library and the Diffusion of Knowledge.* New York: Harcourt, Brace and Company, 1924.

Lears, T. Jackson. *No Place of Grace: Antimodernism and the Transformation of American Culture, 1880–1920.* New York: Pantheon Books, 1981.

Lee, Robert Ellis. *Continuing Education for Adults through the American Public Library, 1833–1964.* Chicago: American Library Association, 1966.

Lester, R.M. *Carnegie Grants for Library Buildings, 1890–1917.* New York: Carnegie Corp., 1943.

Link, Arthur S. *Woodrow Wilson and the Progressive Era, 1910–1917.* New York: Harper & Row, 1954.

Long, Harriet Geneva. *Public Library Service to Children: Foundation and Development.* Metuchen, NJ: The Scarecrow Press, 1969.

Lubove, Roy. *The Professional Altruist: The Emergence of Social Work as a Career, 1880–1930.* Cambridge, MA: Harvard University Press, 1965.

Lustig, R. Jeffrey. *Corporate Liberalism: The Origins of Modern American Political Theory, 1890–1920.* Berkeley, CA: University of California Press, 1982.

Lydenberg, Harry M. *John Shaw Billings: Creator of the National Medical Library and Its Catalogue, First Director of the New York Public Library.* Chicago: American Library Association, 1924.

———. *History of the New York Public Library: Astor, Lenox and Tilden Foundation.* New York: New York Public Library, 1923.

Lykes, Richard Wayne. *Higher Education and the United States Office of Education (1867–1953).* Washington: United States Office of Education, 1975.

Maddow, Ben. *A Sunday between Wars: The Course of American Life from 1865 to 1917.* New York: W. W. Norton, 1979.

McCloskey, Robert Green. *American Conservatism in the Age of Enterprise, 1865–1910: A Study of William Graham Sumner, Stephen J. Field and Andrew Carnegie.* New York: Harper and Row, Publishers, 1951.

Mann, Arthur. *Yankee Reformers in the Urban Age.* Cambridge, MA: Belknap Press of Harvard University Press, 1954.

Mattingly, Paul H. *The Classless Profession: American Schoolmen in the Nineteenth Century.* New York: New York University Press, 1975.

May, Henry F. *The End of American Innocence: A Study of the First Years of Our Own Time, 1912–1917.* New York: Alfred A. Knopf, 1959.

Metcalf, John Wallace. *Information Retrieval: British and American, 1876–1976.* Metuchen, NJ: The Scarecrow Press, 1976.

Miksa, Francis L., ed. *Charles Ammi Cutter: Library Systematizer.* Littleton, CO: Libraries Unlimited, 1977.

Miller, Howard S. *Dollars for Research: Science and Its Patrons in Nineteenth-Century America.* Seattle: University of Washington Press, 1970.

Mitchell, Alma Clarvoe, ed. *Special Libraries Association—Its First Fifty Years, 1909–1959.* New York: Special Libraries Association, 1959.

Mowry, George Erwin. *The Era of Theodore Roosevelt and the Birth of Modern America, 1900–1912.* New York: Harper & Row, 1958.

Munthe, Wilhelm. *American Librarianship from a European Angle: An Attempt at an Evaluation of Policies and Activities*. Chicago: American Library Association, 1939.

Myers, Margaret and Scarborough, Mayra, eds. *Women in Librarianship: Melvil's Rib Symposium*. New Brunswick, NJ: Rutgers University Graduate School of Library Service, 1975.

Nasaw, David. *Schooled to Order: A Social History of Public Schooling in America*. New York: Oxford University Press, 1979.

Nelson, Daniel. *Frederick W. Taylor and the Rise of Scientific Management*. Madison: University of Wisconsin Press, 1980.

Nevins, Allan. *The Emergence of Modern America, 1865–1878*. New York: The Macmillan Company, 1927.

Noble, David F. *America by Design: Science, Technology and the Rise of Corporate Capitalism*. New York: Alfred A. Knopf, 1977.

———. *The Progressive Mind, 1890–1917*. Chicago: Rand McNally & Company, 1970.

Nye, Russel. *The Unembarrassed Muse: The Popular Arts in America*. New York: Dial, 1970.

Ollé, James G. *Library History*. London: Clive Bingley, 1979.

O'Neill, William L. *Everyone Was Brave: A History of Feminism in America*. Chicago: Quadrangle Books, 1969.

Parson, Stanley B. *The Populist Context: Rural Versus Urban Power on a Great Plains Frontier*. Westport, CT: Greenwood Press, 1973.

Pivar, David J. *Purity Crusade: Sexual Morality and Social Control, 1868–1900*. Westport, CT: Greenwood Press, 1973.

Peters, Orpha Maud. *The Gary Public Library, 1907–1944*. Gary, IN: Gary Public Library, 1945.

Predeek, Albert. *A History of Libraries in Great Britain and North America*. Chicago: American Library Association, 1947.

Quandt, Jean B. *From the Small Town to the Great Community: The Social Thought of Progressive Intellectuals*. New Brunswick, NJ: Rutgers University Press, 1970.

Ranz, Jim. *The Printed Book Catalog in American Libraries, 1723–1900*. Chicago: American Library Association, 1964.

Ravitch, Diane. *The Revisionists Revised: A Critique of the Radical Attack on the Schools*. New York: Basic Books, Inc., 1978.

Reed, James. *From Private Vice to Public Virtue: The Birth Control Movement and American Society Since 1830*. New York: Basic Books, Inc., 1978.

Rider, Fremont. *Melvil Dewey*. Chicago: American Library Association, 1944.

Rose, Ernestine. *The Public Library in American Life*. New York: Columbia University Press, 1954.

Roseberry, Cecil R. *For the Government and People of This State: A History of the New York State Library*. Albany, NY: The New York State Library, 1970.

Rosen, George. *The Structure of American Medical Practice, 1875–1941*. Philadelphia: University of Pennsylvania Press, 1983.

Rosenkrantz, Barbara Gutmann. *Public Health and the State: Changing Views in Massachusetts, 1842–1936*. Cambridge, MA: Harvard University Press, 1972.

Rossiter, Margaret W. *Women Scientists in America: Struggles and Strategies to 1940*. Baltimore: The Johns Hopkins University Press, 1982.

Rothman, David J. *Conscience and Convenience: The Asylum and Its Alternatives in Progressive America*. Boston: Little, Brown, 1980.

Rothstein, Samuel. *The Development of Reference Services through Academic Traditions, Public Library Practice and Special Librarianship*. Chicago: American Library Association, 1955.

Rothstein, William G. *American Physicians in the Nineteenth Century: From Sects to Science*. Baltimore: The Johns Hopkins University Press, 1972.

Russett, Cynthia Eagle. *Darwin in America: The Intellectual Response, 1865–1912*. San Francisco: W. H. Freeman & Company, 1976.

Schiest, Martin J. *The Politics of Efficiency: Municipal Administration and Reform in America, 1880–1920*. Berkeley, CA: University of California Press, 1983.

Schwendinger, Herman and Julia R. *The Sociologists of the Chair: A Radical Analysis of the Formative Years of North American Sociology (1883–1922)*. New York: Basic Books, 1974.

Shaw, Robert Kendall. *Samuel Swett Green*. Chicago: American Library Association, 1926.

Shelton, Brenda Kurtz. *Reformers in Search of Yesterday: Buffalo in the 1890s*. Albany, NY: State University of New York Press, 1976.

Shera, Jesse H. *Foundations of the Public Library: The Origins of the Public Library Movement in New England, 1629–1855*. Chicago: University of Chicago Press, 1949.

Shiflett, Orvin Lee. *Origins of American Academic Librarianship*. Norwood, NJ: Ablex Publishing Corp., 1981.

Sinclair, Bruce. *A Centennial History of the American Society of Mechanical Engineers, 1880–1980*. Toronto: University of Toronto Press, 1980.

Soltow, Lee, and Stevens, Edward. *The Rise of Literacy and the Common School in the United States: A Socioeconomic Analysis to 1870*. Chicago: University of Chicago Press, 1982.

Spencer, Gladys. *Chicago Public Library*. Chicago: University of Chicago Press, 1943.

Sproat, John G. *"The Best Men": Liberal Reformers in the Gilded Age*. New York: Oxford University, 1968.

Stone, Elizabeth W. *American Library Development, 1600–1899*. New York: H.W. Wilson Co., 1977.

Sugg, Redding S., Jr. *Motherteacher: The Feminization of American Education*. Charlottesville, VA: University Press of Virginia, 1978.

Sullivan, Mark. *Our Times: The United States, 1900–1925*. 6 Vols. New York: Charles Scribner's Sons, 1926–35.

Sullivan, Peggy. *Carl H. Milam and the American Library Association*. New York: H. W. Wilson Co., 1976.

Tariello, Frank, Jr. *The Reconstruction of American Political Ideology, 1865–1917*. Charlottesville, VA: University Press of Virginia, 1982.

Taylor, Lloyd C. *The Medical Profession and Social Reform, 1885–1945*. New York: St. Martin's Press, Inc., 1974.

Thernstrom, Stephan. *Poverty and Progress: Social Mobility in a Nineteenth-Century City*. Cambridge, MA: Harvard University, 1964.

Thimm, Alfred L. *Business Ideologies in the Reform-Progressive Era, 1880–1914*. University, AL: University of Alabama Press, 1976.

Thomison, Dennis V. *A History of the American Library Association, 1876–1972*. Chicago: American Library Association, 1978.

Thompson, Charles S. *Evolution of the American Public Library, 1653–1876*. Washington: The Scarecrow Press, 1952.

Tomsich, John. *A Genteel Endeavor: American Culture and the Politics in the Gilded Age*. Stanford, CA: Stanford University Press, 1971.

Trachtenberg, Alan. *The Incorporation of America: Culture and Society in the Gilded Age*. New York: Hill and Wang, 1982.

Trautman, Ray L. *A History of the School of Library Service, Columbia University*. New York: Columbia University Press, 1954.

Tyack, David. *The One Best System: A History of American Urban Education*. Cambridge, MA: Harvard University Press, 1974.

Utley, George Burwell. *Fifty Years of the American Library Association*. Chicago: American Library Association, 1926.

———. *The Librarians' Conference of 1853: A Chapter in American Library History*. Chicago: American Library Association, 1951.

Van Riper, Paul P. *History of the United States Civil Service*. Evanston, IL: Row, Peterson and Company, 1958.

Vann, Sarah K., ed. *Melvil Dewey: His Enduring Presence in Librarianship*. Littleton, CO: Libraries Unlimited, Inc., 1978.

———. *Training for Librarianship Before 1923: Education for Librarianship Prior to the Publication of Williamson's Report on Training for Library Service*. Chicago: American Library Association, 1961.

Wall, Joseph Frazier. *Andrew Carnegie*. New York: Oxford University Press, 1970.

Warner, Sam B., Jr. *Streetcar Suburbs: The Process of Growth in Boston, 1870–1900*. Cambridge, MA: Harvard University Press, 1962.

Warren, Donald R. *To Enforce Education: A History of the Founding Years of the United States Office of Education*. Detroit: Wayne State University Press, 1974.

Weinstein, James. *The Corporate Ideal in the Liberal State, 1900–1918*. Boston: Beacon Press, 1968.

Wesley, Edgar B. *NEA: The First Hundred Years: The Building of the Teaching Profession*. New York: Harper & Brothers, 1957.

White, Carl Minton. *A Historical Introduction to Library Education: Problems and Progress to 1951*. Metuchen, NJ: The Scarecrow Press, 1976.

White, Morton Gabriel. *Social Thought in America: The Revolt Against Formalism*. Boston: Beacon Press, 1957.

Wiebe, Robert H. *Businessmen and Reform: A Study of the Progressive Movement*. Cambridge, MA: Harvard University Press, 1962.

———. *The Search for Order, 1877–1920*. New York: Hill and Wang, 1967.

Wiegand, Wayne A. *History of a Hoax: Edmund Lester Pearson, John Cotton Dana and The Old Librarian's Almanack*. Pittsburgh: Beta Phi Mu, 1979.

Wilcox, Benton H. *The Wisconsin Library Association, 1891–1966*. Madison, WI: Wisconsin Library Association, 1966.

Williamson, William Landram. *William Frederick Poole and the Modern Library Movement*. New York: Columbia University Press, 1963.

Wilson, Dorothy Clarke. *Stranger and Traveler: The Story of Dorothea Dix, American Reformer*. Boston: Little, Brown and Company, 1975.

Wilson, Margaret Gibbons. *The American Woman in Transition: The Urban Influence, 1870–1920*. Westport, CT: Greenwood Press, 1979.

Wilson, R. Jackson. *In Quest of Community: Social Philosophy in the United States, 1860–1920*. New York: John Wiley and Sons, Inc., 1968.

Woodford, Frank B. *Parnassus on Main Street: A History of the Detroit Public Library*. Detroit: Wayne State University Press, 1965.

Woytanowitz, George M. *University Extension: The Early Years in the United States, 1885–1915*. Iowa City, IA: American College Testing Publications, 1974.

Wynar, Bohdan S., ed. *Dictionary of American Library Biography*. Littleton, CO: Libraries Unlimited, Inc., 1978.

Young, Arthur P. *Books for Sammies: The American Library Association and World War I*. Pittsburgh: Beta Phi Mu, 1981.

Zurcher, Louis A., and Kirkpatrick, R. George. *Citizens for Decency: Antipornography Crusades as Status Defense*. Austin: University of Texas Press, 1976.

Index

About the Author

WAYNE A. WIEGAND is Associate Professor of Library and Information Science at the University of Kentucky, Lexington. His earlier works include *The History of a Hoax: Edmund Lester Pearson, John Cotton Dana and the Old Librarian's Almanack*, as well as articles in the *Journal of Library History, The Reference Librarian*, and the *Journal of Academic Librarianship*.